Drift Boats and River Dories

Drift Boats and River Dories

Their History, Design, Construction, and Use

Roger L. Fletcher

Illustrator, Samuel F. Manning

STACKPOLE
BOOKS

Published by
STACKPOLE BOOKS
5067 Ritter Road
Mechanicsburg, PA 17055
www.stackpolebooks.com

Printed in China

First edition

10 9 8 7 6 5 4 3 2 1

Photos by the author except where indicated.

Library of Congress Cataloging-in-Publication Data

Fletcher, Roger (Roger L.)
    Drift boats and river dories : their history, design, construction, and use / Roger Fletcher ;
    illustrator, Samuel F. Manning. — 1st ed.
        p.   cm.
    Includes bibliographical references.
    ISBN-13: 978-0-8117-0234-8 (hardcover)
    ISBN-10: 0-8117-0234-0 (hardcover)
    1. Drift boats—History.   2. Dories (Boats)—History.   3. Drift boats—Design and
construction.   4. Dories (Boats)—Design and construction.   I. Title.

SH452.9.B58F58   2007
799.1028'4—dc22
                                                                                      2006039068

Contents

DEDICATED TO SUE,

whose presence allowed me to grow in ways unimagined
and without whom I would not have had the
courage to undertake this project.

Foreword

Drift Boats and River Dories is a rich collection of stories, images, instructions, and drift-boat plans. This is a book for the angler who has drifted in a wooden boat to a perfect spot, slowed the craft with a few pulls on the oars against the heavy flow to present a cast or two, and been swept away through standing waves to the pool below. And it is for everyone who has marveled at the grace and beauty of a wooden drift boat slipping along in the swirling current with its cargo of anglers. In these pages, you will find stories of the river pioneers who designed and built the first drift boats in order to fish and navigate the Pacific Northwest's wild rivers. The boatbuilder who chooses wood for its strength and beauty and the modeler who handcrafts a piece of art may confidently employ the lines plan of any one of the original boats provided herein.

Roger Fletcher is a fisherman and an accomplished river runner. He understands and appreciates the interaction of wood and water, and he knows what makes a good fishing platform that offers a safe and comfortable ride. When I met Roger a decade ago, he was beginning to realize his singular interest in the wooden drift boats of the Pacific Northwest. As he gathered the information necessary to preserve and re-create these unique boats, his interest in their evolution grew and the story of the creation and modification of the drift boat began to take shape. He decided that the lines of these boats must be recovered and recorded before they were irretrievably lost. At the same time, he was becoming enthralled with stories of the people who designed and built the early river dories, and he wanted to preserve their history along with the lines of the original boats. He had compiled measurements of several of the original vessels, and he was hot on the trail of other links in the evolution of the McKenzie River dory. He knew that once he had created lines plans for the boats, they would be preserved for future builders, and he believed that he had a responsibility to organize and share the information he had gathered.

Roger admires John Gardner's work, *The Dory Book,* which presents the history and lines of the eastern dories, distant relatives of the McKenzie boats, and it served as a model for him as he began to write. His research brought him into contact with scores of people who contributed memories, diaries, photographs, expertise, and access to the original boats. Among these individuals is H. H. "Dynamite" Payson, renowned Maine boat builder, modeler, and author. Dynamite shares

Roger's interest in preserving historic boats and had an immense influence on his activity as both an advisor and a participant. The men were in frequent contact as the lines of the originals were rescued, and Dynamite became so involved that he modeled four of the boats. Roger asked marine illustrator Sam Manning, whose fine pen-and-ink drawings are a highlight of the Gardner work, to contribute his art to this book. Manning's illustrations add clarity to the instructions for free-form construction and provide continuity with Gardner's book. I consider this work to be its companion piece.

Roger has produced lines plans for each boat that he considers to be an important link in the evolution of the McKenzie and Rogue River dories. These lines and his instructions for construction are tailored to both the novice and the experienced craftsman, and they should ensure the survival of boats that would have been lost to time. Of the author, Dynamite Payson recently wrote: "For more than fifty years I've had the pleasure of building and using boats here on the coast of Maine. During this time I've seen many boats come and go and have seen some of them gone forever because no one had taken the time and trouble to preserve them. . . . Roger got the job beautifully done, so these little river runners will live on for the pleasure of future generations." I don't think it can be said better than that.

Bill Girsch

Acknowledgments

For helping me keep both oars in the water, I thank Ken and Dorrene Brown, for introducing my family and me to drift boats almost forty years ago; H. H. "Dynamite" Payson, for helping me drop the shackles of academia and replace them with straight talk and simplicity through the art of modeling and boat building; Jim Fletcher, for his three-dimensional perspective of the light board-and-batten McKenzie boat, my first attempt to recover a craft; and Bill Girsch, for his continuous interest, questions, and encouragement and our bimonthly evening bull sessions.

Thanks to the later generations of river folks who opened their doors, histories, family recollections, and other relevant resources to me: the Helfrich siblings, Dave, Dick, Diane, and Dean, especially Dave for family histories and insights into the psyches of guides sensitive to their environment and their dudes; Leroy Pruitt, whose support and response to my re-creation of his daddy's light board-and-batten boat confirmed that this is a project worth doing, and who unselfishly gave me access to recollections, photographs, and other memorabilia; Bobby Pruitt, for stories and insights into the mind-sets of the early guides; the Tom Kaarhus grandchildren, especially Maurya Kaarhus, for information about her grandfather, and family photographs; Ruth Burleigh, who shared with me Ruthie and Woodie Hindman's diaries and histories, and whose interest gave rise to recovered connections with family and friends; the late Frank Wheeler and his widow, LuElla, for preserving a piece of history, and their daughter Mary Ellen for her interest in restoring the boat; Delbert Trew, a rancher, freelance writer, historian, and humorist, who helped confirm the Woodie Hindman–McLean, Texas, connection, and the Alanreed-McLean Area Museum in Texas; Linda Bush of Mount Pleasant, Texas, and her mother, Ruth Hindman, Woodie's niece by marriage, for family recollections and Hindman family photos; Steve Pritchett and his treasure trove of Rogue River history and memorabilia, as well as his dad's last dory, a classic; Virginia Pritchett and her reminders that women also played crucial roles in the use and development of the earlier boats; Jerry Briggs, for family histories and insights about river stories, boat building, and the Colorado Rover dory, and Barbara Briggs, for her interest, patience, and grand lunches; Florence Arman, for her biographical work on Glen Wooldridge; Louise Richards and Robyn Wicks, Bureau of Land Management, for their Rogue River trip and help in recovering the lines of the Zane Grey boat at Winkle Bar; Willard Lucas, for his gifts of humor and insight into river navigation; the late Kenny King, a member of the National Fishing Hall of Fame, for fishing and boating stories and his unqualified passion for the river, and Virginia King, for her love and care of Kenny in his twilight years; and Colorado River dory guides Brad Dimock, Martin Litton, Rudi Petschek, Dan Dierker, and Andy Hutchinson, who helped me more clearly understand the Colorado River connection to Oregon.

I am grateful for the reviewers who generously offered their critiques: Stephen Beckham, Ph.D., Professor of History, Dr. Robert B. Pamplin Jr., Chair, Lewis and Clark College, Portland, Oregon; Cort Conley, Middle Fork of the Salmon River historian, author, and river guide; Brad Dimock, Colorado River boatman and author, Fretwater Press, Flagstasff, Arizona; Ray Heater, traditional frame-construction boat builder, Ray's River Dories, for his contributions to and review of my chapter about how to build the boats; Richard Jagels, Ph.D., Professor of Forest Biology at the University of Maine, Orono, and author of *WoodenBoat* magazine's bimonthly feature, "Wood Technology"; Martin Litton, author, environmentalist, and founder of Grand Canyon River Dories, for his recollections of the Briggs-Litton connection and personal history related to the Colorado River dories; Maeve Kaarhus, a Tom Kaarhus granddaughter, Durango, Colorado, for her thoughtful review of the Kaarhus chapter; Samuel Manning, marine illustrator, Camden, Maine, whose wise counsel about the relationships between traditional building of small boats and that of drift boats gave rise to an understandable chapter about free-form construction and has led to an enduring friendship; Megan Moholt, Research Archivist, Weyerhaeuser Company, Federal Way, Washington, who graciously contributed to my understanding of the history of plywood manufacturing in the Northwest; and Grey Elliot, fellow drifter and budding boat builder in Cayuse, Oregon.

I also appreciate the help of James Babb, the well-known Maine-based fly-fishing author, who convinced me that most of the people who will be interested in this book are those for whom these boats were originally designed and built—sportfishers; Doug Bridges of Sequim, Washington, for his excellent advice and craftsmanship in helping me create a near replica of the Tom Kaarhus 16-foot Rapid Robert, and Susan, for her unqualified support of this project; Ted Leeson, Ph.D., English writing instructor at Oregon State University and widely read fly-fishing author, who unselfishly advised me on the ways of proposals and the organization of a book's content and publishers, and whose writing style helped define a standard for me; Susan Manning, whose frequent vocalizations of the loon over several thousand miles of phone lines brought a sense of comfort and calm during my more hectic moments on this book; David Zielinski, for his interest in building the first-off of the Trapper and ability to do so, Deena, for her support of Dave's project, and Gracie and Andie, as reminders that drift boats, fishing, dads, and moms go together naturally; and an unnamed friend who prodded me into action by telling me I am known as the person who recovers boats that have been lost to time, and he hopes to see this project completed before I am lost to time.

Finally, thanks to Judith Schnell, my publisher, whose enthusiasm for this book drew me to Stackpole Books; her assistant, Amy Lerner, whose guidance shaped the final product; and Stackpole's graphics folks, including Caroline Stover, who helped bring the images and text together here.

Preface

If you have felt the quiet wake of wood on water,
Or the tranquility of a river canyon
Made crisp by your oneness
With that milieu;
If you have danced with white water
Under crystal skies,
Or nested on a velvet sandbar under panoplies of stars,
Then you have felt the river's touch.

The purpose of this book is to present the stories and lines of the original drift boats and river dories as spawned on Oregon's McKenzie and Rogue Rivers. Though now used from Alaska to Maine, south to Georgia, and on at least two other continents, these boats are Oregon's unique contribution to wooden-boat design as fishing platforms and whitewater craft. I wish to preserve the evolutionary lineage of their design, which in a few short years may be irretrievably lost. But my research has also revealed that the history of the boats and their successive incarnations consists very much of the stories of the people who built and used them, with varied fishing interests, personalities, capabilities as craftsmen, and intended uses. It is impossible to separate the boats from the builders. The objectives of this book, then, are to chronicle the logic of the boats' evolution as reflected in the experiences of the individual boat builders and to preserve the lines of eleven boats that represent changes—some subtle, others obvious—in form that followed function. The boat plans provide sufficient detail that any one of the boats may be modeled to scale or built full-size.

The meat and potatoes of the book are found in chapter 11. With the able help of the chapter's illustrator, Samuel F. Manning, I describe a traditional method of drift-boat construction. I call it free-form construction, a simple and cost-effective method. No form, jig, or strongback is required. Each boat presented in the book may be built or modeled using the free-form method. With his intimate knowledge of small-boat construction, tooling, and tools, as well as his skills as a gifted marine artist, Sam brings the construction techniques to life in ways that may encourage even the novice to contemplate drift-boat modeling or building.

My wife and I met Sam and Susan Manning in 1999 at their home in Camden, Maine. Years earlier, Sam had worked with John Gardner to illustrate *The Dory Book,* a definitive work about the seafaring cousins of drift boats and river dories. The first time I picked up *The Dory Book,* I knew it was something special, and in fact, the book became something of a model for me in my recovery of Oregon's whitewater riverboats. It was a pleasure to meet and visit with both Sam and Susan. We knew we were in the presence of serious wooden-boat folks when we saw a dory under construction in their living room! They take traditional dory building seriously. Hardly a day goes by that they don't row their dory around Camden

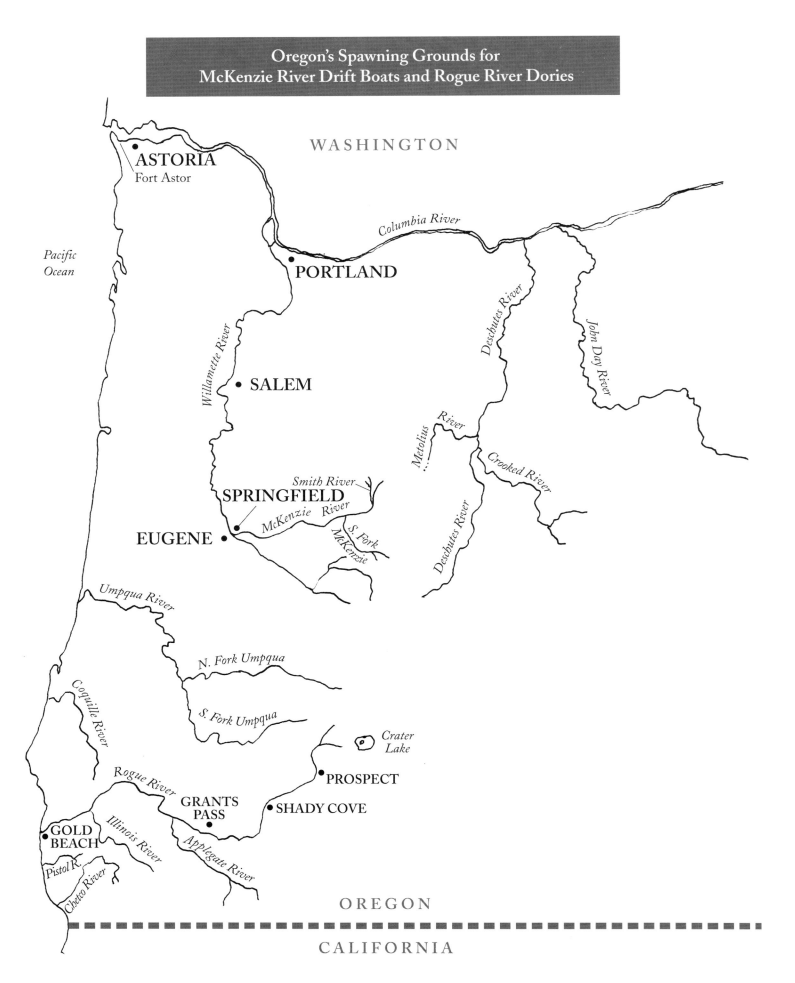

Oregon's Spawning Grounds for
McKenzie River Drift Boats and Rogue River Dories

Harbor and adjacent Penobscot Bay using semaphore to talk with nautical friends, and Susan often carries on vocal conversations with loons. I was thrilled when, two years ago, Sam accepted my invitation to do the illustrations for this book.

Our long-distance collaboration is a story in itself. Sam is a holdout in this computer age. He doesn't own one. He doesn't want one. His joy is in the hand-scribed line and hand-lettered word. Our collaboration across the continent has been telephone and snail-mail dependent. As each packet of drawings arrived from Sam, I was reminded of my Christmas mornings as a youth, and I expectantly opened the package to review his latest work. Our working relationship represents one of the marvels of this book.

The heart and soul of this work are the people who provide the context for the boats and the families who opened their doors to my inquiries about their histories. River guides are focused on their clients, the river, and the job at hand. In their worldview, a singular issue is tied to their boats: performance. The boats changed because of the needs and interests of the people who carved a life out of their environments. They were basically hardworking, caring people whose lives demonstrated that form followed function. Many readers will find the stories of these river pioneers the most intriguing.

The functionality of the book is the boats. The documentation and resurrection of drift boats and river dories has been a work of passion. Much of the credit for my technical success with these projects is attributable to the wise counsel of my good friend and mentor Harold "Dynamite" Payson and a publication by the Museum Small Craft Association called *Boats: A Manual for Their Documentation.* A number of well-intentioned friends have encouraged me to capitalize on the new technologies resident in computer-aided design (CAD) programs and other electronic wizardry to lay out the lines of these boats. No; I am too tactile. Though my aging eyes and less-than-steady hands don't offer the precision of digital technology, as Dynamite reminded me one time—and I found assurance in his words—"These are just boats; they aren't airplanes." I truly appreciate the marvels of computers, but they don't let me feel the boat take shape. I cannot smell cedar shavings on the floor as I carve a plug to get the bilge or panel dimensions. I cannot marvel at a product that isn't solely the result of my eye, head, and hands working together to re-create a thing of beauty. My hat is off to the digital crew, but this aging romantic has chosen to plod the paths of Dynamite Payson, Samuel Manning, John Gardner, Howard Chapelle, Tom Kaarhus, Woodie Hindman, Ray Heater, and others who were unable to get away from the feel of the thing.

PART I

Eddies of Evolution
The Boats' Spawning Grounds

"It is humbling to admit that I, who should know something about dories, having written a book about them, had never heard of the McKenzie River drift boat, or at least had never taken notice of it, until a few weeks ago. It just goes to show you how parochial and out of touch we sometimes can be here in the Northeast, as I am sure some of our friends in the Northwest will agree."

—*John Gardner,* National Fisherman, *July 1980*

CHAPTER 1

Beginnings

These heavily-timbered boats served their guides well, but they were troublesome in whitewater, and their weight and limited freeboard required the guides to ceaselessly work the oars. Though they loved their work, the end of the day brought welcome relief.

To seek sanctuary from the storm, coastal fishermen sought safe harbors. Harbors are sanctums from the sea's threats, places to repair the vessel and reinvigorate the body, sell the catch, and contemplate the next ship.

Safe harbors for men and women of the river are those places where the current is at variance with the prevailing flow, where the river gets confused, reverses itself, and runs upstream along the bank, slips into slack water, and then moves quietly into the whitewater again. They are places to catch one's breath following the maelstrom of the previous rapids, quietly contemplate the surrounding beauty, or consider the graceful lines of the riverboat in which you sit. The boatman is in an eddy. This is a place where an oarsman may ponder the efficacy of his craft and consider ways to improve its efficiency, maneuverability, draft, or ease of handling. The boatman has entered an eddy of evolution, that place where ideas are born and, ultimately, boats are modified to address the changing demands of the river.

The lure of the McKenzie River is tied in part to the lore of its riverboats. The lines of the contemporary McKenzie drift boat are widely recognized as the crème de la crème of river fishing craft. The McKenzie predecessors were equally functional in their time and place. To overlook their relevance today is to miss the boat of opportunity. Their utility is superb for siting a tight fishing hole, negotiating a stretch of bony water, or comfortably handling gear and fly fishers. Each riverboat type is a modification that represents varying demands users have placed on the boats. These eddies of evolution are Oregon's indigenous contribution to riverboat design.

My first encounter with the McKenzie River was in 1946. I was eight years old. With my family, I traveled to Clear Lake, headwaters of the McKenzie. This was a camping expedition to rendezvous with aunts, uncles, and cousins, a family reunion of sorts. The clan enjoyed camping, though they weren't very good at it. No one owned a tent. The two or three tarps to serve as rain flies were used as courtesy curtains for the more modest among the group, a trait few displayed. Sleep was under the stars or a canopy of tall Douglas fir. Those who enjoyed stars awoke to heavy dew on their sleeping bags; those under the trees were a bit drier.

Two things are memorable about that trip. My dad was fond of family, but he was not fond of camping. Campfires were particularly annoying to him, and it was his lot to create and tend to them. His skills produced what we called a smudge pot, because he typically covered our camp area in thick, white smoke. His fires were cool, damp, feeble things that rarely bloomed into anything hotter. Whether he attempted to build a warming fire or a cooking fire, his results were similar: smoke, and lots of it. The primary advantage to his lack of incendiary skills was that it repelled mosquitoes. These dipterous vampires couldn't tolerate Dad's smoke and so were driven back into the woods. So too were the campers, until the mosquitoes drove them back into the smoke.

Dad may not have been a competent fire builder, but he had a penchant for the fly rod and reel. He could drop a number 12 caddisfly into a 12-inch pocket behind a rock from 20 yards without effort. I liked to watch him lay out his line as water droplets formed a fleeting seam in the refracted sunlight, and then the fly would settle like a feather on the small eddy. If a rainbow was there, and it

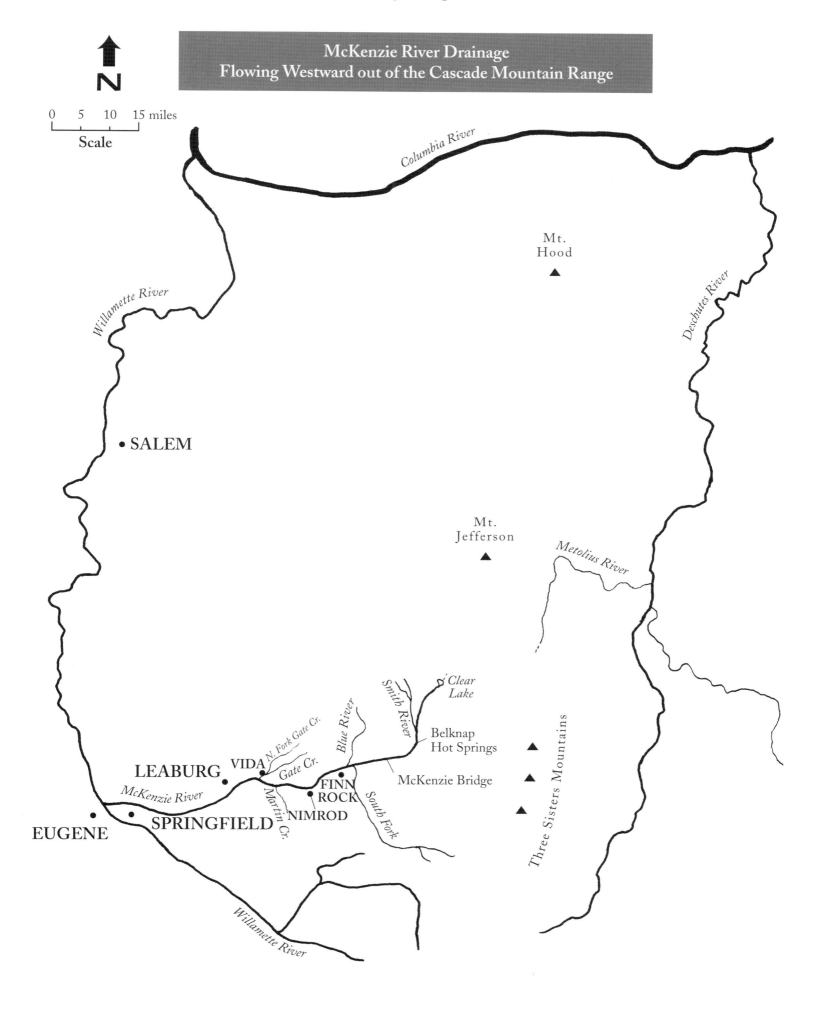

McKenzie River Drainage
Flowing Westward out of the Cascade Mountain Range

N

0   5   10   15 miles
Scale

Columbia River

Mt.
Hood

Willamette River

Deschutes River

• SALEM

Mt.
Jefferson

Metolius River

*Clear
Lake*

Smith River

Blue River

Belknap
Hot Springs

N. Fork Gate Cr.

VIDA

Gate Cr.

McKenzie Bridge

LEABURG

McKenzie River

Martin Cr.

**FINN
ROCK**

NIMROD

South Fork

Three Sisters Mountains

EUGENE

SPRINGFIELD

Willamette River

was tempted, the pocket would explode in a spray of shimmering fury. If the trout was elsewhere or otherwise satisfied, the fly would disappear in a streak as the inside current caught the line and ripped the lure unnaturally into the rapid.

It was here that I first met the McKenzie River, just below Clear Lake. It didn't look or feel like a river. It appeared to me as a series of cataracts, volumes of water constricted into narrow chutes and forced to tumble over lava beds ringed now by tall timber. I couldn't imagine any trout residing in such a place. As I watched dad from safe distances, however, he found pockets of quieter water here and there, enough space that offered sanctuary from the surrounding turmoil, a space where morsels slipped out of the current and caught the cusp of the small eddy. In such places, dad would occasionally catch a fish. If it was pan size, he conveniently lifted it out of the pocket. If the fish weighed a pound or two and it caught the current, he usually threw it a kiss good-bye. Dad seemed too pure to use anything other than a light tippet. Nor was he particularly interested in cleaning his catch. It was the stalk, catch, and release that thrilled him.

My interest in the McKenzie River boats materialized twenty-one years later and was unrelated to any curiosity about that river. Proximity to Oregon's Santiam and Deschutes Rivers and my preoccupation with nearby coastal streams precluded any felt need to investigate the McKenzie. It was after I began to research the origins of drift boats and river dories that my interest in the boats' spawning grounds surfaced. Only then did I dip an oar in her waters. It was a memorable experience.

Dave Helfrich, the noted McKenzie, Rogue, and Middle Fork of the Salmon Rivers guide, squired me through my maiden voyage down the McKenzie. It was early April 2002. Dave is Prince Helfrich's oldest son. The two of us talked about doing a commemorative run down the Middle Fork of the Salmon in two McKenzie River boat reproductions: Veltie Pruitt's light board-and-batten boat and Woodie Hindman's first double-ender. The trip would honor Hindman, the first McKenzie guide to run the Middle Fork, in August 1939, and Prince Helfrich, who first ran the Middle Fork in 1940 with Hindman. Prince preserved the lines and construction detail of Hindman's first double-ender.[1]

Dave is a prudent man. As we visited about the Middle Fork run, he wondered about my river skills. A good riverboat researcher doesn't necessarily make a good oarsman, just as a good obstetrician hasn't necessarily given birth. It was therefore wise for him to evaluate my river skills.

On that pleasant early-April day, I met Dave at his home in Vida, Oregon, which sits on acreage overlooking the McKenzie immediately upriver from a boat landing that carries his family name. Joining us was Frank Wheeler, a lifetime resident of the McKenzie. Though he did not guide professionally, Frank knew the river well and loved it dearly. In 1952, Frank purchased a 12-foot square-ender from Prince, a boat Prince used to run his trap lines in the off-season. Woodie Hindman had built the boat for Prince in the spring of 1939. Frank and his family both used and preserved the boat over the years. It is in pristine condition and is a treasure. Frank allowed me to take the boat's measurements a couple years earlier to accommodate my interest in recovering and recording the lines and construction detail of the earlier riverboats.

We launched two boats a few miles above Belknap Hot Springs, a popular resort on the upper McKenzie. The river at this elevation is busy. It never rests. It tumbles over rocks, twists, and turns as it plies its way toward milder water downstream. Rapids in this pristine stretch are not heavy, but they are continuous, as is the degree of difficulty—much like the Middle Fork of the Salmon. Dave thought it would be a reasonable test of my skills.

Dave and Frank drifted in Dave's 16-foot[2] McKenzie drift boat, a double-ender with a transom built by Keith Steele.[3] Dave is a Keith Steele fan. Dave's boat had more freeboard than a standard drift boat, whose two sides are traditionally cut from one 4-by-16-foot sheet of 1/4-inch plywood. With beefy frames, it was well crafted and was built to stand the abuse of heavy rapids and rocky water. Its continuous rocker offered easy pivots. Dave's intimate knowledge of the McKenzie, Rogue, and Middle Fork at various levels of flow provided courses through safe channels. I was in good hands.

I followed 30 to 40 yards behind in my reproduction of Woodie Hindman's first double-ender. The 14-foot-long boat is narrower in breadth at the bottom and more sheer than most other drift boats. It is therefore more tender, or tippy, and it has the most accentuated rocker of all the McKenzies. I love the boat because it puts me in close contact with the river, and it requires continuous adjustment of the oars as I push and pull to keep it in proper alignment with the currents and away from hazards.

Our 15-mile run down the McKenzie was invigorating and routine, although during our lunch stop, Dave asked if my boat was leaking. Unlike his higher-sided drift boat, mine was prone to accepting some water now and then if my bow angle into a wave was off a bit. I took his ribbing graciously and did not counter, as I should have, that at least I knew how to secure my boat trailer.

As we had left Dave's that morning, his boat and trailer slipped off the pickup hitch and glided gently to a roadside stop. Dave continued on, unaware of his loss. Frank and I chuckled as we hooked the trailer to Frank's truck, wondering how long it would take Dave to discover the absence. It wasn't long before Dave met us. His concerned expression turned to one of relief when he saw his boat in tow. I promised myself that this would remain our little secret—until now. It was refreshing to learn that a man of Dave's stature puts his pants on one leg at a time, just like me.

Dave never said so, but I like to think I passed his test, although we have yet to make that Middle Fork run. The day was satisfaction enough, having conjured up romantic images in my mind of another first-time McKenzie explorer who visited the area 190 years earlier.

One of the first recorded white men to explore the McKenzie was a native Scotsman, Donald McKenzie, who became the river's namesake. McKenzie was one of John Jacob Astor's original partners in the newly formed Pacific Fur Company of 1810. Fort Astor was located at the mouth of the Columbia River on the south shore. Astor's intent was to use this base as a springboard to explore the Northwest interior for fur. On about April 1, 1812, McKenzie launched an expedition from Fort Astor into what is now Oregon's Willamette Valley.[4] Their goal was to explore the tributaries of the Willamette River, including the stream now known as the McKenzie River.

Donald McKenzie has been described as knowledgeable in woodcraft and the "strategy of Indian trade and warfare. . . . He had a frame seasoned by toil and hardship, a spirit not to be intimidated, and was reputed to be a remarkable shot."[5] He was sometimes called "Perpetual Motion" McKenzie, a sobriquet he deserved. It was said that "the chronology of his movements reflect a whirlwind energy."[6] He was viewed by some of his contemporaries, however, as "a very selfish man, who cared for no one but himself."[7] This perception was later shared by Hudson's Bay Company's governor George Simpson. In 1832, Simpson wrote confidential evaluations of his twenty-five chief factors, or senior officers; one was Donald McKenzie. McKenzie was "well on his way to becoming a confirmed Drunkard," he said, and "was one of the most dangerous men I was ever acquainted with."[8]

McKenzie's memoirs, written in the waning years of his life in Mayville, New York, unfortunately were destroyed by fire.[9] We therefore don't have a first-person account of the man. It seems to me that a man with McKenzie's wilderness skills required an enormous ego, a no-nonsense approach to problem solving, and the occasional need for strong drink. His size, at 300 pounds,[10] along with his strength, reputation, and pungent odor, likely would have caused any frontiersman on a dark night at Fort Astor to give him a wide berth. I would have appreciated his company in the wilderness.

McKenzie was considered an excellent boatman and was particularly adept at commanding the large birchbark canoes that were favored by the Hudson's Bay Company field men in central and northeast Canada.[11] He also had experience with keelboats, river drivers, and dugout canoes. The dugouts were his least favorite, though the most available in the Northwest. Red cedar logs were plentiful and easy to work. In 1811, McKenzie and Wilson Price Hunt made an overland trek from Montreal, Canada, to Fort Astor. For part of the trip down the Columbia, they fashioned dugout canoes, which overturned in the rapids, and one man was drowned. So they abandoned the canoes and continued on foot.[12] Whatever boat type McKenzie used on that first exploration of the Willamette Valley and its tributaries, if any, I can find no evidence that the boats left any permanent tracks along the McKenzie River. The trapping grounds of the McKenzie proved unsuitable for the company, and the area was left untouched for several decades.

As settlers migrated into the McKenzie River area in the mid-1800s, the gentle drainage of the McKenzie encouraged trail development along the river. The first wagon road opened in 1862 and was named the Scott Trail, in honor of two brothers, Felix and Marion Scott, who blazed its path. In 1871, John Craig settled at what is now McKenzie Bridge. He worked to improve the trail and held the mail contract from Eugene, up the McKenzie, and across the Cascade Mountains into central Oregon. Sadly, he perished in a snowstorm trying to carry Christmas mail across the McKenzie Pass in 1877.

The first cattle drive along the McKenzie River Trail, amid virgin Douglas fir and snowcapped mountains, occurred in 1859. Rainbow trout rising to mayfly, caddisfly, or stonefly hatches tempted McKenzie Trail users. I envision a couple of cowboys along the trail, pausing from their evening camp chores, being drawn to the river by the sounds of trout slapping the surface in a frenetic frenzy as they responded to an evening hatch. How long would it take a wrangler, regardless of his exhaustion at the end of the day, to become an angler—to try with hook and line to match wits with a wary native rainbow? Word seeped out of the McKenzie drainage about the wonderful sport fishery on the river, as well as its scenic beauty.

By the end of the nineteenth century, the river drew increased numbers of fishermen. The first wayside inn

A 1903 McKenzie River rowboat, the predecessor of the early McKenzie fishing boats. COURTESY LANE COUNTY HISTORICAL MUSEUM

and resort was built on the upper McKenzie in 1886: the Log Cabin Inn. The inn still operates today, although a fire in 1906 destroyed the original structure. Wading the river, with fly rod in hand, was necessary but treacherous. Slick freestones, strong currents, and deep holes made to appear shallow by crystal-clear water dunked many fly fishers and drowned some. It did not take long for enterprising fishermen to find and use flotation.

Flat-bottom rowboats of limited freeboard were the first boats to be used by serious fishermen. Rowing in a river current, however, is quite different from rowing on a lake or other flat water. Boatmen soon discovered that it was prudent to row against the current. This slowed the boat's descent down the river. Oarsmen learned how to move the boat laterally across the current to avoid heavy rapids, rocks, downed trees, and other obstacles.

Carey Thompson Sr., founder of Thompson's Lodge at Vida, may have been the first person to take fishermen down the McKenzie for hire in 1909. If true, Thompson began a tradition of fishing guides who became known for their boating skills, river and fly-fishing expertise, courtesy, and good humor. McKenzie River guides have attracted serious-minded fly fishers, including a president, baseball hall-of-famers, and Hollywood stars. Thompson's boat was a flat-bottom, planked rowboat 18 to 22 feet in length and about 3 feet wide on the bottom amidships. The boat showed considerable flare and nominal rocker fore to aft, except for a slight upward rake under the bow. Vertical freeboard approximated 14 inches. The boat's strakes were planked or lapped, and frames were local material such

as Douglas fir, spruce, or cedar. The stem posts were white oak, Oregon ash, or Douglas fir. Interior appointments were modified slightly to accommodate one or two fly fishers, including an elevated platform at the transom end. The platform became a trademark of the early McKenzie River boats. It served as a perch on which the fisherman stood to cast his fly into attractive pockets as the guide slipped the boat downriver. Fishing attire for some dudes[13] included a coat and tie.

McKenzie River boats were hauled upriver by horse and wagon to suitable launch sites. The guide and his dudes would then drift several miles of river to fish productive pockets. Imagine the guide on the oars as he lowers the boat through the choppy whitewater of a rapid while his fly fisher stands and dances on the fishing deck, deftly casting into small pockets, all the while maintaining his balance. I once described this fishing technique to a group of intermountain guides on the upper Snake River. "My God," one grizzled guide responded, "they don't make fly fishermen like that anymore!"

These heavily timbered boats served their guides well, but they were troublesome in whitewater, and their

"My God, they don't make fishermen like that anymore!" A fly fisher maintains his balance as he fishes likely pockets en route downstream. COURTESY LANE COUNTY HISTORICAL MUSEUM

Dallas Murphy (left) and Charles Harold Richards in the fishing boat typically used from about the turn of the twentieth century through the 1920s. COURTESY LEROY PRUITT

weight and limited freeboard required the guide to ceaselessly work the oars. Though they loved their work, the end of the day brought welcome relief. They soon became broad-shouldered men of considerable stature, regardless of their size when they began guiding.

The bottom of the transom on the downstream end sat below the waterline. To the untrained eye, unseen rocks just below the surface were particularly hazardous. If a boat hit one of these rocks in a current of 3 to 6 miles per hour, it would stop dead momentarily. The impact would fracture the transom, buckle a plank and frame or two, and most likely pitch one or more occupants into the McKenzie's riley, cold water. Characteristics such as these led some guides to refer to the boat type as the old scow, often preceded with an expletive.

John Shirley West began guiding on the McKenzie in 1920 at age nineteen. Raised in Nimrod, he rowed clients for fifty-five years. West described the boats of that day as constructed of 1-by-12-inch boards, with bottoms that were 16 to 18 feet long. "You'd pull your arms off and not accomplish much. They wouldn't turn easily," he said.[14] Even the most skilled boatman had his hands full with this boat. West complained that he was bailing all the time. A river colleague recalls West's complaint: "When you went through some rapids in those days, you'd run 'em with just one oar in the water. You'd

have a bailing can in the other. You never could use both oars because you were bailing all the time."[15] According to West, "At that time there were no real boat builders anyplace. There were people who built boats. They'd build a boat and try it. If it worked, they'd use it. If it didn't they'd try something else."[16]

John West and his brother Roy built the first boat with a bottom length less than 16 feet in the early 1920s: "We decided if we had a wider boat and not quite so long, it would be stable and not tip so much. So we made one 14 feet long and 4 feet across the bottom." The wider bottom did indeed offer greater stability and less draft than the heavier boats. It turned more quickly, and in the fall, when the McKenzie River's volume was at it lowest, the boat floated where the heavier-timbered skiffs wouldn't. The West boat was different enough that a river colleague, Milo Thompson, jokingly called it "a bathtub with oarlocks."[17]

The boat's performance proved attractive, however, and other guides—including Milo Thompson—soon copied the pattern. The John West boat type remained the guides' preference from the early 1920s through the early 1950s. In 1920, the Model T Ford and trailer replaced the horse and wagon for hauling boats upriver, and the McKenzie River grew in popularity as a destination point for fly fishers.

Prince Helfrich and guides with a covey of West-type boats, circa 1930. Also called "bathtubs with oarlocks" by Milo Thompson, these were examples of the first boats less than 16 feet along the bottom. COURTESY OF DAVE HELFRICH

John West's boat represents the first serious pause in an eddy of evolution on the McKenzie River. He set the stage for the McKenzie River boat phenomenon. Twenty-five years later, Tom Kaarhus called his popular square-ender the John West boat in West's honor. It was now up to another man to modify the West boat type further. The adaptation led to a unique friendship and a series of river adventures that elevated McKenzie River boats to an elite status.

Endnotes

1. In the middle part of the last century, Prince Helfrich operated the Skyline Boys' Camp, a program designed to introduce youth to the river and its environments. One piece of the experience included river trips in their own drift boats. Helfrich built several 14-foot double-enders from Hindman's patterns, one of which was displayed for several years at Paradise Lodge on the Rogue River.

2. Unless otherwise stated, measurements of length are around the gunwales, or sheer line, of the boat.

3. Steele was the McKenzie's most prolific boatbuilder from the mid- to late 1950s until his death in the mid-1990s. Their users revere his boats.

4. Keith Clark, "Travelers at The Deschutes, 1813," Letter to the Editor, *Oregon Historical Quarterly* 77, (March 1976): 78–81.

5. Washington Irving, *Astoria* (Philadelphia: Carey, Lea, and Blanchard, 1836), vol. 1, 132.

6. Clark, "Travelers at The Deschutes," 80.

7. Gabriel Franchere, *A Voyage to the Northwest Coast of America,* translated and edited by Milo Milton Quaife (Chicago: Lakeside Press, R. R. Donnelley & Sons Company, 1954), 289.

8. Glyndwr Williams, a commentary on George Simpson's Character Book, The Beaver, *Canada's History Magazine* (Summer 1975), 5–17.

9. Ibid.

10. Clark, "Travelers at The Deschutes," 80.

11. Irving, *Astoria,* 133.

12. Franchere, *Voyage,* 101–111, especially 106.

13. An affectionate term used by guides to identify their clients.

14. Jim Boyd, "The Boat the McKenzie River Spawned," *Eugene Register-Guard,* December 14, 1974.

15. As retold by Dave Helfrich, *The Creel,* a publication of the Fly Fishers Club of Oregon, 40th Anniversary ed. (Portland, OR: Frank Amato Publications, 2001), 40.

16. Boyd, "Boat the McKenzie River Spawned."

17. Ibid.

CHAPTER 2

The Preacher and the Prince
The Light Board-and-Batten McKenzie Boat

"I wouldn't stand in that old scow today if it were tied to a tree."

—HANDWRITTEN NOTE IN LEROY PRUITT'S FAMILY ALBUM
ATTRIBUTED TO HIS DAD, VELTIE

Imagine the light board-and-batten boat broadside in the current. The oarsman pulls evenly on the oars and then does a quick pivot, pulling on the right oar while pushing the left, to align the boat with the flow of the river. He slips past a car-size boulder. Once past, he pulls hard on the right oar but falls backward off the rowing thwart as the pitch of the boat causes the oar blade to grab air instead of water. The man quickly recovers, repeats the move, and draws a full blade of river. The boat angles slightly to the left. He pulls more gently now on both oars. The current carries him downriver as the boat slips laterally across the stream. His eyes scan the rock garden ahead, searching for the navigable channel. The environment looked different when he and his boating partner scouted it from above a few minutes earlier. He is aware of this anomaly, but he is not accustomed to these dissimilarities when running virgin water. He stands momentarily in a half-crouched position to capture a better view of the rock garden ahead. There they are! Three rocks that resemble the dorsal fins of salmon appear in a line 10 yards above the chute, though from this vantage, the channel looks more foreboding.

He sits down, anchors his feet against the guest seat in front of him, releases the oars briefly to dry his sweaty palms on his shirt, and then regains his grip. There, that's better. Dry hands are less apt to slip. He notices a slight tightening in his chest. The adrenaline surge alerts him to every nuance of the rapid, yet strangely, it all seems a blur. He aligns the boat with the current again but pulls a little harder on the left oar as he slows his descent. The boat moves slightly to the right. His goal is to be close to the dorsal fins without obstructing the right oar. Once past this navigational mark, he pulls hard on the left oar

while feathering the right one. The boat slips below the last dorsal and catches the eddy.

He sits there momentarily, gives the chute one last survey, and then pushes the boat into two converging currents. The current on the left, being the stronger of the two, catches the upriver bow, causing it to heel to starboard and casting the boat 45 degrees to the current. He has a second to straighten out the boat and reposition it to hit the narrow chute dead center. A missed stroke of the oar will spell disaster. Perhaps they should have portaged this rapid too, but frankly, he's tired of the work, and if a rapid looks navigable, he will run it.

The oarsman pulls hard left while pushing on the right. The maneuver works. The boat glides down the tongue of water into the chute. He quickly pulls both oars in and leans as far forward as possible so that the blades are parallel to the sheer rails. The oar blades scrape the rock columns as he passes through. Once through, he extends the oars full length. He steadies the boat as it runs a series of standing waves, and then hauls hard left to pull the boat into an eddy. He turns the boat around, grabs an overhanging limb, stands up, and looks upriver for his partner. He watches as his partner emerges from the chute, rides the standing waves, and is reunited with him in the eddy.

The pair is giddy with excitement. They swap their stories, and then begin to examine the boats. One observes that the water sloshing about under the floorboards appears to be yellow. The other chides his colleague for showing his legs as he enters the rapid. Laughter echoes through the canyon when the first one through the chute admits that he missed a critical stroke that caused him to fall off his seat and observes that no

Veltie Pruitt (standing left), his ten siblings, and parents. Veltie's son, Leroy, writes about this picture, "The family of my grandparents, aunts and uncles are the greatest people I have ever known." COURTESY OF LEROY PRUITT

mere mortal could make the recovery he did. The two men boast, fence, and banter with each other for a few minutes, and then they turn serious, bail their boats, and consider the next stretch of this pristine wild river. Contrary to the opinions of their betting friends, they are now confident they will make it safely to the stream's mouth. Their two clients, who did as much walking as drifting, are below the next set of rapids, fly-fishing these virgin waters.

The year was 1938, and these men were on the rugged, beautiful, but treacherous Metolius, a Deschutes

Prince Helfrich runs a logjam on the Metolius River run in 1938. COURTESY OF LEROY PRUITT

River tributary in Central Oregon. The portage from road's end to the first safe point of launch was about a mile. Once they were on the river, portages over downed timber, impassable cascades, and boulder-laden rapids raised questions about the wisdom of this trip. Why would they risk their boats and lives to run this wild water? Was it because of the two dudes who paid for this adventure in order to fly-fish these virgin waters?[1] Was it because no one had run them before? Was it the lure of wild trout that had never seen an imitation fly? Was it their spirit of adventure and the need to peer over the next ridge or around the next bend of the river? The answer was likely yes to all the above. They also had a compelling desire to be first: the first to run the upper Rogue, Deschutes, Metolius, Crooked, John Day, and Owyhee Rivers in a McKenzie River boat. Two things are very clear: Their adventures would not have been possible without the light board-and-batten riverboat, and they developed rowing techniques that are used today to provide safe transport of boats and people down technically difficult rivers. These two men were the Prince and the Preacher, Prince Helfrich and Veltie Pruitt.

Veltie Pruitt was a fisher of souls and trout. Born on April 26, 1900, in Harrison, Arkansas, Veltie and his family moved to Oregon in 1911. Veltie's dad, David Leroy Pruitt, settled his family on a cattle ranch near Merlin, Oregon. Veltie's attraction to the outdoors came naturally. He and his nine siblings loved to hunt. The Rogue River flowed near their ranch, but he spent little time there. His attraction to a river came later, while he was attending college.

The Pruitts were a God-fearing family who attended church regularly. Sunday worship was a weekly ritual for the twelve-member family. This exposure, as well as Veltie's association with nature and his fondness for people, influenced his call to preach. Veltie graduated from Eugene Bible College, later known as Northwest Christian College. While there, he met, fell in love with, and married Ina Collins, a lovely and artistic woman from Kalispell, Montana. Ina was a fellow student. Together they had four children: Bessilee, Veltie Leroy, David Lael, and Janice. One of their children, Veltie Leroy, became a popular fishing and hunting guide in his own right.

Veltie Pruitt was blessed with a crystalline tenor voice and was a popular soloist at churches, public events, and riverside campfires. In 1936, he studied voice under Frank LaForge and Dudley Buck in New York. Following his return to Oregon, he received a "you-fill-in-the-amount" contract[2] from the Metropolitan Opera, but his call to serve, preach, and run the river outweighed his desire to sing professionally. Veltie served several churches and was one of the founders of the Christian Church in Oregon City.

His fondness for the McKenzie River developed while in college, and he maintained a connection with the river throughout his ministry. The stresses of public life caused Veltie in the late 1930s to move his family to a location halfway between Leaburg and Vida on the McKenzie. Until this time, rivers and fishing had been his avocation—part-time interests that rejuvenated his spirit. Now they became his vocation. Although he left the professional ministry, he saw the river as God's church, and he treated it and the people he guided with loving respect and care. For him, the river was a metaphor for life. Scout a rapid, identify the hazards and opportunity, chart one's course, and run the gauntlet. The Preacher was struck by the lessons of the river, and they undoubtedly influenced his perspectives, strengthened his faith, and brought him considerable joy. Veltie died on April 10, 1991, followed ten days later by his wife, Ina.

To fish the McKenzie, the Preacher used the traditional rowboat of the river, though he despised the thing. It looked good, but appearances were deceiving. Like its contemporaries, the boat flared considerably, had limited freeboard, was 22 feet long, and held a fly-fishing platform at the transom on which Veltie or his friend could stand. The river's current had no problem catching the boat and moving it downstream. It was a struggle, however, for the oarsman to maneuver and control the boat, which rowed like an ark.

In the mid-1920s, the Preacher had a revelation. Why not build and use a boat that was lighter, more maneuverable, and portable? He lamented, as John West had a decade earlier, that there must be a better way. The Preacher decided to make his next boat from the lightest and strongest material available, and large enough to accommodate the oarsman and a guest, yet small enough for two people to hand-carry. For this new boat, he chose

A boat very similar to the old scow used by Veltie Pruitt. This 1922 photo shows fifteen-year-old Prince Helfrich on the oars, along with a guest. Prince's dad, Ben, is standing on the fly-fishing deck. COURTESY OF DAVE HELFRICH

to use Sitka spruce and Port Orford cedar. He formed the bottom and sides from spruce boards and the frames from cedar. He knew that ounce for ounce, these two woods were the strongest materials available. Rather than use 1-inch-thick material, he resawed the spruce to an unheard-of $1/4$- to $3/8$-inch thickness for the sideboards and the bottom planks to $1/2$ inch. The 22-foot heavily timbered old scow had eight frames, whereas this smaller light board-and-batten boat required eleven frames in order to shore up the lighter boards. A new friend, who shared Veltie's love of music, milled the rough boards to dimension for the Preacher. He was Torkel Gudmun "Tom" Kaarhus, a recent immigrant who worked at a local planing mill. This is the same Tom Kaarhus who opened his own boat shop ten years later and had major influence on the McKenzie River drift boat (see chapter 3).

Veltie built the board-and-batten boat, which measured 13 feet from stem to stern and was 3 feet wide on the bottom amidships. Three 12-inch planks ran lengthwise to form the bottom. The sides required two boards plus a modest wash strake from the oarlocks to the downstream transom end. This third strake added 4 inches in elevation at the transom. From the stem post to the transom, the vertical elevations from the baseline of the boat to the sheer line rose from about 12 to 23 inches, in a fair line. The boat was 5 feet across the sheer amidships and had about a 9-inch rake under the bow to frame #5. From that point to the base of the transom, there was nominal rocker.

The Preacher used $7^1/2$-foot oars for the boat. His earliest oars had about a 1-inch bore in the center of the blade. The holes may have been made to reduce pressure on the oar when in heavy water, though the practice actually weakened the oar. Another reason may have been merely to allow the oar to be hung in storage. He soon abandoned this custom.

Veltie had to adjust to his new boat. It was tippier than his old scow, and its smaller size limited the load to one guest, fishing tackle, and a modest amount of gear. What it lacked in carrying capacity, however, it made up for in maneuverability and ease of rowing. It was a charm to handle in fast-moving currents, and the Preacher had energy remaining at the end of the day. The boat sat high in the water and slipped handily across the current, making it easy to overshoot an entry point to a rapid, one of the adjustments Veltie had to learn to make. He was able to load and unload the boat without assistance and could reach portions of the river's trout pockets unattainable in

Veltie Pruitt fishes the McKenzie from his newly built light board-and-batten riverboat, circa 1925. COURTESY LEROY PRUITT

The boat was light and maneuverable. This picture was taken on the Rogue River during the duo's June 1931 run from Prospect to Shady Cove. It was the first known attempt to run this stretch. The Preacher holds his boat as Prince negotiates a typical rocky course. It was on this trip that Veltie used oars with a 1-inch bore in the blade. COURTESY OF LEROY PRUITT

the old scow. His learning curve with the lighter boat was steep but short. He fell in love with this boat, whose performance was vastly superior to the old scow. Perhaps what he liked most about the boat was its portability. It easily mounted a trailer, and Veltie built a special frame for his touring car so the boat could be cartopped, making transporting it even more practical.

Prince Helfrich was born to Byron Benjamin and Ruth (Gladys Wright) Helfrich on October 19, 1907, near Prineville, Oregon. Prince was his given name—he was named in honor of a family friend and Forest Service employee, Prince Glaze.[3] Honoring friends in such a way was a custom in the Helfrich family, and one of Prince's sons, James Dean, was named after a good friend and client, Dean Witter.

Ben, Ruth, and young Prince moved to the McKenzie River in 1912 by way of McArthur, California. Ben left Prineville to operate a large ranch southeast of California's Mount Shasta with his brother Jim, but he sold it after a few years. The sale was something Ben and Ruth later regretted. Had they retained the ranch until after World War I and into the California land boom, the property would have brought more money. Ben and Ruth purchased 160 acres of McKenzie River property, which included about 1 mile of riverfront, as well as tim-

ber and meadows. Young Prince explored every aspect of this beautiful environment, from the river to the mountains. He had a natural curiosity that caused him to learn about ecosystem relationships within this setting.

Prince became a skilled outdoorsman as a youth. When he was sixteen, he lived off wild berries and small game for a week because forest rangers were unable to reach his mountain fire lookout with supplies. As a young guide on the Snake River, he was once forced to feed his crew and guests wild game that he harvested after the party's supply boat was lost in rapids, leaving the group without food. Though he harvested the wilderness and its rivers, it was the conservation of these resources that became his central theme, and he soon began to practice and encourage catch-and-release, safely releasing fish he had caught.

Basalt columns, obsidian flows, volcanism, riverbeds, and freestones piqued his curiosity early on. A desire to better understand the land and its formations led him to obtain a degree in geology at the University of Oregon in 1929. With degree in hand, he decided that life on the river and in the wilderness was sufficient for his needs.

In college, he met Marjorie Love Peyton, an undergraduate student from Klamath Falls, Oregon. Marjorie graduated a year before Prince and taught school at Mosher, a small town in the Columbia River Gorge.

Prince pursued a long-distance courtship and asked her to marry him the spring of 1931. She accepted, and they married without her parents' consent. Marjorie's parents had made it clear that they didn't like Prince, believing that as a mountain man, hunter, and guide, he was a man without promise and beneath their daughter. Little did they know then about the accolades he would garner within the fly-fishing world or the wealth he would accumulate through wise investments and hard, practical work.

Prince asked the Preacher to officiate at their wedding. He wanted it to take place on a large rock at the head of the McKenzie River's infamous Martin Rapids, a spot that could be reached only by boat. Veltie dissuaded his good friend and instead married the pair at the First Christian Church in Eugene on May 16, 1931. Together, Prince and Marjorie raised three sons and a daughter—David Prince, Richard Peyton, Diane Virginia, and James Dean—all of whom in their unique ways continue and expand what has become known by fly fishers around the West as the Helfrich dynasty. When asked how she and Prince were able to stay together when so many other guides' marriages failed, Marjorie offered two reasons: First, she was actively involved in supporting Prince's work, and second, she said, "Marriage is a decision. I took it seriously."[4]

Prince began guiding on the river at a young age. His skill on the oars, ability to teach, knowledge of the river and fly fishing, riverside cookery skills, and calm demeanor drew all manner of people to him. He was as comfortable guiding the president of the United States or a business giant as he was guiding a young man and his son on their first joint fishing trip. In 1947, encouraged by a client, Prince opened a weeklong wilderness and river camp for boys. The Skyline Summer Camp became a popular event and continued for fifteen years. Prince's eldest son, Dave, and several of his guide colleagues assisted him. Boys involved in his river camp were treated to a week on the McKenzie, learning how to navigate technically difficult water in drift boats, set up and break camp, cook, and fish. They also learned about the environment. In the early 1960s, Prince built several 14-foot double-enders for the camp, using patterns provided by Woodie Hindman.

Prince became a premier McKenzie guide, respected by those who knew him and revered by reputation. He was always cordial, instructive, and an excellent guide, and he provided people with river experiences that brought a lifetime of memories. Prince understood relationships within and among ecosystems, and he was an articulate spokesman for conversation and outdoor education. He was a person ahead of the environmental curve. Former Oregon governor Bob Straub wrote: "Prince had a sensitive appreciation of nature and of the environment of anyone I have known. Camping out with Prince, I noticed birds would come a little closer to his campfire with their songs, and deer were visible and calm. Nature knew a kindred soul in Prince."[5]

Prince Helfrich died on June 23, 1971, at the age of sixty-three. He left a legacy of adventure, friendship, and respect for his environment.

Prince and Marjorie on the McKenzie Pass in the Oregon Cascade Mountains, circa 1930. The boat atop the car is Veltie's light board-and-batten boat.
COURTESY OF LEROY PRUITT

Prince and his four children ready to fish. From left to right: Dean, Diane, Dick, and Dave.

The Preacher's boat as a cartop made traveling to distant rivers more efficient and practical. The boat was light enough for a couple of people to load and offload easily, and it made accessible rivers hitherto out of reach. This photo was taken in central Oregon, circa 1932. COURTESY OF LEROY PRUITT

It was in 1928 that Prince and the Preacher first met. As Veltie Pruitt fished the McKenzie, a guide with a client hailed him over to an eddy. The guide was Prince Helfrich. Prince had seen Veltie and his light boat previously, but he had not been close enough to engage the man in conversation. Prince introduced himself and inquired about the boat. Being a Pruitt, Veltie likely invited Prince to take it out and row it around a bit. Prince liked what he felt. Unlike his own boat, Veltie's was light and responsive. It could pivot on a dime, seemed to be as tough as nails, had a shallow draft, and was a charm to row. Prince also observed that one person could easily handle the boat on land. This was a huge contrast to his heavily timbered boat, which usually required four people to off-load and load onto a trailer. Prince asked Veltie to build a light boat for him. The Preacher agreed. Thus began a lifelong friendship that engaged these two men, along with a few other friends, in a number of river runs made possible by the Preacher's light board-and-batten boat. Whether it was for fishing or the sheer joy of running a river, Prince and the Preacher used their boats to explore northwestern wild rivers that had not yet seen a riverboat.

Oregon's Deschutes River, like the McKenzie, offered some of the finest fishing in the Northwest. My dad, George, told of his days in the 1920s on Oregon's lower Deschutes. He and his brothers often caught the 3:00

A.M. freight train in The Dalles and traveled into the Deschutes River canyon. The engineer stopped long enough to drop them at the river's edge at 4:30. As soon as it was light enough to tie on a fly, they began their search for the native redsides, a rainbow trout indigenous to the Deschutes. They would fish all day, and then hop the return train around midnight, arriving back at the family ranch in the Hood River Valley in time to put in a full day's work.

McKenzie-based fly fishers could reach portions of the upper Deschutes by foot, but much of it was made inaccessible by canyon walls and distance from passable roads. Native redsides and their anadromous cousins, salmon and steelhead, made the Deschutes and its tributaries their home and spawning grounds. Prince, the Preacher, and their McKenzie friends had fished the banks of the upper Deschutes. They could not help but wonder about the canyons and remote portions of the river. Could the river be run? There was only one way to know. Veltie had rigged a carrying frame for his 1929 touring car to cartop his boat greater distances. He could drive over the McKenzie Pass into central Oregon without having to worry about the vagaries of a trailer. In 1938, the Preacher and Prince ran the Crooked River, a Deschutes River tributary. Later that year, they ran the Deschutes from the confluence of the Crooked and Deschutes Rivers to the Columbia. These were the first times the rivers had been

Upper Rogue River
Run by Prince Helfrich and Veltie Pruitt in June 1931

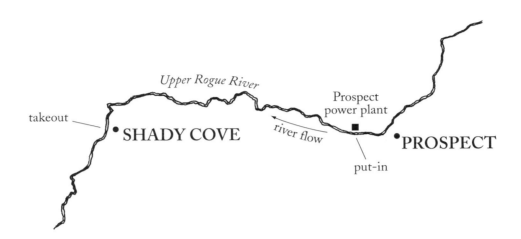

run. The trip brought scenery and fishing into focus that no one else likely had seen before. "Each turn in the stream presented a wildly beautiful picture," Prince later wrote. "This was a fisherman's paradise. Midday, when the insects hatched, the water's surface was constantly broken by rising fish."[6] A pattern developed for the Preacher and Prince: ponder the navigability and fishery of a river, then try to run it and fish it. There was an entrepreneurial reason for their seeming madness—they were looking for and testing new waters on which they might take future clients, a system that proved to be productive for them over time.

Prince and the Preacher were the first to run the upper Rogue in June 1931 from Prospect to Shady. This was a rocky and technically difficult stretch of river that was considered by some people to be impassable. In September of that year, they ran the lower Rogue from Galice to Agness. A friend of theirs, Dr. Earl Rebhan of Springfield, accompanied them on both trips and filmed their adventure. Rogue River guides had plied the lower Rogue for several years in their lengthy, cumbersome river drivers and had to line many of the rapids. Imagine their dismay when a pair of light board-and-batten boats skirted around the fringe of Tyee, a class IV rapid, or ran Graves Creek Falls, Slim Pickens, Upper and Lower Black Bar Falls, Kelsey Falls, or Staircase. These experiences led to envy among some Rogue River guides, and

A pair of Veltie's boats on the river, perhaps the Rogue, circa 1935. Prince is on the oars, and both clients are fishing. The upper boat is positioned to fish the tailout of the hole.
COURTESY OF LEROY PRUITT

in a few cases, resentment. This was particularly true when the Rogue guide's clients would ask, "Why can't we run those rapids?" Much time was wasted lining the Rogue River, driving boats around a dozen rapids that the McKenzie boats could run. The clients were there to fish.

Press Pyle, a respected Rogue River guide, rowed a light McKenzie board-and-batten boat the length of the lower Rogue in the late 1930s. Pyle didn't identify the boat's owner. "It bobbed like a cork," Pyle reported. "Sat real high in the water, it did. It would kind of skitter. Scared the hell out of me. Took me places on that river I never been before. I never rowed one again."[7] River guide Bobby Pruitt, however, disputes Pyle's claim, saying that Pyle rowed a McKenzie boat on one of his Owyhee River trips in the mid-1950s.[8]

One of the more interesting stories about the Preacher and Prince relates to the Smith, a McKenzie River tributary. With help from some friends, the pair hand-carried one of their board-and-batten boats several hundred yards through virgin timber in order to run the stream. Their load included fly rods and tackle, oars, and rope for lining rapids, should they encounter water that the light boat couldn't handle. The intrepid duo was also the first to run the Crooked and John Day Rivers.

The Preacher and Prince likely would have felt uncomfortable about the credit I give them for their pioneering work on Oregon's wild rivers. They were gracious and humble men, and others were involved in their exploits. Veltie Pruitt would have been the first to say that his light board-and-batten was nothing special, merely an attempt to make his river experiences more comfortable and achievable. He knew what he wanted in a riverboat, and he built it. Form followed function. The truth is, however, that Veltie built the first light board-and-batten riverboat, it drew Prince to him, and they launched their boats on a variety of virgin rivers. Together they represent the character of the early McKenzie River fly fishers and rivermen. Veltie Pruitt was one of a few who set the bar for a tradition of maneuverable and safe whitewater boats as fishing platforms.

The board-and-batten boats used by the intrepid duo were not perfect. The boats tended to leak. The timbers used for the side strakes limited the boats' profile. As a result, the boats occasionally shipped water on milder rapids. It took a Norwegian transplant to revolutionize the McKenzie River boats.

The intrepid duo, Prince (left) and Veltie, confer at the close of their 1938 run of the Deschutes River. Their exploits on that trip were filmed and shown at the 1939 World's Fair.
COURTESY OF LEROY PRUITT

Endnotes

1. The two dudes were San Francisco financier John Gallois and a U.S. Marine Corps captain Jackman. The *Portland Oregonian* posted an account of this trip on August 7, 1938. The trip stirred considerable interest and concern for the foursome around the state, especially in the Bend area of central Oregon, during their descent. The Metolius had not been run before. I have found no record that it has been run since.

2. Leroy Pruitt interview, March 16, 2003.

3. Glaze Meadow at Black Butte Ranch in Sisters, Oregon, is his namesake.

4. Marjorie Helfrich interview, May 15, 2000.

5. Prince Helfrich, *Tales of the Oregon Cascades* (Hillsborough, CA: Natural World Press, 1990), a 224-page publication of essays published posthumously by Prince's wife, Marjorie Peyton Helfrich. The essays first appeared in the *Eugene Register-Guard*.

6. Helfrich, *Oregon Cascades*, 73–74.

7. A taped interview with Press Pyle, by Steve Pritchett.

8. Bobby was Veltie Pruitt's nephew and a member of the clan that remained on the Rogue River. He made the comment during a recorded reunion of river guides in Eugene, Oregon, on April 2, 2000.

CHAPTER 3

Torkel Gudmund Kaarhus
The Original McKenzie River Drift Boat

"I'll bet it will make a very fine whitewater boat."

—PRINCE HELFRICH AND VELTIE PRUITT

In one of my interviews with the Preacher's son, Leroy Pruitt, he recalled with fondness the 1940 movie *Abe Lincoln in Illinois,* which covered the life of the country's sixteenth president from his days as a Kentucky woodsman to his election in 1860. It was Leroy's recollections of the movie that drew him to the banks of the McKenzie, where a portion had been filmed. Both Veltie Pruitt and Prince Helfrich, along with a number of other locals, had served as extras. There was nothing young Leroy enjoyed more than being at his dad's shirttail, rarely underfoot but always taking advantage of any opportunity to be with or do something special with the Preacher. A trip with his dad to the filming of this movie to serve as extras was one of those special events.

During a break in the filming, Leroy recalls, his dad and Prince looked down on the river and talked about a boat nestled into the riverbank.[1] "Do you notice that the boat has one side panel?" asked one of the pair. "It's not board and batten." "And look at how nice and high the boat sits in the water," noted the other. "I'll bet it will make a very fine whitewater boat," they both predicted. The Preacher and Prince were looking at their first plywood square-ender built by Tom Kaarhus. Leroy Pruitt knew Tom Kaarhus, who had milled his dad's spruce and cedar for the light board-and-batten boat he pioneered eleven years earlier. Veltie, Prince, and Tom had remained friends over the years.

Prince's oldest son, Dave, told me the same story about his dad's introduction to a Kaarhus boat. He recalls that Prince and the Preacher were impressed that the plywood boat was lighter than the board-and-batten boats, and that the transom sat higher out of the water.

The side panels, transom, and bottom each were one piece. In their board-and-batten boats, the Preacher and Prince occasionally shipped water in modest rapids. That meant having to stop and bail the boat before the next set of rapids in order to navigate them safely. In very busy water, such as the upper McKenzie, it was difficult to find a quiet eddy in which to stop and bail the boat. Shipping water was less of a problem in the high-sided Kaarhus boat. The light plywood boat was no more maneuverable than Prince's board-and-batten boat but it sat higher in the water, had more freeboard on the downriver end, and had greater carrying capacity. Dave Helfrich recalls that it wasn't long before Prince and the Preacher were taken by the river-worthiness of the Kaarhus boat.[2]

Until 1938, McKenzie riverboats were board-and-batten construction. The length, width, and thickness of the planks and the run of the wood's grains helped define a boat's shape. A plank is difficult to conform to a bend that is unnatural, and builders long ago learned to "listen to the wood,"[3] to let it tell them what it will and won't do. Board-and-batten boats were therefore fairly homogenous in appearance, and it was difficult to determine who made each boat. About this time, Kaarhus posted brass nameplates on his boats that read, "Built by Kaarhus." His joinery work was excellent, and generally one could distinguish a Kaarhus-built boat from one cobbled together by a river guide. The nameplate eliminated any confusion.

Among the early McKenzie River boatbuilders, Kaarhus was the most skilled craftsman. Woodworking was his profession of choice, and crafting boats was one of several interests he pursued. In his Kaarhus Craft

Shop, he built kitchen cabinets and other home furnishings, skis, riverboats, lake boats, and sailboats. He had a keen eye for problem solving because he understood relationships between form and function. For example, a powerboat aficionado visited Tom's shop in the late 1930s and asked him to identify and fix a problem with his boat. The man raced the boat, but it was slow to get up on plane. Once up, the boat moved efficiently. Could Tom find a way to modify the boat so it got up more quickly? Tom examined the boat, tested it on the water, and offered a suggestion: The rounded base of the transom didn't provide enough "bite" on the water when the motor was powered up. The owner thought that made sense and asked Tom to modify his boat. Tom adjusted the transom end of the boat to include a slight downward thrust at the chine. It worked beautifully.[4]

The same ingenious eye revolutionized McKenzie River boats. The McKenzie square-ender carries the Kaarhus name today, though he was sensitive to the origin of the boat type by identifying it on his sales list as the John West Model.[5]

In 1935, Tom Kaarhus opened his own business, the Kaarhus Craft Shop, at 1366 Moss Street in Eugene. That year and the next, Tom built his McKenzie River boats in this shop. They were of board-and-batten construction, with spruce ribs, cedar planking, oak chines, and bottom battens. He also had some Philippine mahogany planks resawed at the Ford Nelson Mill and used them for planking on some of his riverboats.[6]

Tom began to explore the use of plywood for boat construction. The introduction of plywood simplified riverboat construction. The flexibility and durability made it an ideal material for boats. More important, it was easy to work and allowed for free-form construction (see chapter 11). A plywood boat could be built in half the time it took to form a board-and-batten boat. Two side panels were cut from a single 4-by-14-foot sheet of ¼-inch plywood, on which the station lines were marked as guides for the application of the frames. The frames were preformed with the appropriate bevels and rectangular notches for the chine. They were installed at the station lines, beginning with the centermost frame.

Veltie Pruitt (left) and Prince Helfrich as extras in the 1939 film Abe Lincoln in Illinois. *It was during the filming of the movie that the two got their first look at a Kaarhus plywood boat.* COURTESY OF LEROY PRUITT

Each frame thereafter was installed fore and aft, until the hull was ready to receive the transom and stem. The frames gave the boat its shape and rocker. To help align the ribs, Tom used a piece of $1/4$-inch plywood 10 inches wide tacked to the inside of the bottom frames along the marked centerline. Simple.

With plywood construction, Kaarhus also was able to provide patterns, materials, and instructions to guides who wanted to build their own plywood boats. Veltie Pruitt was so impressed with the Kaarhus square-ender that he built a Kaarhus boat from kit material during the winter of 1939. Veltie's son, Leroy, built his first boat in 1943. It too was a square-ender from a Kaarhus kit. Near as I can tell, Tom Kaarhus was the first builder to provide riverboat kits. This innovation made riverboats more accessible to people who otherwise might not be able to afford them. According to one of his granddaughters, Maeve Kaarhus, kit customers frequently came back to Tom with questions, and he patiently walked them through each step of the building process. Maeve's dad, Tom's son and partner, Joe

Gudmund, commented that they probably never made any money from them as a result.[7] That's the way Tom was—generous.

There were two problems initially with plywood. First, it was originally manufactured in 8-foot lengths only, and there was no effective way to extend the panels' length. Second, the adhesives that bound compressed veneer together were unreliable when exposed to the elements. About 1937, one of the northwestern manufacturers offered 12-foot panels and claimed that its adhesive was waterproof. Tom built a test boat with these 12-foot panels. He exposed the boat to the weather, loaned it out to a couple of guides, and used it himself. Unlike previous plywood he had tested, this material did not blister or separate. He did notice some minor checking of the plywood, a frequent occurrence with exterior-grade and, later, marine-grade fir plywood, but this was inconsequential to the integrity of the boat.[8] Tom was pleased with the results of his tests.[9] As soon as 14-foot panels became available in late 1938, he moved from board-and-batten to plywood construction.

Veltie Pruitt builds his first square-ended plywood boat from a Kaarhus kit in 1939. Kaarhus was one of the first to employ what I refer to as free-form construction. These Kaarhus boats have come to be known as the original McKenzie River drift boats. The location of Veltie's project is the top floor of the old Eugene City Hall, where the archway reads, "Honor lies in honest toil." COURTESY OF LEROY PRUITT

The Kaarhus Craft Shop opened in 1935. Howard Hall, shown at right in this circa 1938 photo, was Kaarhus's first employee. Walter "Cy" Siebolt is to his left. Note the Olympic-class cat-rigged sailboat in front of the shop. COURTESY LANE COUNTY HISTORICAL MUSEUM

Inset: *Howard Hall in 2003 perusing memorabilia during our first visit to his home in Seattle. Hall carries very fond memories of Tom Kaarhus, for whom he offered to work without pay until he proved his worth. Kaarhus was impressed by the offer.*

The 14-foot plywood square-ender rapidly became the boat of choice among river guides. The boat was well suited for whitewater, had great carrying capacity, and was highly maneuverable and fun to row. Tom Kaarhus had set the new standard for McKenzie River boats.

Tom introduced another feature to the square-ender: a cutaway on the transom that allowed the boat to accept a motor. Brackets were installed on the transom, and then the cutaway was reinserted into the brackets. In this configuration, the boat was used as a whitewater fishing boat. The cutaway could be removed and a motor set in place for lake or river running. The broad base at the transom's chine allowed adequate bite for this boat to get up and plane with a 7- to 9-horsepower motor. The McKenzie square-ender thus became a very good dual-purpose boat. The square-ender with the cutaway transom ultimately became known as the Rapid Robert.

The name Rapid Robert is a conundrum. In 1955, *Science and Mechanics* published "Boat Builder's Handbook, Craft Print Project no. 33," written by Thomas E. Riley, in which the Rapid Robert is identified as the "MacKenzie [*sic*] River boat." The article features the Kaarhus Craft Shop and the McKenzie square-ender, with a detailed description of how to build the craft. Curiously, McKenzie River boatmen know the boat only as the square-ender or the original McKenzie River drift boat; outside McKenzie River country, the boat is known as the Rapid Robert. A well-known and respected Ore-

gon drift-boat builder, Ray Heater, was born and raised on the central Oregon coast, and in the 1950s, he knew this boat as the Rapid Robert. Ray has built this boat for years, and he considers it the unsung hero of the McKenzie tradition. So how is it that this boat came to be called the Rapid Robert? Apparently only Tom knew. The name is a mystery to Tom's granddaughters, McKenzie River guides, and at least two of his earliest employees.

Eugene Register-Guard outdoor writer Mike Stahlburg theorizes that perhaps Kaarhus recognized one of the many famous McKenzie River visitors by awarding the boat his name. Bob Feller began his baseball career in 1936 and soon became known as the pitcher with a great fastball. The first time Leo Durocher faced Feller, the hitter threw the bat down in anger after the second pitch and roared, "This kid looks at third base and stuffs the ball down your throat."[10] Feller's fastball invited the sobriquet Rapid Robert, and the name stuck throughout his career and into retirement. Is it possible that there was a connection between Kaarhus and Feller? The McKenzie River drew a number of well-known people to it.

Bill Lawrence of McKenzie Bridge has another theory: that Kaarhus, in his interviews with the *Science and Mechanics* author, referred to the boat as a "rapid robber" because the boat could navigate many rapids that hitherto were impassable. The author simply misheard Tom and thought he said, "Rapid Robert." Who knows? Both theories are interesting and plausible, though unsubstantiated.

It would not be beyond Tom to pull a fast one on later generations of McKenzie boat enthusiast. A common denominator among McKenzie River men was a sense of humor. Sometimes their humor was self-deprecating, but often it was at the expense of each other, especially if one swamped a boat, broke an oar, or lined rapids instead of running them. Quick to come to the aid of another when in difficulty, they were also competitive. Tom shared their humor. Howard Hall recalls a time when Tom was salmon fishing and an adjacent boatman asked how he was doing. Tom said, "Oh, I've got a couple." The man asked to see them, so Tom reached into the bottom of the boat and hoisted a nice chinook. Tom replaced it and then alternated hoisting and replacing the two fish in his boat, seemingly show-

ing the man a third, fourth, fifth, and sixth fish. The droll Norwegian impressed the inquirer. Hall says he can still hear Tom chuckle over the story.

Another story he liked to tell was of a trip on a cruise ship into the Seymour Narrows. As the tide evacuated the narrows, the captain had to lay off to the side and wait for the riptide to subside. It was a beautiful day, and everyone watched the rushing waters. When the tide had subsided a bit, the captain eased the boat into the current. As he did, the ship started to heel over. Instinctively, everyone on deck scrambled to the high side to counterbalance the boat. A heavyset English lady was the last to reach the rail. As she did, the boat righted and Tom exclaimed, "My God lady, you saved us all!" Tom said she gave him a very disapproving look.[11] Would

Ray and Daphne Heater fish the North Santiam River in Oregon from Ray's 14-foot Rapid Robert, a boat he continues to build today. Ray has known this boat as both the Rapid Robert and the original McKenzie River drift boat. Neither of us knows the origin of the name Rapid Robert, but that's what these boats were called when he was growing up on the central Oregon coast in the 1950s. COURTESY OF RAY HEATER

Tom Kaarhus and a friend with a day's catch of trout. Tom loved to fish, and he ate what he caught. COURTESY OF
MAURYA KAARHUS

Tom chuckle today if he knew how I have puzzled over the name, Rapid Robert? Perhaps.

Tom was born Torkel Gudmund Kaarhus on January 5, 1893, in Nedre Vats, Norway, a small island off the southwest coast, not very far from the birthplace of playwright Henrik Ibsen (1828–1906), an author Kaarhus later liked to quote. Being surrounded by water and fishing, the island made a lasting impression on Kaarhus. Water, boats, and his delight in fishing were grounded there. It was there also that the seeds were likely sown for his love of music, a lifelong interest. Orphaned at sixteen, Kaarhus emigrated to the United States in 1909, landing in Iowa with family friends.

Tom then moved to Silverton, Oregon, where he worked in home construction and began to refine his woodworking skills. His peripatetic nature led him to Alaska, where he fished commercially and was engaged in some boatbuilding, all the while nurturing his interest in music. It's not clear whether his time in Alaska occurred prior to his move to Silverton or after. In Silverton, he met and married Adena Franzen. Music was a lifelong interest, and he studied voice and belonged to and directed several choral groups.

Tom and Adena landed in Eugene, Oregon, in 1923 to help build the Pacific Christian Hospital."[12] McKen-

A young Tom Kaarhus at twenty-three. COURTESY OF
MAURYA KAARHUS

zie River guides affectionately remember him working at the Ford-Nelson Lumber Company, a planing mill. It was here that Kaarhus milled the spruce for Veltie Pruitt's light board-and-batten riverboat. It is unclear when and how Tom Kaarhus connected with the McKenzie River, its fishery, and the river guides. Tom and Adena loved to fish. His granddaughter Maurya Kaarhus recalls that he could eat fish three times a day. It is probable that Tom was on the river soon after his arrival in Eugene.

When Tom opened the Kaarhus Craft Shop, he, Adena, and son Joe Gudmund lived on the second floor. Adena handled the books, and Tom worked at his trade. His eclecticism was evident in the diverse offerings at the shop. He built cabinets and other home furnishings, finely handcrafted skis and snowshoes, and boats. Though he is best remembered among McKenzie River guides for his riverboats, he also built powerboats, lake boats, and sailboats. Two of his former employees, Howard Hall and Ed Reschke, recall Tom building Olympic and lightning-class sailboats, a hydroplane, and a trimaran.

Ed Reschke remembers Tom as a kindhearted and giving person who was sometimes generous to a fault.[13]

Howard Hall has similar recollections. Sometime in the mid to late 1930s, Woodie Hindman asked Tom for a job building boats, and Tom assigned Woodie to work with Howard (see chapter 4). Woodie stayed with Tom about a year to learn the trade and then started building boats on his own. If Tom felt used by Woodie, he didn't utter a word about it in the shop. "Tom was very gracious about it," Hall says. He was like that. Generous, gentle, and kind."[14] Ed Reschke recalls that Woodie Hindman, Prince Helfrich, Veltie Pruitt, and others were Kaarhus shop visitors. They discussed new ideas, boat-handling issues, and the success of a day's fishing.[15] There was camaraderie among Tom, his employees, the guides, and the earlier boatbuilders. They shared ideas, asked questions, posed puzzles, and mutually discussed solutions. Individuals did not always take credit for their contributions to the boats' development.

All of these men by necessity were self-reliant and independent. John West, Veltie Pruitt, Prince Helfrich, Tom Kaarhus, Woodie Hindman, and the other river folks of their era had to employ considerable ingenuity to survive and succeed at what they did. I marvel at the courageous spirit of the sixteen-year-old Tom Kaarhus, recently orphaned, who made a successful life in a new

One of Tom's favorite boats, and the one he kept the longest, was a lake skiff. Here his grandson and granddaughter enjoy the peace of Gold Lake. COURTESY OF MAURYA KAARHUS

Ray Heater runs his Rapid Robert upriver with a customer. The boat nicely handles a 5- to 10-horsepower motor. This is an excellent dual-purpose riverboat, serving as a drift boat or a flat-water fishing craft under power. COURTESY OF RAY HEATER

country. He had to be strongly independent yet willing to accept a helping hand, use the assistance to his benefit, and continue on grateful for the support. Independence and dependence, two seemingly contradictory values, appear to have been central to success for Tom and the other early river guides and boatbuilders. These values reflect a pioneer spirit, and the men imbued it in others. Therefore, I think these folks appreciated and used each other's ideas as they visited, collaborated, and addressed the various issues concerning the boats and the river.

Tom Kaarhus stood above the rest as an innovator. His riverboat and ideas about boats were used, copied, and adapted. Some people consider this the greatest form of flattery. Tom's genius was the application of his experiences with boats and his craftsmanship to adapt and modify the riverboat type innovated by John Shirley West, the "bathtub with oarlocks." West's flat-bottom boats with minimal rocker were the first on the McKenzie with bottom lengths of less than 16 feet. Kaarhus seems to have built on the idea of a lighter, more maneuverable, safer, and more versatile boat. Some McKenzie guides erroneously thought that Kaarhus modified his boats to conform to his recollections of the boats he knew in Norway and Alaska. His son Joe dispels that notion: "All the (Nor-

way) boats he described to me were round-bottomed, clinker built. Dad simply improved on the flat-bottomed row boats he found when he moved to Eugene."[16]

Tom's interest in the potential of plywood and his application of that material as the boats' outer skin allowed him to do several things. He was more easily able to add or reduce rocker to the bottom of the boat fore to aft. This increased the boat's maneuverability in technically difficult water. He took advantage of the 4-foot-wide plywood sheets to give the boat more bottom width. More width was then carried through to the transom. The boat was able to displace more water and thus have considerably more carrying capacity. When Prince Helfrich and Veltie Pruit first saw a Kaarhus plywood boat, they immediately saw "a very fine whitewater boat" because they saw stability, capacity, and maneuverability.

Kaarhus was also innovative in his efficient use of material. He designed his plywood boats so that two side panels were extracted from one 4-by-14-foot, ¼-inch sheet. This feature, two panels from one 4-foot piece, has become a hallmark of most McKenzie River drift boats. Tom was no longer limited by the dimension of planks that gave rise to boats of more limited freeboard. Finally, he tested and proved the suitability of this boat for a

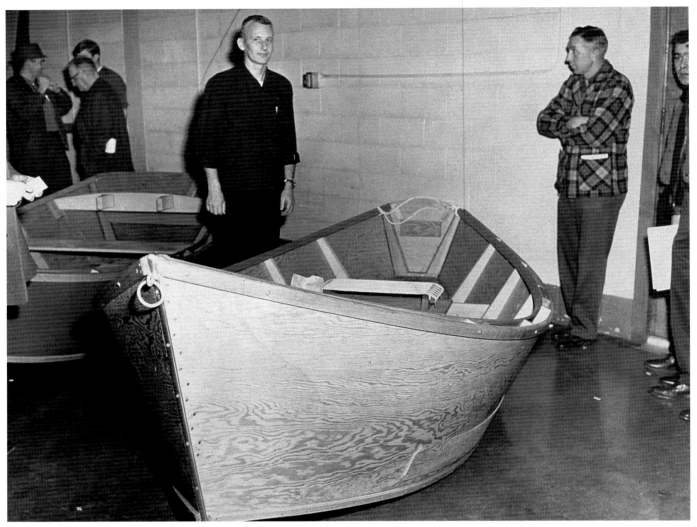

Joe Gudmund Kaarhus, Tom's son, stands beside a Kaarhus-built McKenzie double-ender with a transom in this photo taken circa 1955. Notice the Kaarhus square-ender behind him. Clear Douglas fir as used in the plywood panels is no longer available. COURTESY OF MAURYA KAARHUS

motor. An annoying inconvenience about most drift boats is that they must be put in at one point and taken out at another point downriver. Under some conditions, the Kaarhus boat could run back upriver. Tom's boats were the best whitewater fishing platforms to date. The Rapid Robert was ultimately replaced by the sexier looking double-enders, but in my view, they added little to the stellar performance of the Kaarhus boat.

Tom Kaarhus did not guide professionally. His river skills and fishing success earned both him and Adena the respect of the guides. He was, however, most appreciated for his boats. Tom continued to build McKenzie River boats through the 1950s. His only child, Joe Gudmund, worked with him and continued with the Kaarhus Craft Shop after Tom's death. The Kaarhus square-ender remained a boat of choice among many guides. The McKenzie double-enders, however, grew in popularity after World War II. Tom was quick to pick up this boat and add it to his inventory of offerings. Maurya Kaarhus

fondly recalls being on the river in the early 1960s with her grandfather, who would point out the boats he had built as they drifted. Tom had built most of the drift boats they encountered, and many of them were the double-ender with a transom. Woodie Hindman had departed McKenzie River country in 1954. Marty Rathje's tenure as a McKenzie boatbuilder was short lived. Keith Steele, the most prolific McKenzie River drift-boat builder during the last half of the twentieth century, was just getting started. Tom Kaarhus was the Man, his boats were popular, and his craftsmanship was stellar, so it's understandable that Tom had built many of the boats Maurya recalls seeing that day.

Illness overcame Tom in his final years. Shortly after his untimely death in 1964, his obituary in the *Eugene Register-Guard* eulogized: "To know that attitudes of true craftsmanship shape actions of the heart as well as those of the hands, one needed only to know Torkel G. 'Tom' Kaarhus. . . . Tom was far famed as the originator of the

McKenzie River boat, and widely known as one of the best all-round masters of the woodworking art. But, in this community he was loved as much if not more than he was respected." He was "at once the friends of youngsters who stood enthralled watching him work in his shop and the friend of industrial magnates impressed by his extraordinary, quiet but assured, personality. . . . Everything Mr. Kaarhus did, he did with dignity and with personal devotion to an inner, personal sense of excellence."[17]

Tom Kaarhus's eclectic life as boatbuilder, cabinetmaker, singer, dancer, fisherman, poetry aficionado, and teacher led his granddaughter Maeve Kaarhus to observe, "He was a Renaissance man."[18] That may say it best. Just as the Renaissance marked the transition from the medieval to the modern world, Tom Kaarhus's personification of fine craftsmanship and the arts marked a transition from antiquities to modernity in boatbuilding.

Endnotes

1. Leroy Pruitt's youthful affection and admiration for his dad remain today. This is evident in his consistent references to "Daddy" whenever speaking of Veltie.

2. Dave Helfrich interview, March 20, 2001.

3. This phrase was used by Colorado River guide and author Brad Dimock when we built the *Julius* in my shop in the fall of 2001. The *Julius* was a lapstrake riverboat of the Galloway type, originally built by Oregon's Buzz Holmstrom in the winter of 1936–37. Holmstrom used this boat to solo the Colorado from the headwaters of the Green River through the Grand Canyon to Lake Mead. I had laid the *Julius* out on paper and modeled the forms we would use to build the boat. Only when we allowed the Port Orford cedar planks to lie along lines consistent with their natural bend did we achieve the Holmstrom look. As we rediscovered this phenomenon, Brad exclaimed, "Listen to the wood. It will tell us what to do!"

4. A story reported by Howard C. Hall, Tom Kaarhus's first shop employee (1935–40), interview, September 23, 2003.

5. Hall interview.

6. Howard Hall letter dated April 30, 2005. The mahogany planking supported a beautiful finish. Hall also notes that another popular boat constructed of mahogany planking was a 15-foot Olympic class cat-rigged sailboat.

7. Maeve Kaarhus letter to the author, May 4, 2005.

8. Checking is caused by loss of moisture in the face veneer, resulting in shrinkage of the outer veneer. As the dimensions of the veneer change, the stresses between the face and the under-

Tom Kaarhus in his later years, a Renaissance man.
COURTESY MAURYA KAARHUS

lying veneer or core cause a minute rupture in the fiber to occur. Actually, such stresses are nothing more than a restraining action of the more stable core. These checks usually follow weaker areas, such as lathe marks, pores, or splices in the veneer.

9. Hall interview.

10. Baseball Historian online at www.baseballhistorian. com/index.htm; with Bob Feller, at www.baseballhistorian. com/html/bobfeller1.htm.

11. Hall interview.

12. Kaarhus obituary, *Eugene Register-Guard,* August 1964.

13. Ed Reschke correspondence, April 15, 2002. Ed was a Kaarhus Craft Shop employee in the 1940s.

14. Hall interview.

15. Reschke correspondence.

16. Jim Boyd, "The Boat the McKenzie River Spawned," *Eugene Register-Guard,* December 14, 1974.

17. Obituary, *Eugene Register-Guard,* November 1964.

18. Maeve Kaarhus correspondence, May 15, 2005.

CHAPTER 4

Woodie Hindman
The Double-Enders

"The high curling waves of these rapids do their best to bend a boat to fit their pattern.
. . . All I've done is build hulls shaped to the roll of the river. That's why wooden
boats go through without trouble where even rubber rafts are sometimes swamped."

—WOODIE HINDMAN AS QUOTED BY DAVE ROBERTS
IN THE "ROD AND GUN" COLUMN, *SEATTLE TIMES*, JULY 23, 1952

Woodie Hindman's first trip down a river in the McKenzie River drift boat may have reminded him of his younger days as a cowboy and trail cook in the Texas panhandle and eastern New Mexico. Oregon's McKenzie River drainage, framed with tall timber and towering mountains, was a very different environment from the flat horizons of his McLean, Texas, origins. But as Woodie experienced his first set of standing waves in a boat, perhaps it awakened memories of the gentle, rolling canter of his horse as the pair worked stray cattle. His first time through the McKenzie River's Martin Rapids may have been reminiscent of the harsher pitch and roll of a quarter horse as they separated a calf from its mother. In both cases, Woodie's security depended on his ability to keep his derriere firmly planted—in the saddle or rowing seat. He required a horse and a boat that were responsive to his cues. A slack rein coupled with a light touch of his heels to the flanks brought an instant response from his horse. A deft draw on the left oar coupled with a firm feathering of the right oar gently rotated the boat to port for a perfect entry into the rapids. It was evident in how he communicated with his boat, his horse, and the people around him that Woodie had a gentle but firm hand that reflected a genuinely likable personality. I imagine that as he completed his first run of the McKenzie, he rediscovered a sense of place. The recent divorce from his wife and his separation from family back in the Texas panhandle still pained him. But he remembered the advice of his mother: Leave McLean and find something you truly enjoy doing.[1] He had found a new home.

McKenzie River drift boats reached their apotheosis at the hands of this kindly Texas transplant who prior to 1933 had no experience with riverboats or the McKenzie River. His subsequent river experiences and predisposition to tinker with and tweak his boats, coupled with insights from his guide colleagues, led Woodie to craft two major drift-boat innovations over the next twelve years: the McKenzie double-ender and the double-ender with a transom.

Wood Knoble Hindman was born on March 21, 1895, to John Robert and Mary Ivy (Forte) Hindman. He preferred to be called Woodie. The youngest of five children, he was closest in age and affection to brother Joe, two years his senior.[2] There is some confusion as to his birthplace. Popular belief is that he was born in McLean, Texas, but according to his mother's 1936 autobiographical sketch, the family didn't move to McLean until 1902.[3] Brother Joe was born in Fairley, Texas. It's possible that was Wood's birthplace too.

Pa and Ma Hindman, as John and Mary came to be known in McLean, worked hard and showed an entrepreneurial spirit. Their first McLean home was a half dugout.[4] They remained there for a short period, and then moved into a second half-dugout located near the Rock Island Railroad Line. The line opened in 1900 and became a conduit for passengers in 1901. Many chose to stay overnight in McLean. In 1904, the Hindmans decided to start a small hotel business in their dugout. As one would imagine, prospective guests were reluctant to enter the grotto. Once inside, however, the guests were treated to comfortable accommodations and excellent food. Their hotel grew in popularity, and in a few years they moved to the corner of Main and Railroad Streets, above ground this time. In 1916, the O'Dell Hotel was built and opened. The Hindmans purchased the building

The Hindman Hotel still stands today in McLean. Originally built as the Odell Hotel, the structure was a vast improvement over the Hindman's turn-of-the-century dugout. Photo circa 1930. COURTESY OF THE ALAN REED-MCLEAN MUSEUM

that year, and in 1927 they added fourteen new rooms to the sixteen-room structure. The building still stands today and remains the Hindman Hotel, though there is no longer a family connection to the structure.

Ma Hindman had a deep religious faith. When she and her family migrated to Texas from Kansas, they experienced unspeakable life-threatening hardships, and she found sustenance in prayer. She lost her mother when she was ten, and it fell on her to shoulder all the domestic chores and care for her siblings and father. She became particularly skilled in food preparation and soon reaped praise for her cooking. She refined her culinary skills over time and in her later years was known throughout the Texas panhandle for her fine cooking.[5]

The Hindman children assisted in the operation of the hotel. Though they worked hard, the men of the family enjoyed the area's fishing and hunting, taking prairie chicken, antelope, and deer.[6] In fact, when Pa Hindman died behind the wheel of his car from a heart attack on May 27, 1927, he was returning from a fishing trip. Woodie's death forty years later occurred while fishing, also from a heart attack. Woodie was raised in a family that worked hard, knew how to capitalize on business opportunities, and enjoyed the outdoors, especially fishing and hunting. Woodie's attraction to these sports also may have led to his being a wrangler and trail cook for a time, an interest for which he seemed to have a natural disposition.

A 1928 pencil drawing of Mary Ivy (Forte) Hindman.
COURTESY OF RUTH HINDMAN AND LINDA BUSH

Woodie enjoying fishing, hunting, and bird dogs in the Texas panhandle, circa 1930. COURTESY OF RUTH HINDMAN AND LINDA BUSH

Woodie was a slight man, although hard work produced a muscular frame. His dad and mother were also slight of build, but in her later years, Ma Hindman was much overweight. By her own account she weighed 260 pounds, probably a result of her own cooking at the hotel. Woodie inherited his mother's altruistic nature, although he had a characteristic deadpan expression that revealed little of what he was thinking. Because of this, some thought him to be unfriendly, but in fact, his poker face was the result of his selflessness. During the early stages of World War I, Woodie's brother Joe had been drafted into service. Joe was married and had a child, Joseph Marvin. Woodie was single and twenty-two, so he volunteered in Joe's place, a practice allowed at the time. Once inducted and trained, Woodie was shipped overseas. Onboard ship, however, he developed appendicitis, underwent surgery, and contracted lockjaw. To the relief of his family, and Joe in particular, Woodie never saw battle. He spent most of his service time recovering from the tetanus infection. The episode left some of his facial muscles rigid, something from which he never fully recovered. Thus his deadpan expression was a product of his altruism.[7]

In 1922, Woodie married Moody Newman. Together they ran a café in McLean. According to Ruth Hindman,

Moody left Woodie a few years later. He was heartbroken over her departure.[8] His mother encouraged him to leave McLean, find a fresh start, and do something he enjoyed. It was then that he moved to Eugene, Oregon, leased the Hampton Hotel, and made his connections with the McKenzie River. Woodie's move was difficult for Ma Hindman. She had already lost her husband, John Robert, and a year later, her eldest son, Jack, died. In Ma Hindman's 1936 journal, she comments how much she missed Woodie. Nevertheless, she was a woman who chose to put the welfare of her child first.

There is no record of Woodie's beginnings on the McKenzie River or his initial associations with the fishing guides. However, it's clear that his introduction to both came quickly. His attraction to fishing, his soft and unassuming demeanor, and his riverside skills led to prompt recognition of the man as someone the McKenzie guiding community wanted to know. Dave Helfrich recalled one example of that attraction, when Woodie introduced Dutch oven cooking to the guides.[9] To McKenzie River dudes, the draw to the guides was their fishing expertise, boating skills, and ability to offer comfortable camps and savory meals streamside. Using reflector ovens, and in some cases a deep cast-iron frying pan, the guides would delight their guests with biscuits, fruit cobblers, or other baked edibles, things dudes would least expect to find on a wild river. Woodie's outdoor cookery skills, learned from his mother and as a trail cook for hungry cowboys in the Texas panhandle and eastern New Mexico, included the creative use of number 10 and 12 Dutch ovens.[10] Woodie spaced hot coals from the campfire under the Dutch oven and on the lid to create uniform heat that was evenly distributed and, timed correctly, produced biscuits and desserts. According to Dave Helfrich, it wasn't long before Woodie was ordering Dutch ovens for the guides from his source in Amarillo, Texas. No longer did guides have to work with light reflector ovens, which were susceptible to the wind and blowing sand along the river, or worry about placing them carefully and rotating them toward the fire to capture irregular heat for baking. The Dutch oven found a new home on the McKenzie, and the river guides found a new friend and companion in Woodie Hindman.

In late 1935 or 1936, while operating the Hampton Hotel, Woodie went to work part-time for Tom Kaarhus in order to learn about McKenzie River boat construction. He worked for Tom about a year, and then left to build his own boats, taking his newfound knowledge and the ubiquitous McKenzie-West-Kaarhus boat designs with him. This didn't seem to bother Kaarhus but remains an issue with at least one of Kaarhus's grandchildren today. For a time, he tied his own flies and did well enough with this craft that he sold them to upscale customers who frequented the McKenzie. His passion quickly became the river, and it led him down three parallel paths: river running, guiding, and boatbuilding. All the while, he maintained the Hampton Hotel. By 1936, he was guiding for Prince Helfrich and other outfits, and he was beginning to build his own clientele base as a fishing guide. Between 1938 and 1943, Woodie built two to three boats a month in the off-season. The guides liked Woodie, and they liked his boats. His absorption into life on the river was rapid, and he brought with him an adventurous spirit, a dry sense of humor, a pleasant demeanor, and the insights of an innovator.

Woodie's Oregon story is closely tied to that of Ruth Wilhoit. Woodie and Ruth were attracted to each other shortly after she went to work for him at the hotel. She shared Woodie's interest in fishing, people, and adventures on the river, and they soon developed into a novel team. She ascended as an expert oarsman in a riverboat.

One of Woodie's specialties was cooking over a campfire and using a Dutch oven, circa 1950. Riverside cooking was part of the culture nurtured by the early McKenzie guides.
COURTESY OF KENNY KING

Often when Woodie was boatbuilding or guiding for another outfit, Ruth teamed up with a friend, Ruby Taylor. Ruby was married to Kenny Taylor, another guide, and she was equally skilled on the oars and at the business end of a fly rod. The two of them kept score of their fishing exploits together. Ruth's successes were usually equal to and frequently exceeded Woodie's. Woodie and Ruthie went together like a hand and glove, and the couple was married on June 12, 1937, in Eugene, Oregon.

Ruth was born on June 24, 1904, to Leander Franklin and Susan Cordelia (Dunne) Wilhoit in the isolated community of Ash, near Loon Lake in southwest Oregon. As a child, Ruth experienced the breakup of her parents.

Ruthie (Wilhoit) Rhodes in January 1936, before she and Woodie married. Their mutual interest in outdoor adventures of various kinds helped form their bond. COURTESY OF RUTH BURLEIGH

She remained with her mother, while her sister Nora went with their dad. Despite her family being divided, Ruth was raised in a caring environment and adopted the values of a people and a community that reflected their pioneering spirit: self-reliance and independence, hard work, and honesty. Nora returned to their mother when Ruth was a teenager. The sisters became very close, but the relationship between Nora and her mother was strained, perhaps because of the earlier separation.

In 1922, an attorney entered the remote valley surrounding Ash to do some legal work. Though Ned Rhodes was considerably older than eighteen-year-old Ruth Wilhoit, he showed an interest in her, and she responded to his romantic overtures. Perhaps he was able to meet needs that had been unmet during her childhood. For whatever reason, they were married later that

year, and she moved to Hood River, Oregon, with her new husband. During that time in Hood River, Ned worked little and drank heavily. Unable to tolerate this excess in his life, Ruth left Ned and moved to Eugene to be near her sister, Nora. In spite of Ned's drinking, he maintained a kind and caring demeanor toward Ruth, and Ruth maintained a lifelong fondness for him. When Ned died years later, she expressed considerable sorrow.

Woodie's and Ruth's attraction to each other was predicated in part on similarities of interest: the river, a yearning for excitement, enjoyment of people, and the need for companionship. Their mutual love for the river and Woodie's growing boatbuilding business led them to start looking for property in Springfield, Oregon—the gateway to the McKenzie River and a logical location for his boatbuilding shop. Woodie built his boats in the basement of the Hampton Hotel, and then in a hotel leased by his new sister-in-law, Nora, and her husband. Woodie purchased some Springfield property in 1941 and moved to their new location. It was another couple of years before his shop was completed.

As a person on the oars in heavy whitewater, Ruth was in the company of very few women. In 1950, the president of the McKenzie River Guides Association, Bill Sheppard, praised her skills in rough water. At that time, only three women had mastered the infamous 20-mile stretch of the McKenzie made famous by the annual White Water Parade of guides: Ruth Hindman, Ruby Taylor, and Coralee Thompson.[11] Ruth explained that her joy with the river was the thrill she got when the current gripped her light boat. "It's like a runaway roller coaster without tracks!" she said.[12]

Often Ruth and Woodie slipped away by themselves for quiet and adventurous solos on a mystical river. The rivers always harbored trout that allowed the pair to match the hatches and try to outwit their native friends. One river in particular caught their fancy—the Middle Fork of the Salmon in Idaho, a river that had some influence on Woodie's first riverboat innovation, the double-ender.

The flow of the Middle Fork is born of the runoff from the glacier-studded peaks of the Sawtooth Mountains in central Idaho. By early to midsummer, the ice and snow have retreated from the heights but rarely disappear completely. The river descends from an altitude of about 6,500 to 3,200 feet at its confluence with the Salmon, a distance of 110 miles. The tributary slips through canyon walls, some of which are near vertical, and is rife with rapids and drop-offs, falls and deceptive curl-backs, suck-holes and eddies, as well as limited stretches of calm water in which to catch one's breath. This spectacular cleavage threaded by the discharge of the Sawtooths places the intrepid visitor on holy ground, and one is never quite the same for having been there.

In June 1939, Woodie joined McKenzie River guides Ken Tayler and Ed Thurston on a guided trip down the Salmon River from Salmon (then known as Salmon City) to Riggins, Idaho, a distance of 165 miles. Adolph and Mrs. Spreckles of San Francisco employed the guides. Woodie wrote in his diary about that trip: "When we got down to where the Middle Fork empties into the Salmon, it looked as though the Middle Fork was a real trout stream. She was about 150-feet wide, cold, clear, deep and swift. So right there I began wondering what the river looked like." On that trip, Woodie tried to learn as much about the Middle Fork from the few locals along the Salmon including a forest ranger, who told Woodie that any consideration of a run down the Middle Fork is "not a bright idea." Just below "Salmon Falls we came to where Mr. Handcock[13] lives. He is a veteran of many a barge and boat trips down this river. I asked him if he knew anything about the Middle Fork. He said he had been all along the Middle Fork. He said he had run some . . . of it in a boat and I would find it tough going. That was the extent of our information."

Woodie's curiosity was piqued. Always on the lookout for new trout water, scenic wonders, and a fresh challenge, he couldn't dispel the idea of attempting the Middle Fork. He had only one problem: Ruth. "On arriving back to Eugene, Oregon, my home, the more I thought about a trip down the Fork, the more I wanted to go. So I broke the news to Ruth, my wife, about this trip and asked her if she didn't think that would be a swell trip. Her answer was, 'Well of all the dumb ideas of a good time!' Then she paused a moment and asked, 'When do we start?' That girl is awfully hard to get to go any place.

"So on July 20, 1939, Ruth and I with our 14-foot 200-pound boat built for fast and rough water, arrived after a 500 mile trip by car, with our boat loaded on our trailer in tow. At the headwaters of the Middle Fork of the Salmon is the Bear Valley Dude Ranch. . . . The manager of the ranch came out and asked, 'Where do you think you are going with that boat?' We told him we had a fool notion hit us to run the Middle Fork. . . . I asked him about the chances we had of making it. He told me he had been along it on horses and didn't have a bit of trouble, but he had packed out several parties that had started out in boats. His last advice was, 'Get down the canyon as far as possible before wrecking, for the farther down you get, the more it will cost you to be packed out.'" Undaunted, Woodie and Ruth unloaded their boat and packed their gear, and at 3:00 that afternoon, they

Ruthie on the oars with her sister Nora in the McKenzie White Water Parade, circa 1945. Woodie built this decked square-ender especially for her. Her skills on the oars were known and respected by McKenzie River guides. COURTESY RUTH BURLEIGH

shoved off for their premiere on the Middle Fork. Their first night's camp Woodie named "Lost Camp." It was there that they discovered they had misplaced their geologic map, and it was noon the next day that Woodie missed his $35 fly rod. He wrote in his trip diary, "I think it [the fly rod] is in this camp also. However, we still had one [fly rod] left."

At their second night's camp, they turned the boat over to check the damage. The river in August typically runs low, and not until they passed Marsh Creek's entry into the stream did they have enough flow to accommodate the boat's shallow draft. "We decided three patches would make it look more sea worthy. . . . From there to the falls [Dagger Falls] we did everything but turn over. . . . The holes between the rapids are not long enough to give a fellow time to spit on his hands before he is in another one."

At Dagger Falls, Ruth kept the boat off the rocks from the bank with a long pole as Woodie lowered it through the falls with a rope. They were able to "smile a bit after that," Woodie wrote, although he did complain of being sick during this time with a sore throat and fever. Ruth actually handled the boat during this period, and on another trip down the Fork, she rowed Woodie most of the way when he was ill again. They spent more time fishing after Dagger Falls. "From the falls on down the river has nicer holes for big trout and there are lots of

them. They seemed to me they could not leave a fly alone. We had no use for them so we clipped the barb off our hook so when through playing one, we gave a little slack and he was gone."[14] It was the practice of McKenzie River guides to fish barbless hooks and keep no more fish than were needed for a meal on the river.

Dr. Russell G. Frazier of Bingham, Utah, preceded Woodie and Ruth's launch that year by three days. Dr. Frazier was a company physician for the Utah Copper Company. In that position, with support from some associates, he was able to pursue his passion for adventure. In fact, he was the expedition physician for Adm. Richard E. Byrd's third expedition to the Antarctic in 1939–41, for which he received a congressional medal in 1947. His adventures included runs of western rivers: the Middle Fork of the Salmon, the Yampa, and the Colorado.[15]

Frazier's first attempt at the Middle Fork was in July 1935. Low water and a ravenous river ate their boats. Narrow channels, river debris, and exposed rocks made passage from Bear Valley to Sulphur Falls—later named Dagger Falls—extremely difficult. The boats took a beating. The party abandoned the trip and cached the boats above the falls.

A heavy winter snowpack in the Sawtooth Mountains the next year offered more favorable conditions for a second attempt the following summer, and this time Frazier successfully ran the Fork. Disaster struck on the

Woodie Hindman (standing) and Dayton Thomson in the boat contemplate Dagger Falls, circa 1940. Woodie introduced several McKenzie River guides to the Middle Fork of the Salmon. Note the added wash strake on Thomson's square-ender and the covey of five boats. COURTESY LEROY PRUITT

Ruthie tends camp on the Middle Fork during their first run of that river, in 1939. COURTESY OF RUTH BURLEIGH

main Salmon, however, when the party became preoccupied with a sow bear and cub. The distraction caused them to stumble unprepared into Big Mallard Rapid, upsetting two boats. One man broke his leg.

Frazier and his group ran the Middle Fork again in 1937. High water and inexperienced oarsmen were his nemesis on this trip. It didn't take long for them to decide that the trip was folly. Doc Frazier was disappointed and frustrated. During an evening of drinking, he took an ax to the boats. His final and second successful run was in 1939 with a flotilla of seven boats, which departed from Bear Valley three days before Woodie and Ruth launched their single McKenzie River boat at the same location.[16]

Neither Frazier and his parties nor Ruth and Woodie were the first to navigate the Middle Fork, although it is probable that Ruth was the first of her gender to run the river. In 1926, Henry Wiedner, a wildlife photographer from Payette, Idaho, had spent three months on the Middle Fork and the Salmon filming the area's wildlife. Wiedner navigated the river in two canoes. It is unclear where he began his trip, but it was surely below Dagger Falls. He carried a 50-pound hand-cranked movie camera. One canoe was lost in a river mishap, along with some of the 4,000 feet of film he shot.[17] His was a significant feat. Others may well have navigated the Middle

Fork in earlier days, but the records are sparse. There has been speculation that Harry Guleke, a Salmon River sweep boatman who ran the Main Salmon from about 1896 through 1933, likely made a run down the Fork.[18]

Woodie and Ruth's eventful seven-day trip stirred their souls and prompted many return trips over the next fifteen years. A guest on one of Wood's final trips down the Middle Fork, Dave Roberts, later wrote of the 1939 trip:

> Mr. and Mrs. Hindman, alone and unaided, ran virtually the full length of the River of No Return. There were two or three tough spots, including one thirty-foot waterfall, where their 200-pound craft had to be lined through. When they emerged from the lower stream they knew the character of the stream—its hundreds of rapids, whirlpools and granite rocks. And if Woodie knew them after that first expedition, how much better he must know them now—with a score of new experiences added to the old. He's the man our party long ago decided to trust to take us down safely.[19]

Woodie introduced Prince Helfrich, one of Oregon's famous and endearing McKenzie River guides, to the Middle Fork the next year. The McKenzie River boats,

An unidentified boater on a Hindman trip down the Middle Fork, circa 1940. The broad transom on the square-ender could be a challenge in whitewater if the boat did not have momentum and could not enter a rapid at the correct angle. In part, it was Woodie's experience on the Middle Fork that prompted him to pull into an "eddy of evolution" and consider a change in the boat, which led to the double-ender. COURTESY OF RUTH BURLEIGH

light and maneuverable, high-sided and open, were perfectly suited for the Middle Fork.

How did the McKenzie River and the Middle Fork of the Salmon influence Woodie's perspective on riverboat design? His boat for the Middle Fork trip was a 14-foot[20] Kaarhus square-ender, which he had learned how to build under the tutelage of Tom Kaarhus. The person who tutored Woodie was a young apprentice builder, Howard Hall, Kaarhus's first shop employee. Fir plywood suitable for boatbuilding had recently become available in 12- and 14-foot lengths. Until that time, Woodie and his colleagues built board-and-batten boats, carvel-planked boats with battens that ran along the outside seams. Both the board-and-batten and early plywood boats were comparable in shape, but the plywood boats tended to have higher sides. The more heavily timbered board-and-batten boats were more cumbersome to handle out of the water, but in the water they showed dexterity similar to the plywood boats. The basic design of these boats is attributable to John West.

The term "drift boat" had not yet formed on the lips of the river guides, though it is probable that in planning a trip, the guides talked about drifting from one point on the river to another. Guides then referred to the boat type as a rowboat. The peculiar form of the boat addressed the demands of the river: a flat bottom with a continuous rocker fore to aft and a high, broad transom. The boat was rowed so the transom faced downriver and served as splashboard to keep the boat dry. The boat could pivot on a dime. Woodie reports that the boat he and Ruth used on the Middle Fork weighed about 200 pounds, which is heavier than a 14-foot square-ender built today. This is because he used $3/8$-inch plywood panels, whereas $1/4$-inch panels are used today. The bottom was constructed of Port Orford cedar planks. The boat could maneuver nicely, however, and slip nicely across fast-moving currents. Moreover, the boat's interior space, with its flat, wide bottom and high, flared sides, provided ample carrying capacity for two people of average size and modest amounts of gear.

The design, however, presents two problems in heavy whitewater. First is a tendency for the boat to be slapped about a bit as the broad transom hits a set of standing waves or curlers. The second is the possibility of a stall at the crest of a large standing wave because the boat's broad transom slows momentum. This could be disastrous if the boat slips back into the trough. Neither problem was acute with the boat in the hands of good oarsmen. The McKenzie guides learned that by angling a boat into a curl, the transom's corner cut smoothly through the wave. The oarsman added momentum to the boat with a couple of thrusts on the oars to mitigate the threat of a stall. Because of the square-ender's mobility, the oarsman also had the option of skirting water that appeared too risky.

Woodie experienced these anomalies firsthand. George Godfrey, a University of Oregon journalism professor at that time, told a story about Woodie and his square-ender on the Middle Fork during their 1940 run. Woodie invited Godfrey, Prince Helfrich, and a U.S. Fish and Wildlife friend, Harold Dobyns, to join him on his second trip down the Fork. Godfrey's story was later confirmed by McKenzie guide and early boating pioneer John West in 1975.[21]

Godfrey reported that Woodie's square-ender was slapped broadside by heavy water on the Middle Fork. It is important to keep a boat parallel to the current in heavy water to avoid swamping or worse, so Woodie had two choices: swing the broad transom back around into the downstream position or let the boat do a 180-degree pivot. Rather than waste precious time fighting the natural swing of the boat, he quickly jumped from the rowing seat to the guest thwart—by one account, a bale of hay or straw—and realigned the boat parallel to the current. The boat was now reoriented so that the sharp bow faced downriver. He finished the rapids bow-first. Woodie commented that he liked the way the bow cut through the curls. He apparently tested the bow-first approach on other rapids.

Some people doubt the veracity of Godfrey's story, but I think it is a plausible account. However, it seems clear that Woodie's experiences with the square-ender were cumulative. Other guides talked of their ordeals under similar circumstances. Woodie had probably been thinking of ways to redesign the square-ender. As a good fishing guide will catalog fishing success under a variety of river conditions, so too a good boat builder will catalog his boat's response to demands placed on it by the oarsman under various situations. Accumulated experiences will cause an innovative mind to pull into an "eddy of evolution."

During the winter of 1940–41, Woodie designed and built a double-ended riverboat. Woodie and Ruth had encountered double-ended boats before on the Rogue

Woodie (third from left) and a pair of his 16-foot double-enders nesting on a trailer, circa 1949. COURTESY OF RUTH BURLEIGH

and Umpqua Rivers, as well as the cape dories in Pacific City, Oregon, and those used in the Alaskan fishery. Woodie and Ruth traveled with regularity throughout the Northwest. It is therefore probable that he had been thinking about a boat that navigated the river prow-first.

The lines of his first double-ender suggest that Woodie may have done nothing more than modify the lines of the Kaarhus square-ender. In 1938 and 1939, northwestern plywood manufacturers were producing plywood fir panels in 12- and 14-foot lengths. Woodie was a practical guy who perceived simple solutions to seemingly complex problems. From amidships to the bow of the square-ender, the half-breadth lines matched those of Woodie's new double-ender from amidships to the new prow. He simply replicated the frames. The double-ender maintained the same elevation as the square-ender at the new prow. In fact, of all the McKenzie boats, this one had the greatest amount of rocker. It was his attempt to shape the boat to the roll of the river.[22]

The boat proved to be a dream to row. To achieve greater rocker to the bottom line of the boat, however, Woodie had to cut slightly concave lines into the top and

Everett Spaulding (left) and Woodie with a pair of fish each. Barely visible is the double-ender with a transom, circa 1949. COURTESY OF KENNY KING

bottom of the side panels. Without a template for the side panels, this made the double-ender a little more difficult to build. But the lines of the boat were gorgeous, and Woodie found himself building some of these boats for the guides. The stem and stern posts required a 40-degree bevel each to receive the side panels. It was a lovely and symmetrical boat.

Although guides were attracted to the appearance and handling features of the boat, interior space was much more confined. As a one- or two-person craft, the boat was ideal. It wasn't until the end of World War II that Woodie used 16-foot plywood for boatbuilding. It was then that he built a larger double-ender. The double-ender became Woodie's boat of choice and remained his favorite until he left McKenzie River country in 1954. The 14-foot double-ender remains my favorite when I seek the solitude of my own thoughts on a class III river or a small, isolated stream navigable only in a small boat.

The contemporary McKenzie River double-ender with a transom was born in 1948 when guide and friend Everett Spaulding made a request of Woodie. He guided the McKenzie, Umpqua, Rogue, and Middle Fork of the Salmon River. Spaulding used and liked Woodie's 16-foot double-ender:

> I was boating on the Umpqua, from the highway down to Kellog and on down toward the ocean for salmon, trout and steelhead in August and September. The put-ins and take-outs were far apart. We'd have a lot of rowing to do through those dead stretches. . . . So I went to Woodie and I told him, "I want that bow chopped off." He says, "Well, we'll ruin it." "I don't care if you do. I want it chopped off and put a motor on it so we could go through the dead stretches and save time. So Woodie modified Everett's 18-foot double-ender to include the transom. That's how it started. It was 1948."[23]

A slightly different story has drifted around the McKenzie guiding community. According to Dave Helfrich:

> Everret Spaulding guided for Glen Wooldridge on the Rogue. Glen's early trips were five days with overnights at Galice, Black Bar, Muriel, and Agness. Spaulding used an 18-foot double-ender that Woodie had built for him, and he had trouble keeping up with Wooldridge on the lower Rogue, where he would use a motor from Agness to Lobster Creek, their takeout. So Everett went to Woodie and asked him to cut off the bow of his double-ender and replace it with a transom so he could hang a motor.[24]

Even though the double-ender with a transom grew in popularity, the double-ender remained Woodie's boat of choice. He loved its lines. Here Woodie in his double-ender, followed by McKenzie guide Kenny Taylor, runs the Haystack on the Middle Fork of the Salmon. COURTESY OF KENNY KING

I accept Spaulding's claim. I also suspect that Woodie's objection to chopping off the bow had much to do with altering a boat he had built. It is also important to realize that the boats they saw on other rivers influenced Woodie, Everett Spaulding, and the other guides. A number of the Rogue River drivers displayed small transoms by the early 1920s. This boat didn't evolve in a vacuum.

The double-ender with a transom soon became the standard for McKenzie River drift boats. The elegant lines and handling characteristics of the double-ender were retained, coupled with the advantage of greater interior space. While a motor assists the boat through slow water, it tends to move inefficiently. A double-ender with a transom under power is ungainly and looks like a gooney bird with its awkward takeoff and landing. The continual rocker of the boat and the narrow transom cause the motor to push the upriver end down and the prow up. Stand ashore and watch such a craft under power, and you have a curious conversation piece. The boat did, however, meet the basic needs of the guides.

This riverboat type has stood the test of time. Contemporary McKenzie-style boats copy Woodie's original lines. Over the years, builders have tweaked the interior

appointments of the boat, expanded its size, and used an assortment of materials—various woods, aluminum, fiberglass, and plastic. The basic lines of the original double-ender with a transom, however, have been retained.

In late 1954, just before his sixtieth birthday and twenty years after having moved to McKenzie River country, Woodie sold his boatbuilding business. His health and energy level had slipped a bit. The purchaser, Marty Rathje, continued to build Woodie's boats for a few years. As part of the sale, Woodie agreed not to build any more McKenzie-style boats in Oregon. He packed up his tools and moved with Ruthie to Crescent City, California, where he built more whitewater boats, this time for the Rogue, Klamath, and Smith Rivers in southern Oregon and northern California.[25] McKenzie River guides remained loyal to Woodie, however, and several of them continued to order their boats from him in Crescent City. This didn't please the new owner of Woodie's boat shop in Springfield, but he learned an important lesson: "You can't buy reputation."[26]

Woodie died on March 24, 1967, while fishing with a friend near his home in Parker, Arizona. He is buried in Parker, "with the river close by and craggy mountains

Woodie and Ruthie, hand and glove. COURTESY RUTH BURLEIGH

. . . he seemed to love so much."[27] Ruth maintained her connections with old river friends after his death. She died ten years later on Christmas Eve. As requested, her ashes were secretly scattered atop Woodie's grave. After all, they were hand and glove.

Endnotes

1. Mary I. Forte, unpublished biography, McLean, TX: Alanreed-McLean Area Museum, January 4, 1937.

2. Mattie, the oldest, was born on December 10, 1881; Jack, born February 12, 1883; Leona, November 9, 1884; and Joe, December 11, 1892.

3. Forte biography.

4. McLean is located on the high plateau country of the Texas panhandle, about 75 miles east of Amarillo. McLean became the economic hub for the large ranch country of the area. A dugout was a crude shelter carved out of the ground and roofed with sod. It was a common residence on the Texas plains, where timber for building was scarce. After homes were built, dugouts typically became storage cellars.

5. Forte biography.

6. Ibid. Prairie chickens are Chinese pheasants.

7. Ruth Burleigh interview, May 18, 2001.

8. Ruth Hindman is Woodie's niece by marriage. She married Joe Hindman's son Marvin.

9. Dave Helfrich interview, February 19, 2005.

10. The Dutch oven is sized by the diameter of the oven on which the cast-iron lid sits.

11. The McKenzie White Water Parade started in 1938 as a prelude to the fishing season opener. In the spring, guides gathered to run the upper stretches of the McKenzie to check for river hazards that had been created by the winter and spring runoffs. The event soon became a popular spectator sport, and soon wanna-be river runners and nimrods included themselves in this popular event. Tragedy struck in 1958, with the drowning of two underprepared and overzealous rafters. The White Water Parade was discontinued.

12. *Sunday Journal Magazine,* July 2, 1950.

13. Probably Monroe Hancock, a well-known Salmon River sweep boatman and guide of that time.

14. Woodie Hindman, "We shoot the Middle Fork for a Change," unpublished diary, circa 1939, courtesy of Ruth Burleigh.

15. Russell G. Frazier Papers, 1930–68, Utah State Historical Society.

16. For a more complete story of the Frazier trips, the boatmen and natural history of the Middle Fork, see Johnny Carrey and Cort Conley, *The Middle Fork and the Sheepeater War* (Cambridge, ID: Backeddy Books, 1977), 6–19.

17. To view a clip of Wiedners Salmon River production, visit www.idahoptv.org/productions/salmonriver/movie.html.

18. Carrey and Conley, *Middle Fork and Sheepeater War,* 4–5.

19. Dave Roberts, "Rod and Gun" column, *Seattle Daily Times,* July 22, 1952.

20. As measured around the sheer line. Two side panels could be cut from one 4-by-14-foot exterior-grade (fir) plywood panel.

21. Jim Boyd, "The Boat the McKenzie River Spawned," *Eugene Register-Guard,* December 14, 1975.

22. According to Woodie's diary, he gave Prince Helfrich the patterns for this boat. Prince built several double-enders for his boys camp. I recovered the lines and construction detail from one such boat to replicate Woodie's original double-ender.

23. Boyd, "Boat the McKenzie River Spawned."

24. Dave Helfrich interview, May 17, 2003.

25. Crescent City's newspaper, the *Del Norte Triplcate,* ran an article on November 24, 1955, that featured Woodie and his new part-time boatbuilding business. "After several decades of boat building he can't quite stop, but now he'll take it a bit easy—he says."

26. Marty Rathje interview, 1999.

27. Ruthie Hindman, undated diary entry, courtesy of Ruth Burleigh.

CHAPTER 5

Loose Ends

*Just because something looks like a duck, waddles like a duck,
and floats like a duck doesn't necessarily mean it's a duck.*

Woodie's final innovation—the double-ender with a transom, and the last major eddy of evolution on the McKenzie—has been at the heart of some debate over the years. Which end of the boat is the bow and which is the stern? Appearances can be deceiving. The higher-profiled prow in the downstream position, which looks like the bow, is actually the stern of the boat; the end with the transom, which looks like the stern of the boat, is the bow. The logic for this description is tied to Woodie Hindman's replacement of the downriver end of the boat, the square-ended transom, with a prow in 1940. Further compounding the confusion was his replacement of the double-ender's bow, the upriver end, with a small transom in 1948. To most people unfamiliar with the history of the McKenzie boats, the question is inconsequential—until you wander into Oregon's McKenzie River country. Be warned: Don't argue the point with an old-time McKenzie River guide. People who know and appreciate the story of these boats will politely correct the one who misidentifies the bow or stern. Keith Steele, the most prolific builder of these boats from the 1960s into the 1990s, was told by the U.S. Coast Guard that he must post his identification plate on the "bow" of his new boats, the downriver prow. Keith argued that the evolution of the boats takes precedence over their appearance. They went round and round for a while, but Keith won the argument. One persistent debater ended up on his backside with a sore jaw at the hands of a drift-boat builder who tired of the man's insistence that if the prow looks like the bow, then it's the bow. The argument won't work on the McKenzie River. Just because something looks like a duck, waddles like a duck, and floats like a duck doesn't necessarily mean it's a duck.

Rope seats are a popular feature of drift boats. They are a blessing because they allow rainwater to run off the oarsman's slicker and onto the floor of the boat rather than puddle up on a hard seat and soak one's derriere. The rope seat also provides a comfortable, secure perch as the boat pitches and rolls in heavy whitewater. Howard Hall, Tom Kaarhus's first shop employee, says that Tom talked of using and appreciating rope seats when he trolled commercially for salmon in Alaska. He incorporated this feature in his riverboats when he opened his shop in 1935.[1]

I have been unsuccessful in my efforts to pinpoint a time when the McKenzie River boats came to be called drift boats. The one inconvenience of the riverboat is that the takeout on a river is always downstream. Arrangements must be made to move one's transportation from a put-in point to a takeout point. As guides and other river runners talked about their trips, it was inevitable that they would discuss them in terms of a drift from one point to another. It was also inevitable that over time, references to the drift boat increasingly were made. "Drift boat" gradually became part of the standard nomenclature on the river. Spelling is also a question. Some writers combine the two words and call the craft a "driftboat." I have chosen for this book to use "drift" as a descriptor, hence "drift boat."

There is also local confusion over the boat's type. My good friends of the McKenzie prefer to define the boat type as unique to its name: drift boat. The McKenzie boats are flat and rockered or have cambered bottoms fore to aft, with straight, though flared, sides. In some quarters, they are described as banana boats because of their crescent shape. Dory expert John Gardner wrote about the McKenzie River drift boats after he had recently discovered the boat, asking, "Is the McKenzie boat a dory?" and answering, "It most certainly is." Gardner then cites Dewey Ray's counterpoint from an article that had appeared in a recent Northwest fishing magazine. Ray reportedly wrote that the McKenzie River drift boat "owes nothing to the traditional dory, but was invented by Woodie Hindman." Gardner wasn't persuaded. I'm not either.[2]

Ray was correct about Woodie Hindman, but he failed in a basic understanding of boat types as a way to classify craft that is universally acknowledged among learned boatmen. If you were to describe drift-boat characteristics to a boatbuilder in Nova Scotia, he would respond, "Ah, a dory." The same would be true of a boatbuilder in Santiago, Chile, or Nedre Vats, Norway.

Howard Chapelle might differ with Gardner, instead identifying the drift boat as a river skiff, as he included construction methods in classifying a boat. A dory is traditionally built bottom-first, without a chine log, and the frames and sideboards, or strakes, are then installed. The bottom planks are cambered to define the rocker. The boat is built right side up. A skiff, on the other hand, is usually built upside down around a mold, and then the bottom is installed. Timbered skiffs were usually cross-planked. By this definition, drift boats are skiffs.[3]

I tend to simplify things in my mind. If the boat has a flat and cambered bottom fore to aft, the sides are flared and straight, and the boat moves like a dory, then it's a dory. I think Leroy Pruitt says it best: "I'm sure that the McKenzie River boat can be classified as a dory. But I'm also sure the dories all over the world had various shapes, methods of construction that derived from the minds of that area. The same is true for the drift boat. The McKenzie was derived from the minds of this area. . . . Many drift-boat builders of this day strive to build the McKenzie because it is a proven design and successfully works on the rivers."[4]

The boat type may be that of a dory or a skiff. There is no doubt, however, that these boats are Oregon's unique contribution to wooden-boat design. They are McKenzie River drift boats.

The evolution of the McKenzie River boats is a story of form and function. The boats, as they evolved, represented efforts by people to build and use craft that were specific to their needs. These particular stories, though unique, have been repeated in different ways in other parts of the world where men and women have tried to make a living on the water. Needs on the water, kinds of materials that are available, and collective ingenuity have given rise to these eddies of evolution. The contributions of McKenzie River boat design are unique to the experiences of the McKenzie's people. It's probable that without them, a comparable boat type eventually would have emerged among others interested in running the wild rivers of the Northwest. The genius of the early McKenzie River boatbuilders was in experiencing and understanding their river environment and the materials available to them.

My account of the McKenzie eddies of evolution doesn't cover the full story. There were many other guides and several other attempts to build boats that were uniquely designed to meet specific needs. Nor does it cover the refinements in the continuing efforts of fly fishers, river runners, and boatbuilders to refine the McKenzie drift boat further. In my view, the four McKenzie River boat types reached their apotheosis at the hands of four people: Woodie Hindman, Tom Kaarhus, Veltie Pruitt, and John West. The contemporary double-ender with a transom has become the boat of choice, particularly among sportfishers. Each of the boat types, however, offers features to fit various needs, and its reemergence on rivers across the country and around the world is testimony to its value.

Endnotes

1. Howard Hall letter to Frank Amato of Amato Publications, July 25, 1985.

2. John Gardner, "McKenzie Boats Well Suited for Steelhead or Salmon Fishing," *National Fisherman,* July 1981. Gardner writes that Ray's comment had appeared in an earlier issue of *Salmon Trout Steelheader,* a fishing magazine published bimonthly by Amato Publications.

3. Howard I. Chapelle, *American Small Sailing Craft* (New York: W. W. Norton Company, 1951), 36, 45–53.

4. Leroy Pruitt in a letter to the author, April 30, 2005.

CHAPTER 6

First Encounters
The Rogue River

Each twist of the canyon presented a new vista . . .

My boating partner, Ken Brown, exclaimed, "There is Slim Pickens, and now there is No Pickens!" We were navigating Oregon's Wild and Scenic section of the Rogue River for the first time. Ken was responsible for my initial introduction to drift boats about forty years ago, and there aren't many river runs we haven't done together. On this trip, our boats were McKenzies. Mine was the 16-foot Hindman-style double-ender with a transom. John Ostrom of Salem, Oregon, built it for me eight years earlier. It was wood, of course.

Harry Lagerstedt, a professor of horticulture at Oregon State University, designed Ken's boat in the early 1960s. It was a unique whitewater boat. With a bottom length of 8 feet and width of 4 feet, the craft had the same width and flare as the 16-foot McKenzie drift boat. It was basically the same as my boat, but with both ends lopped off and squared. The high-sided craft could handle anything the Rogue put in front of it. Harry had affectionately named the boat *Tubby* because of its broad transom and stubbed, flat bow. If any boat looked like "a bathtub with oarlocks," it was this one. "But," says Harry, "comparing *Tubby* to a 16-foot drift boat is like comparing a motorcycle to a Cadillac. In *Tubby*, you feel every ripple of the river. You are working all the time, correcting, adjusting, and responding to signals being sent by the river."[1]

Ken Brown's experience with the boat demonstrated its capacity to carry two people, with limited gear, through difficult rapids. The boat was portable in the bed of a standard-size pickup, though for this trip, *Tubby* nested nicely in my boat on the trailer. Ken had built the boat from Harry's plans a few years earlier. It was a boat that

attracted attention. It was sufficiently novel that twenty-two years later, I helped my grandson Matt build that same boat.

With me on my first Rogue run was my daughter Wendy. At fourteen, she was bolder than most her age, and unwisely, she trusted her dad's river skills completely. With Ken was his sixteen-year-old son, Bryan. Both he and Wendy had river experience. Bryan, however, being the older of the two, had the edge on the oars. They were brought up right. Bryan was a tall, strapping, good-looking lad. Recently I learned that Bryan was one of the reasons my daughter decided to join us on this float. I should have known!

We launched our boats that year on June 12, 1978, at Grave Creek. This final launch point before entering the Wild and Scenic section of the Rogue is located about 7 miles downriver from Galice and 30 miles downriver from Grants Pass. Grave Creek was named after the death of a pioneer couple's daughter, Martha Crowley, on the creek near Leland, Oregon, in 1854.[2] Armed with a copy of the *Handbook to the Rogue River Canyon* and a confidence that veiled our apprehensions about the river, we ran the Rogue without mishap but with some consternation at almost every bend. River levels that year were lower than normal for the season. In our log, we renamed Upper Montgomery Creek Rapids "No Pickens." As we scouted the river, we couldn't see a course through the slightly submerged rock garden that extended from the north to the south bank. Evidence of the damage caused by the rocks, a couple of which looked like large shark's teeth, was obvious by their scars from errant boats.

As we pondered our options, a guide with his dudes came through Russian Rapids and headed straight for

N

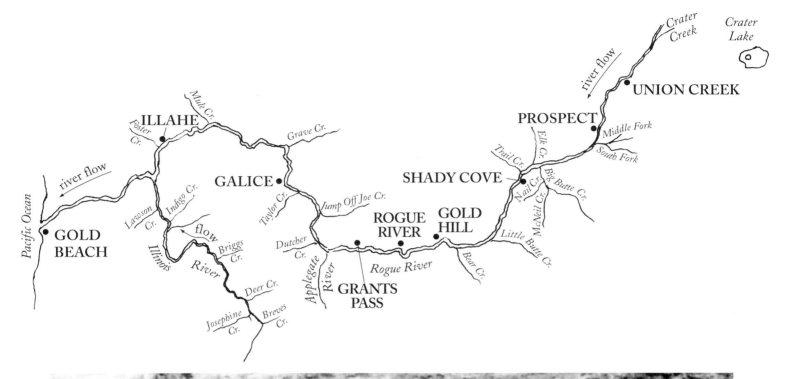

The Rogue River from Its Presumed Source to the Pacific

Daughter Wendy on the oars in Ken Brown's little drift boat, Tubby, *in June 1978.* COURTESY OF KEN BROWN

A boatman makes his entry into Slim Pickens while another approaches upriver. The route is marked by a large rock that cleaved from the bank and rolled into its present position. The remaining chute was blown out with dynamite years ago for safer passage.

Upper Montgomery. We watched as he moved so far left that his boat brushed the bank. Once through the rock garden, he deftly pushed on the right oar and pulled hard on the left to move the drift boat to the center of the river. This maneuver avoided a rock just downriver a few yards. Piece of cake. We followed suit without problem, and shortly we were faced with Slim Pickens, a very narrow and foreboding chute on the north bank.

Slim Pickens was our only option at low water levels. The rapids were so named because the "pickens" are slim. To run Slim Pickens successfully, the oarsman must enter the chute dead center between a fairly high, rocky bank on the right and a house-size boulder on the left. As he makes his entry, he has to lean forward and simultaneously pull the oars in so that the blades rest on the gunwale beside him lest the oars impede the boat's progress. The instant the boat is through the narrow passage, the oars are extended full length to leverage the boat away from the rock wall that juts into the river a few yards downstream. Wendy thought we were going to leave a permanent deposit of McKenzie River drift boat on that wall as she screamed, "Daddy, the wall!" I didn't

need to be told the damn thing was there. An uncontrolled adrenaline surge helped me pivot and pull the boat safely by the hazard. Slim Pickens and No Pickens represent the kind of attention this river demands from any drift boater. These rapids, however, were inconsequential in comparison with Rainie Falls, Tyee, Wildcat, Kelsey Canyon, Mule Creek, or Blossom Bar.

For a time, we wondered if we had erred by not hiring a guide for our first encounter with the Rogue, but we were soon pleased we had not. We felt the way Glen Wooldridge and Cal Allen must have felt when they first ran this river in 1915—anxious, expectant, and invigorated. Unless one has considerable whitewater experience in a drift boat, I would not recommend this river for a do-it-yourselfer.

The beauty and the history of the place enveloped us from the start. Even though preoccupation with safe passage was my priority, the river's mystical beauty invaded my peripheral vision continually and caught my imagination. We felt a sense of expectation at each bend of the river; not only for the river we encountered, but also for the history it held. If we saw a piece of rusting mining

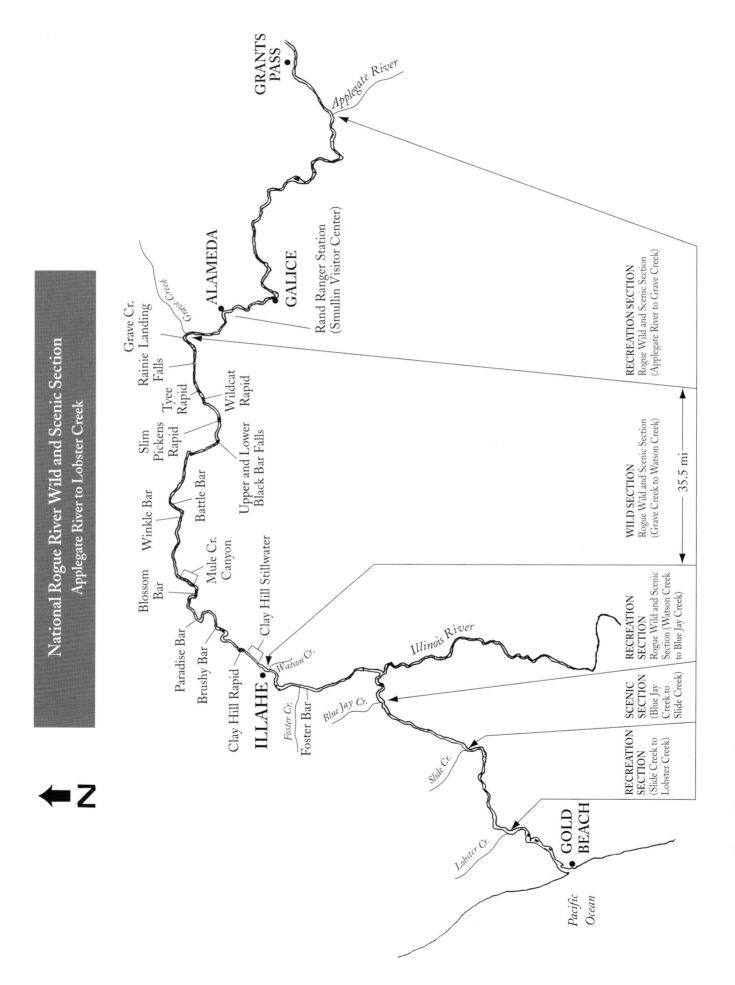

Rogue River map adapted from Oregon Northern California guide book (Cross Advertising and Printing Studio, 1950). Wild and scenic section identifiers from *Rogue River Float Guide*, (Bureau of Land Management and U.S. Forest Service, 2004).

equipment nestled among the rocks, a seemingly natural part of the landscape, we could only imagine the labor and risks involved in moving that equipment into this impregnable canyon. Nor could we escape the sense of isolation the early miners and rare homesteaders of this wild place surely must have felt. Accounts of the few hardy pioneers and interlopers who first arrived here suggest it was the magnificence of the place and the solitude of the canyon that drew them.

Another bend in the river revealed the sweet aroma of wild azaleas. The fragrance drifted over the boat on a stream of cool air that slid down a draw and over the secretive flowering shrubs from somewhere above. Each twist of the river presented a new vista of the canyon or a scene just viewed but from a reverse perspective as the Rogue twisted and turned through the gorge.

Equally interesting was the wildlife: deer, river otters, bears, eagles and osprey, rattlesnakes, and other assorted creatures. The loveliest creature we spied on that trip was one Ken first spotted as we rounded yet another revealing bend. Bryan and Wendy were upriver from us 30 to 40 yards in *Tubby* as we drifted a quiet stretch. Ken nudged me. There she was, nestled in a sandy enclave between two large boulders, hidden from the Rogue River Trail above and unaware of the view her hideaway afforded for a few moments from the river. Uninhibited because of the illusion of privacy, the creature revealed a body whose lines were every bit as a graceful as my boat, a most pleasant scene. Our attention was then drawn to Bryan and Wendy. Bryan was on the oars with a downriver view, and Wendy was resting against the transom looking upriver. From our position, it appeared as though Bryan made a furtive glance toward the creature but quickly averted his eyes. As their boat slid by, we noticed Wendy sit up and look to her left. As she did, her eyes widened, and she pointed and mouthed the words, "Bryan, look! A naked lady!" Ken about swallowed his gum as my daughter invited Bryan to behold the sight he had nobly avoided a moment before.

That year, the number of river travelers through the Wild and Scenic section of the Rogue was restricted. In 1974, a permit system was implemented to limit the numbers of commercial groups on the river. The new system created considerable bewilderment and angst among many river guides, especially those unable to document their history on the river. Some lost their privilege to guide the river. Because of the increased popularity of this section of the Rogue, 1978 also saw restrictions on the numbers of private users.[3] We didn't like the idea of having to apply for private-user permits, but we soon forgot about the inconvenience and uncertainty surrounding our trip when we were notified by mail that our application

had been successful. On that trip, it took little time for us to come to fully understand and appreciate the magnetic effect of this river on people, as well as their impacts on this extraordinary environment. The Rogue River had seen many changes since the first white man approached its banks 186 years earlier.

The headwaters of the Rogue River are in southern Oregon's high Cascades, not far from Crater Lake, a huge caldera formed by the eruption and collapse of Mount Mazama some 7,000 years ago. Many geologists believe that Crater Lake is the Rogue's initial underground source. The lake also sits at the head of two other river basins, the Klamath to the south and the Umpqua to the northwest. After tumbling out of the Cascades, the Rogue weaves its way through the Rogue River Valley, a succulent and temperate area bounded on all sides by mountains—the Cascades to the east, the Siskiyous to the south and southwest, the Coast Ranges to the west, and the Umpqua hills to the north. The river then cuts its way generally westward through the Siskiyou Mountains and Coast Ranges. In some areas, the canyon is 3,000 feet deep. The river tumbles up to 30 feet a mile through this section and presents some of the most technically challenging water in the Lower Forty-eight. The Rogue's severe hydraulics coupled with its scenic beauty make the river a mecca for river enthusiasts. Once through the mountains, the Rogue flattens out a bit and makes a more docile glide to the Pacific Ocean at Gold Beach.

Early inhabitants of the Rogue, prior to the infusion of trappers and traders, were a scattered indigenous people whose cultures and dialects were influenced by the isolation of their environments. According to Stephen Dow Beckham, the people of the Rogue comprised three linguistic groups. The Athapascans, the largest in number, inhabited the southern Oregon coastline, an area extending 30 to 40 miles up the Rogue from the river's mouth, the Applegate River, and Galice Creek. They lived in small bands whose relative isolation from each other is evidenced, in part, by variations in dialect. The Takelman and Shastan resided inland in the middle and upper Rogue River drainage.

Because of the topography and limited areas of habitability, these peoples lived in groups of 30 to 150 individuals. Groups large enough to exhibit political autonomy didn't exist. Favored sites for their dwellings were meadows and sandy bottomland near the river and mouths of streams along the coast. The relative seclusion of the bands gave rise to a strong sense of independence and territoriality.

Beckham calculated the Rogue Indian population when the first white settlement was established in 1851. He estimated that the Athapascans were about 8,800 in

Ken Brown enters Upper Black Bar Falls in his little boat . . .

. . . and then finishes the bottom of the rapid. The pour-off just upriver from his left oar is a favorite spot for kayakers to frolic and match wits with the river. I am serving as a safety net below. COURTESY OF KEN BROWN

number, the Takelmas 500, and the Oregon Shastas about 250. Assuming an average band size of about 90 individuals and a total of roughly 9,550 Indians in the defined region, then there were roughly 106 bands of Rogues. These bands resided in choice locations that were in close proximity to their food sources: migrating fish and eels, clams and mussel beds, and ungulates.[4] The inland Takelmas were dependent on additional sources for nutrition, such as a variety of insects and larvae, pine nuts, and acorns. As miners and settlers arrived in the area, life for the people of the Rogue began to change.

Western author and Rogue River enthusiast Zane Grey claimed that the name Rogue was derived from the French *rouge*, meaning red. The river looked reddish because of silt from placer mines during the late nineteenth century and early twentieth century. Grey didn't cite his source, though it may have been his fishing and river guide, Claude Bardon.[5] Bardon was born and raised on the Rogue River and had a story for just about every occasion or question. According to some oral traditions on the Rogue, Bardon enjoyed baiting his clients. It became customary among some Rogue River guides to tell tales that were embellished by their imagination. To stretch the truth or fabricate a story that was tied to some feature of the river became part of the guiding culture. The stories added to the intrigue of the river. Generally, people—even visitors to the area—could tell the difference between truth and a tall tale, but every once in a while a storyteller wove an anecdote that left the listener a believer. I can envision someone like Bardon, when Grey and his party asked him about the origins of the Rogue name, spinning a tale about early French trappers, placer mining, and river color. Whatever Grey's source for the origins of the name Rogue River, he was mistaken.[6]

According to another source, the Rogue River acquired its name at the hands of early French trappers in the region. They referred to the Indians as *les coquins,* the "rogues," and the river as la Rivière aux Coquins, the River of the Rogues.[7] Certainly the Rogue Indians were identified with the river. The name of the Takelmas, those inhabiting the heartland of the Rogue, translates as "along or beside the river," and Tutuni, the largest bands inhabiting the lower Rogue, means "people close to the river." Beckham noted that the Rogues were "known for their fierce and roguish behavior" and "lived in a land well suited to their character." Perhaps it was the land that shaped their character.[8]

The first white men to enter the "heartland of the Rogue" were a Hudson's Bay Company brigade under the leadership of Peter Skene Ogden, who took his group into the Klamath basin in December 1826. The following March, Ogden and his men crossed the Siskiyous and camped on the banks of the Rogue.[9] They were in search of fresh trapping grounds. There they learned that the Umpquas had been in the area gathering furs to trade with a second Hudson's Bay group under the leadership of Alexander McLeod, who was working the Coos Bay area on the coast. McLeod's was the first Hudson's Bay brigade to visit the mouth of the Rogue, arriving there on January 11, 1827.

Although the Hudson's Bay group was experienced in negotiating trades with indigenous populations, the Rogues were cautious and suspicious. In 1828, Jedediah Smith ventured up the southern Oregon coast. Having been arrested and charged with laying claim to lands he had trapped for the United States, Mexico's provincial governor in California, Governor Echianadia, gave him two months to leave California. He decided to go north to the Columbia River and Fort Vancouver, and he and his party trapped as they went. Following a coastal route north, they reached the Pacific on June 8. The trappers found the Indians of the interior valleys to be fearful of them but peaceful. When they arrived on the coast, however, Smith reported that Indians would periodically shoot arrows into their camp, prompting the party to respond with gunfire. His expedition reached Oregon on June 23. His interactions with the Rogues were mixed, but he was able to negotiate assistance across waterways, and they were generally civil to each other. On July 14, however, as Smith and his party were camped at the mouth of the Smith River on the coastal Umpqua estuary, about 100 Indians entered their camp and attacked the party.[10] Two of their chiefs had been insulted the day before and were angered by the trappers' behavior. Smith was not present at the time of the attack but was attacked on his return. Smith and the few remaining survivors made their way to Fort Vancouver, arriving there twenty-eight days later.[11]

Relations with the coastal Indians were on a slippery slope. The Rogue River Indians had thrived in their Garden of Eden, secure in a world made safe by natural and menacing boundaries of mountains, an impassable and productive river, and the sea—until now. The brushy-faced, odoriferous trappers who crossed the mountains seemed more interested in the fruits of the Indians' natural garden than in them as a people. The natives were not happy, sensing that the intrusions of these early white men were the beginning to an end of their ways of life. Their misgivings were well founded.

With the discovery of gold in 1852, a "reckless population" of miners moved over the Siskiyous and off the gangplanks at Port Orford and Crescent City. Many of the Indian bands resided on the streams' terraces, which were prime spots for placer mines. The Indians were dis-

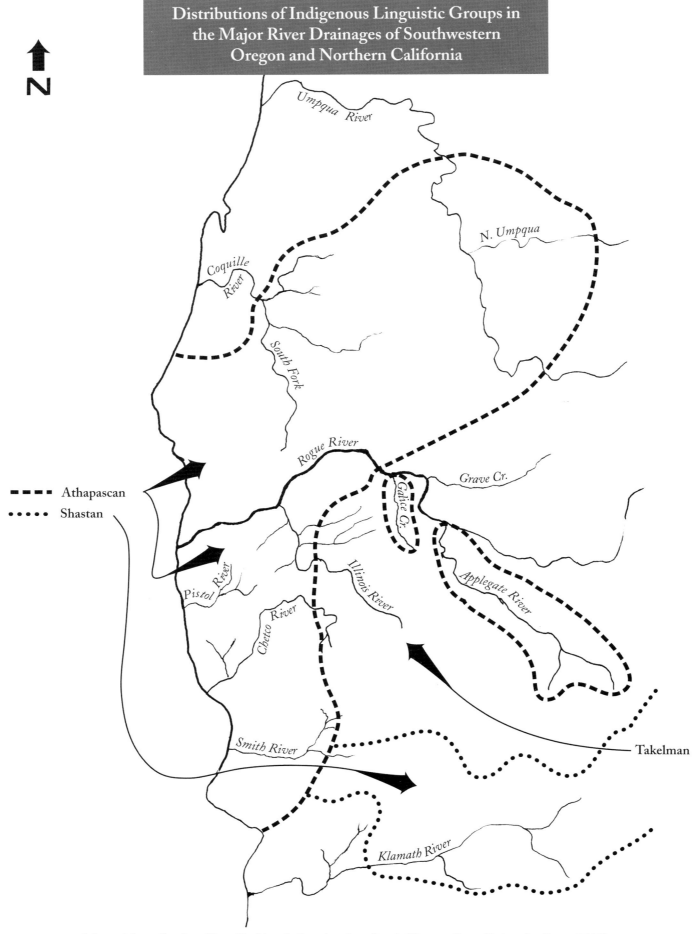

Distributions of Indigenous Linguistic Groups in the Major River Drainages of Southwestern Oregon and Northern California

- - - Athapascan
· · · · Shastan

Adapted from Stephen Dow Beckham's *Requiem for a People* (Oregon State University Press, 2002).

Hydraulic mining occurred in places along the Rogue, and the attendant silt and debris entered the river and affected its color.
COURTESY OF THE BUREAU OF LAND MANAGEMENT (BLM), ROGUE NATIONAL WILD AND SCENIC RIVER

placed, mining debris fouled clam beds and impeded migratory fish, and the eels died.[12] This invasion led to some of the bloodiest encounters in the Northwest.

Further compounding the problem for the Indians was the Donation Land Claim Act. Passed by Congress in September 1850 to promote settlement of the Oregon Territory (present-day Washington, Oregon, and Idaho), it granted a free half section of land to every white settler and American "half-breed Indian" in the Northwest above the age of eighteen if single and a full section (640 acres) to married couples.[13] Beckham observes that the act "ignored the tribal presence altogether and was a law in contradiction to the Organic Act of 1848, which created Oregon Territory. The Organic Act extended the provisions of 'utmost good faith' in the Ordinance of 1757 to Oregon Territory." Confusion, resentment, and anger spread through the Indian communities. Hostilities and atrocities culminated in the Rogue River Indian Wars of 1855 and 1856. Following this war, the tribes of the area were forced to relocate to the Coast Reservation, about 200 miles north of their home.[14]

In the 1830s, President Andrew Jackson had implemented the policy of forced removal of Native Americans. Jackson's actions reflected a national opinion among the white majority of the country during this period: Indians must be dispossessed of their land. Thus began a

"Trail of Tears" that continues to haunt the American psyche today.[15] Stripped of their land and ways of life, the Indians struggled to adjust. John Beeson, one of Oregon's first civil rights activists, wrote letters to the *Oregon Statesman* and *New York Tribune* in 1856 to call attention to the deplorable treatment of the southwest Oregon Indians. He observed in his letter to the *Tribune:*

> Often as I have looked upon these people, dwelling in small communities in the shady grove or along the lipid stream, bountifully supplied with fish and roots and berries for subsistence . . . the conviction was forced upon me that they were living as much in harmony in their beautiful surroundings as their more toiling and anxious brethren of another race. . . . And after being driven from their pleasant homes, and their domains usurped by invaders, I never saw anything in their condition or conduct but what aroused my deepest sympathy and commiseration. To have submitted to robbery and outrage of the gravest kind without resentment would be more than Christian; to have remained passive and indifferent would be less than Men.[16]

It is ironic that at this writing, the most popular tourist attraction in Oregon is Spirit Mountain Casino, a facility owned and operated by the Confederated Tribes of the Grand Ronde. Grand Ronde is just a few miles north of the Confederated Tribes of the Siletz. Both communities' ancestry is traceable to western Oregon's displaced Indians, including the Rogues. The casino has provided a substantial economic boon to the tribe. Unlike the days when they were dependent on their governmental hosts, whose inattention to tribal needs led to severe deprivation in the early years of the reservation, today the new wealth is generously invested in the tribe as well as their nontribal neighbors in surrounding communities. (Perhaps the casino with its beckoning call to the avarice of gamblers symbolizes the return of acorns, clams, and chinook salmon.)

Whatever the origins of the name Rogue River, the moniker is apt for the stream. This is a river of mischievous and dangerous character, restricted by canyon walls that create powerful currents and rapids that will test the most able boatman. It is truly a rogue, full of beauty, rich in history, and completely unforgiving to the foolish and ill prepared. Not only did the Rogue give rise to a mixed and rich history of cultures and traditions, but it also spawned a tradition of riverboats that is unique and cherished.

Endnotes

1. Harry Lagerstedt interview, May 4, 2004.

2. James M. Quinn, James W. Quinn, and James G. King, *Handbook to the Rogue River Canyon* (Medford, OR: Commercial Printing Company, 1978), 5.

3. In the eyes of many, people love the Rogue to death. Implementation of the permit system was a joint decision of the Bureau of Land Management (BLM) and the Forest Service following several years of public hearings. The permit system is managed by the BLM.

4. I am indebted to the good work of Stephen Dow Beckham for the historical background on the Rogue River Indians. See his excellent treatment of the earliest peoples of the Rogue: Stephen Dow Beckham, *Requiem for a People* (Oregon State University Press, 2002). See especially chapter 1, "The Land and the People," for a detailed description of the four linguistic groups that comprised the peoples of the southwest Oregon and northern California. Of the four groups, the Athapascans were the greatest in number (9). Beckham, in *Requiem for a People*, 7, cites Joel V. Berreman "Tribal Distribution in Oregon," *Memoirs,* No. 47, (American Anthropological Association, 1937), 29. Beckham notes that Berreman identified several dialects among the Athapascan linguistic groups and clustered them according to their similarities by

Rainie Falls is a stretch that is impassable to all except the most daring and foolhardy. The middle channel is sometimes navigated by rafters, and a natural fish ladder on the north bank is the place where drift boats and river dories are lined today. Fish continue to migrate up the falls. COURTESY OF STEVE PRITCHETT

geography: Galice Creek and Applegate River; Shasta Costa, those bands living on the Illinois River up to the Rogue Valley; Upper Coquille and upper Umpqua basins; Tolowa, from the Smith River in northern California and Oregon's southern coast; Tutuni, those bands residing up the Rogue to the Illinois and from Pistol River to an area just below the Coquille River on the coast.

5. Zane Grey, *Tales of Fresh Water Fishing* (Lanham, MD: Derrydale Press, 2001), 211.

6. River Guides' stories told during Rivers' Reunion, Eugene, OR, April 2, 2000.

7. Quinn et al., *Handbook to the Rogue River Canyon,* 81.

8. Beckham, *Requiem for a People,* 8, 27.

9. Ibid., 26.

10. Karen Bassett, Jim Renner, and Joyce White, Jedediah Smith Route, for the Oregon Trails Coordinating Council, www.endoftheoregontrail.org/oregontrails/jedsmith.html.

11. Stephen Dow Beckham, "Oregon History-Indian Wars," *Oregon Blue Book,* http://bluebook.state.or.us/cultural/history/history14.htm.

12. Ibid.

13. *Donation Land Claim Act, 1850,* An Act to create the Office of Surveyor-General of the Public Lands in Oregon, and to provide for the Survey, and to make Donations to Settlers of said Public Lands. A copy of the act is available at www.ccrh.org/comm/cottage/primary/claim.htm.

14. Comments from Beckham, chapter review, in an email dated May 15, 2006. Beckham also notes that the Coast Reservation was created by executive order and had three administrative units: Southern (Umpqua, later known as the Alsea, Sub-Agency). central (Siletz Agency), and northern (Grand Ronde Agency). The Coast reservation was reduced by executive order in 1865 and by Congress in 1875, leaving only a diminished central unit, the new Siltez reservation.

15. Walter Williams, "From Independence to Wardship: The Legal Process of Erosion of American Indian Sovereignty—1810–1903," *American Indian Culture and Research Journal,* 7:4 (1984), 6.

16. Beeson to Editor, *New York Tribune,* September 30, 1856, in United States, Office of Indian Affairs, Letters Received by the Office of Indian Affairs, 1824–1880, National Archives Microcopy 234, Roll 609, NADP Document D43. View letter online at www.csusm.edu/nadp/d43. htm#1.

Old Man Rainie (left), for whom the falls was named, had a cabin nearby. During salmon and steelhead migration, he eked out a living gaffing fish at the base of the falls, circa 1900.
COURTESY OF THE BLM, ROGUE NATIONAL WILD AND SCENIC RIVER

CHAPTER 7

The Rogue River Drivers

*The happiest lot of any angler would be to live somewhere along the banks
of the Rogue, the most beautiful stream in Oregon. Then, if he kept close watch
on conditions, he could be ready on the spot when the run of steelhead began.*

—Zane Grey, *Tales of Fresh Water Fishing*

Zane Grey's first attempt to hook and land a steelhead with a fly and rod on the Rogue was unsuccessful. The year was 1922. A dentist by training, an author by trade, and a fly fisher at heart, Grey was determined to learn about the Rogue and the ways of its wily inhabitants. With his 9½-foot, 8-ounce Kosmic fly rod, he set about his hunt that year with flies that were "too small" and an American manufactured reel "that would not do for this great fish." English reels that held 100 yards of linen backing were needed, or so he was told. The river captured his imagination. As a self-described world-class fisherman, Grey soon learned that no matter where he was fishing in the world after that first Rogue experience, the aqua green river framed with white and busy riffles infiltrated his thoughts. It was like being with one woman while thinking about another. Rather than hooking, he had been hooked. Grey returned to the Rogue each fall over the next several years, became somewhat successful in outsmarting his prey, and finally realized "the happiest lot of any angler" when he purchased a piece of property on the Rogue's north bank at Winkle Bar in 1926.

The property, however, was in the heart of the Rogue River canyon. Inaccessible to most people, save for miners and reclusive settlers, this stretch was a haven for salmon and steelhead in search of their spawning grounds. Grey's introduction to Winkle Bar came in 1925 on his "never to be forgotten trip down the Rogue." He had heard stories of the wild Rogue where it slips, slides, and cascades through the Siskiyous and Coast Mountains to the west, a foreboding but beautiful place that offered the most pristine environment. A fishing trip through the canyon became his goal, and it was on that trip that he first encountered Winkle Bar and the miner from whom he ultimately purchased the property.

My interest in Zane Grey's trip and cabin, of course, is the boats. For the 1925 voyage, Grey arranged for seven boats to transport his party and an overabundance of gear. It was to be a two- to four-week fishing trip down the Rogue to the Pacific. The arduous and dangerous trip was justified with the expectation of the steelhead runs. The trip also required that there be no pressing time demands on the tail end of the expedition for any of his ten-member party. The guide for this trip was Claude Bardon, accompanied by his helper Van Dorn, nicknamed Debb.[1] Bardon so impressed Zane Grey on that and future trips with his fishing tales, physical attributes, and river expertise that Grey's central character in his 1929 novel, *Rogue River Feud*,[2] Kevin Hill, was based on the guide.

Three of the seven boats were built for the trip, and Bardon had arranged for the remaining four. Wrote Grey:

> The four boats Bardon had secured for me were of a type new to me, and certainly unique. They were about twenty-three feet long, sharp fore and aft, rising out of the water, very wide and deep, with the gunwales having a marked flare, twelve inches to the foot. They looked heavy and clumsy to me, but upon trying one I found, to my amaze, that, empty, it rowed remarkably easily, turned around as on a pivot, and altogether delighted me. Each boat was equipped with two sets of oars, a hundred feet of rope, and a sixteen-foot pole with iron spiked end. In these seven boats we aimed to transport our large outfit and 10 persons.[3]

This was a substantial flotilla, destined for adventure, mishaps, and superb fishing. The rewards outweighed the risks.

The four boats Grey described were river drivers, somewhat similar to the river driving bateaux[4] of our own northeastern colonies. The boats are poled and rowed upriver, but they are more easily moved downriver as the current propels the boat in a descent controlled by the oarsmen. The three new boats were the same type as the four older bateaux, except that each had a small transom on the upriver end, and bulkheads were built into the stem and stern to assist with flotation and provide some semblance of dry storage. Grey referred to the boats as canoelike in profile. The boats were typical of those built and used on the lower and middle Rogue ever since miners, settlers, and commercial fishermen discovered the river's resources.

One of Zane Grey's bateaux remains, though it is in a sorry state of disrepair. It sits under a protective cover on his former property at Winkle Bar and remains an attraction to Rogue River travelers. It is a flat-bottomed, carvel-planked double-ender with a bottom length just over 20 feet. In beam, it is just under 3 feet at the bottom and 5 1/2 feet at the rail. There are no other longitudinal supports. My analysis of the bateau suggests that construction of this boat began with several redwood planks running fore to aft on the bottom. The stem and stern posts were attached first, followed by the frames. The outside edge of the bottom planks and side frames were beveled to receive the garboard, the bottommost sideboards. The garboard was nailed into the edge of the one-inch-thick beveled bottom plank and the frames. A couple forms likely were used as spreaders to guide the garboard into place for nailing, and then the frames were installed. Each plank was added in succession, the last one being the sheer board. The intended use of the craft and the lengths of available lumber determined boat lengths. These boats were simple, easy to build, and seemed to fit the rugged requirements of the Rogue River canyon. A few drivers, however, were lapstrake constructed as opposed to carvel-planked. Their performance was comparable but the lapped boards took greater care to install.

Documentation of the early Rogue drivers is scant. It was, and remains, the custom of Rogue River boatbuilders to build from patterns drawn on a piece of cedar or other wood that is hung in the shop. The very few

The river driver at Winkle Bar on the Rogue. This is probably one of the boats Grey kept on hand for local use when he and his party were at the cabin. It could be poled and rowed upriver or floated downriver and then returned.

pattern boards I have studied do not show lines or off-sets, but merely the frame angles and bevels, stem and stern post bevels, and length of the frames. The station lines are not specified. The rest of the data was in the head of the builder and in the length and flexibility of the material to be used. Most of the drivers that plied the Rogue River canyon are gone. Prior to the 1920s, many of these bateaux were built for one-way trips into the canyon. If the boats were taken through to the Gold Beach area, they may have been sold to local fishermen, left to rot along the riverbank, or set adrift. In the canyon, the boats were often dismantled for their lumber.

The more docile stretches of the Rogue, like those in the Rogue River Valley and the lower 40-mile stretch from Illahe to the Pacific at Gold Beach, required a flat-bottom boat that could carry goods, equipment, fishing nets, and men upriver and then safely negotiate the return trip. These keelless boats were occasionally assisted by a

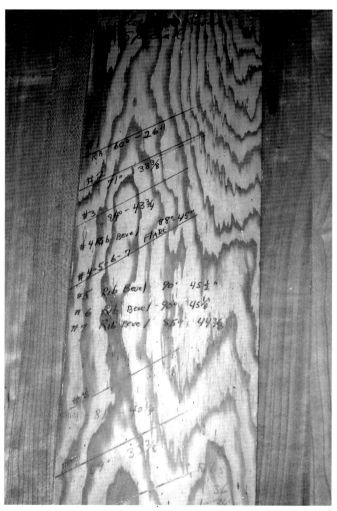

The pattern board for Jerry Briggs's Colorado River dory shows frame angles and bevels. The record of this boat and the other Rogue and McKenzie River boats hung in the shop on a board or shingle such as this. To date, I have not located any lines drawings of the early boats.

sail on their upriver migration when tides and onshore breezes encouraged the hoist of a cloth. Their profile may have resembled that of a canoe, but the breadth was far greater. The lines moved in a symmetrical arch from stem to stern. My analysis suggests, however, that there was a little more flare to the downriver end of some boats, especially those that were used to brave the canyon. This flare helped keep the water out of the boats in rapids. Grey commented that the flare on his boats approximated 12 inches to each vertical foot of the side planks.[5] The length of the boards determined the length of the boats, most of which were 20 to 25 feet long. Frames were Douglas fir, redwood, white oak, or Port Orford cedar.

As with the McKenzie riverboats, there has been some confusion over which end was the bow and which was the stern. Raising the question on the Rogue, however, does not elicit a firm opinion, but instead a comfortable dialogue about the boat's function. My discussions have led to mutual conclusions that the slightly sharper upriver end of the double-ender, the end that cuts through the current as the boat is rowed and poled upriver, is the bow. The subject remains open for discussion. One thing is certain: The boats were stable but very heavy.

I am curious about the origins of these boats. They were the workhorses of the Rogue River canyon second only to the strings of pack mules used to haul supplies and goods overland.

As with boatbuilders in other areas, economies of ease, available tools, and suitable logs led the Rogue Indians of southwest Oregon to build and use dugout canoes. Stephen Dow Beckham reports that the Rogue Indians used dugouts built from single logs that were split and then carved out using stone adzes and fire.[6] A cedar log was the wood of choice, but redwood was also used. The dugouts worked reasonably well for local use along a stretch of calm river or estuary. They were generally shallow, difficult to manage, unseaworthy, and inadequate in whitewater. Nonetheless, the early traders bartered with the Indians for use of their canoes in crossing rivers and estuaries. Beckham notes that the dugouts among the various bands of Indians of southwest Oregon were comparable in shape and function. The craft were generally used for transport, clam and mussel collection, and fishing. It was the custom of the Cheti Indians, residents of present-day Chetco and Windchuck Rivers, just south of the Rogue River, to split cedar logs into rough planks and erect them vertically as walls of their domiciles.[7] Their ability to craft rough planks led me to wonder if they found a way to make planked boats, but my review of the literature indicates that they had neither the skills nor the resources to

Rogue River driver under sail, circa 1900. Fred and Frank Lowery use their pike poles to move the boat upriver with assistance from an onshore breeze. The Lowerys owned a lodge midway between Agness and Gold Beach. The river driver navigated downriver more comfortably than upriver, but the boat's design made upriver navigation possible. In the late nineteenth century, mail was delivered from Gold Beach to Agness with this same boat type, often with support of a sail.
COURTESY OF VEVA STANSELL

cobble together such a boat. The seeming ease with which the dugouts could be paddled and poled against and with the river's current was an asset the early settlers wanted to mimic in a boat, but the only thing.

The origins of the Rogue River drivers reside in the miners and settlers who moved there in the last half of the nineteenth century. Collectively, they were an eclectic group of immigrants. In 1884, Antone Walker was one of the first permanent settlers at the Big Meadows, several miles upriver from Agness. Walker was Portuguese and had spent twenty years as a whaler on the high seas. Though there is no evidence to suggest that he built a boat for the Rogue River, people with his kind

of background and experience found their way there. Walker would have been familiar with the working whaleboat of the nineteenth century and its suitability for transporting goods and services in coastal waterways and rivers.[8] In May 1916, Capt. John Aubery captained a "gondola model" boat from Grants Pass to Gold Beach. The boat was "modeled along the lines of a double Venetian gondola . . . with a length of 38-feet and $9^{1}/_{2}$-feet at the beam." This was a huge boat for the canyon. Spring runoff raised the river to levels that made ordinarily impassable rapids negotiable in a large boat under skilled hands. The purpose of the trip was to deliver a 1-ton mining stamp mill to Blossom Bar. This

The boat used by Capt. John Aubery to transport about 2,000 pounds of mining equipment to Blossom Bar on the Rogue River. The trip was made in the spring of 1916, when snowpack runoff from the Cascade Mountains created above-average river flow. COURTESY OF THE BLM, ROGUE NATIONAL WILD AND SCENIC RIVER

Captain Aubery's boat at the Alameda mine footbridge. Equipment had to be offloaded, and then the boat was hand-hauled to the downriver side of the bridge and reloaded. The same routine was carried out at each significant rapid, of which there were many. Note that the boat has tumbled sides, is lapstrake, and has great carrying capacity. COURTESY OF THE BLM, ROGUE NATIONAL WILD AND SCENIC RIVER

spot on the Rogue is at the lower end of Mule Creek Canyon, a 2-mile stretch of precarious class IV water. Blossom Bar today is also a class IV rapid; however, in 1916, boats had to be portaged up, over, and around large boulders that impeded the river at this point. The few pictures of this boat that exist show a double-ended lapstrake boat that looks to me like a whaler. Without a record of the boat's lines, it is difficult to judge from poor-quality photo plates.[9]

Lou Reuben Martin is a miner who spent several years in the Whiskey Creek Cabin, not far downriver from Grave Creek. Though a relative latecomer to the Rogue, he was born and raised in Sprucehead, Maine, home port for a variety of oar-powered boat types, including flat-bottom dories.[10] My point is that though the origins of these river drivers are undocumented, their creation was in response to the demands of the river and the context of experiences and traditions of the area's immigrants. The Rogue River drivers paralleled a tradition of flat-bottom double-ended boats, and there were several possible threads of influence.

One thread relates to the Hudson's Bay Company. Company traders were among the first to ply the coastal areas of southwest Oregon. The company had its own tradition of boats, including river drivers and canoes. In 1821, the York boat emerged. Built for larger rivers and lakes, this boat was used across central Canada and the territorial Northwest as a means to transport furs and goods from remote locations to the company's many points of demarcation, including Fort Vancouver on the Columbia River. The York boat could carry more than 3 tons—three times the capacity of the largest canoe of the north. Six to eight oarsmen propelled the boat, each one located on the off side of the oar pins. The flat-bottom boats had pointed bows and sterns of 45 degrees. This allowed the crew to easily beach the boats and pull off the sandbars as needed. Upriver movement of the boats was by pole in shallow water, sail and oars in deep water, and rope and brute strength through rapids. The boat was named after the York Factory, the principal staging area and collection point for the Hudson's Bay Company's goods. The York Factory was located near the mouth of the Nelson River on Hudson Bay in Manitoba. The latticework of rivers and streams in central and northwestern Canada required a boat of this type. The Yorks served the Hudson's Bay Company well through the initial part of the twentieth century. Early versions of this boat were operating out of Fort Albany on the Hudson in 1746.[11]

Another thread of possible influence was the colonial river driving bateaux. John Gardner traces the origins of the river drivers to the governor of New France, M. de Courcelles, who in 1671 commissioned a flat bateau.

The governor desired a boat to drive up the rapids of the St. Lawrence River to Lake Ontario, and then safely return downriver. The governor's goal was twofold: to demonstrate to the Iroquois Indians an ability to move men, equipment, and armaments efficiently in the event of future problems, and to develop a capacity to access the wilderness interior for future trade and development. Though the bark canoes of the day could move upriver with relative ease, their carrying capacity was limited, and the prevailing opinion was that a planked boat could not be taken up through rapids. On June 3, the bateau, thirteen bark canoes, and fifty-six people headed upriver from Montreal. The party completed the 175-mile journey in nine days, then immediately turned around and made the return trip in five days. The venture marked a new era for trade and warfare. Gardner referred to the flat-bottom bateau, which had the multidirectional capabilities of a bark canoe and carried a much heavier payload, as the "white man's canoe."[12]

The British colonials saw value in this versatile craft, and within a hundred years, the boat type was a major part of the New England and upper Hudson River transportation system. Indeed, the river driver was key to military successes between the French and the British colonials during their struggle for North America. In 1756, Massachusetts governor William Shirley who was also the commander of British forces in North America, called for the formation of a "Battoe Service" and set out to recruit 2,000 experienced "battoemen." They were to report to Albany by March of that year.[13] The turning point for the British forces was the daring assault two years later of 2,737 men in river drivers on the French Royal Fort Frontenac on Lake Ontario. Commanding this group of battoemen was Col. John Bradstreet.[14] Although the river driving bateaux rubbed gunwales with other boat types, such as the whaleboat and scow, the river drivers made a lasting impression. In concert with the expansionist mindset of the colonials, river transport was essential to moving people and materials into the wilderness, and these bateaux became a craft of choice for navigating the rivers of the northeast.

The northeastern fisherman's dory appears to be closely related to the bateaux in both construction and history. The Bank dory emerged as the fishing trawler's boat in the mid-1850s and was the first boat of its type to be mass-produced. This dory is generally credited to Simeon Lowell at Salisbury Point on the Merrimack River.[15]

Many river boatmen of the Northwest see the origins of drift boats and river dories in the Bank dory. The crescent profile of the Bank dory, flared and straight sides coupled with a very modest rocker fore and aft, does remind one of the present-day drift boat. Another

The traditional Bank dory, as modeled by Harold "Dynamite" Payson. Some northwestern drift boaters erroneously assume there is a direct connection between this dory and drift boats. At best, they might be considered distant cousins, but both are beautiful nonetheless.

similarity is the relative ease of construction and ability to store the boat efficiently, especially aboard ship. Drift boats and river dories are occasionally seen in transit by trailer, with two or more boats nested inside each other, just as the Bank dories were nested on the deck of a mother ship. The boats, however, have very different functions, and though there may be similarities in profiles, that is the extent of the likeness. A drift boat on the high seas, with its high flared sides, flat bottom with rocker fore to aft, and shallow draft, behaves like a butterfly in a stiff breeze, blown here and there, its own course set with great difficulty. The narrower and deeper, flat-bottom draft of the Bank dory has a stabilizing influence in a surly sea when fully loaded with fish and net. They are two very different boats that serve two different functions. The poetry of their profiles, however, brings a smile of acknowledgment to the drift boater.[16]

It is the log-driving bateau that I find most fascinating as a potential thread of influence on the Rogue. This boat was developed, perfected, and used on Maine's Kennebec and Penobscot Rivers and is a lineal descendant of the French Canadian and colonial river driving bateaux.[17] Poled and rowed upriver to ferry men and equipment to logging sites, the boats were often used to shepherd logs downriver and transport log-driving crewmembers and gear. Before the development of road and rail, rivers were the principal means to move logs from landing sites to the mill.

On a drive, the log drivers or river hogs, as the men were called, kept the cut timber moving in the flow of the river or stream. As Eldon Marple described it: "The job of the driving crew was to get the logs down river . . . as fast as the current could carry them. Each river and each drive required different methods and sizes of crew. . . . They spent much of their time on the logs in mid-stream and had to be quick on their feet. . . . Other men on the drive were two man crews of several bateaux to move men from work area to another."[18]

Marsh Underwood, a man of the woods who worked in Vermont, Wisconsin, Washington, and Oregon from the mid-1880s to 1938, kept a diary of his experiences as he migrated across the country. For a time, he manned a log-driving bateau. It was harrowing work that required utmost skill. "Only 'catty men' could be drivers," he said, "and their ability to move quickly with all kinds of body contortions was tested when it came to leaping from the boat to a rapidly moving log or diving from the log to the boat. I've landed on the boat in all kinds of shapes, sometimes with part of a man on top of me." The man up front on the boat was called the bow man and the pilot was called the stern man.[19]

The log-driving bateau had a bottom length ranging from 18 to 36 feet. The material that was available in a given location, the boat's function, and the builder's proximity to navigable water determined the length. Among the Maine log drivers, a bateau with a bottom length of

A Maine log-driving bateau in repose at the Leonard Mills farm in Bradley, Maine. Note the lapstrake construction and the severe stem and stern angles for riding up onto a log deck or riverbank to offload men and equipment. COURTESY OF BOB DICKENS

A log driver at work on an upper midwestern or Canadian river. Life for these waterborne log drivers was risky, but the boats served them well. They could be easily driven upriver, parked on a logjam, and quickly removed once the logs started to move. COURTESY OF THE FOREST HISTORY SOCIETY

A log driver at work on the Clearwater in Idaho, circa 1940. The log driver was owned and operated by Clearwater Timber Company. The interior construction of this boat was similar to that of the Rogue River drivers.
PERMISSION BY WEYERHAEUSER

20 feet had a stem-to-stern length of about 30 feet topside. The elongated extension of the sharp bow and stern allowed the boatmen to ride up on a logjam and hold the craft in position while one or more men attempted to break apart the logs with their pike poles. The design also improved the ease of movement upriver. As the boat migrated across the northern United States and Canada, the extended bow appearance of the log drivers became less pronounced.

Log-driving bateaux were employed on northern Idaho and some Washington rivers, but their use in Oregon was very limited. Rivers were a major transport system for cut logs, but in western Oregon and western Washington, logs were moved by way of splash dams, rafts, flumes, and later, rail and trucks.[20] River hogs, however, remained in high demand. Generally the highest paid in the logging camp, and the most nimble, these men were the bread and butter of most timber companies. One of the final drives using log-driving bateaux occurred on Idaho's Clearwater River in 1946.[21]

There are striking similarities between the construction of the Rogue River drivers and the log-driving bateaux. In both cases, the builder formed and cambered the bottom, added the frames as on a keel, and then planked the sides.[22] Was this simply a function of the logic of boat construction, or were there men in residence on the Rogue who had experience with log-driving bateaux and river drivers? Just as the river drivers and dories of the Northeast have roots in the knowledge and experience of the British colonial immigrants, so too the early river drivers of the Rogue may reflect the threads of migratory influence.

The river drivers served the Rogue River Valley and canyon for about a hundred years. One popular fishing guide in Grants Pass used this boat type into the 1950s. In spite of Zane Grey's observation that the boat handled easily and moved "as on a pivot," it was heavy, cumbersome, and difficult to handle. Improvements in the Rogue River whitewater boats were inevitable.

Endnotes

1. Zane Grey, *Tales of Fresh Water Fishing*, (Lanham, MD: Derrydale Press, 2001), 109, 257, and 180.

2. Zane Grey, *Rogue River Feud*, (New York: Harper, 1930).

3. Grey, *Tales of Fresh Water Fishing*, 182.

4. I use the term "bateau" in reference to this boat type, and I use it interchangeably with "driver" and river driver. To the early French Canadian settlers, the term meant no more than boat until the early eighteenth century, when bateau came to refer to as the type name for double-ended, flat-bottom, chine-built boats on Eastern Canada and northeastern colonial waterways and lakes, designed to be driven upriver and floated downriver.

5. Grey, *Tales of Fresh Water Fishing*, 182.

6. Stephen Dow Beckham, *Requiem for a People*, (Oregon State University Press, 2002), 18.

7. "First Residents were the Chetco," *Curry Coastal Pilot*, Brookings, OR, February 23, 2001. Article may be found on line at www.currypilot.com/news/story.cfm?story_no-1495.

8. Kay Atwood, *Illahe: The Story of Settlement in the Rogue River Canyon* (Northwest Reprints, Oregon State University Press, 2002), 137–38.

9. "Capt. Aubery Pilots Boat down the Rogue River to Gold Beach," *Grants Pass Courier,* May 24, 1916.

10. Atwood, *Illahe,* 166.

11. *Our History, Transportation and Technology,* (Hudson Bay Company Heritage), 1. www.hbc.com/hbcheritage/history/transportation/yorkboat.

12. John Gardner, with illustrations by Sam Manning, *The Dory Book,* (Mystic, CT: Mystic Seaport Museum, 1987), 18–19.

13. Boston Weekly Newsletter, February 5, 1756, published from November 5, 1730, through August 25, 1757, Library of Congress, Box 10, Fol. 5.

14. Gardner, *Dory Book,* page 22.

15. Howard I. Chapelle, *American Small Sailing Craft,* (New York: W. W. Norton and Company, 1951), 25, 85–86.

16. For a more detailed treatment of the Bank dory and her cousins see Gardner, *Dory Book,* 25–40.

17. Chapelle, *American Small Sailing Craft,* 80. Also see Lore Rogers' "The Bateau," *Northern Logger and Timber Processor,* Vol. 24 (May 1976), 6–29.

18. Eldon Marple, "Logging," Hayward, WI: Sawyer County Historical Society.

19. Marsh Underwood, *The Log of a Logger,* Portland, OR: published by the author, 1938. A river driver's account of loggers, logging, and logging camps from New England to Wisconsin, Oregon and Washington since the 1880s, 23–55.

20. For an excellent treatment of log transportation is Oregon see *Swift Flows the River,* (Coos Bay, OR: Arago Books, 1990), a first person account by Dow Beckham with an introduction by his son, Stephen Dow Beckham.

21. Artie F. Lentz, "Potlatch Forests, Incorporated," *Pacific Historian* 16 (Summer 1972), 37–46, describes log drives on the main branch and North Fork of the Clearwater to Lewiston, ID.

22. Chapelle, *American Small Sailing Craft,* 46.

CHAPTER 8

Glen Wooldridge and Bob Pritchett
The Classic Rogue River Dory

*The shallow draft, extended chine contact with the river, and flare provided for
a dory that was stable, held its course in the current, and was easy to row.*

Zane Grey was an interloper. He loved the Rogue River, but it wasn't home. He came for relatively brief visits, and then he was gone. He brought notoriety to the river, a blessing for some. The people who lived and worked along the course of the Rogue to the coast were unafraid of isolation or the confinement caused by towering topographies, recalcitrant streams, or a foreboding Pacific Ocean. The earliest rush for furs and gold brought other interlopers too. Many were inconsiderate of the land and its indigenous peoples. To the remnants and those who sought permanent settlement in the area, the Rogue became home. Somehow they dealt with the isolation. An unsung poet laureate of the southwest Oregon coast, sequestered by surrounding hills, pondered her own milieu:

> "Thus far" say the hills about me.
> "Thus far" say the boughs of trees
> Weaving their lattice above me,
> But my heart is not held by these.
>
> My heart goes tunneling under
> The ground, where the still roots are:
> Slips out to a screened peak yonder:
> Soars up—straight up—to a star.
>
> Therefore this sweet small valley
> Builds walls in vain for me,
> For walls are quite impotent
> If but the heart is free.[1]

This is a curious paradox. Some people seek isolation to be free yet seem to be imprisoned by what they seek, until we learn it is their spirit that soars. In some cases,

however, especially in the canyon, the sequestration drove a few people mad, or their madness was quarantined by their isolation, I'm not sure which. For others, the Rogue River represented the lure of the unknown and adventure. In addition to the commercial viability of gold, the river itself became a target of entrepreneurs as spawning salmon and steelhead were harvested by the millions in the area of present-day Gold Beach.

Commercial fishing was also a practice 120 miles upriver at Grants Pass that often led to contentiousness between the two fishing communities. But it was the allure of the river and its environs that seduced a few into thinking that in the pulchritude of the Rogue River there might be a future for those who learned how to navigate its course for the gratification of the experience. These isolates had a heuristic side who seemed to hear the river's call: "If you can learn to go with the flow, you can have me and what I have to offer." It was a beguiling invitation, and it was fortuitous that a few answered the call, for it was their response to the river that ultimately led to the Rogue River dory as the whitewater boat of choice.

Glen Wooldridge was one such person. Wooldridge was born of Oregon pioneer stock in 1896 at his grandfather's placer mine on a small Rogue River tributary, Foots Creek, upriver a few miles from Grants Pass. He was fascinated by the river from the beginning, influenced in part by his grandfather's stories of migrating salmon that spawned in the creek. He marveled that they had found their way to the Rogue, matured enough to migrate to the Pacific, and then returned to this exact spot alive enough to spawn before dying. Perhaps it was the salmon that interested him in the Rogue. He discovered that the river was alive. He was also attracted to the wonders of its flow. "I'd get up mornings before the family was awake and fill my pockets with cold biscuits and meat, then sneak off down to the river. I'd bellyflop on a big, flat rock, studying the water. The current doesn't always run the same; rocks and logs are washed in and out, causing changes. Sometimes I'd make little boats out of pieces of bark and set them adrift, watching to see how they moved in the current or swirled in the eddies." Wooldridge seemed destined to bring the river to life by making it accessible to others.

By age nineteen, Wooldridge had been fishing commercially for a couple of years, gillnetting. That year, 1915, he and his good friend, Cal Allen, decided to challenge the Rogue by running its course from Grants Pass to Gold Beach. The trip would require that they build their own boat. "Boats weren't easily come by then. Each man usually had to build his own. They were narrow, like a canoe, sharp on both ends with hardly any rake so they could be poled up riffles with the pike, or easily rowed." So he and Cal Allen built a boat, and "it was a hell of a looking thing. Heavy! It was made of cedar planks and 2 x 4s, and was about 20 feet long. We caulked up the cracks and dragged it down and heaved it over the bank. . . . We rustled up some oars some place and got ready to start." The previous year, two men had died in separate attempts to negotiate the river. Both sets of parents and friends warned the pair about the dangers and counseled them not to attempt the trip.

"We were just a couple of green kids, didn't know half as much about boating as we thought we did. But we sure learned." Over the next five days, they navigated, portaged, ran, relished, and cursed every rapid the river threw at them. There was an economic motivation to their trip—salmon—which they fished en route and on arrival at Gold Beach. They sold their catch to the local cannery and after a time headed back to Grants Pass on foot. "One guy told me a story. . . . He said he hiked down the Rogue Trail. Sometimes it was on gravel bars, sometimes up the side of a mountain. He kept going and it turned into an Indian trace. He followed that and it turned into a game track. Later on it became a squirrel trail. He followed that and it went up an oak tree and into a hole. . . . That's sort of the way our trip was. . . . After the troubles . . . and all that energy . . . we didn't bring much home."[2]

Wooldridge's 1915 encounter with the length of the Rogue spawned at least three things in him: an insatiable thirst for understanding the river's dynamics, an interest in turning his passion for the river into an economic enterprise, and the ability to spin tales of the Rogue that were appropriate for a variety of occasions. In fact, his

tall tales equaled those of another Rogue River storyteller, Hathaway Jones, a tradition kept alive today by Rogue River commercial jet boat pilots and river guides.

For the next sixty years, Wooldridge explored and manipulated the Rogue. He came to know the river intimately, and his popularity as the river's first guide grew exponentially. He guided anyone interested in adventure and fishing. His notoriety grew, and his clients included Clark Gable, Herbert Hoover, Betty Grable, Victor Moore, Guy Kibbee, and Ted Trueblood, to name a few. Trueblood wrote in his Foreword to the Wooldridge biography, "His first love remains the Rogue and if you move a rock anywhere along I'm sure he would notice the change."[3]

Indeed, Wooldridge knew the Rogue's rocks. In an attempt to make the river safer for travel, it was his custom to remove perilous rocks from rapids that were particularly troublesome, a practice silently questioned by a few but often supported by the Forest Service with contributions of blasting powder. He would drop a weighted charge of dynamite on the upriver side of an offending boulder, and then move like hell downriver to escape the blast. Eddies below targeted boulders allowed him to edge the boat against the rock. His partner, often Bob Pritchett or another stalwart, hopped onto the rock and placed the lit charge at the base of the boulder on the upriver side. The current always splits just above a rock, and they placed the package in this calm area. Depending on the size of the boulder to be blown, the charge included from two to ten sticks of dynamite, tightly bundled with two blasting caps crimped and encased in axle grease and two $2\frac{1}{2}$-foot fuses. The fuses burned at a foot per minute, thus giving the duo two and a half minutes to find safety before the explosion.[4]

On one occasion, Wooldridge left Pritchett's good friend Press Pyle stranded on a rock after the charge had been placed. Glen had inadvertently allowed the boat to drift away but was able to motor back up to the rock. Pyle dove into the boat as Wooldridge whirled the craft around and headed downriver. The concussion of the blast and the cascade of rock chunks falling around them was something they didn't soon forget.[5] It was perilous work.

The most burdensome set of rapids was Blossom Bar, so named because of the wild azaleas growing on its north bank. The place was a rock garden that required the boats to be portaged 50 yards over and around cabin-size boulders. Over time, Wooldridge and his buddies dynamited a small channel along the south bank that enabled them to line the boats rather than portage them. Ultimately, he opened a channel that allowed the rapids to be run by expert oarsmen.

Preparing to portage at Blossom Bar, also called the "rock garden." Moving the heavy boats 50 yards over treacherous and slippery boulders was arduous and dangerous work. It didn't take many such portages before Glen Wooldridge was thinking about ways to clear a passage for lining the boats. COURTESY OF THE BLM, ROGUE NATIONAL WILD AND SCENIC RIVER

Glen Wooldridge's most significant contributions during these years, in my view, were the riverboat modifications he made. The river was his life, and his goal was to make it accessible to as many fishers and adventurers as possible. He cobbled together his own boats, and in each successive craft he incorporated changes that were influenced by his experiences on and demands of the river. Through the 1920s and 1930s, he gave his planked river driver more flare on the downriver prow. The flare helped throw water away from the boat as he encountered a heavy rapid, rather than allow it to lap into the vessel. The boats were heavy enough without the addition of errant river water. Later he added a 6- to 8-inch wash strake that extended from just aft of the bow to the first set of oar-locks. Its purpose was to help keep clients dry in heavy water. His boats retained the bottom profile of the river drivers, flat as a pancake except for a modest rake under the prow and stern. The lengthier chine contact with the river made it more difficult to maneuver quickly, but the boat was more likely to hold its course if a set of rapids was entered correctly. This was unlike the emerging McKenzie boats, whose continuous rockers made them highly maneuverable but demanded constant attention to keep them aligned with the current. Another advantage the boats provided was their carrying capacity. Originally

intended as river mules, they were capable of carrying gear and a pair of clients for the ten-day trip to Gold Beach. This capacity was an asset Wooldridge chose not to lose.

His boats also included a small, tombstonelike transom on the upriver end. Commercial fishermen used motors on their boats prior to 1920 on the lower Rogue. The use of motors on his boats became something of an obsession with Wooldridge. When he and Cal Allen returned to Grants Pass after their 1915 trip, they hitched a ride on the mail boat from Gold Beach to Agness, about 30 miles upstream. "Elihu Fry ran it. It had a motor, about a 5 to 8 horse, and he carried several pike poles in the boat. When we came to a riffle everyone had to use a pike pole to push us over the white water, then we'd go bumping along to the next riffle." From Agness, they hiked the 50 miles over the mountains to Galice. Wooldridge told Florence Arman, "I think right there was when I decided to make a run upriver someday."[6]

Over time, the "Old Man of the River," as Glen Wooldridge came to be affectionately known, pioneered the use of motors—prop and then impeller driven—to navigate upriver. He seemed intent on keeping the promise he had made to himself on his 1915 trek back to Grants Pass from Gold Beach. Though his first love

Wooldridge runs a particularly bony stretch. Note the addition of a wash strake on the transom end. The boat no longer resembles a double-ended canoe; it has been shortened a bit and is built for durability and carrying capacity. At some point, Wooldridge began running the boat prow-first rather than transom-first, perhaps for the same reasons Woodie Hindman converted the Kaarhus square-ender to a double-ender. COURTESY OF THE BLM, ROGUE NATIONAL WILD AND SCENIC RIVER

A river mule laden with supplies being lined through what is now called Mule Creek Canyon. These river drivers had considerable carrying capacity, and managing the boats in this kind of water was onerous. COURTESY OF THE BLM, ROGUE NATIONAL WILD AND SCENIC RIVER

Top left: *Wooldridge at the tiller on his first run upriver from Gold Beach to Grants Pass in 1947. Bob Pritchett was in the boat too. His job was to take the oars and navigate the boat to safety should the motor fail. It was a perilous run.* COURTESY OF THE BLM, ROGUE NATIONAL WILD AND SCENIC RIVER. Top right: *The "old man of the river."* Left: *Glen Wooldridge and Ruell Hawkins during Glen's 1948 run up the River of No Return from Riggins to Salmon City, Idaho. Wooldridge used a long-handled tiller with throttle so he could stand and scan the river ahead. Tom Staley accompanied the pair to take pictures.* COURTESY OF THE BLM, ROGUE NATIONAL WILD AND SCENIC RIVER.

was the Rogue, his attention turned to other rivers too, and over the next couple of decades he perfected upriver running under power to conquer such wild rivers as the Klamath, Salmon, Frasier, and Yukon. He was an extraordinary promoter, and it paid him and the Rogue great dividends. Anyone who today takes advantage of a Rogue River jet boat trek up the Rogue from Gold Beach or down from Grants Pass must thank Glen Wooldridge for his pioneering work in this area.

A quiet, self-assured stoic worked with Wooldridge through the 1940s. He was a river man too, but he was uncomfortable with flamboyance and hyperbole. Bob Pritchett was twenty-four years Glen's junior, but Wooldridge's confidence in his river skills was testimony to Pritchett's competence on the Rogue. Pritchett worked with Wooldridge through most of the decade and was involved in his first and second runs upriver from Gold Beach to Grants Pass in 1947 and 1949. The second run was filmed and used to promote Wooldridge, the Rogue, and this new form of whitewater travel. One of Bob's jobs was to man the oars of the boat should the motor fail in the midst of rapids or anywhere else.

In 1951, Wooldridge sold his guide business to Pritchett, including a Rogue dory. One of Pritchett's first acts was to repaint the boat Oregon State University's colors, orange and black. Bob had attended Oregon State in 1938 and 1939, and he maintained an affection for the school throughout his life. As a senior in high school, Pritchett had earned five letters, and he went on to play two years of football for Lon Stiner at Oregon State. The new colors didn't please Wooldridge, however, who insisted that Pricthett keep the Wooldridge color: red. Pritchett firmly informed Wooldridge, "I'll paint the boat any color I please."[7] He did not buy the Wooldridge opinions, colors, or style of flair. Bob was unpretentious, quietly confident, his own man, and ready to demonstrate his superlative qualities as a guide. He was a man who walked in quiet confidence.

Bob's partner in his new enterprise was his wife, Virginia. In my conversations with her about Bob and his life as a guide, she always used the pronoun "we." Having met in junior high school, Virginia King and Bob Pritchett rediscovered each other when Bob was in college. They married in 1941. It is clear that she was a keystone in both their relationship and the guide business. They had four children: Lynn, Larry, Bob, and Steve. In addition to caring for the family, Virginia managed the business behind the scenes. She bought the food, prepared meals for the day's fishing excursion, and along with other guide spouses, shuttled the trailers to the put-in and then, in late afternoon, back to the takeout. Trips through the canyon to Gold Beach were in the fall, usually mid-September through October, and were four to ten days long. When Pritchett worked for Wooldridge, Virginia usually didn't shuttle the vehicles for the long downriver trips, but after they purchased the guide business, she was very much engaged.

In April 2001, my wife, Sue, and I hosted a reunion of Rogue and McKenzie River guides and their spouses in Eugene, Oregon. Over the previous two years, I had interviewed many of the guides and their spouses. The reunion provided me an opportunity both to thank them all for their contributions to my research up to that time and to see what would happen when two or more old-time guides and their spouses were in the same room. Such social events were rare in the life of the guiding community. It proved to be a wonderful time, and as I had hoped, stories flowed like water over Rainie Falls. One of the observations Virginia made that day was that

Bob Pritchett in his characteristic orange and black Oregon State University colors. COURTESY OF STEVE PRITCHETT

Virginia Pritchett assists her husband, Bob, in terminating a day trip. Like most of the guides' wives, she scheduled trips for clients, shuttled vehicles, prepared and packed lunches, and tended the children. In Virginia's case, she also helped build the boats. COURTESY OF STEVE AND VIRGINIA PRITCHETT

Virginia visits with another guest at the 2001 river guides' reunion. COURTESY OF PATRICK FARRELL

a book could be written about the wives and their experiences in support of their husbands' work. She chuckled at some of her shuttling experiences over tightly winding muddy roads and trails that today would make a grown man cower. Spouses were generally key elements in the guides' success.

Virginia is descended from pioneer stock. Her grandfather was a well-known Oregon pioneer, George Meek, who traveled the Oregon Trail to the area in the 1850s. She exhibited the self-assurance, independence, and determination of her forefathers. She recounted several stories of shuttling her husband's vehicle and trailer, of which one stands out. With her Buick Roadmaster, Virginia, accompanied by two of her young children, traveled the muddy road to Galice to a pickup point. Halfway across the old Hells Gate Bridge, a logging truck entered the bridge from the other side. The driver jumped from the cab "and cussed me out: 'Back that thing out of here!'"

The bridge's roadway was narrowly planked, with little room for error. Virginia replied, "Do you want to spend all night here on this bridge? That's just what'll happen if you don't back that truck off the bridge and let me pass." And that's what he did. Though Virginia was independent, she usually traveled caravan-style with the other guides' wives. There was security in numbers, not from logging truck drivers, who were generally a courteous bunch, but in the event any one driver ran into difficulty.

Virginia was also a partner in Bob's shop. She has clear recollections of how he built his boats, and she regularly assisted him with the projects, especially during the installation of the side and bottom panels. Bob's custom was to use a boat for a few years, and then build replacements when needed or as he had time. The boats were worked hard on the Rogue. Lining Rainie Falls was particularly tough on the boats' chine caps, but they did their job of protecting the boat. Each winter, Bob repaired, refinished, and repainted his boats so they were crisp and ready to go for the next season. Pritchett built his own replacement boats, and during his early years, he also built boats for fellow guides. His boats were typical of the emerging Rogue River dory style, and his own river experiences helped shape changes in each boat he built. The most challenging part for Virginia was the bottom panel. Once the panel was cut to size, it was her job to align the large piece of plywood so that predrilled holes matched in the stem and transom. Any miscalculation would result in a misaligned panel and a very leaky boat. Virginia speaks with pride of the boats' durability and the continued existence of several craft, two of which are owned by her grandchildren.[8]

Bob's method of dory building was novel among his peers. Most boats of the Rogue were built upside down, but Bob built his right side up. According to his son Steve, "He liked to watch the boat take shape."[9] The jig on which the boat was built provided for upright frames. The rocker of the boat could be adjusted by placement of shims under the bottom frames. Once Bob was satisfied with the feel of the boat, he secured the frames and wrapped the plywood side panels around the structure to form the hull. It was an unusual method for the Rogue. Bob's patterns and angles were recorded on a 1-by-6-inch board that hung in his shop. Most of the other details of the boat were in his head, and when he considered an idea to improve a feature, he would mentally log it away and then incorporate it into his next dory.

Most of the Rogue dories I have examined show a couple of anomalies. The first is the chine log. I have yet

Bob Pritchett built his boats using an upright jig. A man with an engineer's mind, Pritchett liked to see his boats take shape. In this apparatus, he was able to adjust the rake of the boat under the stem and stern. Near as I can tell, he retained a lengthy flat spot at the chine from stem to stern, which increased the boat's displacement and thus ensured good carrying capacity.
COURTESY STEVE PRITCHETT

to see a chine that is beveled, including those on Bob's boats. The chine sits in the squared chine notch flush with the side panel. This creates a small catch basin at the top of the chine and may lead to problems with dry rot. Pritchett's boats were properly cared for and stored dry when not in use. The second anomaly relates to the construction of the frames. The side frames are in two pieces, with one piece lying on top of the chine against the side panel and serving as a shim for a second piece that ties into the bottom frame. This technique eliminated the need to cut a chine notch in a completed frame. The procedure was made possible by building the boat around a form or jig. This procedure would not be possible in today's free-form construction.

Pritchett built his boats to last. The boats' chine caps, as they were intended, protected the chine area from rock abuse. They were easily replaced when necessary during the off-season. If demanding currents, back eddies, or whirlpools didn't get you, the rocks did. In his later years, Pritchett added a steel cap that ran the length of the outside chine. This added considerable life to the chine cap.

The demands of Bob's guide business were weighty. Not only did his clients expect to catch fish and enjoy the Rogue experience, but he was always preoccupied with safety. Anything can happen on the river. Pritchett knew it, and he continually was on the watch for the unexpected. If one is anticipatory enough, many problems can be avoided. Mother Nature, however, occasionally slips up from behind. Bob Pritchett stood 6 feet, 3 inches tall, weighed 200 pounds, and "was Jack Armstrong, the all-American Boy . . . in action and physique. He could break a pair of 10-foot ash oars with his bare hands if he had to."[10]

Prudence on the river is equally important, and Pritchett was known for good judgment. His oarsmanship, strength, and judgment were put to a major test in October 1950. He and co-guide Charley Foster were on the second day of a trip for Glen Wooldridge when it started to rain. Rain is an expectation in Oregon, but not the deluge the party was about to experience. The river colored up quickly, and the party made its way to Black Bar Lodge. Hal and Bea Witherwox had built this isolated haven in the mid-1930s, and it was a popular stay for the guides. It still is, although Hal and Bea are long gone. The friendly ambience and hospitality of the place remain, however. For seventy-nine hours, it rained hard. The water rose, and the 600 feet from the river uphill to the lodge disappeared as the Rogue approached the doorsteps. Bob and Charley's guests—Rowly and Viki Lohman, and Pope and Ruth Hilburn, all from San Francisco—were awestruck by the ferocious attempt of the river to clear its throat of logs and other debris and deposit them in the

Bob Pritchett lines his boat down the natural fish ladder at Rainie Falls. The boat's outside chine caps took most of the abuse in the lining. He added a metal strip to the cap for added protection. COURTESY OF STEVE PRITCHETT

Blossom Bar today. Glen Wooldridge first opened a passage to allow for lining the boats, and later opened another through the midsection. A boat is entering the horn, with the "picket fence" located to port side. Once through the horn, the boatman navigates the Rock Garden for 200 to 300 yards. Imagine Pritchett running this at flood stage.

Pacific 50 miles downstream. On the fifth day, Glen Wooldridge got word to the guides that the river was passable although still running very high, so at 9:00 on Thursday morning, they left Hal and Bea to push on out. "Push" is a misnomer, because it was more like riding a roller coaster. The river at flood stage presented a very different Rogue, where the usual landmarks weren't visible, formerly treacherous rapids were becalmed, and flat stretches of lower water became cascading rollers.

The one exception was Blossom Bar. Blossom Bar under any set of circumstances is treacherous, but the type of treachery changes as river levels shift. At lower river levels, the oarsman is confronted with technically challenging maneuvers to navigate the 300-yard-long rock garden. At flood stage, the confining walls and resident boulders in the riverbed create huge waves, suckholes, reversals, and whirlpools. After studying the rapids, Pritchett decided they would empty the boats and portage their gear, and then he would take the two empty boats through the rapids alone. As Ruth Hilburn described it:

So now, as we looked down, we were all pulling for him every inch. . . . Pulling the oars with all his strength and skill, Bob started out. The boat disap-

peared from sight again and again as the bow went into huge waves. It looked like a tiny cork that bobbed up and under. None but a super man could have made it. Bob beached the boat and walked back up for the second. Knowing he must have been exhausted, we wished he didn't have to tempt fate again. . . . Again he fought the waves and disappeared from view. . . . First we saw him and then he was gone. When we saw him again his arms were working but lacked the punch they had had. He got through the worst of it but was too exhausted to land and had to keep on going with the current [until he could work the boat to a safe landing].

By Ruth's estimate, the waves from trough to crest exceeded 30 feet that day. It's unlikely the rollers were that large, but from Hilburn's elevated downriver vantage, as she watched Bob's boats disappear into the trough of each roller and reappear on the crest of the wave, only to disappear again, her perception of size is understandable. It was huge water.[11]

Press Pyle, another highly regarded old-time Rogue River guide, said of the incident, "I don't think anyone ever pulled a pair of oars like Bob did."[12] Press and Bob were Rogue River colleagues, and each had respect for the other. Their mutual regard led to discussions about their dories and how they might be improved. Pritchett's engineering mind caused him to incorporate subtle changes in his dories over time. His boats assumed considerable flare, for example, more so than most. The flare lowered the profile of the boat a bit, but it offered two advantages: It slapped whitewater away from the boat like a wash strake, and it offered greater stability. Stand on either set of sheer rails, and the flared sides become an extension of the bottom, thereby refusing to let the boat tip over.

Another feature of his dories that he kept tweaking was the bottom line. Bob was concerned about a couple things. First was the boat's carrying capacity, especially with a 75-pound motor hanging off the transom. It was the custom of the early Rogue guides to motor through the longer quiet stretches, especially on the lower end of the river. Two clients, the guide, and their gear necessitated a dory that would remain a high-performance vessel in spite of significant weight. To address this issue, Pritchett retained a flat spot on the bottom that ran fore to aft of amidships 30 to 40 inches. The overall length of the flat area was 60 to 80 inches, depending on the boat. This added considerable displacement to the boat and

significantly increased its capacity. I have film of a Pritchett boat loaded with two clients, gear, and motor on the transom, with a draft that I would estimate at 4 to 6 inches. Equally significant was the base of the transom: It sat just above the waterline, as did the base of the stem. The shallow draft, extended chine contact with the river, and flare provided for a dory that was stable, held its course in the current, and was easy to row. It was a highly functional boat and served Pritchett's needs well.

Pritchett operated his guide business through the 1970s. His reputation as a respected and competent guide became known worldwide. Virginia recalls that Bob always stayed in touch with his customers in the off-season via handwritten personal notes of friendship. Once clients experienced a fishing trip with Pritchett, they were hooked on him. If, on the other hand, clients proved to be difficult to please, off-color, or otherwise unpleasant, Pritchett would not guide them again. He treated people as he treated the river: quietly, confidently, and respectfully.

As the years wore on, other river aficionados, sometimes called the "splash and giggle" group, invaded the Rogue; Nonfishers frequently disrupted the peace and quiet of the place. They had every right to be there, but many showed little regard for those who plied the river

Pritchett running a rapid. Note the motor on the transom. This dory was able to comfortably accommodate two guests, the guide, their gear, and a 75-pound motor. The bases of both transom and stem remained out of the water. PHOTO COURTESY OF STEVE PRITCHETT

Bob Pritchett's final dory, a boat that reflects his accumulated experience of forty years on the river. I call it the classic Rogue River dory.

commercially. They seemed unaware of the contributions these guides had made to safe navigation of the Rogue. By 1974, river traffic through the canyon had become such that a permit system to govern commercial traffic was imposed. In 1978, a permit system for private boaters was implemented. Discouraged by the increase in discourteous traffic and the loss of remoteness, Pritchett retired in 1979. It was a difficult decision, and the Rogue lost one of its most respected river guides.

Five years after his retirement from the Rogue, Bob Pritchett decided to build one more dory. His goal was to incorporate his forty years of experience into a boat that would serve as the cream of his crop of boats. He built the boat, but the dory was never launched. Instead, it sat in his shop for five years as monument of sorts to his skills and experiences. The boat epitomized the classic Rogue River dory.

An environment as beautiful as the Rogue carries other hazards, and over the years, several river guides succumbed to the sun. A lifetime on the river with inadequate protection from its rays can lead to skin cancer. In Bob's case, he developed melanoma that went undetected until it had spread too far. Within a short time of the diagnosis, he was gone. Bob Pritchett died on January 3, 1989. An article about Pritchett written after his death said he was "probably the finest old time guide on the Rogue. He had a tremendous following of people from all over the world."[13]

After his death, Virginia and her son Steve dusted off Bob's final boat. The only thing Bob Pritchett hadn't built for the boat was a wash strake, an 8-inch piece that runs along the sheer line from just aft of the prow to a point in front of the oarlock. This was added protection to keep guests dry in heavy rapids. Perhaps Bob thought the strake was unnecessary, since he had no intention of using the dory. Steve and Virginia decided to add the piece, as the boat seemed incomplete without it. Steve painted the wash strake to match the boat's orange and black colors, and then installed it. The dory has remained with Steve since, regally sitting in his garage as a tribute to his family's Rogue River heritage. It's the classic Rogue River dory.

Endnotes

1. Frances Holmstrom, *Oregon Mist* (Portland, OR: Binfords & Mort Publishers, 1951), 17.

2. Glen Wooldridge as told by Florence Arman, *The Rogue: A River to Run* (Grants Pass, OR: Wildwood Press), 11, 31, 51–52, 57.

3. Ibid., foreword by Ted Trueblood, 8.

4. Ibid., chapter 9, "Blasting a Channel down the Rogue," 161–176.

5. Interview with Bob Pritchett's son Steve, March 1999.

6. *The Rogue: A River to Run,* 56.

7. Virginia Pritchett interview, April 7, 2004.

8. Ibid.

9. Steve Pritchett interview, November 1999.

10. As told by Jack Anderson, Rogue River Ranch, in "A River Guide's Guide," by Jeff Duewel, *Grants Pass Daily Courier,* February 7, 1989.

11. Ruth Hilburn wrote an unpublished account of the river trip, titled "Marooned," which she presented to Bob Pritchett and Charley Foster. I received a copy courtesy of Steve Pritchett, Bob Pritchett's youngest son. Quote cited from page 12.

12. As quoted in Jeff Duewel's article, "A River Guide's Guide," *Grants Pass Daily Courier,* February 7, 1989.

13. Ibid.

CHAPTER 9

Jerry Briggs
The Colorado River Connection

"Life sure passes quickly when you're having fun."

—JERRY BRIGGS

It started low, below the diaphragm, and migrated upward until it erupted in a series of high-pitched chortles that trailed off. This was followed by a succession of similar tremors, until everyone in the shop was in the same state of seemingly uncontrolled convulsions. The laughter was spontaneous but clearly required some effort, as his face turned red, his lips curled, and his eyes narrowed. If I closed my eyes and heard the sound in tall timber, I would have assumed it to be the receding call of a bull elk's chuckle at the close of his bugle. But my eyes were open, and through my tears, I saw the proud sphinxian stance of a China rooster assured by the attention he draws and unmistakably in charge of things at the moment. Rogue River guide and boatbuilder Jerry Briggs was responding to one among our group who cut a notch in a frame with hammer and chisel for the inside sheer rail. The hilarity was immediately preceded by Jerry's observation that "what the world needs is more whittlers and fewer chiselers." He enjoyed this witticism as much as everyone else in the shop, or more. His laugh was infectious, like his personality, and we were unmistakably pleased by his presence.[1]

Jerry isn't an old-time Rogue River guide. Though he arrived early enough to know every one of the old-timers, he's second generation. Still, Jerry is considered one of the good old boys by present-day Rogue runners. The Rogue River runs through his veins. Rightly so. His dad, Elmer Briggs, made his first run through the canyon to Gold Beach in 1922, at twenty years of age, to try his hand at gillnetting for salmon. He teamed up with one of his brothers. Elmer, better known as Squeak, couldn't recall a day when he didn't have a fishing pole in his hands. Jerry recounts that as young boys, his dad and two brothers would leave their poles leaning against the side of their house in Grants Pass. When school let out in the afternoon, the Briggs boys ran home and without breaking stride, grabbed their poles and headed for the river.[2]

What's in a name? When Elmer Briggs was a baby, his father gave him the sobriquet Squeaky because he squeaked a lot. The moniker stuck, and Elmer carried it throughout his life. The name's uniqueness connoted an inimitable reputation as a fishing guide, an occupation Squeak gravitated to in lieu of commercial gillnetting.

Squeak's first few guided trips were ten-day adventures from Grants Pass through the canyon to Gold Beach. His boat was the Rogue River driver. This was the traditional boat of the Rogue, which could be navigated downriver with oars or driven upriver with pike poles and oars. Today guided fishermen are treated to stays in wilderness lodges along the river. When Squeak did his early ten-day trips, he and his clients had to camp along the way. Wilderness camping on the Rogue is a treat in itself, but it's also hard work when clients look to the guide for sole support. The length of time required for the downriver trips, and a new bride, caused Squeak to rethink his circumstances. He decided to limit his guiding to the upriver region around Grants Pass. For the next twenty years, Squeak guided on the river locally. In the 1950s, he resumed his long downriver trips, but by this time he was able to capitalize on the hospitality of the few wilderness lodges that were available. For a guide, the long downriver trip was much more enjoyable if he could concentrate on the fishing and not be preoccupied with meals, camp setup, breakdown, and portage of gear and equipment. The guide could travel lighter and more safely.

Jerry Briggs rests against the hull of the Julius *in the author's shop. When Jerry talked, folks stopped their work to listen.*

It was into this Rogue River environment that Jerry was born in 1932. He grew up among the giants of his day: Squeak, Glen Wooldridge, Bob Pritchett, Wayne Riggs, Press and Sid Pyle, Claude Bardon. "I got to know each of them real well," he says. "They were always friendly and ready to help each other out. Everyone knew everyone else on the river. It was kind of like family." The Rogue and its river guides were a regular part of Jerry Briggs's life.

One constant Jerry treasured, and still does to this day, was fishing. He doesn't claim to have the same knack for finding fish as his dad did, but he is very good. He seemed equally adept at finding good people. He landed a beauty on June 25, 1954, at the tail end of the spring chinook run. Her name was Barbara Davenport. A nice catch, even for Jerry. A personality and strength of character that complemented her diminutive presence caught Jerry's attention. "Barbara is a great partner. She was an important part of my success in this business in two ways: I knew she'd hold the fort down when I was on the river, and I had an extra set of hands when I needed them." Booking and shuttling were two important roles Barbara assumed. "I knew the guides' wives as well as I knew the guides," Jerry told me, "because they were always at the boat landings. We'd socialize right there, and when we put work parties together to improve a boat launch site, the wives were right there too." Together Jerry and Barbara raised two daughters, Leann

Rogue River guide Fred Popkins, on the oars of double-ender with a pair of dudes. August 17, 1947. COURTESY OF JERRY BRIGGS

Squeak preparing to shove off for a day trip with his dude, in the late 1940s. The boat is a carvel planked, double-ender and shows considerable flare. Note the absence of an inner sheer rail. The side frames are braced with 1-by-2-inch pieces at the sheer. The boat was surprisingly stable but heavy. COURTESY OF JERRY BRIGGS

and Lori, and at this writing they have one granddaughter, Karli.

Jerry's first trip down the Rogue through the canyon occurred after his marriage to Barbara and a hitch in the army, when he was twenty-three or twenty-four. He accompanied Squeak, and together they made several fun trips over the next couple of years. It wasn't until Squeak's business partner moved away in the late 1950s that Jerry joined his dad's guide business and led fall excursions and local fishing trips. Concurrent was Jerry's developing interest in riverboat construction. An irascible character with a peculiarly large and good heart, George Hood, invited Jerry to join him in his boatbuilding business in 1956. "George could be like a bandy rooster, feisty and in your face, but he knew boats," Jerry explains. Briggs had an eye for boatbuilding, and he viewed Hood's invitation as a great opportunity to learn the trade from an old-timer. Fewer guides had an interest in building their own boats, and the newer generation of guides and local fishermen created a demand for river fishing craft. This was a niche George Hood and Jerry Briggs could fill. The Rogue River Boat Shop was born.

Jerry's eyes sparkle as he tells about the year or so they worked together. They enjoyed each other, and he picked up a lot of knowledge about boats, boat design, and boatbuilding from George. The greatest challenge in boat

Squeak with his young family, circa 1938. From left to right: Squeak, daughter Genesse, Nellie, and Jerry. COURTESY OF JERRY BRIGGS

design, from Jerry's perspective, was transforming ideas into concrete reality. Lines on paper or lofting were tools unheard of on the Rogue. Their technique was touch and feel. Unlike the McKenzie River boat builders, Jerry and George designed and built jigs, forms around which the boats were built. Once they were satisfied with the lines of the boat, they finished off the jig. It was a heavy-duty structure that provided locations for the frames, transom, and stem. The side panels were attached to these components, the chine log heeled in, and the hull then lifted off the jig. It was a surefire way to ensure that each boat was the same when it came off. George Hood, according to Jerry, would say, "Time sure goes by fast when you're having fun."

During one of my visits with Jerry and Barbara, Jerry introduced me to a George Hood boat. It was a river skiff designed to handle a motor as well as or better than a set of oars. Jerry got sentimental as he told how an acquaintance reported that this boat had been sitting in a barn for years and was in excellent shape. Jerry felt compelled to buy it even though he didn't have use for it. Heart over mind. I immediately arranged to capture the boat's lines, and the three of us—Jerry, Barbara, and I—took a couple hours to record each essential measurement. I decided that someday this boat too might be built again. Its lines are safely secured in my inventory.

One of the lessons Jerry learned during his early years of boatbuilding was that the wood will tell you what can or cannot be done. "Go with the flow of the wood. It will kind of direct you into the correct direction.

Young Barbara Davenport, a nice catch. COURTESY OF JERRY BRIGGS

George Hood. COURTESY OF JERRY BRIGGS

The wood will assume the lines that work best. Go with the wood. I think this is what boatbuilders have been doing since the first boat was built. In fact, building a boat is kind of like running a river. Go with the flow!"

Jerry sees many parallels among boatbuilding, running a river, and life. Success in life depends on an ability to read the river ahead and navigate it to one's best advantage. You can't fight the current, because it will eventually wear you down and leave you to the vagaries of its curlbacks, rocks, and suck-holes. Fail to read the river of life's path correctly, and the consequences can be problematic. Jerry turns melancholy as he describes the first 16-foot Rogue River dory he built. Until then, his dories were typically 18 feet. Barbara called the boat, a pretty thing that pleased her eye, the *Pink Lady*. It was the first of what has come to be known as Jerry Briggs's Rogue River Special, a lighter dory that in the hands of able oarsmen provides excellent service.

Briggs sold the *Pink Lady* to a Grants Pass attorney. The river is a beautiful place, but if the oarsman lacks the confidence, skills, or knowledge to run a river, it is unwise to tackle the Rogue or any stretch of challenging water. Within a year or so of purchasing the *Pink Lady*, the new dory owner entered Mule Creek Canyon for the first time. Mule Creek Canyon is in the heart of the wild section, a mile-and-a-half stretch of river that is sorely constricted by vertical canyon walls, creating powerful hydraulics. At the entrance to the canyon is the Jaws, a pair of menacing, monolithic boulders that stand as sentinels to the danger ahead. The river's gradient increases sharply and enters a seemingly lazy S-curve, straightens out a bit and shoots the Narrows, a tight restriction in the canyon that if entered incorrectly will cause the boat to catastrophically bridge the gap. Within another hundred yards or so is the Coffee Pot, a boil of troubled water that presents random and powerful currents that may hold a boat for an indeterminate time in its uncontrolled convulsions. The Coffee Pot gives you up only when it's damn good and ready. I have run this gauntlet many times, and I cannot recall a trip when the Coffee Pot did not toy with me. The entire run of Mule Creek is an adrenaline rush that demands the best one can give.

The new owner of the *Pink Lady* entered the Jaws. Aboard were his wife and the wife of an area dentist. At the last bend of the S-curve, the oarsman failed to keep the boat off the shock wave of a large boulder on the left wall of the canyon. The current carries headlong into the boulder, and oarsmen are required to rotate the boat 45 degrees to the current, pull on the oars, back ferry, and move the boat laterally to sweep around the obstacle. He didn't make it. The dory tipped and swamped, ejecting the three occupants.

Bob Pritchett and his party were in Mule Creek Canyon at the time. He, his party, and the occupants of the *Pink Lady* had stayed the previous night at Marial Lodge, located below Mule Creek eddy and immediately above Mule Creek Canyon. The *Pink Lady*'s owner had visited with Bob Pritchett about the canyon. This was his first trip down the Rogue River, and he was curious about how best to run it. Bob visited with him and then suggested that they follow his party though the canyon the next morning. The *Pink Lady*'s oarsman could mimic what Bob did for a safe journey through the canyon.

Bob wondered where the *Pink Lady*'s party was when he shoved off at the appointed time. Within a short time, he was through the Coffee Pot and was idling in an eddy waiting for his boating colleague, Wayne Riggs, to enter the Pot. About this time, fishing gear, duffels, oars, and other items swept past Riggs as he lowered himself into the Coffee Pot. Pritchett hollered at Riggs to get out of the way. Coming up behind him was a boat whose bow was barely visible above the surface. Hearts raced, boats

bumped, and the submerged dory crashed through the Coffee Pot and then continued down the canyon. Pritchett spotted a black boot. He reached out and grabbed it. It was one of the women. He pulled her aboard. She was dead. The submerged boat's other two occupants went unseen downriver and were not recovered until several days later. The Pritchett party made their way to Paradise Lodge, greatly shaken by the events.[3]

Jerry Briggs was distressed over the tragedy, but he carries no guilt for having sold the *Pink Lady*. For him, it was a profound reminder that safety and boating competence are two requisites to a positive river experience. "You have to respect this river, and if you don't, things can go terribly wrong," he says. The infamous rock at that upper bend of Mule Creek has since been called by boaters Telfers Rock, named after the *Pink Lady*'s owner. No lifejackets were found on the bodies.

Notwithstanding the tragedy, Jerry nurtured his fledgling boatbuilding business. His Rogue River Special became a popular dory among its users. The boat was

Jerry and Barbara in the Pink Lady, *the first 16-foot Rogue River Special that Jerry built.* COURTESY OF JERRY BRIGGS

smaller than the more traditional Rogue dory and had great stability and carrying capacity. Like the guide-made varieties built by Bob Pritchett and Press Pyle, the Rogue Special accepted a 15-horsepower motor. Jerry had found a boatbuilding niche.

Guiding and boatbuilding were demanding work. In the late 1960s and early 1970s, interest in summertime Rogue River trips grew. Jerry responded to this emerging demand for a Rogue River experience. Fall fishing trips through the canyon, boatbuilding during the winter months, spring chinook runs, and summertime float trips for the splash and giggle folks evolved into year-round work. Jerry Briggs was fully engaged, and he occasionally pinched himself and recalled George Hood's declaration, "Time goes by fast when you're having fun."

Martin Litton stumbled onto Jerry Briggs sometime in the mid- to late 1960s by chance. It was a fortuitous meeting. Litton was from another river tradition, and Jerry unknowingly was to become a part of that tradition. To this day, I'm not sure Jerry is fully aware of his influence on the Colorado River dory tradition. "Briggs boat" is a common term used by Colorado River people who have never heard of Jerry.

The Green and San Juan Rivers converge with the Colorado, and the drainage ultimately dumps into the Gulf of California. At least it once did, until southwest-ern water needs and a pair of monolithic dams con-strained and viaducts diverted the Colorado so that the last remaining miles of the streambed are often dry. *Colorado* is Spanish for ruddy or reddish, a color assumed by the river as side streams and gullies awash with the canyon's red silt during rains that color the river. This erosion has been exacerbated since livestock has been introduced along some stretches of the canyon. At times the river looks more like a mudflow. Rumors abound that some people who drowned in its currents became so laden with silt in their clothing that they sank into the river-bottom sediment, never to be found. "Too thick to drink and too thin to plow" was the observation of some early visitors.[4]

Like the McKenzie and Rogue Rivers, these south-western streams have their own personages. Maj. John Wesley Powell, a student of nature and geology and a Civil War veteran who had lost part of his right arm at Pittsburgh Landing, launched a scientific expedition from the headwaters of the Green River down the Colorado through the Grand Canyon in 1869. The area was unex-plored. It was a monumental expedition. Powell had in mind to test his geologic theory that the river carved the canyon as the landmass slowly uplifted.

With nine men, Major Powell undertook the heroic journey in boats poorly suited for such river travel. The Colorado presents the largest water in the Lower Forty-

Muddy water at Hermit on the Colorado River. Mike Taggett on the oars crests the fifth wave in a Briggs dory. COURTESY OF RUDI PETSCHEK

eight. Powell's boats were of the Whitehall type. Heavily keeled, they had to be propelled downstream at a speed faster than the river's current in order to maintain control and direction of the boat. This technique would mortify a McKenzie River boatman. Except for Powell's boat, the *Emma Dean,* the vessels used two sets of oars in a large rowing cockpit, as well as a sweep oar, to gain leverage against the river. The oarsmen kept their backs to the rapids ahead. One can only imagine the kinks they had in their necks! Loaded with ten months of supplies, they were more stable but poorly suited for the demanding maneuvers required in river running.[5] The team carried supplies, equipment, and boats around most rapids. A month into the trip, one of the group quit the party and hiked out to a settlement. Three more abandoned the exploration at what is now called Separation Canyon, never to be seen again by Powell's party. In spite of this, Powell and the remainder of his men demonstrated that the river could be run with a hell of a lot of heavy lifting and grunting, slipping and sliding over rocks, and the loss one of their four boats. Another was abandoned at Separation Canyon, leaving only two. Powell repeated much of the trip two years later.[6]

It wasn't until the late nineteenth century that a trapper from Vernal, Utah, Nathaniel Galloway, developed a better way to navigate this river. Galloway built a lighter boat, gave it a modest rocker fore to aft on the bottom, and decked the hull save for a rowing cockpit. The boat was buoyant, easy to maneuver, and offered dry storage behind the two bulkheads that formed the rowing cockpit. Galloway lived and breathed the river. I don't know how long it took him to develop a better technique to navigate the river, but my guess is, like his compatriots on the McKenzie and the Rogue, not long. Rather than rush headlong into the rapids as Powell's group did, Galloway pivoted his boat so the transom end faced the maelstrom, slowed it, and lowered himself through the rapids."[7] "Lowered" is perhaps too mild a descriptor; it was more like a controlled free fall, but you get the idea. This technique is much like the way the John West and Tom Kaarhus boats performed on McKenzie River rapids. Galloway found that rowing against the current gave him better control and maneuverability. It was a superb idea, and the rowing method he developed carries his name today among some guides of the Grand Canyon. The rowing method was a logical consequence of his river experiences.

In 1909, an industrialist from Ohio, Julius F. Stone, visited one of his investments in Glen Canyon on the Colorado River. He fell in love with the area, met and hit it off with Nathaniel Galloway, and the two planned a trip down the Colorado through the Grand Canyon.[8] Stone underwrote the cost of the trip, and they used the

Portrait of John Wesley Powell at the age of thirty-six, done in 1869. COURTESY OF GRAND CANYON NATIONAL PARK

Galloway-type boats. They departed from Green River City, Wyoming, on September 12, 1909, following the same path John Wesley Powell had taken forty years earlier. The party arrived in Needles, California, four months later. Galloway's boats proved suitable for the trip, and this was the first encounter with the Green and Colorado Rivers simply for pleasure and adventure. Twenty-eight years later, in 1937, an Oregon man named Buzz Holmstrom, using plans sent to him following correspondence with Emery Kolb, built a modified Galloway-type boat and made the same trip down the river—alone. His too was a Herculean feat. A solo. It had not been done before. It has not been done since.[9]

The next noticeable Colorado boat modification was at the hands of Norman Nevills. In 1936, Nevills ran the San Juan River from Mexican Hat, Utah, through the confluence of the San Juan and Colorado Rivers to Lee's Ferry. A Stanford University archaeologist who was interested in seeing, examining, and photographing Rainbow Natural Bridge funded the expedition. Nevills claimed his boat was built from material scavenged from a Navajo water trough. It looked more like a coffin. Over time, he refined this San Juan riverboat to include a modest rocker. This increased the boat's maneuverability, but it still looked like a coffin, as if to symbolize the consequences from challenging the river.[10]

John Wesley Powell's boat, the Emma Dean, *with his armchair and life preserver in the Grand Canyon, 1872. Powell's boats were the Wherry type, with a modest keel.* COURTESY OF GRAND CANYON NATIONAL PARK

Norman Nevills came in contact with the San Juan and Colorado Rivers when he went to work for his dad at Mexican Hat. He was immediately attracted to the geography, history, and natural wonders of the area and was destined to carve out a name for himself on the Colorado. Nevills launched the first commercial venture down the river in 1938. Perhaps influenced by his dad's Alaskan experiences, and perhaps envious of the boat Buzz Holmstrom built and used for his 1937 and 1938 trips, Nevills built a boat akin to the Galloway boat type,

Coby Jordan, Lars Niemi, and Stewart Reeder run Granite Falls on the Colorado in a Powell boat replica. The helmsman, Reeder, has popped an oarlock and is bracing the oar against the gunwale. The run was successful. COURTESY OF RUDI PETSCHEK

except that it had more breadth across the transom, the downstream end.[11] He included a wider rowing cockpit to better accommodate the oarsman and passenger, and the length was comparable to that of the Galloway boat. He called it a cataract boat. The boat's breadth provided more stability, and its low profile made it less susceptible to the influence of the river's wind, but it was more likely to swamp in rapids.

Norman Nevills ran seven expeditions through the Grand Canyon up to the time of his death in 1949. He and his boats set the stage for those who followed. The boatman of greatest influence in succeeding years was—and at this writing still is—Martin Litton.

Martin was born in Gardena, California, in 1917. He served in World War II as a glider pilot and through

A re-creation of the Julius, *a homemade boat built and used by Oregon's Buzz Holmstrom for his famous 1937 solo from the headwaters of the Green River through the Grand Canyon to Lake Mead. The boat is somewhat similar to Nathaniel Galloway's boat type. This picture was taken at Grave Creek landing during a commemorative run down the Rogue River in May 2002.* COURTESY OF JERRY BRIGGS

much of his early adult life explored the outdoors, worked as a freelance writer and magazine editor, and evolved into a hard-nosed, articulate conservationist. His reputation cuts a wide swath on two fronts: as an advocate for environmental sanity, and for the introduction and use of river dories on the Colorado. He was involved in the fight against the Glen Canyon Dam and derailed proposals by the Bureau of Reclamation to build two more dams on the Colorado in Grand Canyon. The structures would have relegated the river to frog water along most of its course, a fate that would have forever changed the face of that place.

In 1955, Litton met P. T. (Pat) Reilly. Reilly had worked for Norm Nevills in the 1940s and continued to make river trips after Nevills's death. Reilly was a competent boatman. He very much disliked Nevills's cataract boat, with its broad transom and tendency to take on water through the whitewater runs. Reilly considered the boat difficult to maneuver. In 1954, he took matters into his own hands—like most serious boatmen—and built two double-ended boats. He claims these were the first double-enders on the Colorado.[12] He kept the breadth of the Nevills boat amidships and added closed compartments with sealed hatches for storage and additional

buoyancy. The most significant change, however, was the stem and stern posts that gave the boat its double-ended configuration. These first two boats, the *Flavell* and the *Susie R,* were formed around molds Reilly had constructed to achieve the shape and design he desired.[13] It was in these boats that Reilly took Martin Litton on Martin's first downriver run in 1955. Litton had hoped to row but couldn't. He had recently dislocated a shoulder in a horseback accident while in the Sierra Mountains, so he did the whole river trip with his right arm strapped tightly to his side and did not change his shirt for twenty-three days. Litton's wife, Esther, was on that first trip, and because of Litton's ailing shoulder, Reilly enlisted a friend, Brick Mortenson, to row the *Flavell.*[14] Litton and Reilly repeated the trip in 1956. This time Litton rowed the *Flavell.* He was hooked.

It wasn't until 1962 that Litton decided it was time to do the river again. In 1961, he had visited the McKenzie River to write an article about the McKenzie White Water Boat Parade. He became acquainted with the drift boat. He rowed one and liked the way it handled: "So I got the idea that I could get some bigger boats made right there by the guys who make them all the time."[15] He contacted P. T. Reilly to suggest they do the river

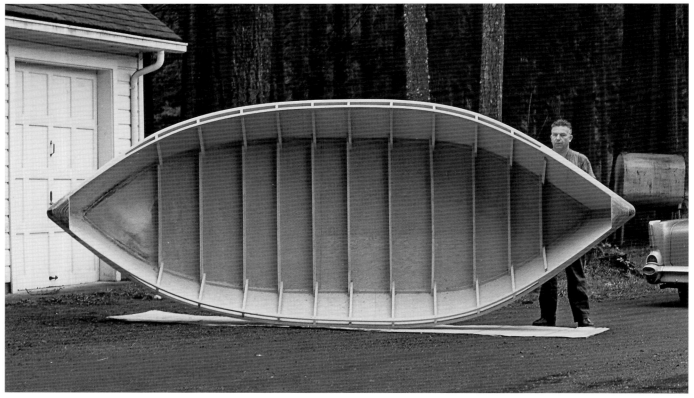

Martin Litton stands next to the hull of the first boat he had built by Keith Steele for the Colorado River at the fish hatchery at Leaburg, Oregon, in 1962. Unlike the traditional McKenzie boats, this one has a bottom line with a significant flat spot fore to aft, giving the boat great stability and control. The parallel lines at the chine define the flat area on the bottom. This design made the boat more comparable to the Rogue River dories than to the full-rockered McKenzie drift boats. Martin scored with this one, and it has stood the test of time on the Colorado. COURTESY OF MARTIN LITTON

The two boats Litton had Steele build are nested on the trailer after Litton's return home to Porta Valley, California, in 1962. Martin's teenage son, John, flexes the oars from the rowing seat. Steele decked one boat for Litton, and P. T. Reilly received only the hull. COURTESY OF MARTIN LITTON

together again. Reilly reported that he didn't have any boats.[16] Litton introduced him to the idea of having two oversize McKenzie River drift boat hulls built. Reilly was slow to warm to the idea but finally agreed.

On his 1961 visit to the McKenzie White Water Parade in Oregon, Litton had met Keith Steele, a young builder turning out superb drift boats in the little town of Leaburg, Oregon. Steele worked for the Oregon Fish and Game Commission at the time and built drift boats on the side. Litton commissioned two drift boats. "I told him [Steele] I wanted a double ended hull, 16-feet along the centerline, and flat for a ways in the mid-section." P. T. Reilly purchased the hull. He wanted to finish the boat himself. Litton told Steele how he wanted the boat decked and compartmentalized, and he purchased the completed dory. "Once those boats were on the water and P. T. got in one of them and started rowing it, he

said that was the best-feeling boat he'd ever been in." Reilly named his boat *Susie-Too,* a sequel to *Susie R,* and Litton named his dory *Portola* but later changed its name to *Diablo Canyon.* Litton's boat was the first in a long line of boats that he named after environmental disasters, a tradition that spoke to his ongoing interest in ecological issues. Unfortunately, Litton's relationship with Steele collapsed when Litton drove to Leaburg to pick up a third boat he thought was ready. On arrival at Steele's, he learned that Keith hadn't started the boat yet. "So that was that."[17]

Enter Jerry Briggs.

According to Litton, he left Leaburg disappointed in Steele and wondering what he would do about future dories. By this time, Martin had developed a strong passion for the boats and foresaw the day when he would incorporate his love for the river and dories into a unique

Keith Steele (left) and Martin Litton, at Leaburg, Oregon, in 1962. COURTESY OF MARTIN LITTON

boating experience unequaled anywhere else in the country. As he drove down U.S. 99 from Eugene, Oregon, on his empty return to California, he stopped in Grants Pass for a short break. As he entered Grants Pass proper, he spied a sign that read, "Rogue River Boat Shop." He followed the sign and located the shop and Jerry Briggs.[18]

Jerry Briggs recalls that "Martin just dropped in one day out of the blue, and he started talking about this boat he wanted built. We drew some preliminary plans in the dust in front of the shop. Litton recalls that it was drawn in mud. The design he talked about was very much like my Rogue River Special." As Martin and Jerry concluded their visit, Briggs agreed to build the dory for him. "A friend of mine constructed a jig to build the Rogue River Special. He let me take the jig and modify it to meet Litton's requirements."[19] Jerry removed some of the flare to

the side panels of his Rogue River Special and added 2 to 2¹⁄₂ inches in the side panels' elevations. The reduced flare lessened the angle of the oars into the river. Because of tight quarters in many places on the Rogue, 9- to 9¹⁄₂-foot oars worked best. On the big water of the Colorado, however, more leverage was needed, and Briggs provided 10-foot oars. Later, 11-foot oars became the norm. Contrasted to the McKenzie boats, the Briggs dory had more breadth that ran its length, giving rise to a broader yet more symmetrical upriver end. This would make a huge difference in the big water of the Colorado. Litton says he called his first Briggs boat *Peace River,* and he notes that it has logged more miles than any other dory in the Grand Canyon. The boat is still in use today.[20] Briggs concluded, "When I finished the boat, Martin carried it off to Arizona, and away we went!"[21]

The Colorado River guides compiled a record of the dories for publication in the 1994 issue of *Hibernacle News,* an erratically published periodical. By that time, according to their list, about seventy-five dories had been built for the Grand Canyon since Steele built the first two in 1962. Between 1971 and 1982, Jerry Briggs built thirty-three wooden Grand Canyon dories. At the time of the 1994 *Hibernacle News* publication, all but one of those wooden dories was still in use. The first Briggs dory posted in the *Hibernacle* list is the *Emerald Mile.* Rudi Petschek, a guest on that boat's maiden voyage, remembers Litton commenting that he would be happy to get twenty trips out of the boat.[22] Litton got that and then some before it crashed in Lava Falls in 1976. Guide Kenton Grua painstakingly rebuilt the *Emerald Mile,* and the boat went on to set a record through the canyon of 36.5 hours. The affection and care these boats receive from their guides is impressive, as well as the boats' longevity. Three or four three-week trips through the Grand Canyon per season is very hard on a boat.[23]

In the late 1970s, Jerry unavoidably strayed from wood and started dabbling with aluminum. The demand for aluminum boats was increasing, and wood was get-ting less desirable and harder to procure. Wooden boats also are very labor-intensive, and labor costs were going up. Briggs took a little heat from one friend, who said, "Dammit, Jerry, if God had wanted aluminum boats, he'd made aluminum trees!" Jerry's first aluminum Grand Canyon dory appeared on the Colorado in 1979. He built and sold nine more in 1980 and 1981. And then he was done.[24]

Judging by the number of inquiries I have received about plans for Jerry's Grand Canyon dory and the genuine affection exhibited toward his boats, it is clear that Jerry and his boats stand tall among Colorado River dory folks. After all, more than half the Grand Canyon dories were Briggs's boats. His dories handle extraordinarily well, have great carrying capacity, and present as beautiful a set of lines as any dory on the planet. There is nothing prettier than a fleet of these boats on a riverbank or the water. The only complaint I've heard about the boat is the traditional tombstone-like transom that is a Rogue River trademark. A few of the Colorado guides preferred that the boat be double-ended and modified them. I find the transom aesthetically pleasing, and for some guides, it offers the

Mark Johnson hits the fifth wave in Hermit in a Briggs dory. All the decking is slanted toward the foot wells. The oarsman's foot well is a self-bailer, but any passengers would have to bail theirs. The hatches are watertight, and the gear is safely stowed in the holds for security and ballast. COURTESY OF RUDI PETSCHEK

advantage of allowing them to hang a motor and ply across those pesky reservoirs. All of Jerry's aluminum dories were built as true double-enders.

Other Oregon builders contributed to the Grand Canyon fleet. Willy Illingsworth and Glen Wooldridge built two each in 1973. McKenzie River's Don Hill built a large dory that year, *Diablo Canyon II*. It was about 7½ feet across amidships and required 12-foot oars. Litton liked the boat, saying it was "very slick and responsive, with the sole disadvantage that you had to get down on your belly to reach a beer in the side hatch."[25] Some guides who rowed her, however, didn't like the boat because they felt it was too cumbersome.[26] The boat ended in a private Durango museum and, according to Litton, has since been rescued, restored, and placed back on the river.[27]

Jerry Briggs has never run the Colorado River, though he has received several invitations. Thus far, he is unwilling to trade one piece of heaven, the Rogue River, for another, the Colorado.

Martin Litton says of Jerry: "He was always affable, always listened, and he never, ever let on that we were dumber than he was. He built great boats, was always dependable, and what he said you could count on."[28]

Jerry smiles when he speaks of Litton and their first meeting. "Here this guy drops in out of nowhere, appar- ently because he saw my sign. He gave me business that was really helpful, and I thoroughly enjoyed making the boats." He pauses a moment, and then with that well- known Briggs wrinkle for a smile and a chortle, he says, "Life sure passes quickly when you're having fun."[29]

Endnotes

1. The location was the author's shop in September 2001. Colorado River guide and author Brad Dimock and I were building a re-creation of the *Julius,* a boat long lost. The *Julius* was originally built by Buzz Holmstrom of Coquille, Oregon, for his 1937 solo run from the headwaters of the Green River through the Grand Canyon on the Colorado to Lake Mead. The boatbuilding project was a collaborative effort and included Colorado River guides Dan Dierker and Andy Hutchinson; my boating partner, Ken Brown; Oregon drift-boat builder Ray Heater; and Jerry Briggs. For the complete story about Buzz Holmstrom, see his biography, Brad Dimock et al., *The Doing of the Thing: The Brief, Brilliant Whitewater Career of Buzz Holmstrom,* (Flagstaff, AZ: Fretwater Press, 1978).

2. Jerry Briggs interview, April 11, 2004. Biographical information and quotes are from my taped interviews with Briggs on May 20, 2002; May 18, 2003; and April 11 and 12, 2004.

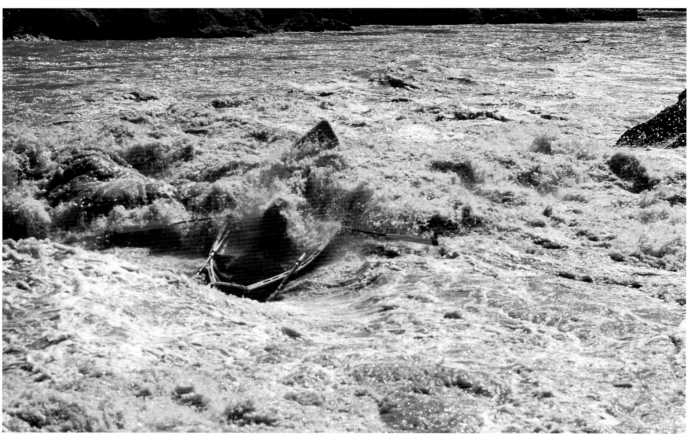

The rationale for decked Briggs boats on the Colorado become clear in water like this. Regan Dale hits the big one at Lava Falls and buries his boat. He emerges wet and afloat. COURTESY OF RUDI PETSCHEK

3. As recalled by Bob Pritchett's wife, Virginia, in a 2004 interview.

4. See www.powellmuseum.org/MajorPowell.html.

5. Former Colorado River guide Rudi Petschek participated in the 1983 re-creation of Powell's trip in replica boats. Petschke reports in a May 6, 2006, telephone interview with the author that the Powell boats were very tippy. The crew got the idea to dump sand in the *V*'d hulls under the floorboards. This lowered the center of gravity, and the boats became surprisingly stable. Powell's heavily ladened boats, Petschek reasons, were probably also very stable. Petschek recounts that the boating crew purposely tried to flip a Powell boat but was unsuccessful.

6. See www.powellmuseum.org/MajorPowell.html.

7. Brad Dimock, "A Nest of Dories: a Meandering Inquiry into the Origins of the Grand Canyon Dory," *Hibernacle News* (1994), 8.

8. Visit the Northern Arizona University Library online at www.nau.edu/library/speccoll/guide/S/Stone.html.

9. Dimock et al., *Doing of the Thing*, 84. Holmstrom was eclectic in his approach to building the boat, drawing on the Colorado River experiences of a number of people. Following his 1937 solo down the Colorado, a reluctant Holmstrom was persuaded to repeat the run again in 1938. His reluctance was tied to the notoriety he received following the 1937 trip, and the objective of his second trip was to film the event. A major benefactor for that second trip was Julius F. Stone. Holmstrom named his little Galloway type boat the Julius F. See Dimock et al., *Doing of the Thing*, 125–170.

10. See Gaylord Stavely, Norm Nevills, *Boatman's Quarterly Review: The Journal of Colorado River Guides*, Vol. 17, No. 1, (Spring 2004), 26–43. Also, visit Gaylord Stavely's website and page, From Nevills to Nowadays, at canyoneers.com/pages/canyoneers.html#principals.

11. Ibid., 26. Stavely reports that Norm Nevills's dad spent time in Alaska, where he became acquainted with drift boat design and the method of "backing down" the river.

12. See Brad Dimock's edited conversations with P. T. Reilly conducted by Lew Steiger, Karen Underhill, and Richard Quartaroli between 1993 and 1995. "I've Got Some Definite Opinions on It—Most of my Opinions Are Definite," *Boatman's Quarterly Review: The Journal of Colorado River Guides*, Vol.15, No. 4, (Winter 2002–2003), 28–42.

13. Ibid., 35.

14. Martin Litton interview, April 28, 2006.

15. Dimock, "Nest of Dories," 10.

16. P. T. Reilly had a penchant for running the Colorado at high water, due in part to his aversion to running it at low water. In 1957 and 1958 he chose to leave the boats and hike out, and he recovered them later. In 1959, however, on another high water voyage, the fiberglass he used on the boats failed again, and he decided to scuttle them at Pipe Creek and then hike out.

Jerry Briggs on the oars of a Briggs-type dory built by Andy Hutchinson of Durango, Colorado. Here, Briggs is participating in a 2001 commemorative run down the Rogue River.

17. Dimock, "Nest of Dories," 10.

18. Martin Litton interview, October 18, 2004.

19. Briggs interview, April 11, 2004. There are actually several different stories about the initial Martin-Litton meeting. Different people hear stories and, like the childhood telephone game, they get twisted. Litton's story may also differ from one tale to the next. As full as his life has been, how can he keep all his recollections straight? My narrative is his most recent iteration. Jerry Briggs's recollection isn't any better. When I pointed this out to Jerry, his response was classic Briggs: "In the late 1950s, a friend and I had a fantastic trip of fishing and hunting at Odell Lake. We both told our friends about it on our return, and by our stories you'd think we were on two entirely different trips!" The differences do not surprise Jerry, nor are they of any consequence to him.

20. Litton interview.

21. Briggs interview, April 11, 2004.

22. Rudi Petschke, Colorado River boatman and photographer, telephone interview, May 6, 2006.

23. Litton interview, April 28, 2006.

24. Briggs interview, April 12, 2004.

25. Litton interview, April 28, 2006.

26. Petschke interview, May 6, 2006.

27. Litton interview.

28. Litton interview, October 18, 2004.

29. Briggs interview.

PART 2

How to Build a Drift Boat

"For more than fifty years, I've had the pleasure of building and using boats on the coast of Maine. During this time, I have seen boats come and go and have seen some of them gone forever because no one had taken the time and trouble to preserve them. So when Roger Fletcher told me he was tracking down old river runners, some that were facing extinction, I was all ears. Bob Lane and I are doing the same thing ourselves, just different boats on the East Coast. Roger's river runners and our East Coast dories have a lot in common, with their flared sides and strong sheer. When he asked me if I'd like to join in on resurrecting these old boats, I said, 'Sure, let's do it.'

"Over the years and through many phone calls, Roger and I have swapped info back and forth, along with a few side trips solving the world's problems (nobody listened). At any rate, Roger got the job beautifully done, so these little river runners will live on for the pleasure of future generations. It is my pleasure to have been a part of this process."

—Dynamite Payson

CHAPTER 10

About Wood

*The drift-boat revolution began with the production of exterior-grade
and then marine-grade plywood in the late 1930s and 1940s.
The material lent itself to simpler methods of construction.*

As was the case in most parts of the world, indigenous wood material in Oregon helped define and shape the early boats. Long, straight-grained redwood *(Sequoia sempervirens)* was one reason the Rogue River drivers ran 18 to 20 feet in length. The lean, tall timber provided for longer river drivers. Longer boats were possible but impractical, save for the lower, wider reaches of the stream. While the wood's texture varies, redwood was desired for its weight-to-strength ratio and decay resistance. Port Orford cedar *(Chamaecyparis lawsoniana)* is unique to the southern Oregon coast, roughly from Coos Bay to northern California. The cedar is lightweight, stiff, and moderately shock and decay resistant. Sitka spruce *(Picea sitchensis)* is the largest of the spruces, with heights up to 180 feet. Its range is the coastline from Alaska through Oregon. On the basis of weight, it rates high in strength properties. Douglas fir *(Pseudotsuga menziesii)* ranges from the Rocky Mountains to the Pacific coast and from Mexico to British Columbia. Douglas fir today can vary in weight and strength, so most boatbuilders are careful to select tight, clear vertical grain (CVG) material. Port Orford cedar, Sitka spruce, and Doug fir are Oregon favorites for boat frames. These woods were also favored for planking.

Hardwoods of choice among early Oregon builders were Oregon white oak *(Quercus garryana)*, canyon live oak *(Quercus chrysolepis)*, and Oregon ash *(Fraxinus latifolia)*. Some red oaks were imported from the Southeast (e.g., *Quercus falcata*), but they were problematic below the waterline because of a lack of a membranous growth known as tyloses. Tyloses is an occlusion in the earlywood pores. The sparseness of tyloses in red oak makes the wood more porous, causing it to act like a sponge, a problem for wood continually exposed to moisture. The pores of the white oak, on the other hand, are usually plugged with tyloses, making the material much less susceptible to water absorption.[1]

Discriminating boatbuilders, interestingly, preferred canyon live oak because of its high shock resistance.[2] Many boatbuilders believe that white oaks are stronger than red oaks, but controlled testing doesn't support that notion. Dr. Richard Jagels of the University of Maine points out that red and white oaks, on average, are of equal strength. If live oak is removed from the white oak equation, these oaks, on average, are somewhat weaker.[3] Oregon ash is heavy, hard, and strong, with a high resistance to shock. It too proved popular, especially as stock for oars. These woods were used for stem and stern posts, chine logs, outside chine caps, and sheer rails, along with Douglas fir.

Local wood materials in your area may be suitable for drift-boat construction. I recommend that each of the boats in this book employ a marine-grade plywood skin, so careful selection of material for the frames, chines, stem and stern posts, and rails is prudent. It helps to know a bit about the basic structure of wood in order to evaluate the suitability of a material for your boat.

The microscopic layer of cells that divide and add dimension to the tree is called the cambium. This cell layer annually produces growth rings. The widths of these rings indicate the rate of growth on a tree and can provide the tree's life history. Generally, growth rings that are tightly spaced in some conifers, especially Douglas fir, indicate slow growth and a dense, strong material. Growth rings that are widely separated in such trees suggest that the finished lumber is comparatively weaker.

On the other hand, for porous hardwoods such as red and white oaks and Oregon ash, the reverse is true: If the rings are wide, the sapwood is stronger. Jagels suggests a useful trick when buying oak to maximize strength: Sort the lumber into two piles—those boards with wide growth rings and those with narrower growth rings. Then select your hardwood from the pile with the wider rings for strength.[4] For Doug fir and other conifers, sort the material also, but select knot-free boards with narrower rings.

Sapwood resides adjacent to the cambium and may be 1 to 6 inches thick, depending on the species. Vigorous

tree growth tends to be reflected in thicker layers of sapwood in some species. Heartwood, on the other hand, is composed of inactive cells and is formed by the gradual change in sapwood.

Hardwood and softwood refer to the two broad classes of trees. Broad-leaved trees, usually deciduous, are classified as hardwoods; trees with needles, such as pine and fir, are softwoods or conifers. Don't rely completely on this classification, however, to determine the relative hardness of a wood. Generally, hardwoods are denser than softwoods, but there are exceptions. Douglas fir and

Structure of a Log

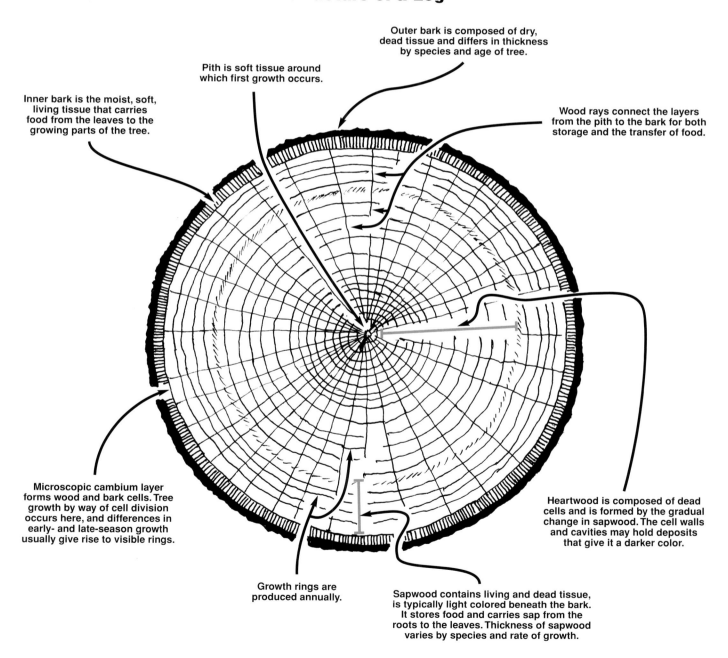

Pith is soft tissue around which first growth occurs.

Outer bark is composed of dry, dead tissue and differs in thickness by species and age of tree.

Inner bark is the moist, soft, living tissue that carries food from the leaves to the growing parts of the tree.

Wood rays connect the layers from the pith to the bark for both storage and the transfer of food.

Microscopic cambium layer forms wood and bark cells. Tree growth by way of cell division occurs here, and differences in early- and late-season growth usually give rise to visible rings.

Heartwood is composed of dead cells and is formed by the gradual change in sapwood. The cell walls and cavities may hold deposits that give it a darker color.

Growth rings are produced annually.

Sapwood contains living and dead tissue, is typically light colored beneath the bark. It stores food and carries sap from the roots to the leaves. Thickness of sapwood varies by species and rate of growth.

Distilled from the *Wood Handbook*, USDA Agriculture Handbook No. 72, page 2-2

larch, for example, typically are denser than poplar, red maple, and black ash.

Douglas fir in mature, naturally established old-growth forests has faded into history. Second- and third-growth trees, often grown commercially in plantations, have become the source of logs for most mills. These woods generally contain a higher percentage of sapwood and have wider rings. This means that heartwood is available in less quantity. So for those parts that are keystones to the boat—stem and stern posts, chine log, and frames—try to avoid the sapwood of Doug fir. Red oak, ash, or other conifers, such as the spruces, don't have decay-resistant heartwood, so the distinction between sapwood and heartwood is less important.

Lumber is removed from a log in two ways: Cuts made at a tangent to the annual rings are called flat or plainsawn lumber; cuts made perpendicular to the annual rings, or parallel to the rays, are called riftsawn or quartersawn. The comparative strength of lumber sawn either way is similar. There are, however, some characteristics that may make quartersawn lumber more attractive to the boatbuilder. It shrinks and swells less in width, it cups and twists less, there is less splitting as it seasons, and it wears more evenly when in use. In some species, it doesn't allow moisture to pass through it and tends to hold paint better.[5]

According to Howard Hall, Tom Kaarhus's employee from 1935 to 1941, Kaarhus started using Philippine mahogany in his boats in the late 1930s. Over the years, tropical woods have become increasingly popular as structural material and plywood for drift boats. As the quality of Douglas fir plywood panels has waned because of the scarcity of old-growth trees, tropical hardwood plywood has become popular. Asian, American, and African tropical hardwoods are now available worldwide.

True mahogany, or American mahogany *(Swietenia macrophylla),* grows in the West Indies, southern Mexico, and Central and South America. It is also known as *caoba* throughout Latin America and *acajou* in French-speaking areas. The trees can reach 150 feet in height and 6 feet or more in diameter above heavy buttresses, with clear boles 60 to 80 feet. It is a premium wood for furniture and shipbuilding. The material is sought for its beautiful dark red appearance, dimensional stability, termite and decay resistance, and machining qualities. Wood density as measured by specific gravity (oven-dry/green volume) ranges from .40 to .68. Air-dry density ranges from 30 to 52 pounds per cubic foot.[6]

Tom Kaarhus may have thought he was using a true mahogany when he purchased his first batch of Philippine mahogany. He wasn't. The wood was lauan, Philippine woods belonging to three genera: *Shorea, Parashorea,*

and *Pentacme.* These woods are generally grouped into three categories: dark red, light red, and white.[7] Kaarhus was attracted to this dark red Philippine wood because of its color and suitability for his boats. The wood provided a nice contrast to his Sitka spruce and Port Orford frames and Douglas fir plywood panels. Kaarhus had an eye for aesthetics and appreciated contrasting wood colors as complementary to his boats. Generally, the dark red Philippine lauan has proved to be a popular boatbuilding material. In machinery trials, this wood is comparable to or better than most hardwoods in the United States.[8]

Today several of these Philippine woods are sold under the trade name meranti and include dark red meranti (dark red lauan group), light red meranti (light red lauan group), white meranti group, and yellow meranti group. All are in the *Shorea* family. Meranti varies widely in decay resistance, but many wood retailers can't tell you the decay resistance or relative merits of their meranti. As a rule of thumb, try to locate dark red meranti, the dark red lauan group. This method isn't foolproof, because some dark red meranti also lacks decay resistance, but selecting by color makes it a little less than a mindless crapshoot.[9]

Other tropical woods have become popular as boatbuilding material. One is African mahogany *(Khaya ivorensis).* This material is shipped from west-central Africa and is found in the coastal belt of closed or high forest.[10] The wood machines well and has a pale pink to dark reddish brown heartwood. In decay resistance, it is generally rated about the same as American mahogany.

Sapele *(Entandrophragma cylindricum),* sometimes spelled sapelli or sapelii, is another tropical wood favored by some drift boaters. Common names for this wood in their tropical homes are *aboudikro* (Ivory Coast), *penkwa* (Ghana), *muyovu* (Uganda), *sapelii* (Cameroon), and *libuyu* (Zaire). The tree may reach 150 to 180 feet, with a bole that is straight, cylindrical, and clear to 100 feet. Density is comparable to that of white oak, but the mechanical properties are generally higher.[11] The heartwood is dark reddish or purplish brown, with lighter-colored sapwood, and is moderately decay resistant. The sapwood can be up to 4 inches thick.[12] The material glues and finishes well. It is most extensively used as veneer for decorative plywood, but some northwestern drift-boat builders use the material for stem posts, chines, and rail stock.

A third tropical wood is okoume *(Aucoumea klaineana).* Its natural range is restricted to west-central Africa and Guinea. The wood is known as gaboon in the United Kingdom. The tree reaches a height of 100 to 130 feet. Diameters of the trunk may go 3 to 8 feet over large buttresses. Boles are cylindrical and clear to 70 feet or

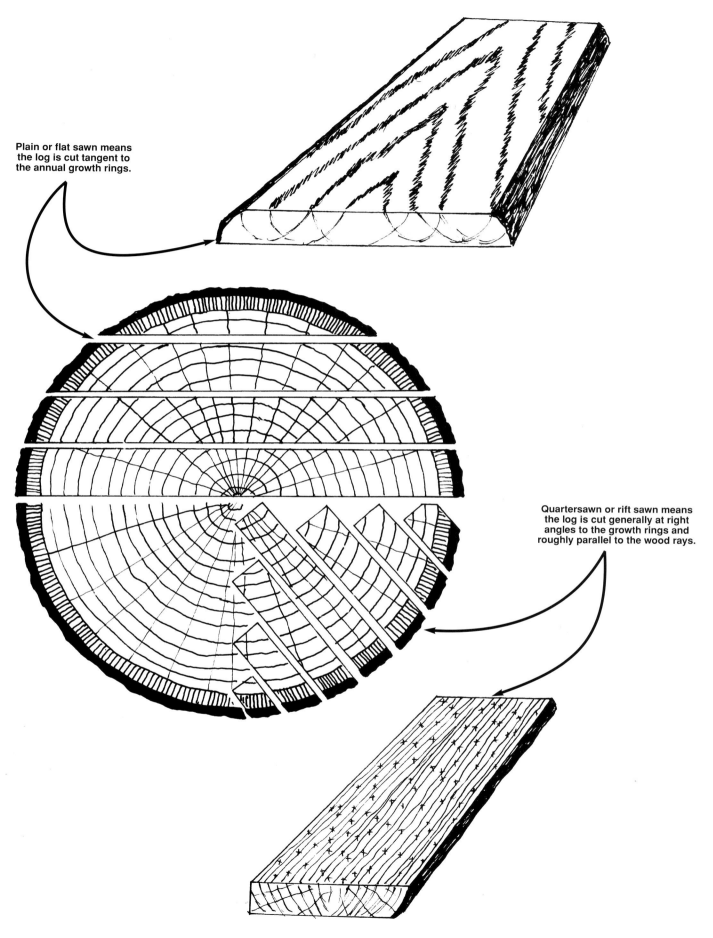

Plain or flat sawn means the log is cut tangent to the annual growth rings.

Quartersawn or rift sawn means the log is cut generally at right angles to the growth rings and roughly parallel to the wood rays.

Adapted from *Wood Handbook*

more.[13] Okoume has been popular in Europe for years and now has found markets on the North American continent. The heartwood is salmon pink to light pinkish brown. The ring of sapwood is usually narrow and lighter in color, though often the line of demarcation is not easily identified. Silica content of the wood has been reported to be about .12 to .16 percent.[14] This makes its use as solid lumber a bit problematic, as it will quickly dull saws and blades. Veneered and compressed as plywood, however, okoume is very popular among some drift-boat builders. Unlike sapele, okoume is not resistant to decay fungi, so some additional treatment to exposed surfaces is usually required.

As you ponder material to use in your drift boat, think about the source of your stock. If indigenous wood is suitable and available, give it serious consideration. It is likely more cost-effective for you. On the other hand, if you are attracted to the tropical hardwoods, bear in mind that some of these woods are in short supply. Unfortunately, we have overharvested many native forests without due consideration of the consequences. In some areas, sapele and okoume are classified as threatened. In central Chile, radiata pine (Pinus radiata), a transplanted species from California, has become the predominant species, often at the expense of Chile's diverse native population. Radiata pine is one of Chile's leading wood exports. It feeds a substantial demand for wood products in the United States.[15] Though radiata pine is unsuitable boat material, this example hints at the need for consumers of wood products to be informed about the potential implications of their purchases. The Forest Stewardship Council (FSC) is one source of information for people who are concerned about these kinds of issues. The purchase of wood "certified" by a third-party certifying organization, approved by the FSC, is one way of knowing that the wood has come from a sustainable source.[16]

Early river guides were the self-taught few whose passion for fishing, adventure, and river transport motivated their mastery of rivers by using and modifying the riverboats of their day. Guides became possessive of their rivers. They had mastered the rivers and, by God, they owned them. As riverboats were refined and became easier to build, rivers became more attractive to larger numbers of novices, who discovered that they too could master the art of whitewater navigation in a drift boat. Some guides resented the presence of these abecedarians. I recall several of my early trips in my own boat as frigid affairs, made icy by a few guides who took umbrage at my presence. I understand their displeasure, but like the air we breathe, rivers are as accessible to the responsible visitor as they are to the professional guide.

The drift-boat revolution began with the production of exterior-grade and then marine-grade plywood in the late 1930s and 1940s. The material lent itself to simpler methods of construction. Builders could now produce two or three boats in the time it took to build one board-and-batten, lapstrake, or carvel-planked river driver. Plywood also provided innovative builders the opportunity to design and test drift-boat modifications. While the basic lines of the McKenzie and Rogue River boats remained unchanged, builders were now able to adjust the rocker, flare, and trim of the boats with relative ease. Guides were more than happy to test these designs, and their stamps of approval or disapproval were useful to the builders.

The early plywood drift boats, as was the case with their predecessors, were constrained by the size of the material. Plywood in the Northwest was, and still is, manufactured in layered veneer sheets of Douglas fir that measure 4 by 8 feet. Not until builders had confidence in plywood adhesives and were able to acquire plywood panels in 14- and 16-foot lengths did they begin to build boats with plywood skins, though Tom Kaarhus built a 12-foot boat in the mid-1930s to test the effectiveness of the plywood. Moisture-resistant plywood in the Northwest became reality only after the advent of phenolic resin adhesives, which became stronger than the wood after the application of heat. More than half the industry in the Northwest had installed one or more hot presses before World War II stopped the acquisition of new machinery. By 1947, practically all factories were using the hot-press method for a substantial part of their production.[17]

Plywood panels could be lengthened once Northwest mills developed a scarfing technology for plywood, a process in which several pieces were joined together end to end to form a larger panel up to 50 feet long.[18] The Washington Veneer Company installed and operationalized its scarfing department in 1945, where beveled edges and glued joints were used to join sheets together to create longer plywood panels.[19] Longer exterior-grade and marine-grade plywood panels were a boon to drift-boat builders.

At this writing, fir panels in excess of 4 by 8 feet are difficult to find, and when they are found, the costs are considerable. Frankly, for boatbuilding, the larger scarfed fir panels are not worth the trouble. Frequent gaps in the core of the plywood—something you definitely want to avoid—and questionable scarfs present risks to the builder. In recent years, there have been increased numbers of incidents among home boatbuilders where commercially scarfed panels have fractured at the scarf joint during installation. Some larger tropical hardwood panels can be found in 10-foot lengths and 54-inch widths.

Scarfing technologies now allow home woodcrafters to economically join pieces of plywood in their shops into sheets of greater dimension. It is not unusual to see drift boats on the river with a bottom width amidships of 54 and 56 inches and lengths exceeding 16 feet. A well-crafted scarf joint in your shop will probably be more secure than one done commercially. The scarf joint is addressed in chapter 11.

Some purists will prefer to build one of these original gems using the same materials as in the original boats. Good luck. It is difficult to locate clear vertical grain (CVG) redwood, Sitka spruce, Port Orford cedar, or Douglas fir in the widths and lengths necessary to build a board-and-batten or planked boat. There is no shame in using contemporary materials that allow you to build an affordable and usable version of one of these early gems. I spent two years in an unsuccessful search for a Sitka spruce log that would yield the required 14-inch-wide CVG boards. Finally I asked myself this question: If I am interested in recapturing the lovely lines and rowing efficiencies of these early boats, and contemporary materials will let me do that, then why not? The question is more practical than academic. What difference does the material make if you capture the lines and the performance qualities of the boat? The marine-grade plywood requires less maintenance and will take more abuse, and the boat's life will far exceed that of the original. If you are hell-bent on replicating the original boat using endemic materials, then consider modeling the boat as an alternative. Materials in the original boats can be acquired for models in dimensions and quantities that are more affordable, and you can enjoy the boat in the comfort of your home.

Endnotes

1. Forest Service Products Laboratory, Forest Service, *Wood Handbook: Wood as an Engineered Material,* Agriculture Handbook No. 72, Washington, D.C.: U.S. Government Printing Office, 1–11.

2. "'Live oak' refers to the fact that the tree was evergreen." It was once known as "'maul' oak because farmers and loggers once sought the extremely heavy, tough wood to make mauls." Canyon live oak has little commercial value today. See *Trees to Know in Oregon* (Corvallis, OR: Oregon State University Extension Service EC 1450), 2003.

3. Dr. Richard Jagels is Professor of Forest Biology at the University Maine. He regularly authors "Wood Technology," a featured column in the bimonthly *WoodenBoat* magazine. See "Red versus White—Plumbing the Depths of Oak," *WoodenBoat* issue 184, 99.

4. Ibid.

5. *Wood Handbook,* 3–2.

6. Forest Service Products Laboratory, "Technology Transfer Fact Sheet," Center for Wood Anatomy Research, from Chudnoff Martin, "Tropical Timbers of the World," *Ag. Handbook,* 607.

7. For more detail about these species, and these are only the tip of the iceberg, see *Wood Handbook,* 1–29.

8. Ibid.

9. For a broad introductory overview of tropical hardwoods, go online to www.fpl.fs.fed.us/documnts/techline/iv-1.pdf.

10. *Wood Handbook,* 1–28.

11. "Technology Transfer Fact Sheet."

12. *Wood Handbook,* 1–36.

13. "Technology Transfer Fact Sheet."

14. Ibid.

15. www.forestethics.org/forests/chile.html.

16. "In many forests around the world, logging still contributes to habitat destruction, water pollution, displacement of indigenous peoples, and violence against people who work in the forest and the wildlife that dwells there. Many consumers of wood and paper, and many forest products companies believe that the link between logging and these negative impacts can be broken, and that forests can be managed and protected at the same time. Forest Stewardship Council certification is one way to improve the practice of forestry." www.fscus.org.

17. *Seattle—First National Bank, Industry Analysis Section report on Northwest Industries: Plywood,* April 22, 1948, Weyerhaeuser Archives, RG#3 C.H. Ingram Box 80.

18. Ibid.

19. *Washington Veneer Company 1945 Annual Report,* Weyerhaeuser Archives, RG#3 C.H. Ingram Box 65.

How to Build the Traditional Drift Boat

"The way to preserve small craft is not to embalm them for static exhibits
or to tuck them away in mothballs, but to get their reproductions out
on the water, use them, wear them out and replace them anew. . . . Treated
in that way, small craft are immortal or as near immortal as anything
can be. Historic small craft are for the young and old and in between.
They are to use and enjoy, and to pass on for future generations to use and enjoy,
ad infinitum. Preservation through use, in the long run, that is the only way."

—JOHN GARDNER

The beauty of traditional drift-boat building is its simplicity. The carvel-planked, lapstrake, and board-and-batten boats were built around mold stations or constructed on strongbacks. A strongback is a heavy timber cut and set the length of the boat's centerline into which the frames are set, secured, and readied for the stem and stern pieces. If a builder decided to experiment with the rocker and shape of the boat, adjustable frames were shimmed in the strongback. It often took longer to form a strongback than to build the boat. The dimensions provided on the profile coupled with the offsets offer that option. In most instances, the plans' side panel layouts will not conform to the strongback's frames set perpendicular to the baseline of the boat. To obtain a match with the original boat, the frames in the strongback should be canted to match station lines on the side panel layout. This is a lot of work. If, however, the strongback is set with squared, perpendicular frames, the differences between a boat so built and the original boat presented in the plans will not be significant. It's important to realize there will be a slight difference in the boat if it is built from a strongback.

The advent of plywood skins for these boats gave rise to a simpler and less expensive method. I call it free-form construction. Forms or strongbacks are not required. The frames, stem and stern posts, or transoms are preformed, and the hull is formed using two side panels that have been cut and marked to specification. The frames, as they are installed onto the side panels, provide the boat its unique shape and rocker.

This chapter presents in detail the free-form building method. This method is cost- and time-efficient, and the details on the boat plans provide the information needed to complete the boat.

The illustrations on pages 102 and 103 show the boat coming and going and give the drift-boat terminology that Sam Manning and I use in this chapter. The terms are important to understand the construction steps that follow.

Jig or form for constructing this boat in the conventional way —

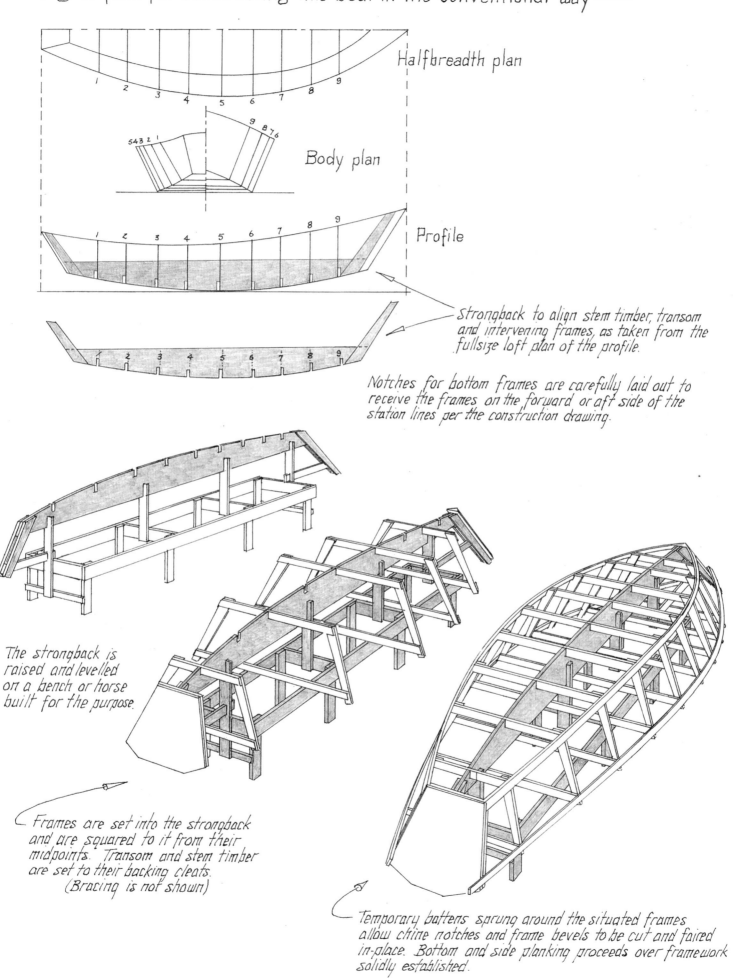

Halfbreadth plan

Body plan

Profile

Strongback to align stem timber, transom and intervening frames, as taken from the fullsize loft plan of the profile.

Notches for bottom frames are carefully laid out to receive the frames on the forward or aft side of the station lines per the construction drawing.

The strongback is raised and levelled on a bench or horse built for the purpose.

Frames are set into the strongback and are squared to it from their midpoints. Transom and stem timber are set to their backing cleats. (Bracing is not shown)

Temporary battens sprung around the situated frames allow chine notches and frame bevels to be cut and faired in-place. Bottom and side planking proceeds over framework solidly established.

Driftboat terminology —

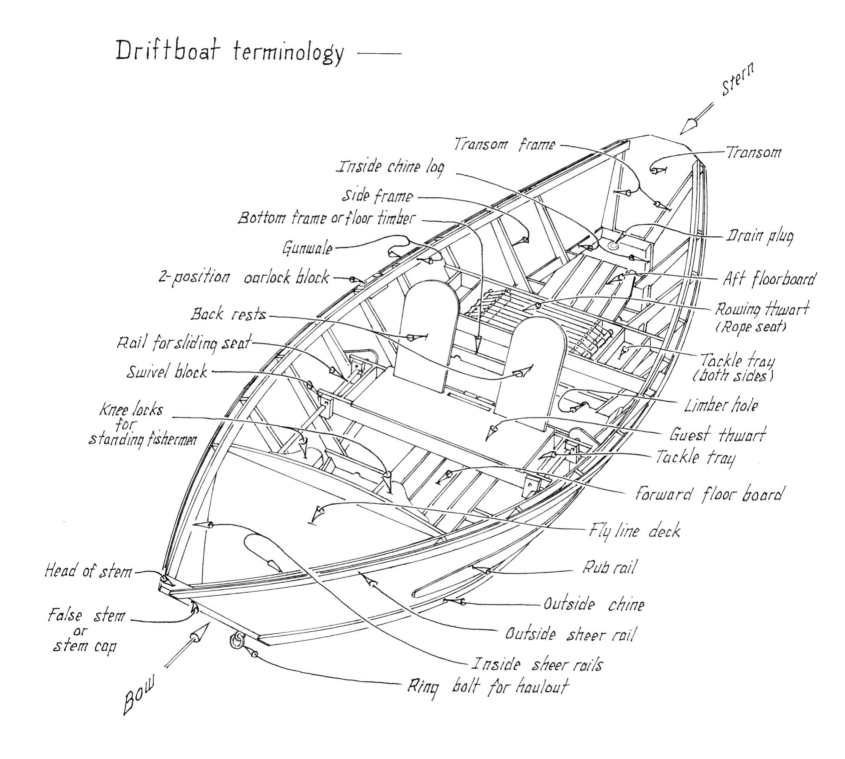

Stern

Transom frame

Transom

Inside chine log

Side frame

Bottom frame or floor timber

Gunwale

2-position oarlock block

Back rests

Rail for sliding seat

Swivel block

Knee locks
for
standing fishermen

Head of stem

False stem
or
stem cap

Bow

Drain plug

Aft floorboard

Rowing thwart
(Rope seat)

Tackle tray
(both sides)

Limber hole

Guest thwart

Tackle tray

Forward floor board

Fly line deck

Rub rail

Outside chine

Outside sheer rail

Inside sheer rails

Ring bolt for haulout

Driftboat terminology ———

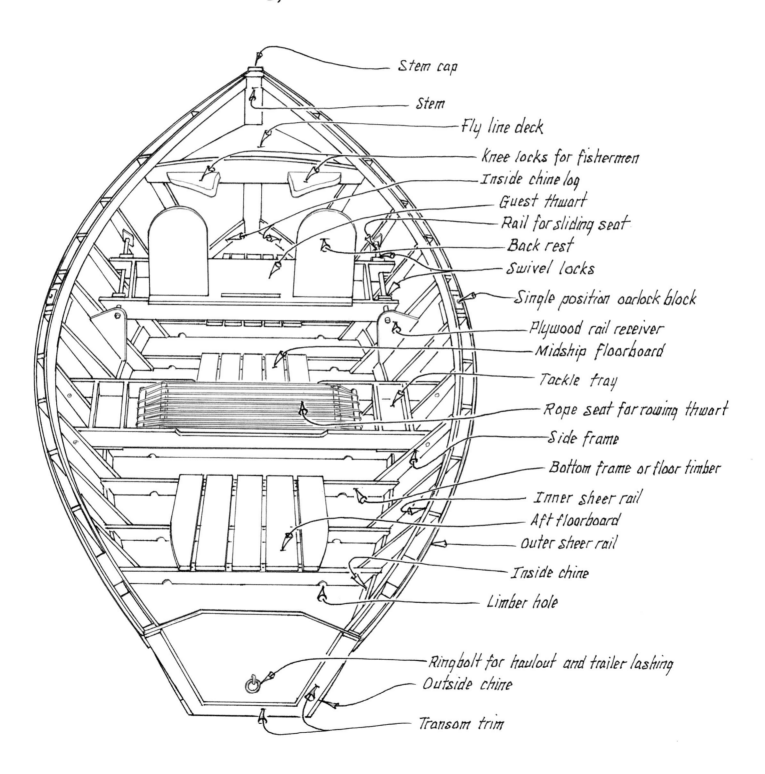

Stem cap

Stem

Fly line deck

Knee locks for fishermen

Inside chine log

Guest thwart

Rail for sliding seat

Back rest

Swivel locks

Single position oarlock block

Plywood rail receiver

Midship floorboard

Tackle tray

Rope seat for rowing thwart

Side frame

Bottom frame or floor timber

Inner sheer rail

Aft floorboard

Outer sheer rail

Inside chine

Limber hole

Ringbolt for haulout and trailer lashing

Outside chine

Transom trim

Until now, there have not been lines drawings of these boats. Lines are a record of the hull shape of a vessel. Lines are easily interpreted and are essential to preserve the boats' designs. As important, they are the basis for construction. Most drift-boat and river dory builders were also users, either as fishing guides or river runners. Their interest was in building a functional riverboat to meet their specific needs. They built from patterns that were recorded on a board or cedar shingle that hung in the shop. Frames—their length, angle of flare, bevels—along with stem and stern measurements were noted on the board. Lose this board and the boat too is lost. None of the boards I have located include elevations or measurements between frame placements. That information was either in the head of the builder or recorded elsewhere.

Design Terminology ——

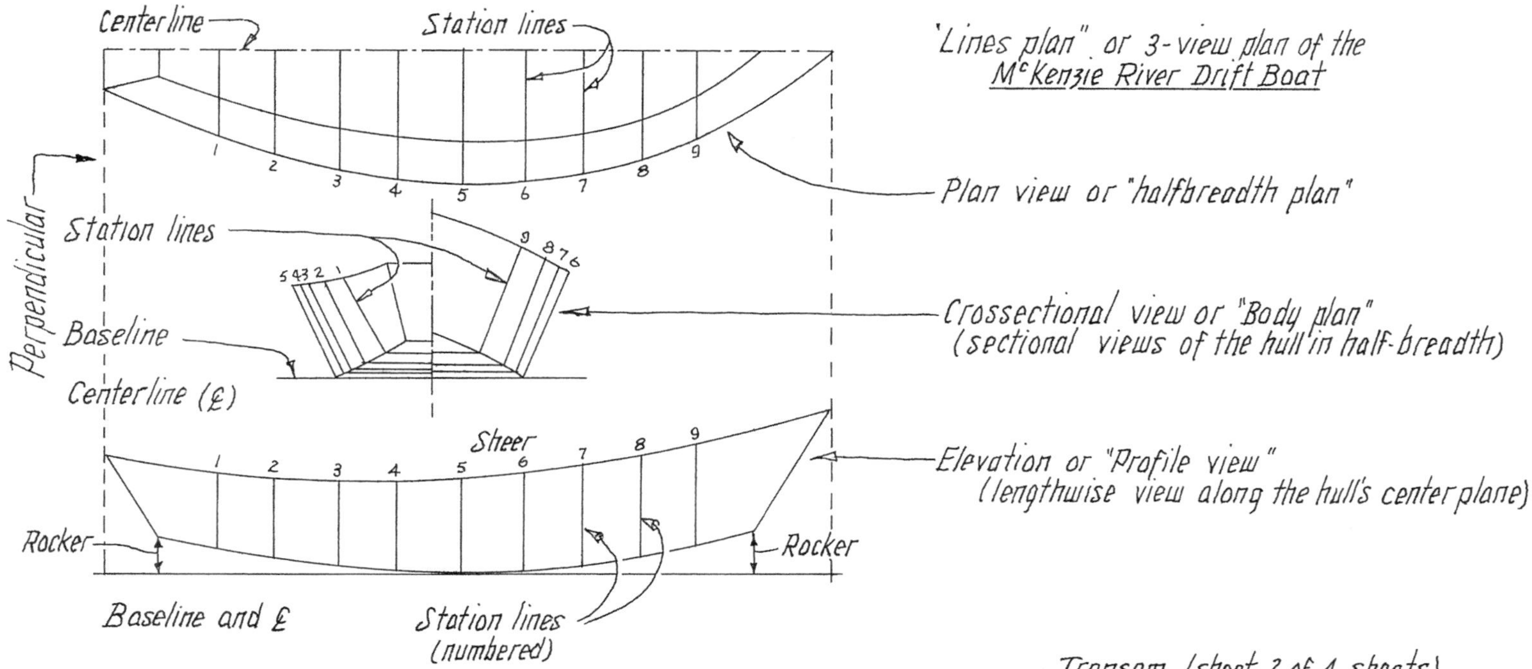

Centerline —   Station lines

'Lines plan" or 3-view plan of the <u>McKenzie River Drift Boat</u>

Perpendicular

1   2   3   4   5   6   7   8   9

Plan view or "halfbreadth plan"

Station lines

5 4 3 2   9 8 7 6

Baseline

Centerline (£)

Crossectional view or "Body plan" (sectional views of the hull in half-breadth)

Sheer

1   2   3   4   5   6   7   8   9

Elevation or "Profile view" (lengthwise view along the hull's center plane)

Rocker —   Rocker

Baseline and £   Station lines (numbered)

Transom (sheet 2 of 4 sheets)

"Lines plan" in 3-dimensions ——

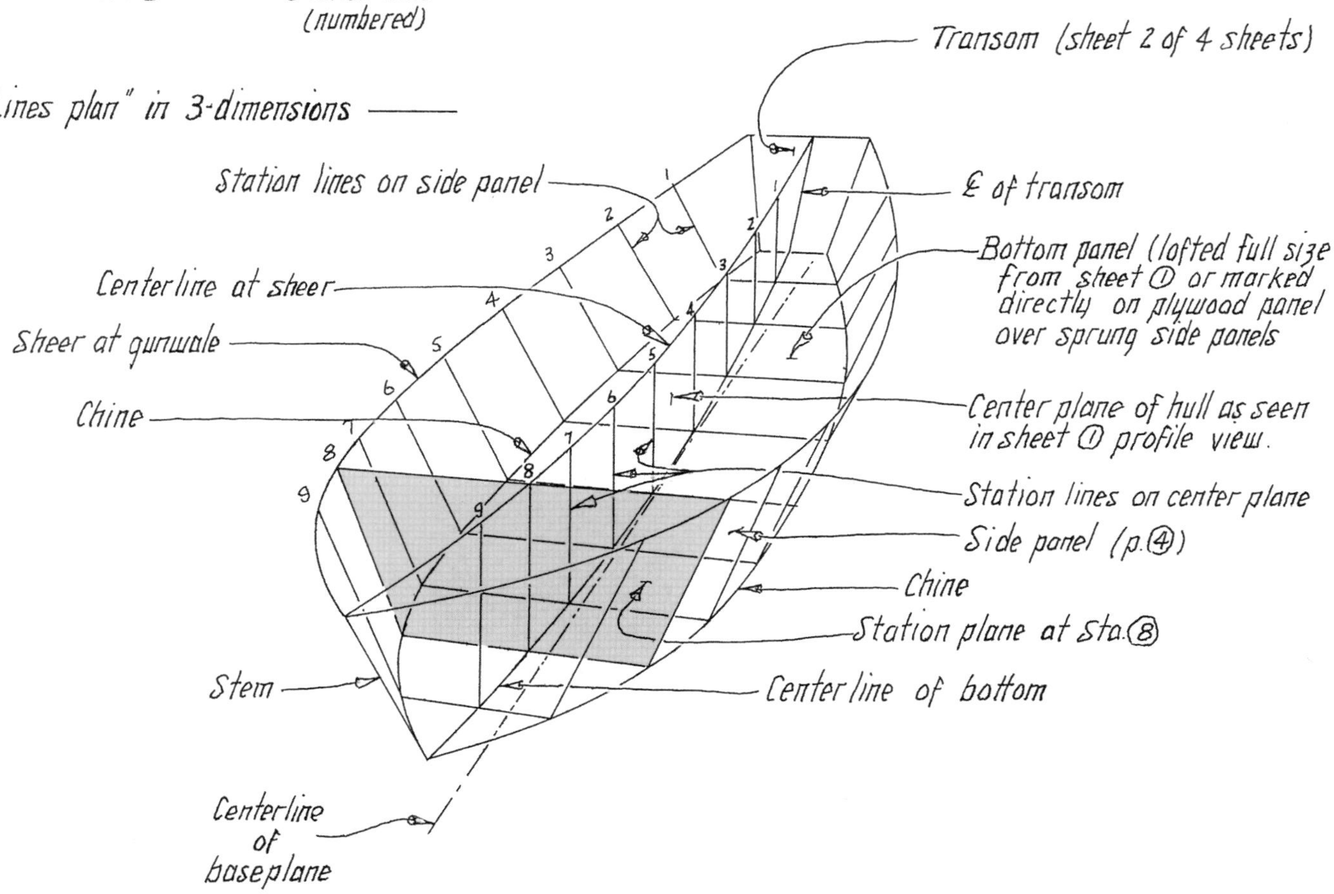

Station lines on side panel

£ of transom

Centerline at sheer

Bottom panel (lofted full size from sheet ① or marked directly on plywood panel over sprung side panels

Sheer at gunwale

Chine

Center plane of hull as seen in sheet ① profile view.

Station lines on center plane

Side panel (p.④)

Chine

Station plane at Sta.⑧

Stem

Centerline of bottom

Centerline of baseplane

Boats are measured: <u>upward</u> (sometimes downward) from a <u>baseline</u>
       <u>Sideways</u> (width) from a centerline (£)
       <u>Lengthwise</u> from a perpendicular

A boat's basic measurements are given by its <u>lines plan</u>

The designer's construction plan is based on correct implementation of the lines plan.

If no construction plan is available for your chosen design, you must proceed from the lines plan if the boat is to be built accurately.

Plans Views

The first sheet of each plan is the lines plan, or three-view plan, the measurements of which control the exterior shape of the hull. First is the half-breadth plan; second, a body plan, or cross-section view; and third, the profile, or elevation plan. Each of these three drawings helps the builder visualize the boat in three dimensions. Drawn to scale or lofted full-size, most bevels and angles can be calculated, or extracted with a bevel square, and used with confidence. Since the book's trim size doesn't allow the plans to be published at the scale at which they were drawn, all measurements and angles are posted on the plans in part 4 for the reader. I have hand-drawn the plans. Just as I like to feel a boat come together in my hands, so too I like to "feel" the boat take shape on paper. Scaled drawings of the plans (1″=1′) are available at The River's Touch (www.riverstouch.com).

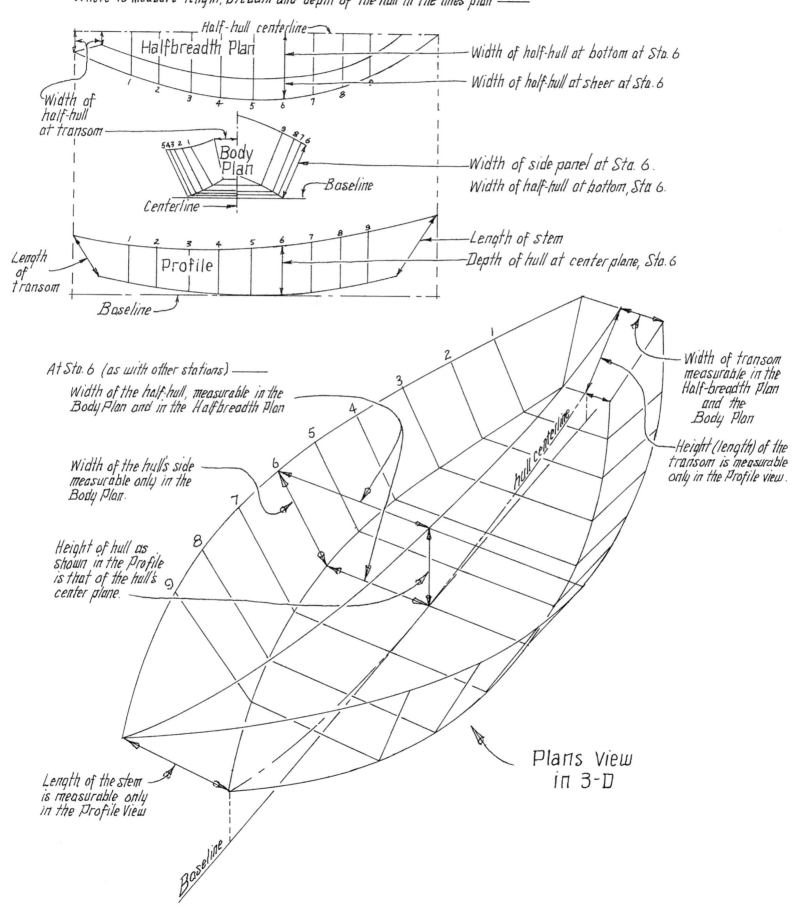

Plans View

Where to measure length, breadth and depth of the hull in the lines plan ——

Half-hull centerline

Halfbreadth Plan

Width of half-hull at bottom at Sta. 6

Width of half-hull at sheer at Sta. 6

Width of half-hull at transom

Body Plan

Baseline

Width of side panel at Sta. 6.

Width of half-hull at bottom, Sta 6.

Centerline

Length of stem

Profile

Depth of hull at center plane, Sta. 6

Length of transom

Baseline

At Sta. 6 (as with other stations) ——

Width of the half-hull, measurable in the Body Plan and in the Halfbreadth Plan

Width of the hull's side measurable only in the Body Plan.

Height of hull as shown in the Profile is that of the hull's center plane.

hull centerline

Width of transom measurable in the Half-breadth Plan and the Body Plan

Height (length) of the transom is measurable only in the Profile view.

Length of the stem is measurable only in the Profile View

Baseline

Plans View in 3-D

Hull

Understand the key parts of the drift-boat hull, and you will better comprehend these instructions. The hull is the heart and soul of the boat and is composed of the stem, frames, transom, side and bottom panels, and inside chine piece, called the chine log. The frames give the boat its shape. Since the frames are set 90 degrees to the centerline of the boat, the outside edge of each one is beveled at the appropriate angle to receive the side panel. As the panels converge to the ends of the boat, the stem and transom also require a bevel. The key pieces that give the boat its rocker fore to aft, flare, and profile are frames, stem, and transom or stern post. The keystone of the boat—that piece that connects the sides to the bottom—is the chine log. This is a continuous piece that runs the length of both sides of the boat from the base of the stem to the base of the stern. Each frame is notched to receive the chine log. The bottom edge of the side panel and the outside edge of the bottom panel are anchored to the chine with fasteners. A chine that lacks integrity in strength and hardiness gives rise to a boat that lacks the same.

Study the Plans Carefully

Your time spent in preparation will minimize confusion and mistakes once the project starts. The performance characteristics of the boats are influenced by the hull design and relate to maneuverability, suitability for fishing, stability in rapids, carrying capacity, and durability. To the extent that I've been able to define them, the plans display the boats' original internal appointments. I encourage you, however, to lift ideas from others, incorporate your own ideas, build to suit your needs, and have fun with the project. Personal modifications also reflect a primordial need once thought to be extinct among the human race: a way to mark your territory. There are two things to remember when siting a boat's internal parts. First, the boat should remain trim in the water. That is, weight should be balanced fore to aft so the stem and stern are balanced in profile as the vessel sits on the water. Second, don't mess with the boat's lines unless you are an experienced builder. An adjustment of the lines will affect the side panel dimensions.

First-time builders may find it helpful to model the hull first. Chapter 13 describes the protocol for modeling any one of the hulls in a manner similar to building one full-size. Modeling does at least two things: It builds confidence to tackle the full-size project, and the product is a nice prototype of the boat that will become your passion.

It is important to know the material requirements, availability, and costs before undertaking a project. If you decide to model the hull, the scaled material will provide good information about quantities of material needed for the full-size project. Chapter 12 provides more information about materials.

Location of "parts"

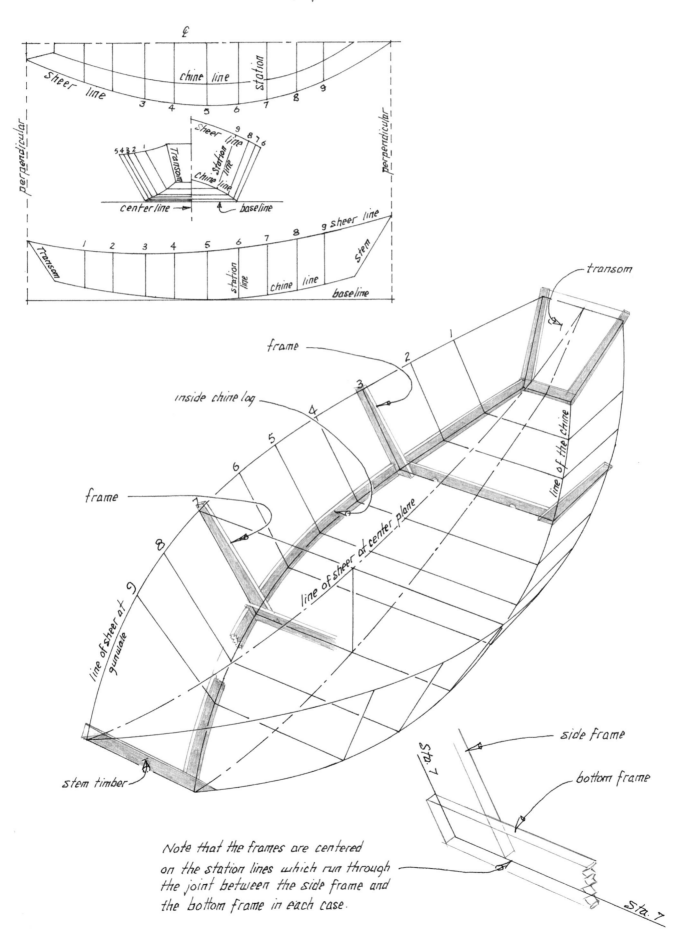

Note that the frames are centered on the station lines which run through the joint between the side frame and the bottom frame in each case.

Lofting

Lofting is a full-size layout of the boat scaled up from the table of offsets, the body view of the plans, or the dimensioned sections of the frames. In free-form construction, lofting is generally confined to the frames. The lines are laid out on a flat, clean, contrasting surface. Shop-grade plywood painted white or any flat clean surface will suffice. A 4-by-8-foot tabletop or level open space on the floor will provide enough room to loft the frames. The frames' lines are to the inside of the panels, those points where the side and bottom panels meet the frames.

Pay attention to the bevels that a set of frames may require (see pages 119 and 120). If a standing bevel is needed, more meat will be needed along the outboard and bottom frame edges.

Lofting ——

Lofting of frames on plywood or paper —— a fullsize layout of the boat's sections scaled up from the Body Plan on plan-page 1, or from the dimensioned sections shown on plan-page 2.

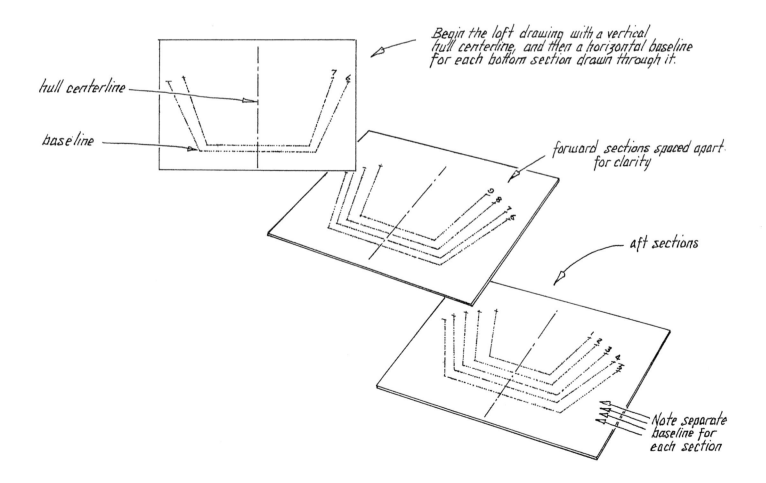

Begin the loft drawing with a vertical hull centerline, and then a horizontal baseline for each bottom section drawn through it.

hull centerline

baseline

forward sections spaced apart for clarity

aft sections

Note separate baseline for each section

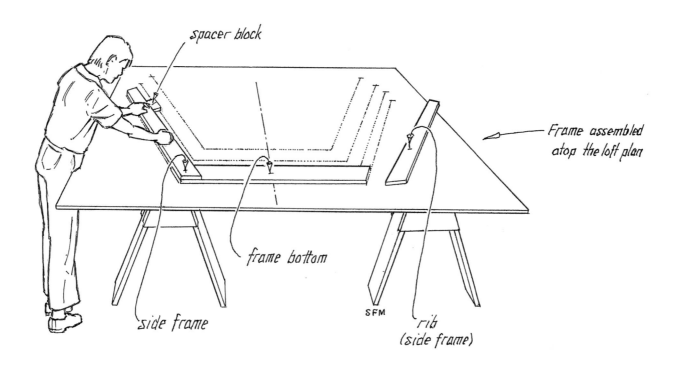

spacer block

Frame assembled
atop the loft plan

frame bottom

side frame

SFM

rib
(side frame)

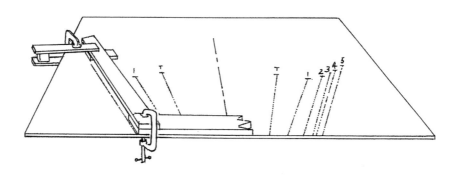

Using a milled edge of the plywood scrive board for the
baseline common to all sections allows easy clamping
of the frame stock during layout and fastening. But
this convenience can lead to errors where the side lines
of the sections fall close together in some of the drift
boats.

Preforming the Hull Parts

A first step to building the boat is to preform the parts for the hull: the side panels, frames, stem and stern posts or transom, and chine logs. The hull is then assembled, and the bottom is installed after the shell is formed and squared.

Side Panel

For most drift boats, side panel material must be 4 feet wide and 12 to 20 feet long. As most plywood panels are purchased in 4-by-8-foot sheets, it will be necessary to marry two or more 4-by-8-foot panels. Some builders prefer to butt-join the panels; I recommend that you scarf-join instead. The joint is clean, smooth, and reliable under stress. This is a relatively easy process. You create a scarf joint, and then marry the two panels with an epoxy resin and resin-fiber compound.[1]

Feather-bevel one end of each panel ends so the length of the bevel from the ends of the panels to be joined is twelve times the thickness of the panel, a ratio of twelve to one. On a $^1/_4$-inch panel, the distance will be 3 inches. Feather-bevel the two panels so the overlap is flush. Keep the leading edge of the bevel true. Lay the plywood edge to be beveled at the edge of your worktable. The bevels can be successfully completed with a hand plane, belt sander, or random orbital sander. Use the veneer lines of the plywood as a guide to maintain fairness of the joint. A belt sander is a little more difficult to control, so I prefer the hand plane and random orbital sander. If you are restricted to the use of a sander, lay a flat metal strip at the edge of your worktable to assist in monitoring the leading edge of the bevel. Don't use the metal strip when employing a hand plane.[2]

Sides ————

To lengthen plywood panels by scarfing them together —

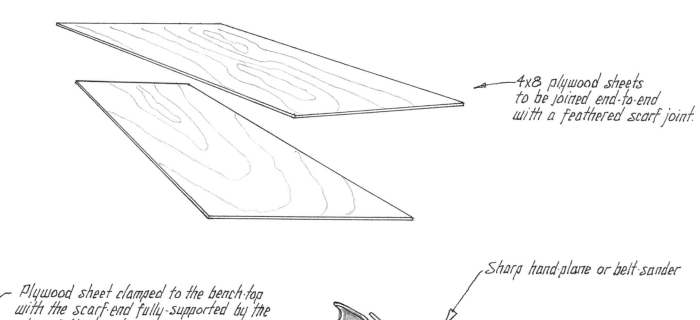

4x8 plywood sheets to be joined end-to-end with a feathered scarf joint.

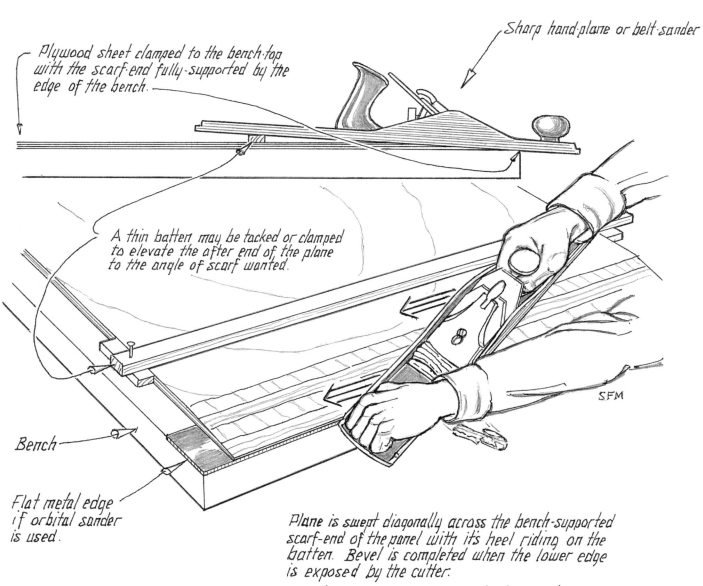

Sharp hand-plane or belt-sander

Plywood sheet clamped to the bench-top with the scarf-end fully-supported by the edge of the bench.

A thin batten may be tacked or clamped to elevate the after end of the plane to the angle of scarf wanted.

Bench

Flat metal edge if orbital sander is used.

SFM

Plane is swept diagonally across the bench-supported scarf-end of the panel with its heel riding on the batten. Bevel is completed when the lower edge is exposed by the cutter.

A belt sander would be hand-held without guidance of the batten.

Once the two panels are beveled, lay them on a flat surface and square them up. Apply the resin and fiber as directed by the manufacturer. Use waxed paper under and over the seam. Clamp the panels so there is no lifting at the joint, and let them set for the recommended time. Panels alternatively may be weighted and secured by other creative means. The builder will lose 3 inches of panel length with a twelve-to-one scarf. Two 8-foot, $1/4$-inch panels, when joined, will measure 15 feet, 9 inches. This may be less or more than is needed, depending on the boat.[3] Some builders like to place their joints so one of them is aligned on a frame. This is unnecessary, except for aesthetic purposes. A scarf joint that is well done will be the strongest point on the panel.

Sides ——

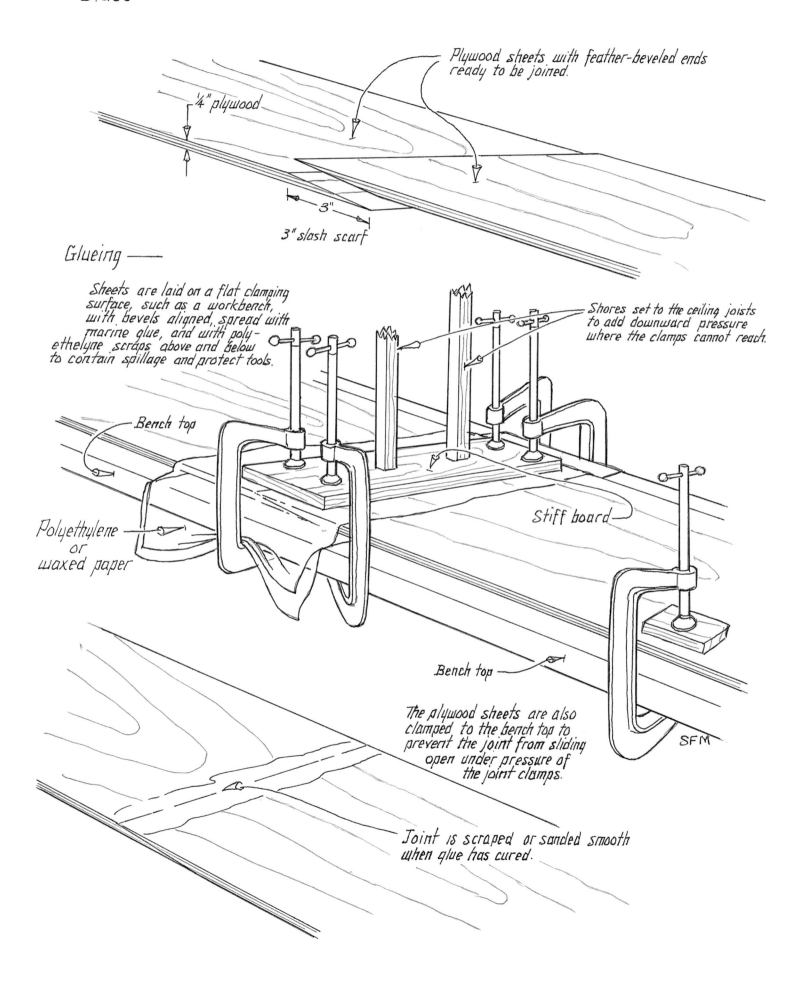

Plywood sheets with feather-beveled ends ready to be joined.

¼" plywood

3"

3" slash scarf

Glueing ——

Sheets are laid on a flat clamping surface, such as a workbench, with bevels aligned, spread with marine glue, and with polyethelyne scraps above and below to contain spillage and protect tools.

Shores set to the ceiling joists to add downward pressure where the clamps cannot reach.

Bench top

Stiff board

Polyethylene or waxed paper

Bench top

The plywood sheets are also clamped to the bench top to prevent the joint from sliding open under pressure of the joint clamps.

SFM

Joint is scraped or sanded smooth when glue has cured.

Mark the side panels on the sheet of scarfed plywood. In most plans, two side panels are extracted from one sheet. Measure and mark the vertical lines that locate the placement of each frame. These are the centerlines of the frames, where the bottom frame joins the side frame and extends vertically up the panel. After the first panel is marked, make the cuts and place pencil tick marks on the panel's edges for each frame line. The panel is the template for the second. Carefully mark and cut out the second side panel. The two panels must match. If they don't, fair the offending panel until they do. Establish the frame lines on the second panel so they are to the inside of the boat when it is assembled.

Side Panels ——

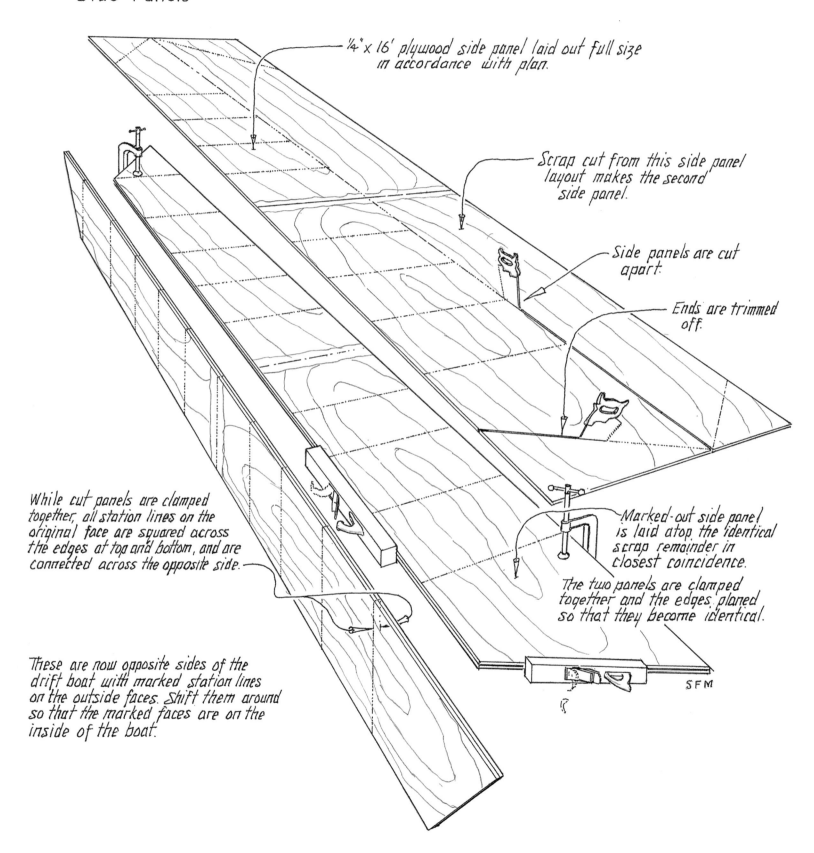

¼" x 16' plywood side panel laid out full size in accordance with plan.

Scrap cut from this side panel layout makes the second side panel.

Side panels are cut apart.

Ends are trimmed off.

While cut panels are clamped together, all station lines on the original face are squared across the edges at top and bottom, and are connected across the opposite side.

Marked-out side panel is laid atop the identical scrap remainder in closest coincidence.

The two panels are clamped together and the edges planed so that they become identical.

These are now opposite sides of the drift boat with marked station lines on the outside faces. Shift them around so that the marked faces are on the inside of the boat.

SFM

Alignment for location of frames within the hull —

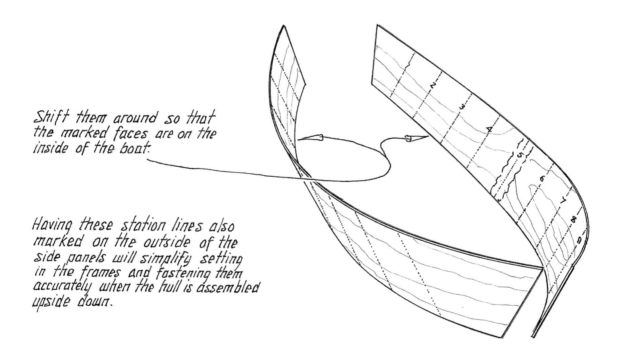

Shift them around so that
the marked faces are on the
inside of the boat.

Having these station lines also
marked on the outside of the
side panels will simplify setting
in the frames and fastening them
accurately when the hull is assembled
upside down.

Note that this layout of side panels illustrates the cutting array possible for the
McKenzie Double Ender with Transom. Not all drift boats considered here have
straight chine and sheer lines.

Understanding Bevels

Many parts of a boat, including the frames, are beveled to provide nice, tight fits. Bevels are usually cut before the frames are formed. Generally, the side frames require standing bevels, and the floor or bottom frames require underbevels to receive the side and bottom panels. From the midpoint of the boat, the bevels will be in the direction of the stem or stern. Some builders include a parallel bevel cut on the inside of the side frame. This provides a face on which the inside sheer rails will lie nicely. The traditional method, however, is simply to notch those portions of the frames that receive the inside rail. Topsides of the bottom frames usually were not beveled to receive the floorboards. Round them with a $1/4$-inch roundover bit.

Understanding bevels ———

Bevels ——— The angles (other than square) put on the edges
or butts of boat frames and planking to ensure
tight fits.

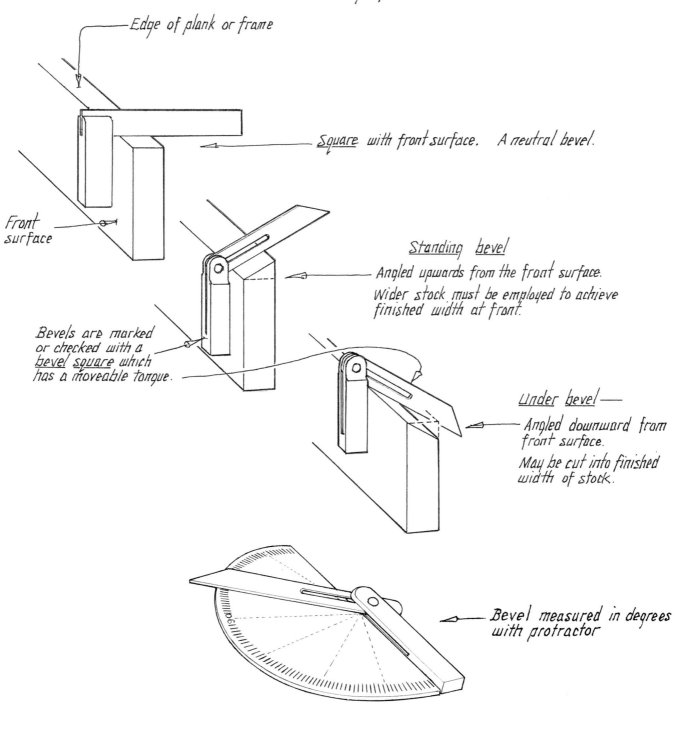

— Edge of plank or frame

Square with front surface.　A neutral bevel.

Front
surface

Standing bevel
Angled upwards from the front surface.
Wider stock must be employed to achieve
finished width at front.

Bevels are marked
or checked with a
bevel square which
has a moveable tongue.

Under bevel ———
Angled downward from
front surface.
May be cut into finished
width of stock.

—— Bevel measured in degrees
with protractor

Understanding bevels ———

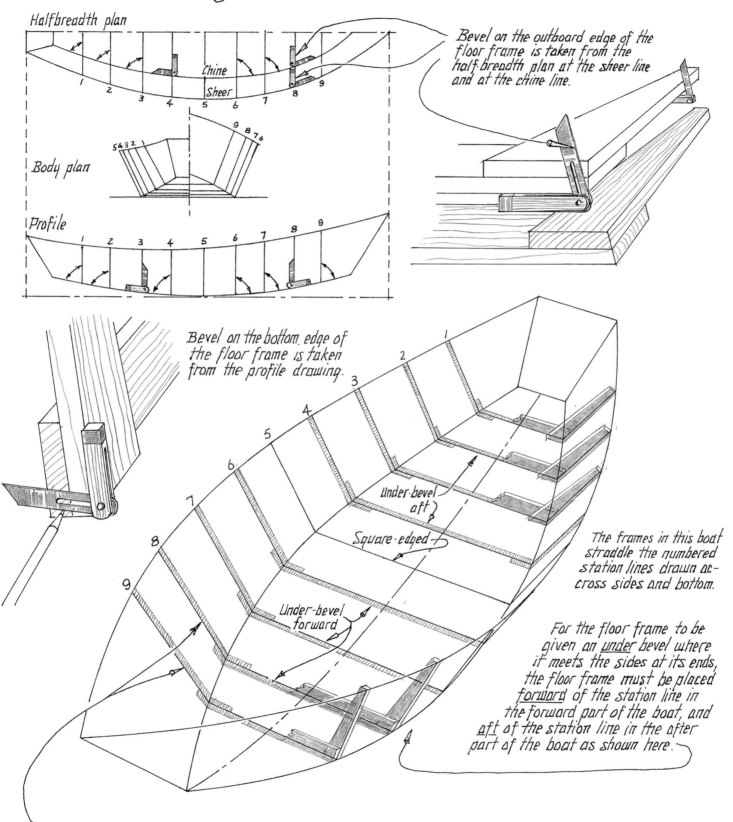

Halfbreadth plan

Chine

Sheer

Body plan

Profile

Bevel on the outboard edge of the floor frame is taken from the half-breadth plan at the sheer line and at the chine line.

Bevel on the bottom edge of the floor frame is taken from the profile drawing.

Under-bevel aft

Square-edged

Under-bevel forward

The frames in this boat straddle the numbered station lines drawn across sides and bottom.

For the floor frame to be given an *under* bevel where it meets the sides at its ends, the floor frame must be placed *forward* of the station line in the forward part of the boat, and *aft* of the station line in the after part of the boat as shown here.

Note that station lines throughout the boat lie in the joint between the floor frame and the side frame and along their mated opposite edges.

If placed in the hull as shown, all floor frames will have an *under* bevel. All side frames will have a *standing* bevel for which "meat" beyond the lofted line must be allowed.

Floor frame and side frames of mid-frame (#5 here) are square to sides and bottom.

Frames

Select frame material that has a good weight-to-strength ratio and is moisture resistant. Clear vertical grain is best. Generally, 1-by-4-inch blank material is adequate, but the builder may decide to extract two side frames from one 1-by-6-inch or 1-by-8-inch blank. Remember that 1-by-4 material actually measures $^3/_4$ by $3^1/_2$ inches, and 1-by-6s are $^3/_4$ by $5^1/_2$ inches. In my neck of the woods, the framing materials of choice are clear vertical grain Sitka spruce, Port Orford cedar, Alaskan yellow cedar, or Douglas fir. A 16-foot drift boat that is built with such material may weigh as little as 225 pounds. While most builders prefer $^3/_4$-inch frames, Woodie Hindman, in his later years, dressed the frames in some boats to $^5/_8$ inch. His trips on the Middle Fork of the Salmon River may have made him more weight conscious.

Use the lofted frame lines to form the frames, and clamp them in place. Because the lines represent the centerline of the frame, take care with the alignment. If the side frames lie on top of the bottom frame, place spacers beneath the side frames to keep them on the same plane. Predrill pilot holes with the proper pilot bit for number 10 or 8 screws or other fasteners you plan to use. Study the illustrations to note the placement of the fasteners. Beware the chine notch—avoid placing a fastener where the notch will be cut. Lightly number each frame for future reference.

Frames assembly —

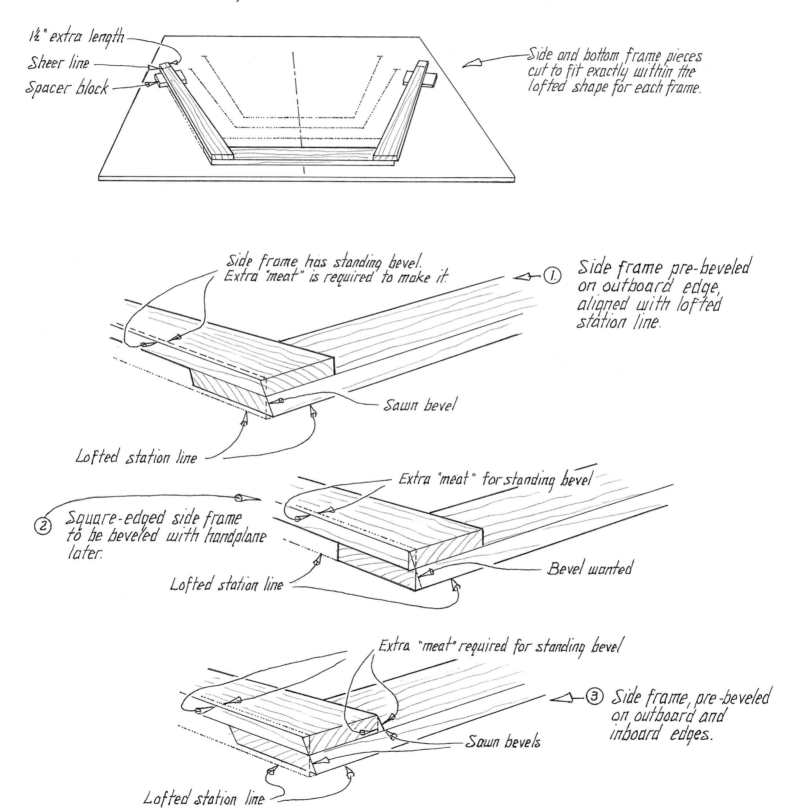

1½" extra length
Sheer line
Spacer block

Side and bottom frame pieces cut to fit exactly within the lofted shape for each frame.

Side frame has standing bevel. Extra "meat" is required to make it.

① Side frame pre-beveled on outboard edge, aligned with lofted station line.

Sawn bevel

Lofted station line

② Square-edged side frame to be beveled with handplane later.

Extra "meat" for standing bevel

Lofted station line

Bevel wanted

Extra "meat" required for standing bevel

③ Side frame, pre-beveled on outboard and inboard edges.

Sawn bevels

Lofted station line

Chine notches are cut after the frame is formed. Carefully define the angles and bevels for the cuts. The chine should fit nicely into these notches at time of installation. Cut the notch slightly wider than the chine. The notches were traditionally marked and sawn by hand. I still prefer this method. First complete the horizontal cut to the vertical chine line, then cut the vertical line, but not enough to remove the chine waste. It will be removed after the frames are installed. If the notch is mistakenly removed, a straight piece of lath may be used to help align the frames' corners to the inside bottom edge of the side panel at time of installation.

Frames Assembly, cont'd —

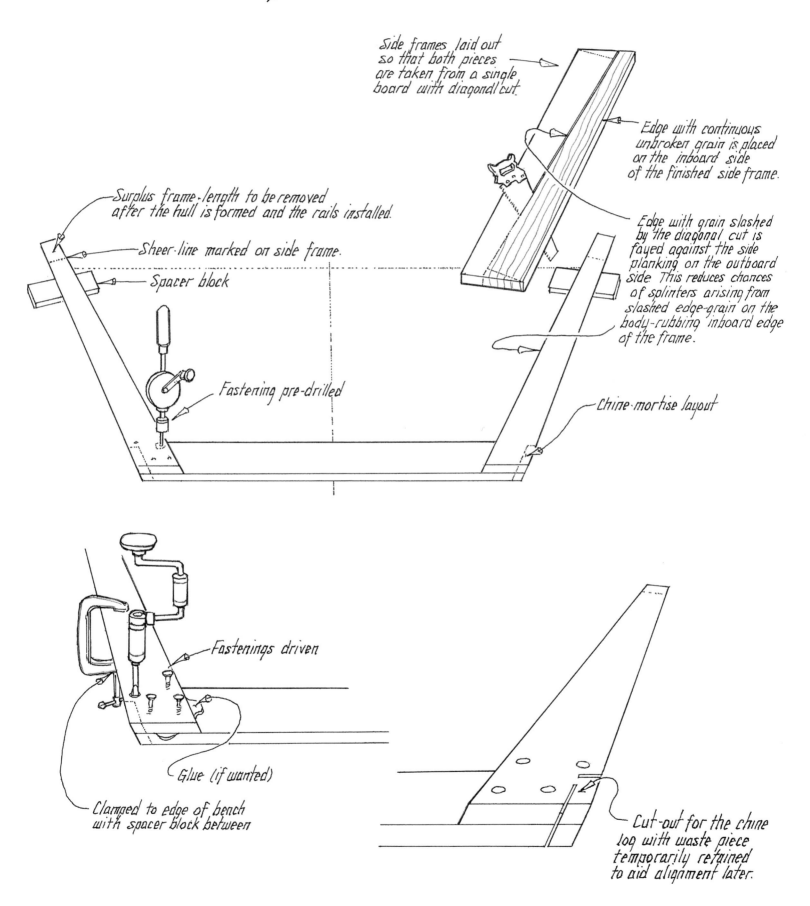

Side frames laid out so that both pieces are taken from a single board with diagonal cut.

Edge with continuous unbroken grain is placed on the inboard side of the finished side frame.

Edge with grain slashed by the diagonal cut is fayed against the side planking on the outboard side. This reduces chances of splinters arising from slashed edge-grain on the body-rubbing inboard edge of the frame.

Surplus frame-length to be removed after the hull is formed and the rails installed.

Sheer-line marked on side frame.

Spacer block

Fastening pre-drilled

Chine-mortise layout

Fastenings driven

Glue (if wanted)

Clamped to edge of bench with spacer block between

Cut-out for the chine log with waste piece temporarily retained to aid alignment later.

Stem and Transom Bevels

The bevels that form the sides of the stem and the side edges of the transom are provided on each set of plans. These bevels cannot be taken directly from the lines plan. The following illustration shows how the bevels can be measured on a boat once constructed. This is the technique I used when determining bevels on some of the boats I have recovered.

When building the boat, the stem timber should extend beyond the sheer line and chine line. The base of the stem, once the hull's shell is formed, will be cut and sized to snugly receive the bottom panel.

Stem and transom bevels ———

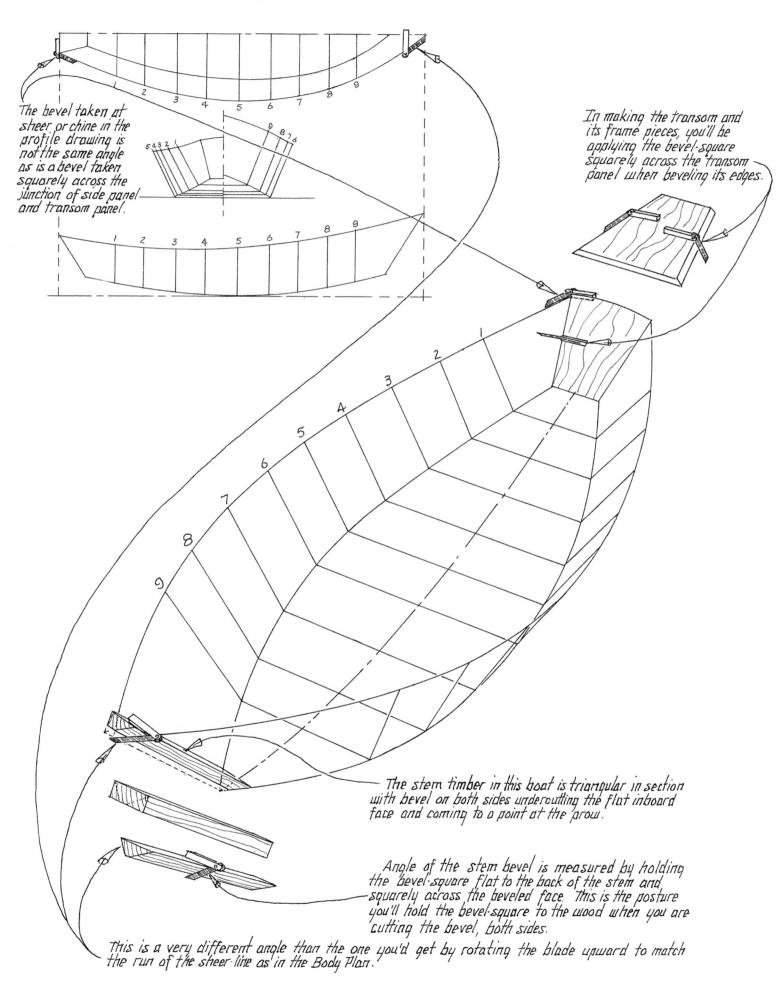

The bevel taken at sheer or chine in the profile drawing is not the same angle as is a bevel taken squarely across the junction of side panel and transom panel.

In making the transom and its frame pieces, you'll be applying the bevel-square squarely across the transom panel when beveling its edges.

The stem timber in this boat is triangular in section with bevel on both sides undercutting the flat inboard face and coming to a point at the prow.

Angle of the stem bevel is measured by holding the bevel-square flat to the back of the stem and squarely across the beveled face. This is the posture you'll hold the bevel-square to the wood when you are cutting the bevel, both sides.

This is a very different angle than the one you'd get by rotating the blade upward to match the run of the sheer line as in the Body Plan.

Although the stem's side bevels and the side edge bevels on a transom cannot be taken directly from a set of lines plans, they can be established accurately by indirect means. The following illustration demonstrates the technique. All you need is a scaled set of lines plans with the horizontal base lines squared up on a drafting board or table. You need a T square, a set of dividers, a protractor, and a tool to establish perpendicular lines. This technique is a reliable means of obtaining the bevels if all you have is a set of lines plans and offsets.

Stem and transom bevels —— How to establish them from the loft drawing ——

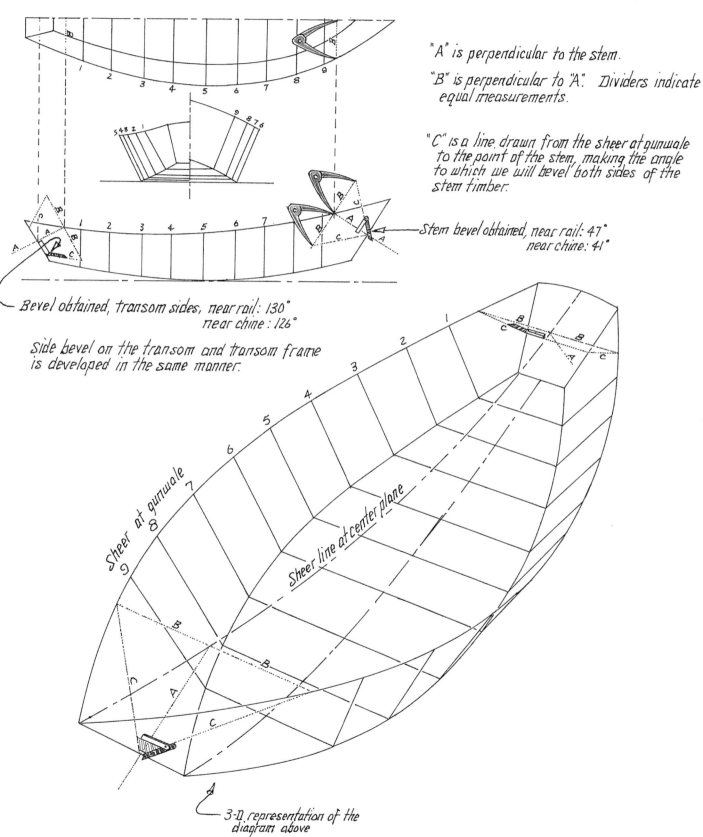

"A" is perpendicular to the stem.

"B" is perpendicular to "A". Dividers indicate equal measurements.

"C" is a line drawn from the sheer at gunwale to the point of the stem, making the angle to which we will bevel both sides of the stem timber.

Stem bevel obtained, near rail: 47°
near chine: 41°

Bevel obtained, transom sides, near rail: 130°
near chine : 126°

Side bevel on the transom and transom frame is developed in the same manner.

Sheer at gunwale

Sheer line at center plane

3-D. representation of the diagram above

Assembling the Hull

Boatbuilders generally form the hull upside down. One exception was Rogue River guide and builder Bob Pritchett, who preferred to build his Rogue River dory right side up on a jig because he wanted to see the boat take shape. He shimmed the frames to attain the desired rocker. Upside-down free-form construction, however, is my preferred method. The frames give shape and rocker to the boat as each is installed.

Pilot holes should be predrilled for most fasteners. This will do two things: It ensures that the fasteners will be anchored where intended, and it minimizes the threat of splitting a frame, chine, stem, or rail. Where screws are used, countersink the pilot holes slightly so that the screw heads will be flat to the surface. Use the following assembly sequence:

Align the side panels so they are precisely juxtaposed on the stem post. Install one panel at a time. Predrill, apply a sealant,[4] and nail (using ring nails) or screw in place. Use an alternating offset pattern for the fasteners as illustrated, about 2 inches on center. There should be surplus stem above and below the panel. The second panel is then aligned to the first. Note that it is splayed outward, bottom sides up, so the panel lies flush to the stem bevel.

Fastening side panels to stem timber —

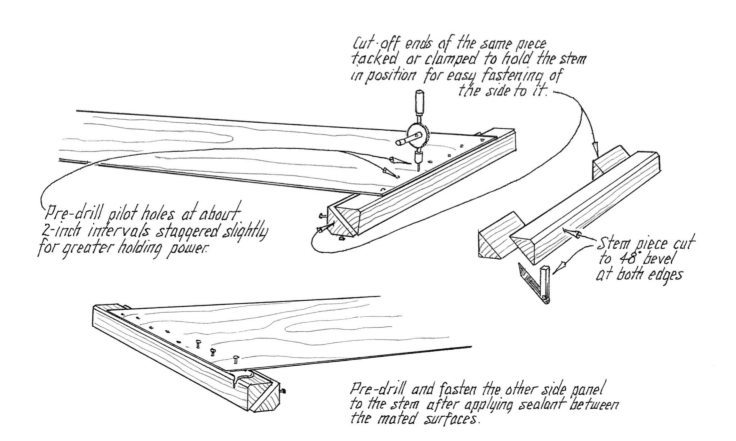

Cut-off ends of the same piece tacked or clamped to hold the stem in position for easy fastening of the side to it.

Pre-drill pilot holes at about 2-inch intervals staggered slightly for greater holding power.

Stem piece cut to 48° bevel at both edges

Pre-drill and fasten the other side panel to the stem after applying sealant between the mated surfaces.

Fastening side panel to stem, the other side ——

Hold the side panels bottom-edge upward and splayed outward with the stem-bevel, along their length. Match the stem fastenings through the panel with their pre-drilled holes in the stem. Apply sealant to the mated surfaces, set clamps at top and bottom of the stem, and drive the fastenings home.

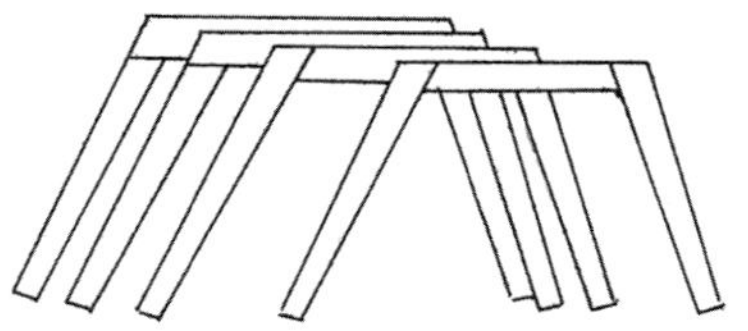

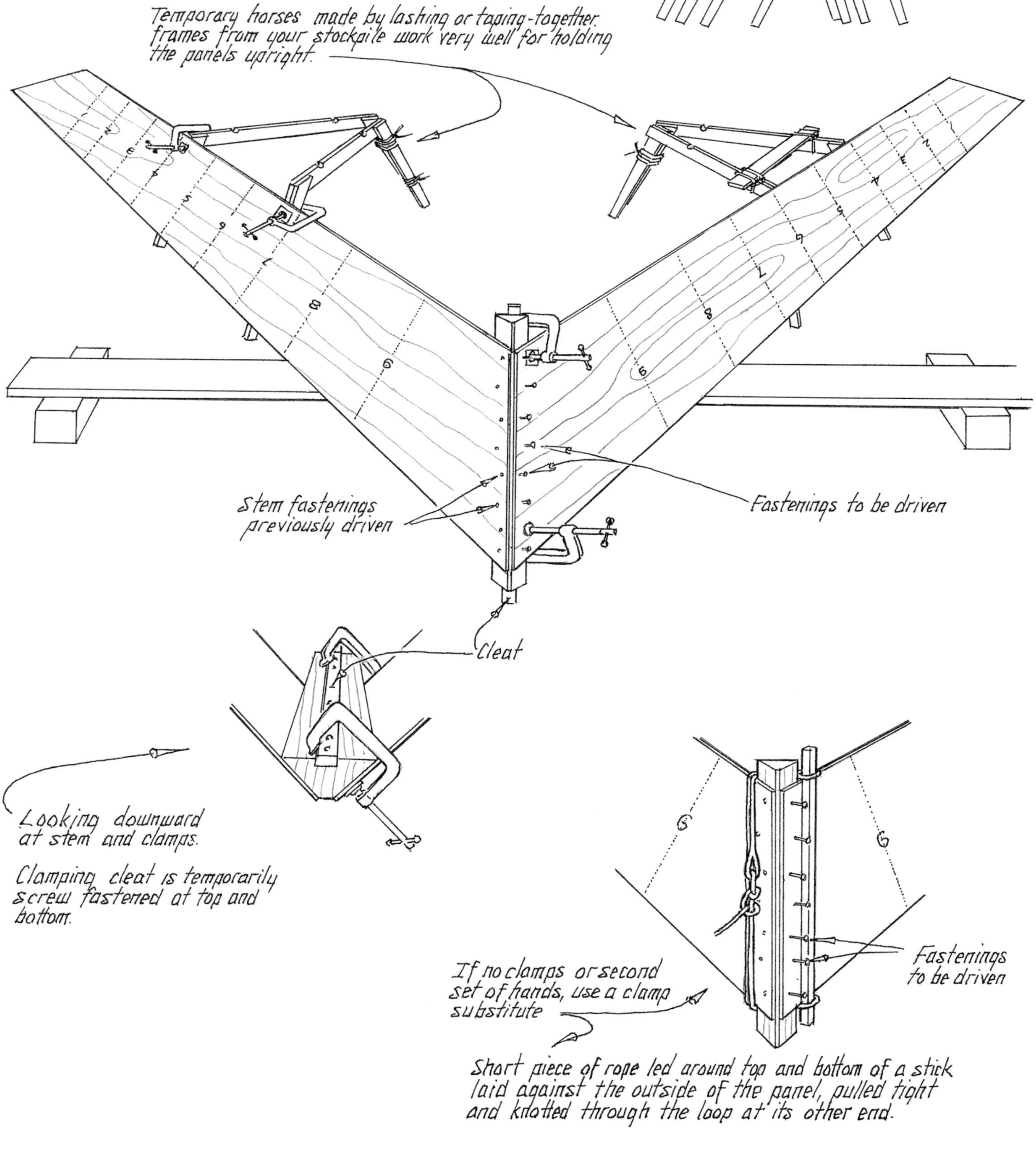

Temporary horses made by lashing or taping-together frames from your stockpile work very well for holding the panels upright.

Stem fastenings previously driven

Fastenings to be driven

Cleat

Looking downward at stem and clamps.

Clamping cleat is temporarily screw fastened at top and bottom.

If no clamps or second set of hands, use a clamp substitute

Fastenings to be driven

Short piece of rope led around top and bottom of a stick laid against the outside of the panel, pulled tight and knotted through the loop at its other end.

Pull the side panels together. Temporarily clamp in place the frame closest to the stem post, and then successively two or three of the centermost frames. For the McKenzie double-ender with a transom, these would be frames 9, 7, 5, and 3. The frames may be temporarily strengthened with cross spalls (braces) set to the frame extension just above the sheer line. If you have too few clamps, temporarily secure one or more of the frames with removable fasteners.

Pulling side panels together around pre-set frames —

1. Set frame #9 in place — bottom flush with bottom edge of sides and with the station mark on the side panel pressing the joint between side and bottom frame pieces. Hold it there with clamps at sheer and chine.

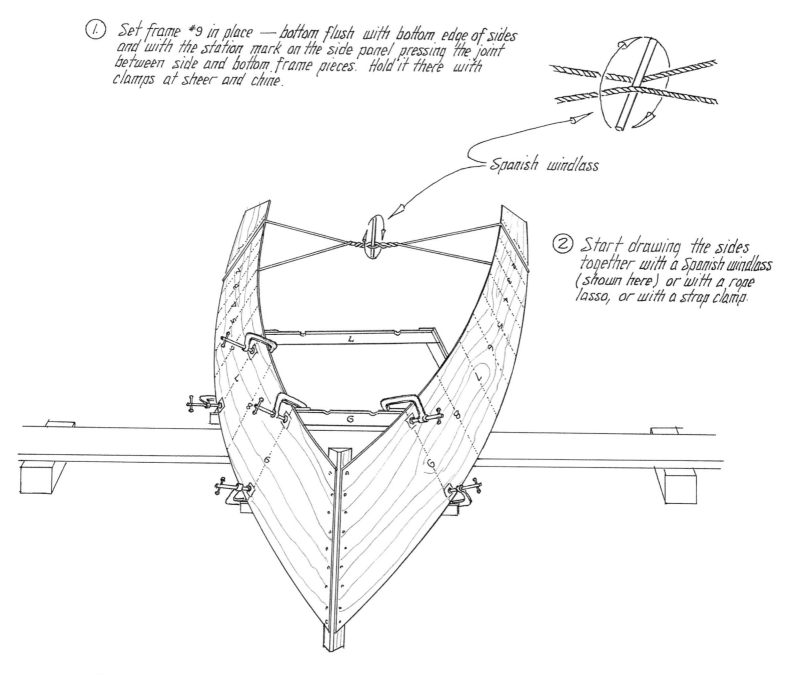

Spanish windlass

2. Start drawing the sides together with a Spanish windlass (shown here) or with a rope lasso, or with a strap clamp.

3. Set frame #7 in place as the side panels draw in to that spot. Clamp side frames at top and bottom as before.

4. Go back to frame #9 and hold it there with temporary fastenings such as pullable thin nails.

5. Set frame #5, clamp top and bottom, set temporary fastenings in frame #7. Remove clamps and use them on frame #3 as the side panels close in to that spot.

6. Set frame #3, then frame #1. Permanent fastenings will be pre-drilled and driven when the transom is in place. To set them during the side-bending process is to have them wear oversize holes in the thin plywood.

Other cordage options. For some, boatbuilding becomes a community or family project and ample hands are available when needed. For those who don't have that luxury or simply prefer to handle the project alone, installing the transom can be done as a joint venture or singlehandedly. If you handle the project by yourself, there are a couple other cordage options in addition to the Spanish windlass: the lasso or the strap clamp, which is also known as a band clamp.

Pulling in the side panels with cordage or strap·clamp —

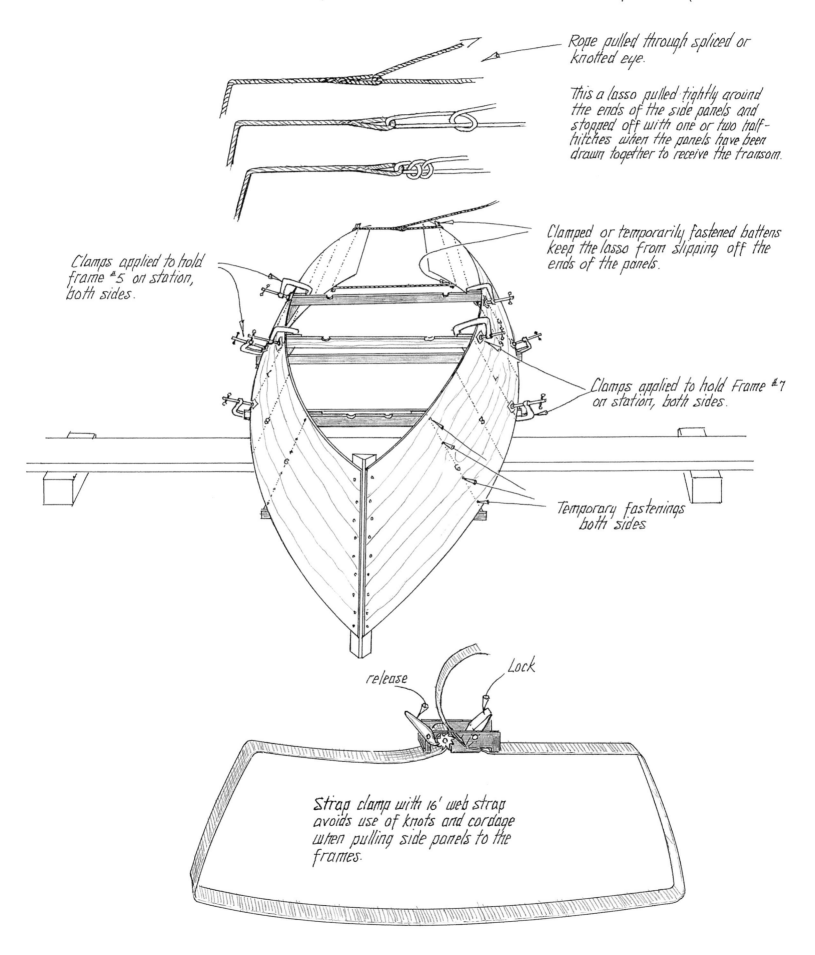

Rope pulled through spliced or knotted eye.

This a lasso pulled tightly around the ends of the side panels and stopped off with one or two half-hitches when the panels have been drawn together to receive the transom.

Clamped or temporarily fastened battens keep the lasso from slipping off the ends of the panels.

Clamps applied to hold frame #5 on station, both sides.

Clamps applied to hold Frame #7 on station, both sides.

Temporary fastenings both sides

release

Lock

Strap clamp with 16' web strap avoids use of knots and cordage when pulling side panels to the frames.

Frame and install the transom. Most boats require a transom. The plans are clear about their design. If the transom includes a frame, match the bevels to the transom bevels. I suggest you also bevel the inside face of the transom frames. This will be easier than notching them later to receive the inside rail.

The beveled frames and transom receive the side panels in a flush manner. When the transom is aligned with the closing panels, make certain the transom bottom bevel aligns nicely with corner and panels' bottom edges. Apply a sealant to the outside edges of the transom and side frames, clamp the piece in place, and apply the fasteners. Attach the side panels to the transom or stern post.

Framing and installing the transom —

Edges and side frames of the transom are beveled to receive the side panels closing upon them.

Bevel (see p. 129) is found to be 126° at the bottom of the transom and 130° at top.

Side frames are fastened along both edges of the transom to provide landing for fastenings from the side panels.

Side frames are given the same bevel on both edges.

Cut-outs for the chine logs are made in the bottom piece. (Optional)

Bottom bevel (129°) is taken from the lines plan Profile. Same bevel on both edges.

The lashing is pulled tight and knotted so that the sides enclose the transom tightly. The lashing holds these members together while clamps are applied.

Temporary cross-spall (optional)

Fastenings are set at 90° to the surface of the side panel.

Transom

Frame #1

Additional frames are set to their marks and are fastened-in through the side panels until the hull is completely framed.

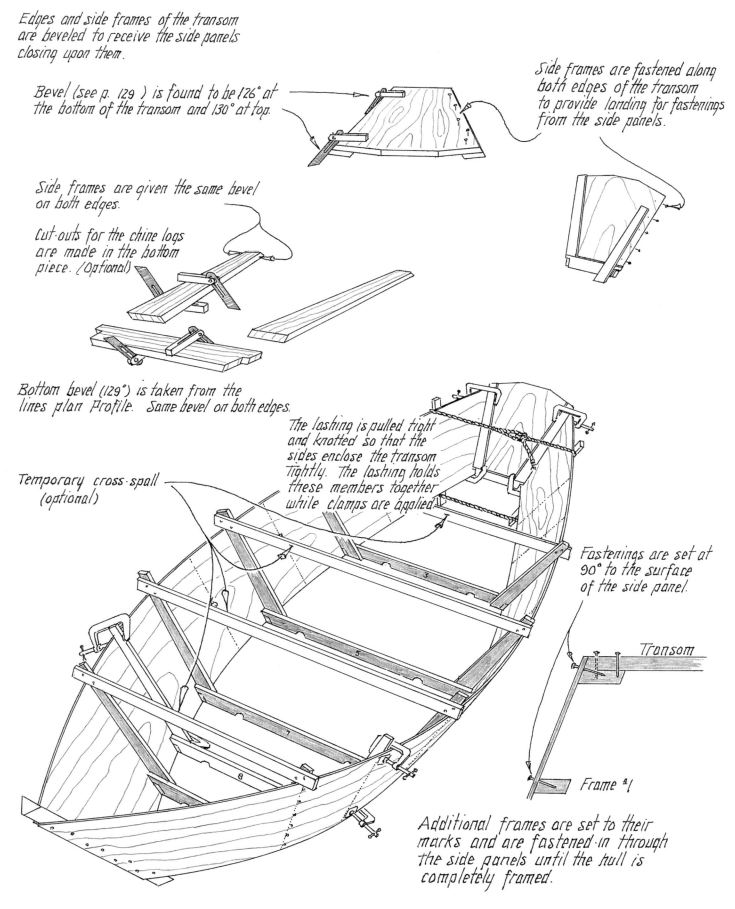

(This view is a peek beneath a boat actually being built upside down!)

Complete the frame installation. Beginning with the centermost frame, set the frames to their marks. The tick marks you placed on the top and bottom of the panels will help deal with the blind spot created by the bottom frame. Check the alignment of the bottom frame to the inside edge of the panel. You now know why the chine notch was not removed. If the notch waste was removed, clamp a short, straight batten to the bottom of the frame to serve as a guide. A bead of sealant may be applied to that portion of the side frame that is below the waterline. Clamp in place. Apply fasteners 4 inches on center. Avoid the chine notch. Frames are alternately installed fore and aft of the centermost frame until all are in.

Frame installation detail —

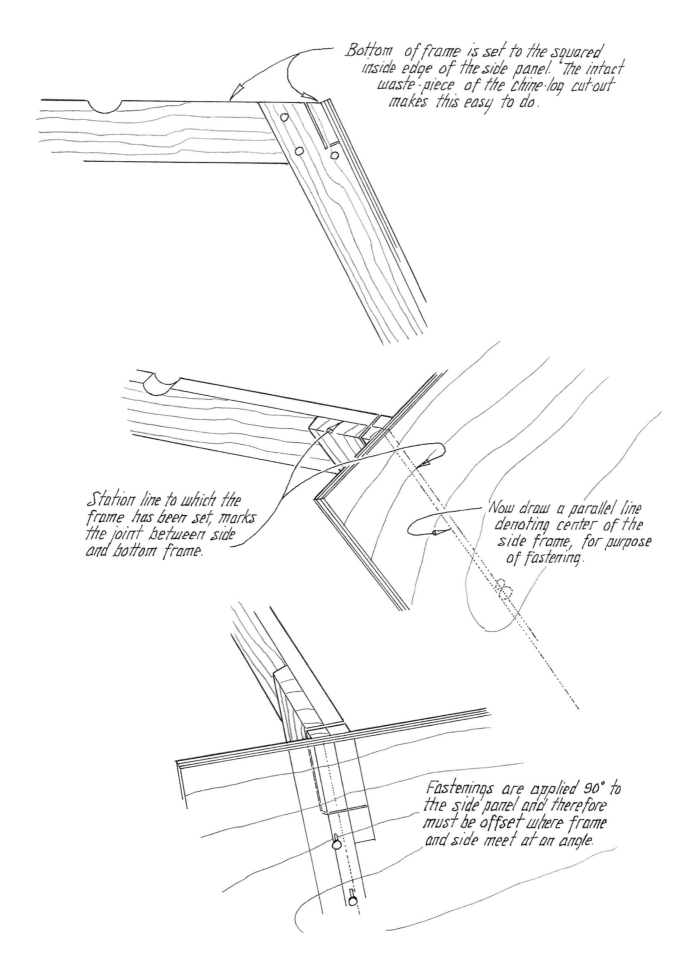

Bottom of frame is set to the squared inside edge of the side panel. The intact waste-piece of the chine-log cut-out makes this easy to do.

Station line to which the frame has been set, marks the joint between side and bottom frame.

Now draw a parallel line denoting center of the side frame, for purpose of fastening.

Fastenings are applied 90° to the side panel and therefore must be offset where frame and side meet at an angle.

Chine Logs

Most of the plans require inside chine pieces called chine logs, one for each side of the boat. These pieces run the length of the boat, from the base of the stem post, along the bottom edge of the panel, to the base of the stern post or transom. They provide stability to the hull structure and serve as anchor points for the fasteners. In architectural terms, chines are the boat's keystones.

Remove the chine notch waste by completing the vertical cut of the chine notch, then removing the waste material. Check the notches for uniformity, and make whatever adjustments may be necessary.

Install the chine logs one at a time. The chine logs are first beveled so the topside is roughly parallel to the floor of the boat once they are installed. The bevel minimizes the collection of water at the inside top edge of the chine. Over time, water that is allowed to collect may eventually soak in and lead to dry rot. The underside of the chine may be beveled with a hand plane after the chine is installed. It is important that the finished chine be flush to the bottom frames to receive the bottom panel. The chines are bent into place without steaming.

Removing chine-notch offcut —

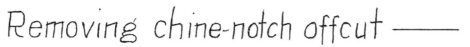

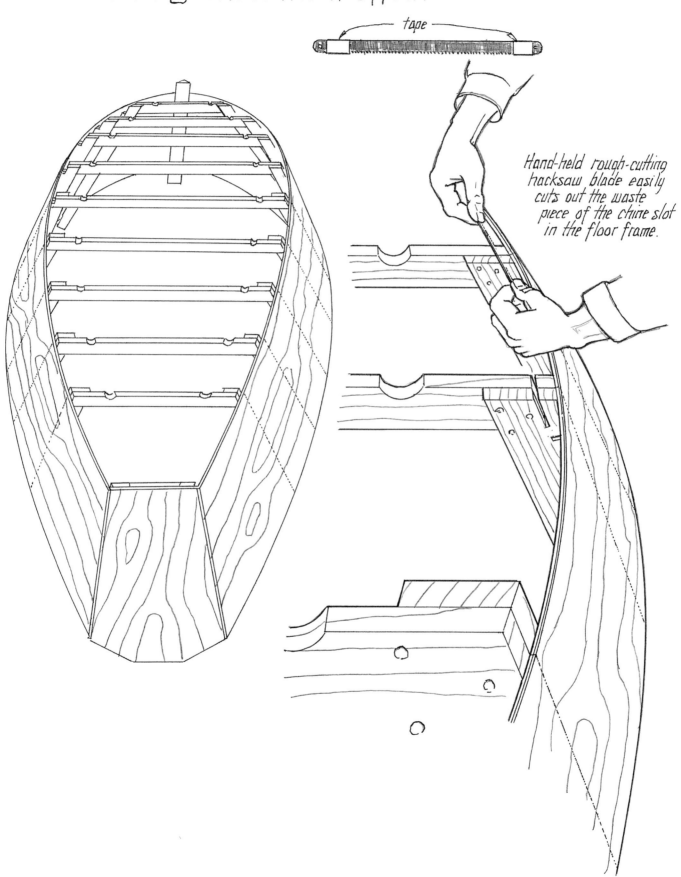

Hand-held rough-cutting hacksaw blade easily cuts out the waste piece of the chine slot in the floor frame.

Cut and fit the chine log so it joins nicely to the stem and stern and fits snugly against the side panel and into the frames' chine notches. Several methods are traditionally used: slip sticks, adjustable sticks, and single stick. The illustrations demonstrate the use of two flexible sticks to lay out, mark, cut, and tight-fit the chine log. Short pieces of lath may be clamped to the inside edge of the frame at the notch to help guide the chine into place.

Apply the marine sealer along the inside face of the chine, and fasten number 8 ($^3/_4$-inch) screws from the panel into the chine 3 or 4 inches on center. This is called a floating chine, because at no point is the panel anchored through the chine into a frame.

Tight-fitting chine log in one piece ——

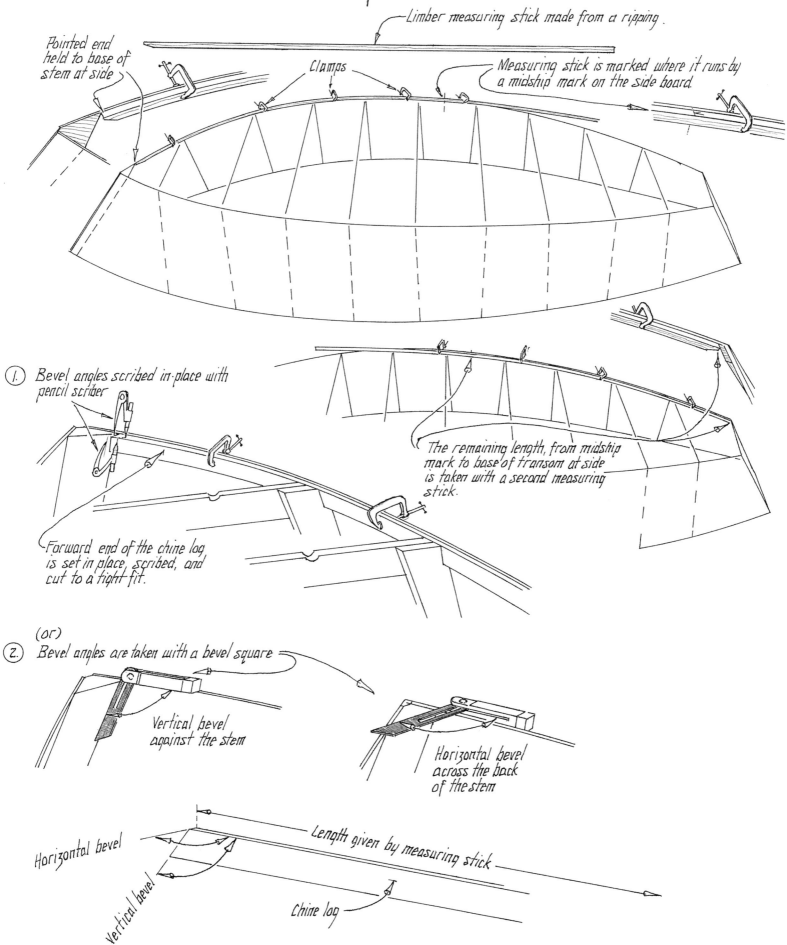

Limber measuring stick made from a ripping.

Pointed end held to base of stem at side

Clamps

Measuring stick is marked where it runs by a midship mark on the side board.

1. Bevel angles scribed in-place with pencil scriber

The remaining length, from midship mark to base of transom at side is taken with a second measuring stick.

Forward end of the chine log is set in place, scribed, and cut to a tight fit.

(or)

2. Bevel angles are taken with a bevel square

Vertical bevel against the stem

Horizontal bevel across the back of the stem

Horizontal bevel

Vertical bevel

Length given by measuring stick

Chine log

Tight-fitting chine log in one piece — cont'd —

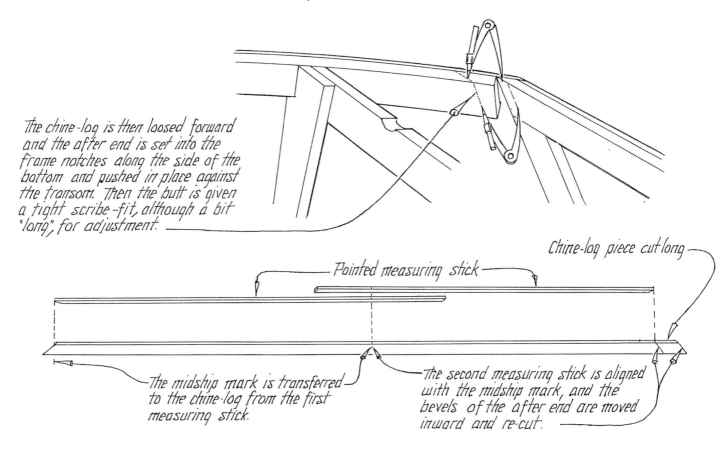

The chine-log is then loosed forward and the after end is set into the frame notches along the side of the bottom and pushed in place against the transom. Then the butt is given a tight scribe-fit, although a bit "long", for adjustment.

Chine-log piece cut long

Pointed measuring stick

The midship mark is transferred to the chine-log from the first measuring stick.

The second measuring stick is aligned with the midship mark, and the bevels of the after end are moved inward and re-cut.

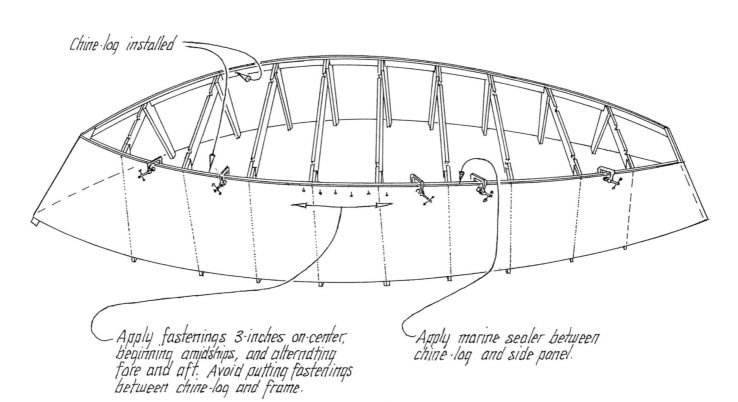

Chine-log installed

Apply fastenings 3-inches on-center, beginning amidships, and alternating fore and aft. Avoid putting fastenings between chine-log and frame.

Apply marine sealer between chine-log and side panel.

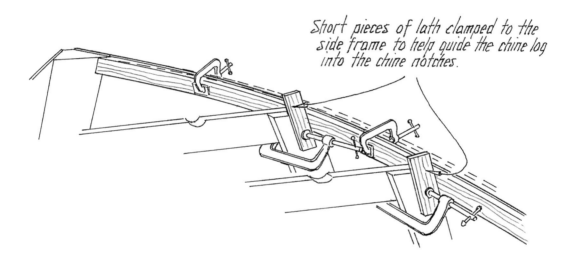

Short pieces of lath clamped to the side frame to help guide the chine log into the chine notches.

Prepare the hull to receive the bottom panel. Have any of the bottom frames bowed? Temporarily straighten an offending frame by clamping a 1-by-4 or 2-by-4 board along both sides so the frame will hold to a straight line. Place the clamps and strengtheners so they don't interfere with the bottom panel.

The bottom panel must lie flush to the chines, frames, stem post, and transom at all points. Remove the excess stem or stern post and chine. Use a hand plane and straight batten for the chines and occasional offending frame. The batten must lie across the bottom breadth of the boat. Use it to measure the progress of your work. Glue a strip of 40- or 60-grit sandpaper to the underside of the batten. The straight edge will help keep your work true, and the reverse side with sandpaper will help fine up your work along the chine. With care, you will ensure a nice, tight fit to the bottom panel. There is nothing more pleasant than curled shavings collecting around one's feet from the use of a sharp hand plane.

40 or 60-grit sandpaper glued to a straight board laid flat across the bottom frames and used as a fairing tool along the chine log and side-panel edge.

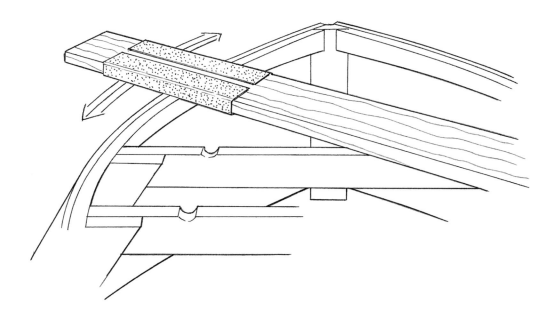

Fairness of chine log and side panel-edge checked with straight edge extended across the hull ——

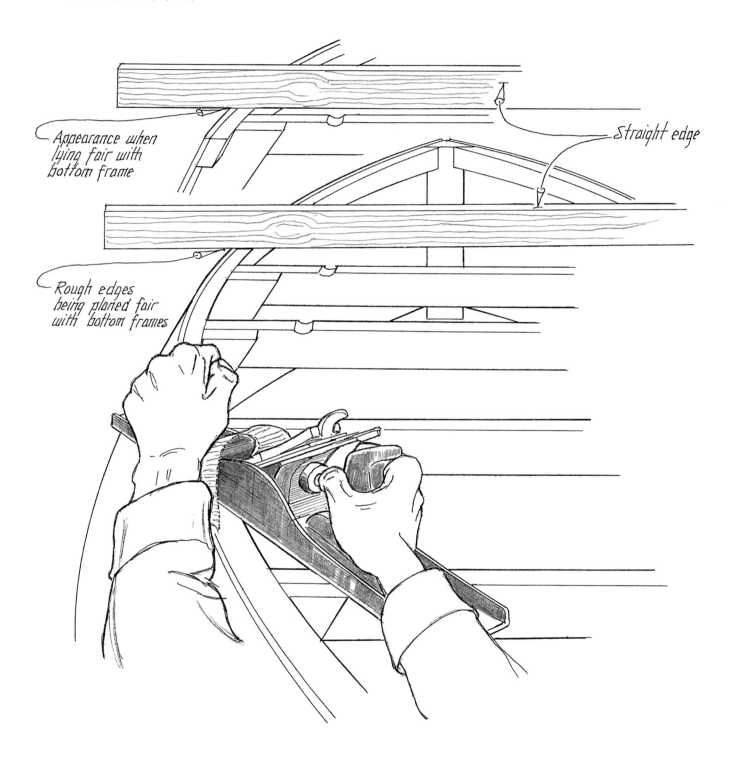

Appearance when lying fair with bottom frame

Straight edge

Rough edges being planed fair with bottom frames

Fairing chines, frames, and bottom of the stem-post with a hand plane to receive the bottom panel flush.

Sander, unless mechanically guided, is apt to produce a convex surface. All surfaces must be flat.

Is the hull square? Establish a centerline mark on each frame, the transom, and the stem. Stretch a line from the center point on the transom to the center point on the stem. If the line stretches over the center marks on the frames, the boat is square. If things are off a bit, twist the still limber hull until the alignments are correct. Shore the hull with multiple sets of hands, or if you are working alone, shore it against the walls or ceiling as shown in the illustration. Once the hull is square, affix a 1-by-6 batten to the top of the bottom frames as shown on page 151. The batten will keep the now-squared hull in place.

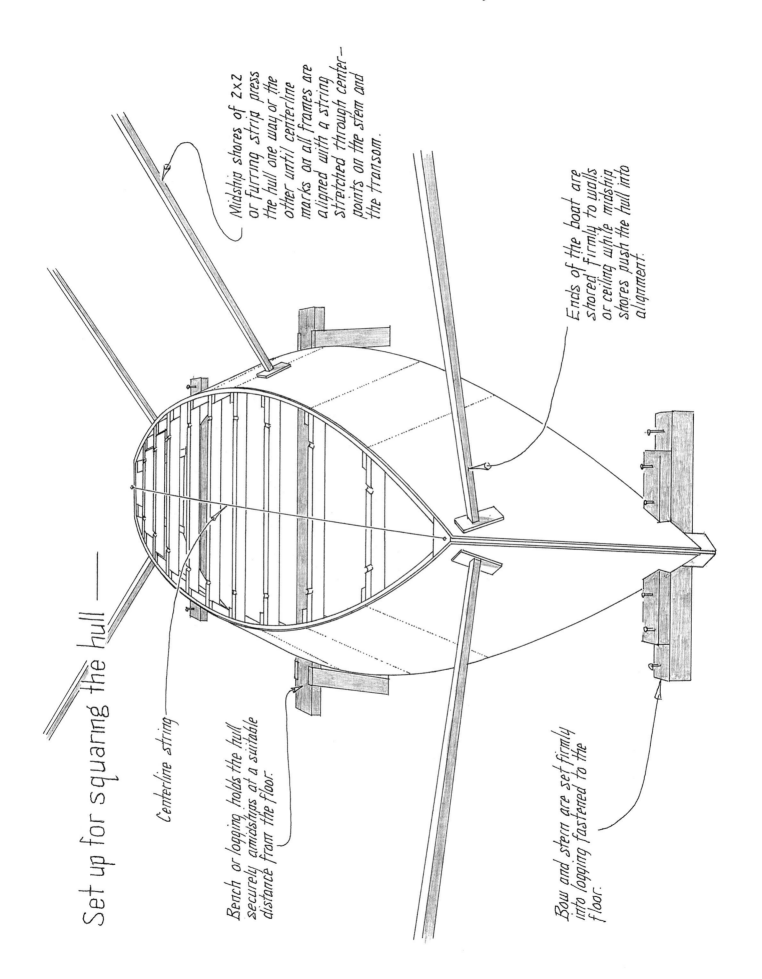

Set up for squaring the hull —

Midship shores of 2x2 or furring strip press the hull one way or the other until centerline marks on all frames are aligned with a string stretched through center-points on the stem and the transom.

Ends of the boat are shored firmly to walls or ceiling while midship shores push the hull into alignment.

Centerline string

Bench or logging holds the hull securely amidships at a suitable distance from the floor.

Bow and stern are set firmly into logging fastened to the floor.

Rub rails may be added to any boat, and one set of plans in part 4 calls for them. They were originally used to protect the boat from tire rub as boat and trailer bounced over rough access roads and trails. The boat, no matter how securely it may have been tied down, often migrated to a spinning tire. Trailers were usually fabricated from Model-T axles. Suspension was limited. Tire rub created more damage to the boat than the river. Early boatmen installed rub rails along the midsection of the boat a couple inches above the top of the chine cap to protect the craft. Today the rub rails are added for their aesthetics or the belief that they add protection to the side panel. Actually, rub rails are unnecessary if the boat is in the hands of a competent river oarsman. But they are attractive, and for an errant boat, they add a little more protection. You may want to add this feature to your boat.

If you plan to install rub rails, now may be a good time to do the job. Traditionally, they are added after the hull is formed, but they are easier to fit and clamp in place before the bottom panel goes on. One downside to installing them now is that their presence may increase the difficulty of installing the outside chine caps when the time comes. If you desire rub rails, install them either now or after the bottom and chine caps are in. It's your choice.

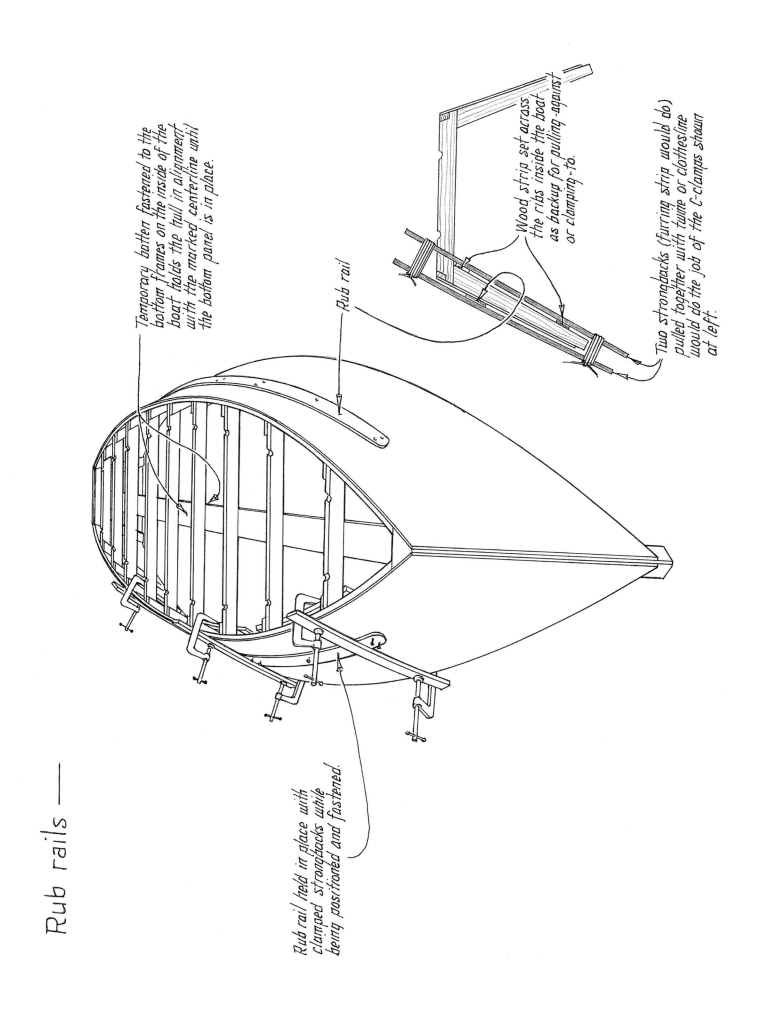

Rub rails —

Temporary batten fastened to the bottom frames on the inside of the boat holds the hull in alignment with the marked centerline until the bottom panel is in place.

Rub rail

Wood strip set across the ribs inside the boat as backup for pulling-against or clamping-to.

Two strongbacks (furring strip would do) pulled together with twine or clothesline would do the job of the C-clamps shown at left.

Rub rail held in place with clamped strongbacks while being positioned and fastened.

Bottom panel —
(½" or ⅝" panels are recommended for most boats)

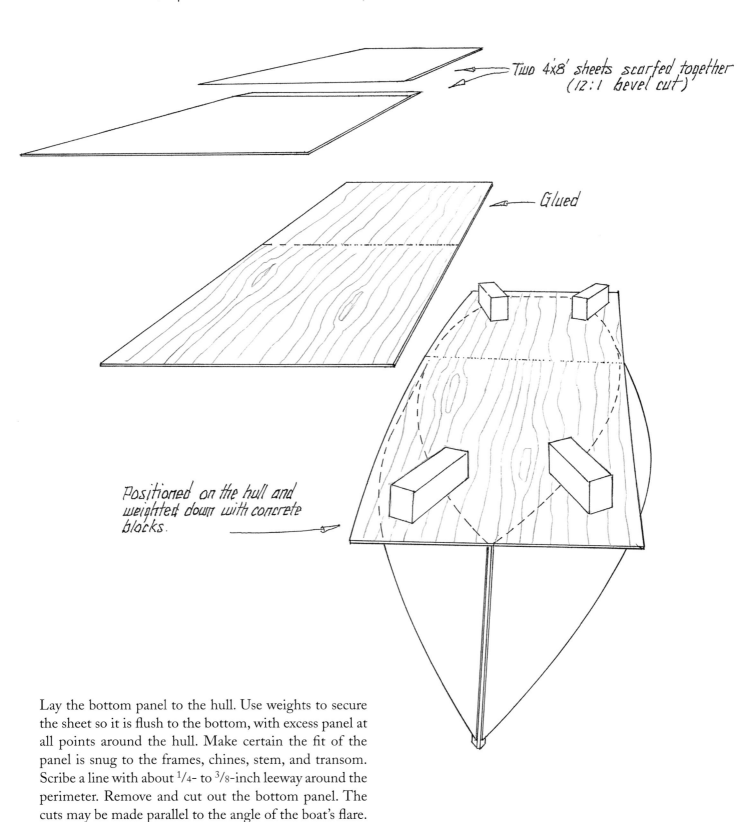

Two 4×8′ sheets scarfed together (12:1 bevel cut)

Glued

Positioned on the hull and weighted down with concrete blocks.

Lay the bottom panel to the hull. Use weights to secure the sheet so it is flush to the bottom, with excess panel at all points around the hull. Make certain the fit of the panel is snug to the frames, chines, stem, and transom. Scribe a line with about 1/4- to 3/8-inch leeway around the perimeter. Remove and cut out the bottom panel. The cuts may be made parallel to the angle of the boat's flare.

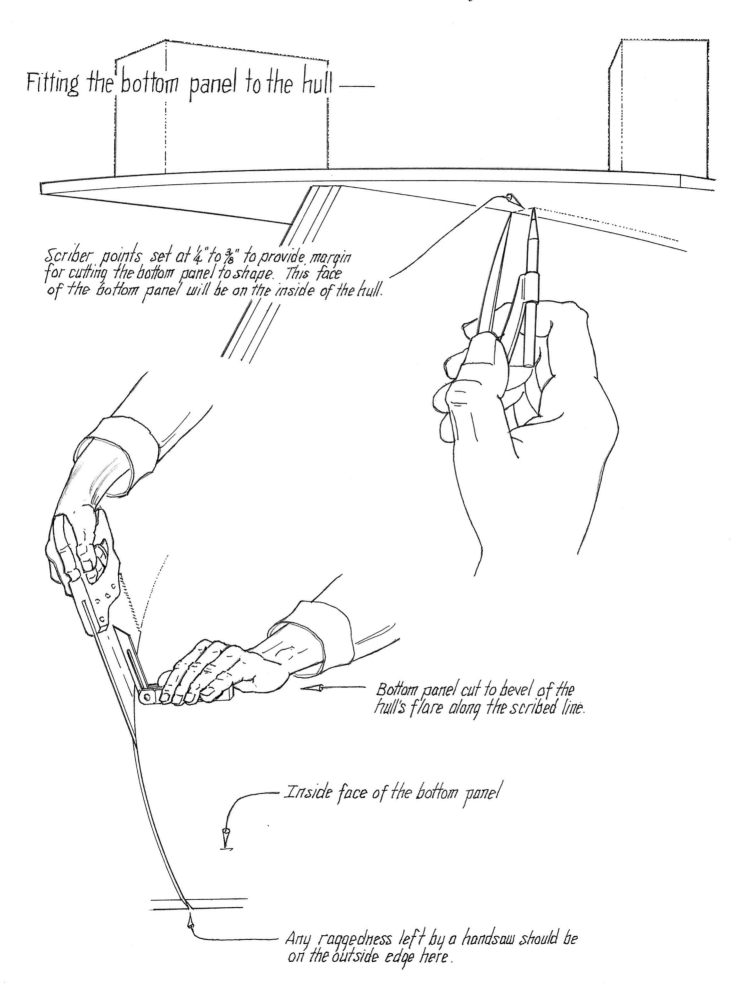

Fitting the bottom panel to the hull ——

Scriber points set at ¼" to ⅜" to provide margin for cutting the bottom panel to shape. This face of the bottom panel will be on the inside of the hull.

Bottom panel cut to bevel of the hull's flare along the scribed line.

Inside face of the bottom panel

Any raggedness left by a handsaw should be on the outside edge here.

Realign the freshly cut panel to the bottom, and establish reference points on the side panels and bottom panel. The reference points will be helpful when the panel is lowered into its final place after the sealant has been applied and minimize smearing the sealer beyond the outlines of the frame. Also mark the center point of each bottom frame on the outside side panels near the chine. These marks will assist in establishing the centerline for each bottom frame after the panel is laid down and aligned for fastening.

Apply the marine sealer to the chine, bottom frames, transom, and stem. Realign the bottom panel to the hull. Temporarily secure the panel, then scribe the centerline to each frame and mark the centerline of the chine around the bottom panel. Craft a scribing block to mark the chine line. These lines will serve as guides for the fasteners into the chine log.

Double-check that all alignments are correct, and apply the fasteners. Some builders prefer to work from the center frame, alternating fore and aft; others prefer working from stem to stern. Apply fasteners 3 inches on center along the chine and 4 inches on center for the bottom frames.[5] Avoid the limber holes.

Once the bottom is installed, carefully fair the bottom panel to the side panel. Do not round the edges. Keep all edges sharp.

Fastening the bottom panel to the hull —

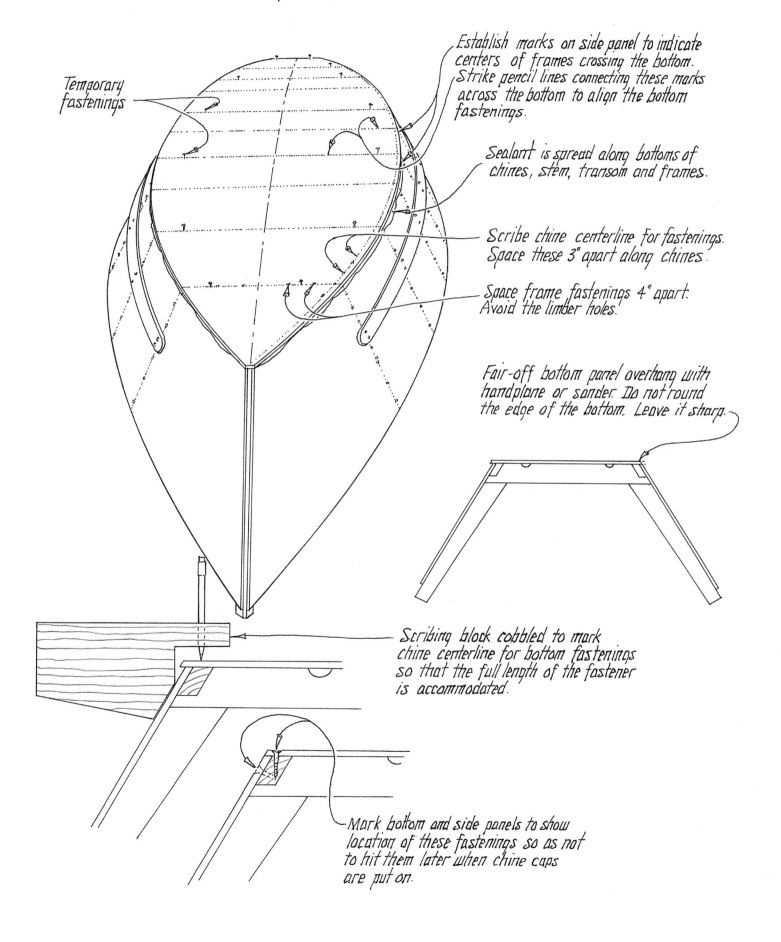

Temporary fastenings

Establish marks on side panel to indicate centers of frames crossing the bottom. Strike pencil lines connecting these marks across the bottom to align the bottom fastenings.

Sealant is spread along bottoms of chines, stem, transom and frames.

Scribe chine centerline for fastenings. Space these 3" apart along chines.

Space frame fastenings 4" apart. Avoid the limber holes.

Fair-off bottom panel overhang with handplane or sander. Do not round the edge of the bottom. Leave it sharp.

Scribing block cobbled to mark chine centerline for bottom fastenings so that the full length of the fastener is accommodated.

Mark bottom and side panels to show location of these fastenings so as not to hit them later when chine caps are put on.

Add bottom protection to the hull. The boat will take abuse on the river, especially the bottom as the craft glides over rocks or is dragged to and from the river, so it is wise to add this protection to the hull. It was once customary to add 3-inch oak strips the length of the bottom. This proved problematic, since it was more difficult to slide over obstacles and often would catch the boat bottom and upset the boat. Beginning in the late 1930s or early 1940s, builders instead added a $1/4$-inch plywood shoe. The shoe covered the entire bottom of the boat, was smooth, and worked well. This remains a preferred method among some traditionalists today.

A more contemporary method is to fiberglass the underside with 20 to 24 ounces of triaxial fiberglass cloth and multiple applications of epoxy resin. The last few coats of resin include graphite. This gives the bottom a black sheen and significantly reduces resistance when the boatman slides over an obstacle. Add the bottom protection before proceeding further.

Install the stem cap. Plane or sand the end panels so they are flush with the face of the stem. The cap should cover the exposed ends of the side panels. If you apply a sealer here, use a marine polysufide product and fasten 3 to 4 inches on center. Leave the cap square or bevel the edges.

If *transom trim* is intended, now is the time to install the pieces, bottom piece first and then the two side members. Install to the inside edge of the bottom and side panels, then hand-plane them and sand flush.

You have already made decisions about the finish applied to the interior. Now, with the hull almost complete, before the outside chines, transom trim, and rails are installed, is a good time to apply the outside finish.

Protective sheathing, edges of bottom panel faired, stem cap fitted —

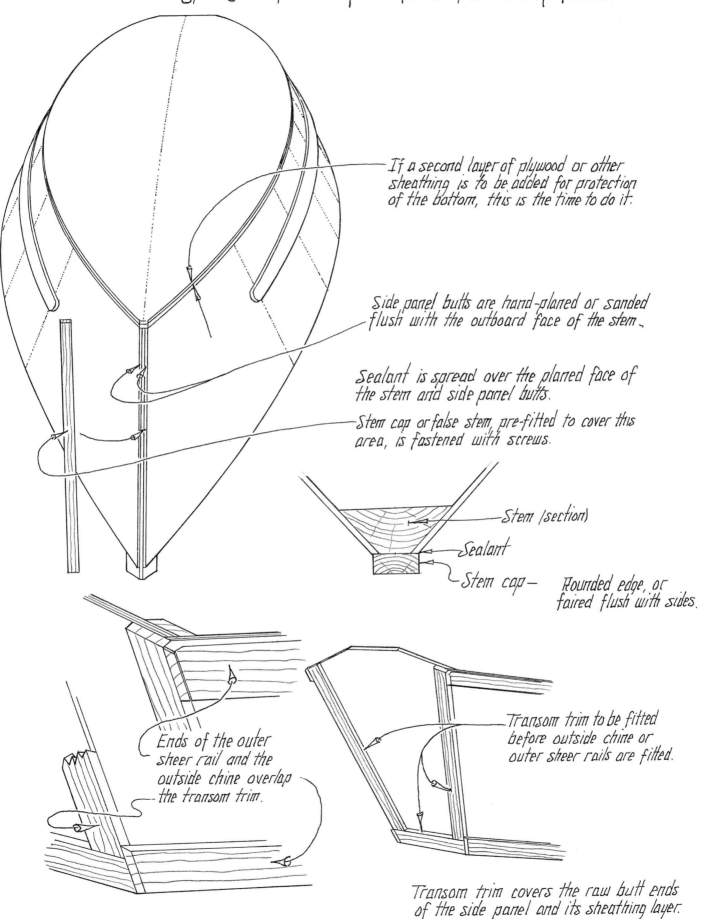

If a second layer of plywood or other sheathing is to be added for protection of the bottom, this is the time to do it.

Side panel butts are hand-planed or sanded flush with the outboard face of the stem.

Sealant is spread over the planed face of the stem and side panel butts.

Stem cap or false stem, pre-fitted to cover this area, is fastened with screws.

Stem (section)

Sealant

Stem cap —   Rounded edge, or faired flush with sides.

Ends of the outer sheer rail and the outside chine overlap the transom trim.

Transom trim to be fitted before outside chine or outer sheer rails are fitted.

Transom trim covers the raw butt ends of the side panel and its sheathing layer.

Install the outside chine cap so the inside edge is aligned to bottom edge of the plywood shoe or protective covering. Cut and fit the chine cap to stem. The piece will lay over the transom trim at the aft end of the boat and then cut flush to the transom after it is installed. The chine cap may be beveled before installation so it lays flush to the bottom panel. Most builders prefer to shave the chine caps flush to the bottom with a hand plane and sander after they are installed. Underseal the chine with a marine-grade poly-sulfide sealer.[6] With some extra sets of hands (your spouse, friends or children may be tiring of you about now), bend the chine cap into place and establish a center mark. Apply the fasteners from the center mark and work toward each end, alternating the fasteners fore and aft.

Except for the sheer rails, the hull is now complete. Turn the boat right side up. Find a chair, sit awhile and admire your work. Though there is much yet to do, this is a satisfying moment.

Fit and clamp the outside rails into place. Predrill and drive number 8 $5/8$-inch screws to secure the rail to the panel. Apply screws from the inside of the panel 4 to 6 inches on center.

Chine caps and outside rails —

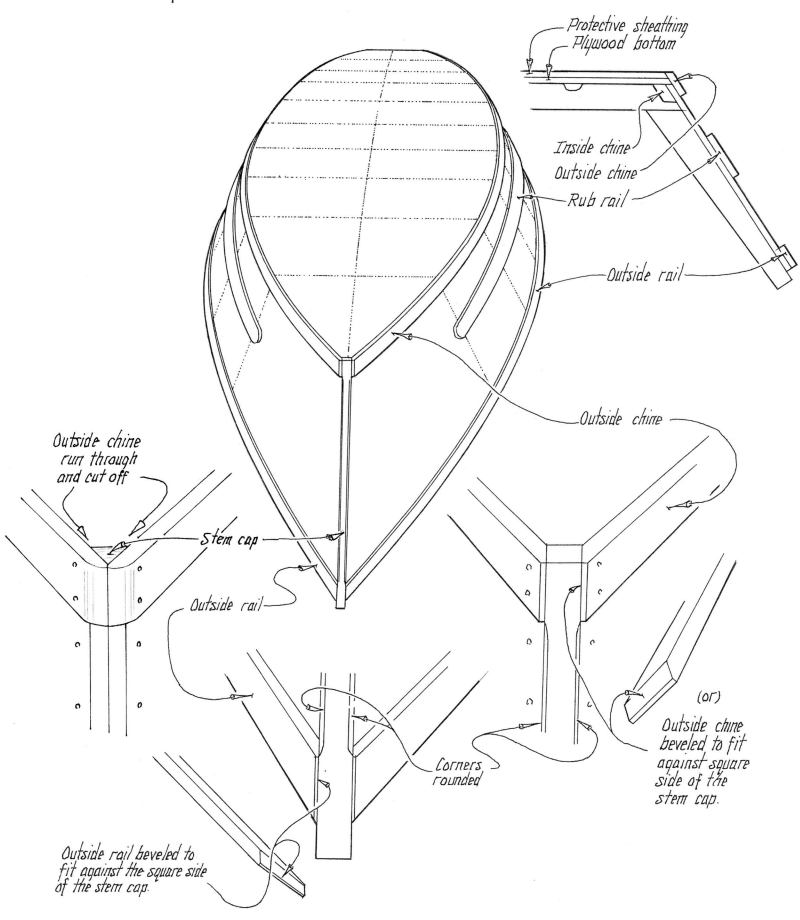

Protective sheathing
Plywood bottom

Inside chine
Outside chine
Rub rail

Outside rail

Outside chine

Outside chine
run through
and cut off

Stem cap

Outside rail

Corners
rounded

(or)

Outside chine
beveled to fit
against square
side of the
stem cap.

Outside rail beveled to
fit against the square side
of the stem cap.

Install Inside Rails. Except for the centermost frame, each frame must be beveled to receive the inside rail. The rail will lie in a fair line if the frames have been properly notched. They will lie against the side panel where it meets the stem. A tapered wedge may be cut and installed for additional support of the rail if necessary. Use your eye to be certain the rails are equally juxtaposed on the stem and stern. Use the same cut-and-fit technique as for the inside chine logs. Hold in place with clamps.

Additional rail support between frame #1 and the transom frame may be needed. A 4- to 6-inch block may be added at mid-distance. Use $1/4$-inch bolts, washers, and nuts to secure the rail at each frame. Note that the fasteners are set at 90 degrees to the panel and must therefore be offset a bit through several of the frames. Remove the excess bolt along with any sharp edges caused by the bolt cutter or hacksaw. Many builders like to replace the nuts with cap nuts. The cap nuts dress the inside rail nicely.

Inside rails —

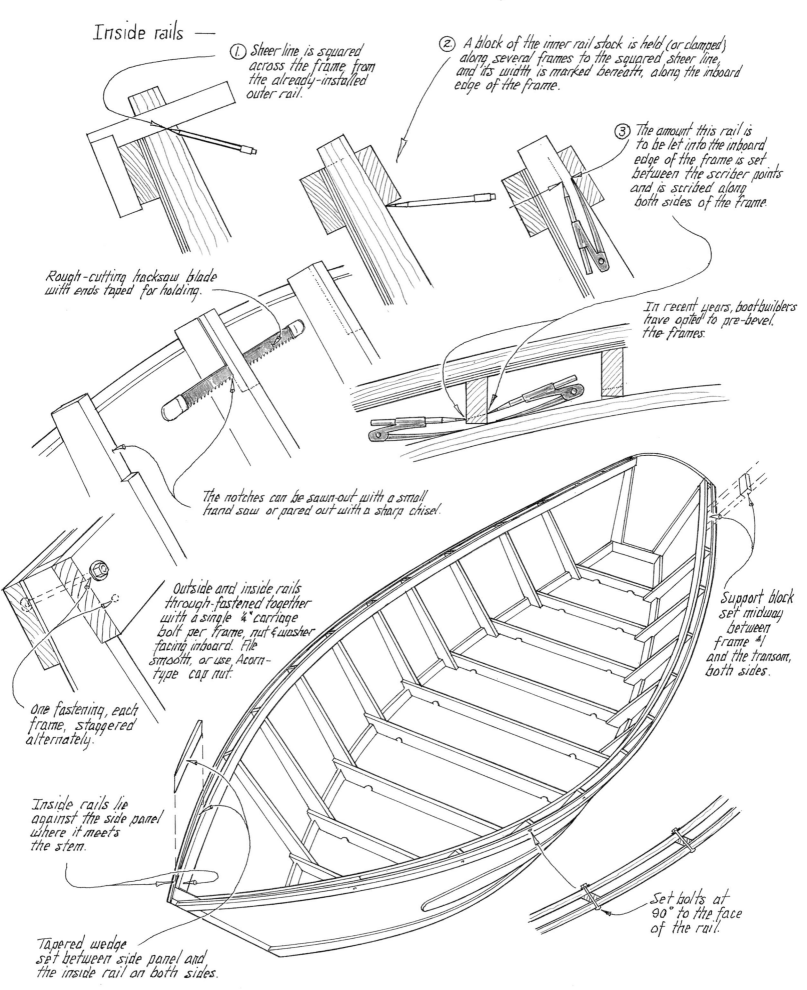

1. Sheer line is squared across the frame, from the already-installed outer rail.

2. A block of the inner rail stock is held (or clamped) along several frames to the squared sheer line, and its width is marked beneath, along the inboard edge of the frame.

3. The amount this rail is to be let into the inboard edge of the frame is set between the scriber points and is scribed along both sides of the frame.

Rough-cutting hacksaw blade with ends taped for holding.

In recent years, boatbuilders have opted to pre-bevel the frames.

The notches can be sawn-out with a small hand saw or pared out with a sharp chisel.

Outside and inside rails through-fastened together with a single ¼" carriage bolt per frame, nut & washer facing inboard. File smooth, or use Acorn-type cap nut.

One fastening, each frame, staggered alternately.

Inside rails lie against the side panel where it meets the stem.

Tapered wedge set between side panel and the inside rail on both sides.

Support block set midway between frame #1 and the transom, both sides.

Set bolts at 90° to the face of the rail.

Trimming the Excess. The excess side frames and stem may now be removed. It has become clear by now why the added length to the ribs was necessary. Carefully cut them flush with the sheer line and sand smooth. Some builders prefer to round the edges of the sheer rails inside and out with a small, round bit.

Cut and shape the stem so the natural flare of the boat is extended through the stem. It will look nice if you can do it. If unsuccessful, simply round off the top of the stem.

Next, shape the top of the transom. Woodie Hindman simply cut the excess transom square to the boat. You can modify the appearance if, as with the stem, you follow the natural flare of the boat. Study it a bit. You'll see what I mean.

Trimming tops of side frames, stem, and transom —

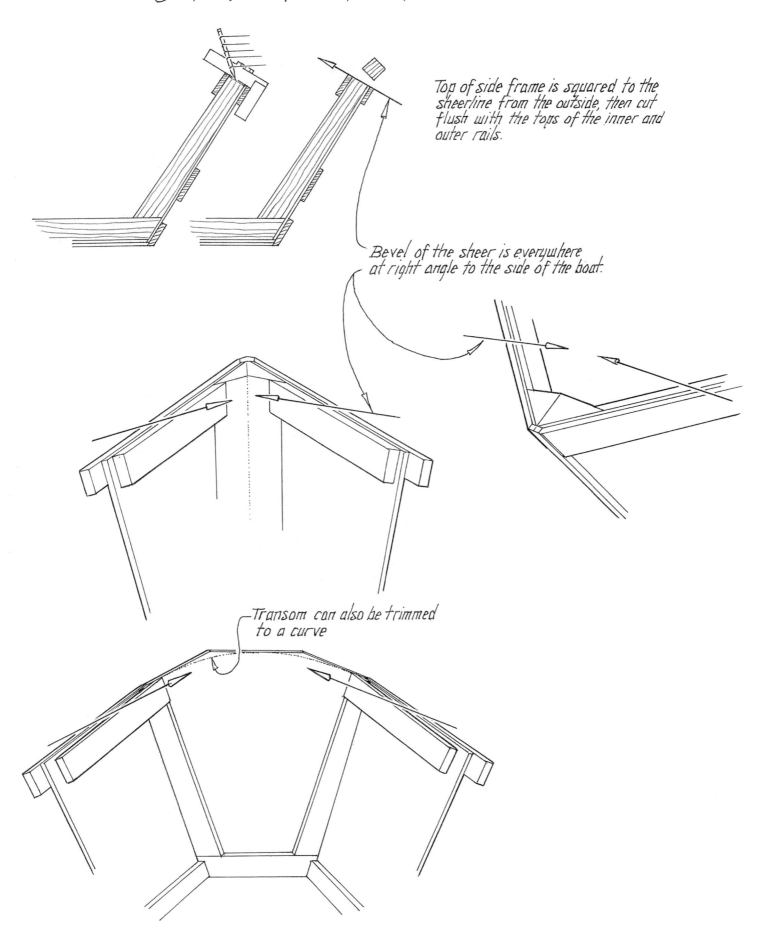

Top of side frame is squared to the sheerline from the outside, then cut flush with the tops of the inner and outer rails.

Bevel of the sheer is everywhere at right angle to the side of the boat.

Transom can also be trimmed to a curve

Interior Appointments

Each set of plans lays out the interior appointments, such as floorboards, thwarts, and fly-line deck and knee locks, if called for. One of the beauties of these boats is that the interior configurations can be adapted to the builder's personal needs and tastes. Be prepared to spend more time on completing these parts of the boat than you did the hull. Sam Manning reports that John Gardner said about a boat's interior, "It's just carpentry from here on."[7]

Floorboards

As a river runner, you will ship water. Floorboards will keep your feet dry as well as add some protection to the bottom's interior. Install the floorboards for easy removal for cleaning or refinishing the boat's floor space. The floorboards rest on the frames, not the bottom panel. Leave enough open space along the chine so that the boat may be easily bailed when necessary. The illustration portrays a configuration popular among earlier guides. The open area between frames #4 and #5 made rowing in a standing position a little more comfortable. Contemporary boatmen like more coverage of the floor, and floorboards may be slatted or solid, using $^3/_8$-inch plywood sheets cut to fit.

Fly-line Deck and Knee Locks

Use $^1/_4$- or $^3/_8$-inch marine-grade plywood for the fly-line deck. The knee locks serve a purpose: to help the fly fisher remain upright when fishing the river. Should the oarsman accidentally hit a submerged object, inertia can catapult a standing fisherman out of the boat, even in slow-moving water. The knee locks provide enough support to keep the fisherman in place.

Oar Blocks

Site the oar blocks for both comfort and leverage. If you plan to run rivers with many rapids, it may be prudent to install two sets of oar blocks—one for an extended reach and another for a more relaxed voyage. Use a good hardwood. Oar blocks should be drilled to receive a $^5/_8$-inch-diameter shaft. If you can locate them, install plastic or metal sleeves.

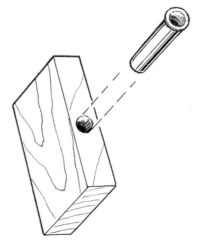

Alternatively to the standard galv. iron or bronze oarlock fitting, this ⅝"-diameter plastic oar-block sleeve reduces wear in the oar-block bore and makes for quieter rowing.

Fly line deck, floorboards, etc. —

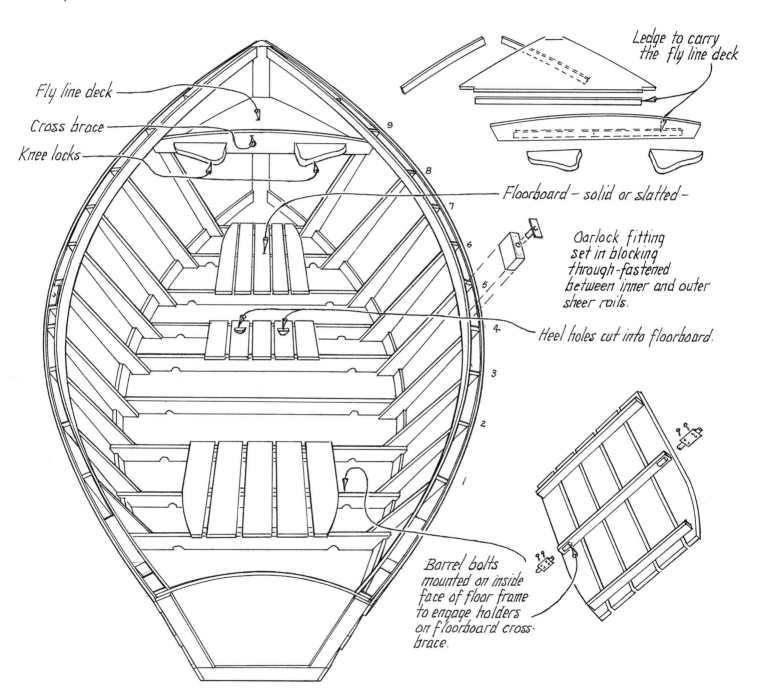

Fly line deck

Cross brace

Knee locks

Ledge to carry the fly line deck

Floorboard – solid or slatted –

Oarlock fitting set in blocking through-fastened between inner and outer sheer rails.

Heel holes cut into floorboard.

Barrel bolts mounted on inside face of floor frame to engage holders on floorboard cross-brace.

Thwarts

The guest seat in several boats is set on rails for ease of adjustment fore and aft. This allows the oarsman to trim the boat when necessary. Alternatively, many guest seats are anchored permanently to the frames, this being the easier method of installation. There are three things to remember when designing your guest seat: First, don't build it higher than the rowing seat, which would impede your downriver view when on the oars. Second, the rails should run roughly parallel to the imaginary baseline of the boat and precisely parallel to each other. Finally, angle the backrests for comfort. Generally, a 15-degree tilt toward the oarsman will work okay.

For the oarsman, it is important that the rowing seat provide a nice fit. In all cases, the rowing seat should be slightly higher than the guest seat. The oarsman must be able to view downriver. I prefer a rowing-seat elevation that allows me to slightly bend the knees while keeping a comfortable upright posture. Heavy leverage on the oars is sometimes required, so you can cut heel holds in the floorboard, form and install foot braces, or if the distance between the rowing seat and guest seat is adequate, simply brace your feet against the back frame of the guest seat.

Drain Plug

Many builders install a 1-inch drain plug on the centerline near the transom or stern post. This is a convenience for the larger boats. Install the plug flush with the underside near the chine amidships or at the centerline just fore of the transom. I dislike drain plugs and prefer to keep the boat dry using other methods.

Guest seat —

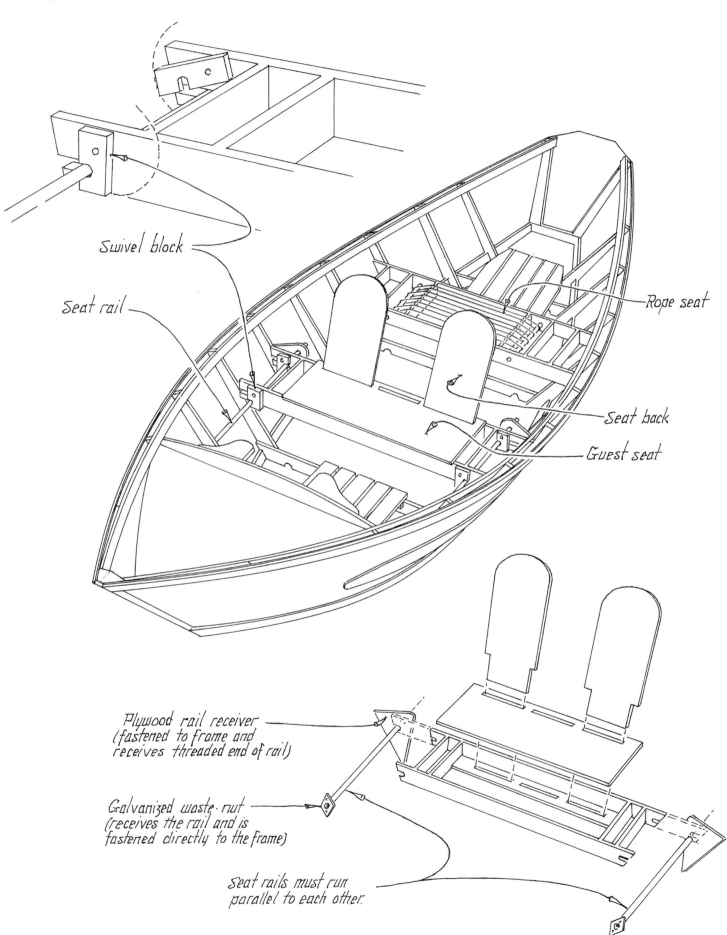

Swivel block

Seat rail

Rope seat

Seat back

Guest seat

Plywood rail receiver
(fastened to frame and
receives threaded end of rail)

Galvanized waste-nut
(receives the rail and is
fastened directly to the frame)

Seat rails must run
parallel to each other.

Rope Seat

A rope seat is called for in several of the boats. There are practical reasons for them. The rains of the Northwest have never kept fishermen off the river. Rope seats allow the rain to run off the oarsman's parka onto the floor rather than puddle under his derriere. More important, the rope is a great nonskid surface and keeps the oarsman securely planted as the boat pitches and rolls in heavy rapids. The seats are surprisingly comfortable.

Rowing thwart — rope seat —

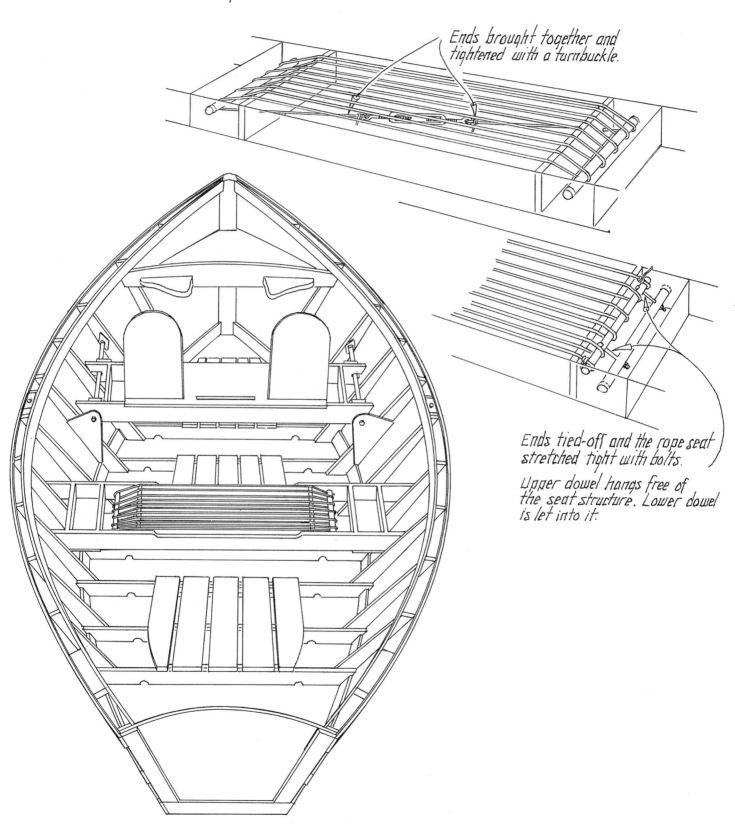

Ends brought together and tightened with a turnbuckle.

Ends tied-off and the rope seat stretched tight with bolts.

Upper dowel hangs free of the seat structure. Lower dowel is let into it.

Oars

Length of oars will vary by boat size. The McKenzie boats can handle 8- to 8^1/$_2$-foot oars comfortably. The Rogue boats will do well with 9-foot oars, and the Colorado River dory is best served with 10-footers. If you are going to the trouble of recreating one of these boats, for the sake of tradition, stick with wood oars. Oars milled from ash are excellent. They are strong, resilient, and reliable, and they flex well under stress in heavy whitewater. My preference is oars with a good weight-to-strength ratio. In other words, I like them light and strong. That's why I tend to use spruce. Whatever type of oars you use, it is prudent to carry a spare of equal quality. Oars can break or be lost in the middle of rapids.

Over time, the oars will wear without protection, and early drift boaters installed leather wraps to prevent oarlock rub. The leather was tacked to the loom using brads. The problem with this method is that moisture will seep into the loom along the brad, eventually inducing dry rot and weakening the oar, which could break at the worst possible moment. Today most drift boaters use rubberized oar stops and wrap their oar shafts with ^{3}/$_{16}$- to ^{1}/$_8$-inch nylon cord. The cord offers great protection without damage to the oar.

Oarlocks

Oarlocks are another consideration. Use bronze with a ^{5}/$_8$-inch-diameter shank. Some prefer round horned locks so that the oar cannot pop out of the oarlock in heavy water. If the oarlock is pinned or tied in place, as it should be, and the oar becomes lodged somehow in moving water, one of two things might happen: The oar might break, or the force may be enough to rip out the oar block and a portion of the side panel. This is not good, so for this reason, I prefer the open ribbed oarlock. An open horn that is secure and tamped to hold the oar shaft in the oarlock will spring under pressure and allow the oar to pop free without damage to oar or boat. If the oar is lost, it can be readily replaced with the spare oar.

Oar bindings

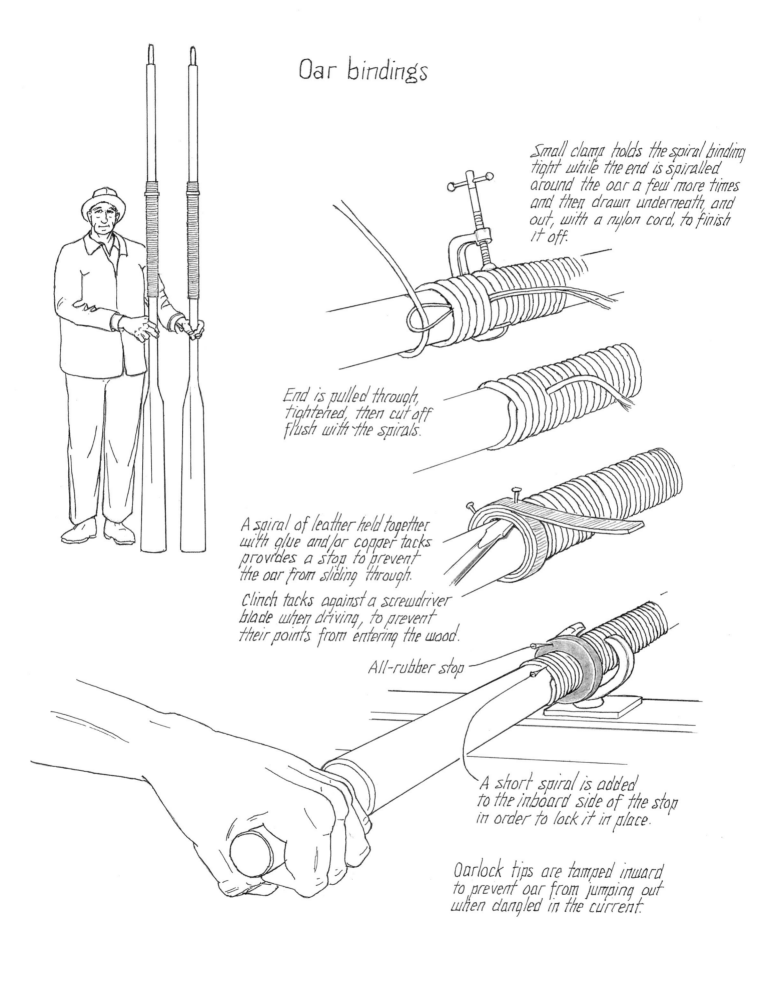

Small clamp holds the spiral binding tight while the end is spiralled around the oar a few more times and then drawn underneath, and out, with a nylon cord, to finish it off.

End is pulled through, tightened, then cut off flush with the spirals.

A spiral of leather held together with glue and/or copper tacks provides a stop to prevent the oar from sliding through.

Clinch tacks against a screwdriver blade when driving, to prevent their points from entering the wood.

All-rubber stop

A short spiral is added to the inboard side of the stop in order to lock it in place.

Oarlock tips are tamped inward to prevent oar from jumping out when dangled in the current.

Anchor

Not all boats require an anchor system. Anchors were not used in the early drift boats and rarely used with the dories. They were awkward and cumbersome. Guides preferred to use the oars to hold the boat in the current and maneuver the fisher to likely habitat. Alternatively, they might beach the boat above a fishing spot and walk down to the hole. Once the spot was fished, the oarsman would run the boat through and then proceed to the next spot. Most drift-boat fishers today employ an anchor system. They prefer an anchor that is easily and quietly released, can be recovered readily, and keeps the rope out of the way.

Danger may lurk around an anchor system. The inadvertent release of an anchor in rapids can have tragic consequences. Launching oneself out of a stable drift boat by stumbling over an anchor rope pulled taut by the strain of the boat against the current may, depending on the circumstances, be humorous or frightening. If you plan to fish a river, however, it may be necessary to secure the boat in an eddy, along the bank, or in a mild current. There are three questions to ask yourself when considering an anchoring system: Is the weight of an anchor appropriate for the boat and the current? Is it a system that is easy to handle? Does it impede or enhance movement inside the boat? Design a system that will work for you.

There you have it: a traditional free-form constructed riverboat. The boat can serve as a fine fishing platform, a whitewater runner, or simply as therapy in mitigating the stresses of life. Regardless of its intended use, there is something special about a boat—or a model—handcrafted from scratch. Nothing will thrill me more than to witness the reemergence of a few of these highly functional, practical riverboats.

Endnotes

1. There are several manufacturers and sources for epoxy, fiber, and fiberglass cloth. Visit a distributor and review the user manual to better understand the uses and application of this material.

2. Jigs for a skill saw or router may also be made to create a clear scarf joint. I prefer the freehand method.

3. Plans for the 16-foot Rapid Robert have been modified to accept a 15-foot, 9-inch panel. The McKenzie 16-foot double-enders have not. If you don't want to scarf three sheets of plywood, you may instead delay forming the transom until all the frames are installed. The transom can be formed to fit.

4. Use a good marine polyurethane sealant-adhesive on all parts, especially below the waterline. Use a marine polysulfide sealer for any part that may need future replacement, such as the chine caps, transom trim, or stem cap.

5. Number 14 $1\frac{1}{4}$-inch ring nails are a good choice.

6. The outside chine cap will accept most of the abuse on the river and may from time to time be replaced. A marine-grade polysulfide sealer will not let moisture weep into the wood, especially along the fasteners, and will allow for easy removal of the chine when necessary.

7. Sam Manning illustrated John Gardner's *The Dory Book* (Mystic, CT: Mystic Seaport Museum, 1987), a book worthy of everyone's boatbuilding library.

CHAPTER 12

Determining Material Needs

An important decision is the material you use.

Early Oregon river boatmen learned that there is a relationship between workload and boat weight. The heavier the load, the less nimble the boat, and the more one strains on the oars. They selected local material that had a good weight-to-strength ratio and weathered well: Sitka spruce, Port Orford cedar, Douglas fir, and California redwood. Hardwoods such as white oak and Oregon ash were used for the stem and stern posts, chine logs, and rails. Depending on your location, these materials may not be available. Other wood indigenous to your area may be adequate (see chapter 10 for a basic review of wood). The boats in this book may be built with 1/4-inch marine-grade plywood panels for the sides. Bottom panels will be 3/8 to 5/8 inch thick, depending on builder preferences.

Finish

Think about the boat's finish before construction begins. Most early rivermen oiled their boats. A favorite recipe with broad appeal was one part gum turpentine, one part boiled linseed oil, one-half part pine tar, and one-quarter part Japan drier. Larry Long of Brunswick, Maine, reports that this concoction has been used for years on the decks of his family's home. One northwestern builder complains that the linseed oil, whether boiled or raw, may grow mildew in a wet and cool environment. Mildew is not a problem with good commercial oils used today. One of my McKenzie boats at this writing is thirty-five years old. It has been oiled annually and is in very good condition. Many boatmen desire a boat that is easy to maintain. Clean the boat, apply the oil liberally, let it set for a few

minutes, wipe off the excess, and the boat is good to go. I like oil for ease of maintenance. I'd rather spend time on the river than in the shop messing with my boats. Excellent commercial oils are available today. The oils are generally applied after the boat has been formed.

Oil, however, is not satisfactory on all materials. If you are forced to use wood that is susceptible to decay or lacks strength, or you want a bright finished or painted boat, then you are advised to encapsulate the wood in epoxy resin. If using epoxy, apply the resin to the boat's interior parts before assembly.[1]

Plywood

Douglas fir, if you are able to locate AA or AB marine- or exterior-grade panels, offers excellent strength and durability, probably the best among plywood. The material will check, however, when exposed to the sun. Checking occurs when the top veneer loses moisture and shrinks a bit. This may cause ruptures in the fiber and create blemishes on the surface. The structural integrity of the panel isn't affected, but checking can be unsightly. One way to prevent it is to apply a 4- or 6-ounce layer of fiberglass cloth to the inside panels before the hull is formed.[2] It is not necessary to glass the other types of plywood, although epoxy resin application is suggested for some panels. If resin is used, apply three or four coats to the inside panels and other hull parts before the hull is formed. Finish on the exterior of the boat is addressed after the hull is built.

Boatbuilder Ray Heater developed a matrix to reflect his experience with four plywoods that are popular with drift-boat builders.[3]

Comparisons of Four Popular Marine-Grade ¼-Inch Plywood Panels

Listed in order of strength-to-weight value and durability

SPECIES	NUMBER OF PLIES	WEIGHT PER SHEET	FINISH OPTIONS
Douglas fir, AA or AB grade	3	23 pounds	Oil. Fir plywood will check, so you may alternatively apply 4-ounce fiberglass cloth to the inside panels.
Sapele, 1088 grade	5	24 pounds	Material will not check; oil is okay.
Red meranti, "Philippine mahogany"	5	23 pounds	Unless you are confident in the specific source and know it to be red meranti, encapsulate in epoxy. Otherwise, oil.
Okoume, 1088 grade	5	20 pounds	Should be encapsulated in epoxy.

Beginning in the mid to late 1940s, increased numbers of boats were painted. Many Oregon guides preferred to use shades of forest green so that their boats blended rather than contrasted with the surrounding environment. They were fishermen, and their goal was to catch, not frighten, their quarry. Paint or varnish applied directly to the wood is, as a general rule, no longer done with drift boats. This system is more difficult to maintain. Be prepared to spend the time and work needed to sustain your boat. Oil, paint, or varnish over an epoxy resin base, on the other hand, provides you with better service and less time on maintenance. When a boat is refinished, plan on its being out of commission for a period of time if it is varnished or painted. With oil, however, you can be back on the river in a day or two.

Estimating Your Material Needs

When you decide to build a boat, the first step is to calculate your material requirements. Only then can costs of the project be estimated with any accuracy. Estimate your material needs from the data given on the plans. Material needs may also be determined from the requirements for a scaled model, should you choose to model the boat first. Needs may be defined from the information provided in each set of plans.

Side Panels

Examine the side panel layout for the boat. Do not confuse this layout with the profile view of the boat. For most boats, two side panels will be extracted from one 4-foot-wide marine-grade plywood panel. The three exceptions are the Rogue River boats: the river driver, the classic Rogue River dory, and Briggs's Colorado River dory. Marine-grade plywood panels are typically manufactured

in 8-foot lengths. Therefore, two or more 8-foot panels will be required. (Review the technique for joining together two or more panels in chapter 11.)

Bottom Panel

All the boats will accept a 4-foot-wide bottom panel. The smallest boats may be constructed with ³/₈-inch panels. I have a preference for ¹/₂-inch. Determine the required length of the bottom panel by examining the profile view of the boat. Here again, two or more panels will be joined together to achieve the desired length.

Stem or Stern Posts

Select blank material with enough dimension to mark and cut stem. Take care to select wood that has good strength, shock resistance, and is slow to absorb water. Clear vertical grain Douglas fir, white oak or live oak, and some tropical hardwoods are good bets.

Frames

Use knot-free lumber for the boat frames and thwart frames. Clear vertical grain (CVG) fir, white cedar, Alaskan yellow cedar, and spruce may be good choices. (See chapter 10 for a primer on wood.)

Chine Logs

The chine log is the boat's keystone. This piece anchors the boat to itself. Don't skimp on quality here. White oak, Oregon ash, CVG Douglas fir, and several tropical woods are good choices. Select a material that is both water and shock resistant. If it is possible to select among plainsawed and quartersawed lumber, choose quartersawed.

Sheer Rails

These rails are also called gunwales. Two pieces run in parallel along the topsides of the side panels. Here too, CVG fir, ash, or a tropical hardwood may be used.

Fastenings

Fastenings may be galvanized, stainless steel, brass, or silicon bronze. If you want to keep the boat truly traditional and use fasteners employed by the early riverboat builders, then use only galvanized material. Brass screws were frequently applied, but I would discourage their use. Over extended periods of time, brass will corrode. Fastenings that will stand the tests of time, in addition to galvanized items, are silicon bronze and stainless steel. I prefer silicon bronze ring nails (#14, 1 to $1^1/_4$ inches long) and screws (#8 or #10, $^3/_4$ to $1^1/_2$ inches long), and stainless steel bolts ($^1/_4$ by 4 inches), washers, and nuts for the inside and outside rails. Marine fasteners such as these may be difficult to find locally, but an Internet search will yield several reliable sources.

Sealer-Adhesive

Use a good marine-grade polyurethane sealer-adhesive for all joined wood surfaces, especially those that fall below the waterline. For those boat parts that may be replaced, such as the chine cap, use a polysulfide marine sealer. The wood receives comparable levels of protection, but this sealer remains flexible over time and provides for easier removal of the part. Some excellent sealers are available. You will probably have a selection of colors. Cleaning excess sealer off the wood can be a challenge. If the sealant color complements the color of the boat, then any surplus sealer will be less noticeable. Get my drift?[4]

Bottom Protection

It did not take long for the early guides to discover the hazards of oak strips applied to the bottoms of their boats as additional protection to the boat's underside. Once confidence in the new plywood material was reached in the early 1940s, oak strips were abandoned. The builder either installed a heavier plywood bottom $^1/_2$ to $^5/_8$ thick and then replaced the bottom when necessary, or installed a $^1/_4$-inch plywood "shoe" over the bottom's underside. The shoe was fitted similarly to the bottom and fastened with $^3/_4$-inch screws around the chines and across the bottom frames. No glue or sealer was applied, though some builders dipped their fasteners in a sealing compound to prevent moisture from seeping into the wood along the screw. The false bottom was oiled on the inside face before installation, and the outside face was oiled later. The shoe was easily replaced if it became necessary to do so.

More contemporary bottom protection is fiberglass cloth and epoxy resin. Twenty to 24 ounces of triaxial cloth on the underside coupled with several coats of epoxy resin offers excellent protection. It has the advantage of easy maintenance and patching. Once the cloth is wetted in, a builder today typically will apply four to eight additional coats of epoxy resin. Graphite powder is frequently added to the last three or four coats of resin. Always consult the resin manufacturer for applications and treatment guidelines.

Forums

You may be surprised by the number of small wooden-boat builders on this globe who represent various levels of boatbuilding experience. The forums are a give and take between men and women who are professional, intermediate, and novice builders. I have found these boatbuilding forums instructive. For the most part, forum participants are engaged because they sincerely want to help and be helped. Several can be accessed through the Internet, of which I recommend two. The first is found at www.woodenboat.com, sponsored by *WoodenBoat* magazine. Few boards are left unturned, and just about every topic from restoring a boat to new construction can be located on this forum, which is dedicated to wooden-boat aficionados. The second forum is specific to drift boats. Many of the people engaged in this forum are stitch and glue builders, but a number of frame builders also participate, and there is good interaction between both interests. At this writing, Sandy Pittendrigh manages the forum, Montana River Boats in Bozeman, found at www.montana-riverboats.com. Links to these forums can also be found at www.riverstouch.com and www.montanaboatbuilders.com.

A boat built from scratch is an accomplishment to make one proud. You will be in good company.

Endnotes

1. Epoxy resin may crack along the sharp edges of the wood. I and many other boat builders round the edges before the resin is applied. A $^1/_4$-inch round bit will do the job.

2. The cloth is wetted in with epoxy resin. Two to four additional coats of resin are usually added for both protection and to mask the cloth fibers, especially if the builder plans a bright finish for the boat.

3. Ray Heater of Ray's River Dories in Portland, Oregon, has over thirty years' experience building drift boats. The table reflects his practical experiences with these wood products.

4. Sikaflex, 3M, and Boat Life offer both polyurethane and polysulfide sealer-adhesives.

PART 3

Modeling the Free-Form Way

One of the best ways to learn drift-boat building the free-form way is to model one first.

CHAPTER 13

The Free-Form Drift-Boat Model

*There's no better way to learn the intricacies
of a river dory hull than to model it.
If you can do it on a small scale,
then you can do it full-size.*

A first-time drift-boat builder may find it helpful to model the hull first. The purpose of this chapter is to walk you through the process of modeling the hull you plan to build as a precursor to building the boat full-size. The modeling method I describe follows closely the free-form construction method. Modeling can be a great confidence builder to anyone contemplating a river dory.

As in chapter 11, this section concentrates on the hull. The hull is the heart of the craft. You will have the option of completing the boat's interior based on the skills learned modeling the hull. For now, though, we concentrate on the hull.

Modeling material may be anything from heavy construction paper or poster board to tropical veneer and basswood or balsa. To learn the most from the modeling experience, use wood. If you are an experienced, serious modeler, you may choose to mill your own stock to scale. There are two great companion pieces I'd recommend to the person who wants to focus on the model: *Boat Modeling with Dynamite Payson* and *The Dory Model Book*.[1] Both are written by Harold "Dynamite" Payson. He likes to keep things simple, and his straightforward writing style is appealing because it is understandable.

For this project to be the most helpful, use scaled lumber. To replicate the natural color of the boat, mahogany sheets for the panels and basswood strips for the lumber work best. If the local craft store doesn't offer the wood, go to your favorite Internet search engine and type in "scaled lumber for miniatures." You are also welcome to contact me through www.riverstouch.com.

List of Scaled Lumber for a Drift Boat or River Dory

The table on page 179 lists the material for a boat that is built to a 1-inch scale. A modest "oops" factor is built into the list. This inventory will also be a useful tool in calculating material needs for the full-size project.

To most closely replicate the colors of the original boats, use mahogany sheets for the panels and basswood for the lumber. Order material in 24-inch lengths. You will have uses for the extra material.

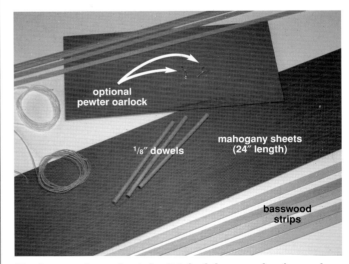

For best results, order 4-by-24-inch basswood strips and mahogany sheets.

Hull

DESCRIPTION	NUMBER OF PIECES
Mahogany side panel stock: $1/32''$ x $4''$ x $16''$	1^a
Mahogany bottom panel stock: $1/16''$ x $4''$ x $16''$	1
Mahogany transom stock: $1/16''$ x $2''$ x $3''$	1
Stem post blank basswood: $3/16''$ x $3/4''$ x $4''$	1^b
False stem blank: $3/64''$ x $1/8''$ x $4''$ basswood	1
Frames: $1/16''$ x $5/16''$ x $12''$ basswood	8
Inside chine: $1/16''$ x $3/16''$ x $18''$	2
Transom trim, inside and outside rails, and chine cap: $3/64''$ x $3/16''$ x $18''$ basswood	8
Floor slats: $1/32''$ x $5/16''$ x $12''$ basswood	5
Floor slat braces: $1/16''$ x $1/8''$ x $12''$ basswood	1
Rub rails: $1/32''$ x $5/16''$ x $9''$ basswood	2

^{a}*Two sheets are needed for the Rogue and Colorado River boats.*
^{b}*Two posts are needed for the double-ended boats.*

If you are interested in moving beyond the hull to model the interior appointments, you will also need the following materials. The Colorado River dory requires additional material for bulkhead frames, decks, and hatches, and is not included in this list.

Thwarts

DESCRIPTION	NUMBER OF PIECES
Frames: $1/16''$ x $5/16''$ x $12''$ basswood	4
Rowing thwart risers: $1/16''$ x $3/8''$ x $4''$ basswood	1
Rail receivers (ears) blank: $1/16''$ x 2 x $3''$ basswood	1
Guest seat rails and rowing seat dowels: $1/8''$ diameter x $12''$	1
Backrests for guest seat blank: $1/16''$ x $3''$ x $3''$ mahogany	1
Seat tops and tackle trays: $1/32''$ x $4''$ x $4''$ mahogany	1
Rowing seat "rope," yellow cotton string: $3'$	1

Fly-line deck

DESCRIPTION	NUMBER OF PIECES
Cross brace: $1/16''$ x $1/2''$ x $5''$ mahogany	1
Strip wood to support deck on cross brace: $3/64''$ x $1/8''$ x $4''$ basswood	1
Knee lock blank: $3/16''$ x $3/4''$ x $2''$ basswood	1
Fly-line deck blank: $1/32''$ x $4''$ x $4''$	1

Oars

DESCRIPTION	NUMBER OF PIECES
Oar blocks: $1/8''$ x $3/4''$ x $2''$ basswood	1
Oar blank for optional handcrafted oar: $5/16''$ x $3/4''$ x $9''$ basswood	2
Optional scaled oar locks: pewter	2
Optional oar shaft wrap: white cord (cotton string), $3'$	1

Stand

A stand for the model may be crafted from wood or Plexiglas. The base should be $3/16''$ x $1^1/2''$ x $6''$, with two uprights that measure $3/16''$ x $1^5/8''$ x $3''$. The uprights are sited one-inch from the ends of the base.

Most of the tools needed to model the hull are items you may already have in the house, garage, or shop. These are the instruments I use. To successfully model the boat, learn to use the architect's rule at the 1-inch scale. The only fastening required is the CA glue.

List of Suggested Modeling Tools

Architect's rule. This instrument is easy to use, and it is essential to lofting the frame lines and side panels to scale.

Hand-held magnifier for marking points using the architect's rule (especially for those whose sight has dimmed a bit).

A $15''$ x $18''$ piece of corkboard, $3/16''$ or $1/4''$ foam board, or heavy cardboard. This material is used to pin and hold the frames and thwart pieces in place.

Craft pins to assist in holding material in place.

Clothespins, spring-loaded. As you need some clamps for the full-size boat, so too clamps will be useful with the model.

Razor saw for trimming and cutting material.

X-acto knife with a pair of new blades for whittling and cutting material to specification.

Number 2 sharp pencil for laying down lines and marking material.

Metal straightedge for scribing lines or cutting edges.

Assorted sanding paper (80- to 120-grit) and an emery board. Cut $3''$ x $6''$ board and glue 80-grit sandpaper to the underside. It will make a great sanding board for the frames and other uses.

One-inch masking tape for temporarily securing pieces.

A $1/8''$ round file for limber holes. Alternatively, cut $1/8''$ square notches in frames.

(continued)

Assorted Tools

Optional ⁵/₆₄″ drill bit for oarlock shaft in oar blocks.

Tweezers, to replace fingers where needed.

Optional small wood vise for hands-free cutting of frames.

Optional modeler's block plane. The X-acto knife, carefully applied, will achieve the same results.

Cyanoacrylate (CA) glue: ¹/₂-ounce bottles each of thin and gap-filling.

Optional accelerator for the CA glue. The CA usually sets up within a minute or two, but the accelerator provides an instant response.

Waxed paper to cover your work area when gluing the frames. You don't want to glue the frames to the foam board!

Cloth dust mask. Hand-sanding the parts creates enough dust that some respiratory protection is advised.

Safety in the shop is always a priority. So, too, is safety around the modeling area. Pay special attention to glue and sharp tools. If there are small children in the household, take care to keep the materials and tools out of reach.

Let's get started on the hull.

Side Panels

Use the ¹/₃₂-inch mahogany sheet. Except for the Rogue and Colorado River boats, one 4-by-16-inch sheet will do for two side panels. Excess material may be used for tackle trays and fly-line deck. A 16-foot side panel translates to 16 inches for the model. Two side panels will be extracted from one piece for the McKenzies. Mark and cut the panel to the desired length.

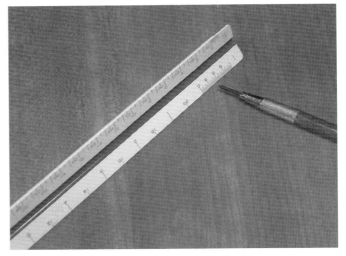

Architect's rule. Use the 1-inch scale, where 1 inch equals 1 foot. The first foot is calibrated into twelve equal parts, or inches. The first inch on the ruler is divided equally into four parts: quarter, half, three-quarter, and full inch. If, for example, the plans show a measurement of ³/₈ inch, then mark the point between the ¹/₄ and ¹/₂ inch marks on the ruler.

Use the plan's side panel layout to mark and draw the panel to scale. It is best to create a template on a piece of poster board or heavy paper with a sharp pencil. Double-check your work for accuracy. Use a piece of strip wood set on edge as a batten to connect the points on those boats that have a curved sheer or chine line. Otherwise, use a straightedge. Once the perimeter and station lines are established, carefully cut out the side panel template so the lines remain on the excess material. Pencil lines cause a model to grow. An X-acto knife plied carefully works well.

Resize the ¹/₃₂-inch mahogany sheets to 16-inch lengths (the section on the right) for the McKenzie boats. The excess may be used for other parts, such as the fly-line deck and tackle trays.

Use the first panel as a template for the second. Make pencil tick marks on the sheer and chine line edges for each station line. Use the first side panel to mark the perimeter of the second panel, and then cut the second panel. Compare the two panels to ensure they match. If one of the panels is slightly off the mark, modify the offending panel with the sanding board. Mark the station lines on the second panel to match those of the first. Establish or reestablish tick marks on the panels' edges atop and at the bottom of each station line. Your panels are now ready. Set them aside.

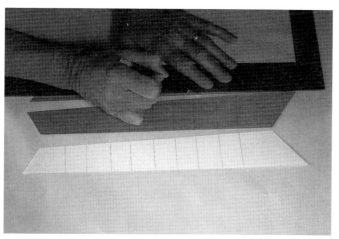

Transfer the lines from the cardboard or paper side panel template onto the ¹/₃₂-inch mahogany sheet. Most panels cut to 16 inches will yield two sides. Place the template to ensure that you will get two sides wherever possible. Use an X-acto knife and metal straightedge. Make the cross-grain cuts first (prow and stern), and then cut the sheer line.

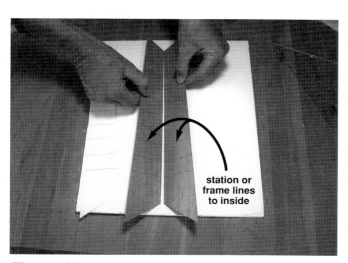

The two side panels match in every respect, including the frame lines. The station lines will guide you in placement of the frames.

Stem Post

Study the plans and note the bevel angle of the stem post. If you have a band or scroll saw, the job of cutting the bevels is simplified. Unless you are skilled at crafting a jig to hold the material, don't use a table saw. Use ³/₁₆-by-³/₄-by-4-inch basswood.

Alternatively, you may hand-carve the stem post. To accomplish this, mark a centerline the length of the stem blank, and repeat the line on the opposite side. Scribe two parallel lines that are an equal distance from the centerline. See the stem cross section in the plans to obtain the stem angle and measurements. Use the X-acto knife or other carving tool to handcraft the stem blank to the lines. A sanding board will be useful to fair the stem bevels if necessary. Be very careful with the blade, working the tool away from you.

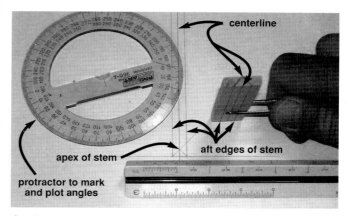

Study the stem's cross-section plans. Plot the measurements to scale as shown. If the apex of the angle is less than ³/₁₆ inch, sand the ³/₁₆-by-³/₄-by-4-inch stem blank to the desired thickness. If the apex is ³/₁₆ inch, leave the blank as shown; if greater, scribe two lines, one on each side of the centerline.

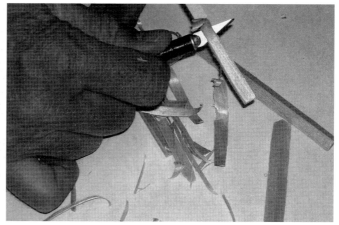

Hand-carve the stem blank to the lines. Basswood handles nicely. The flat edge of the knife helps keep the beveled surface flat. Use a sanding board to smooth the bevels if necessary. The result is your stem or stern post.

Transom

In free-form construction, some builders prefer to form the transom after the hull's frames and stem are installed to the side panels. This is one way to double-check measurements and angles before forming the transom. For the model, however, it is best to form the transom now.

Study the plans and determine the size of the transom blank needed to craft the piece to scale. Use $^1/_{16}$-inch mahogany. On the model, the greatest strength of the mahogany is achieved when the wood grain runs vertically up the transom. Mark the sides of the transom as measured from the centerline. The centerline must be perpendicular to the transom's baseline. Extend the transom's sides line a scaled inch beyond the sheer line. Once the hull is formed, the transom top may be shaped to suit you.

The transom's sides and bottom will receive an under-bevel. The outline established on the transom blank is the inside measurement. The bevels each fall away from those lines. Study the half-breadth view of the plans to visualize the direction of the bevels. The same technique for calculating the stem bevel may be used in determining the transom bevels. Again, absent a scroll or band saw, carefully carve to the lines with your knife and finish them with your sanding board. Try to keep the edges crisp and sharp.

Once the transom is beveled, form the transom frames. Use the same pattern as for the frames with $^1/_{16}$-by-$^5/_{16}$-inch frame material. On the model, a trick I use is to glue the three frame pieces (bottom frame first) with enough overhang that the bevels may be sanded or cut to match the transom's bevels. Set the transom aside.

If you do not have a scroll or band saw, use a metal straight-edge and X-acto knife to remove the transom from the blank. Make several passes with the knife to achieve the cut.

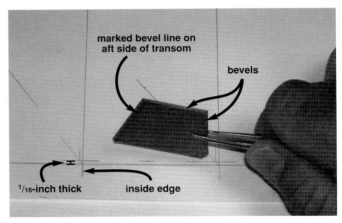

Establish and mark the transom bevels in a manner similar to the stem. With the sanding board or X-acto knife, establish the bevels for the sides and the bottom. The transom's lines are inside measurements to the panel, and the bevels fall away from those lines.

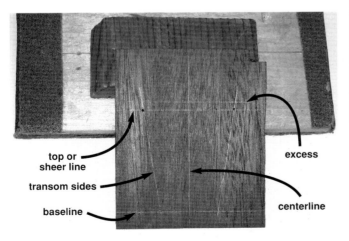

Mark and scribe lines on the transom blank. The centerline must be perpendicular to the base and top lines of the transom. Extend the sides' lines 1 or 2 scale inches beyond the sheer line. This excess will be removed after the hull is formed.

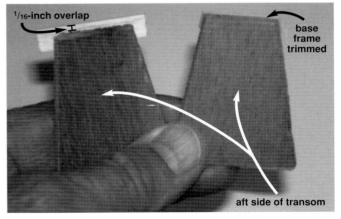

Most transoms require an inside frame. For the model, it will be easier to complete the bevel for each frame after it is glued to the transom. Lap the frames slightly beyond the edges so that the bevels may be cut after they are in place.

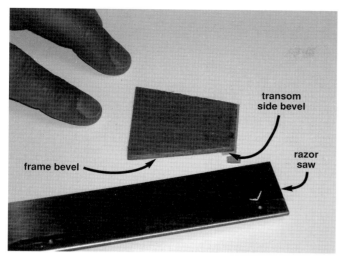

To cut the frame bevels, hold the razor saw flush to the transom bevel. Alternatively, you can use your X-acto knife to make the cuts. Refine the cuts with a sanding board.

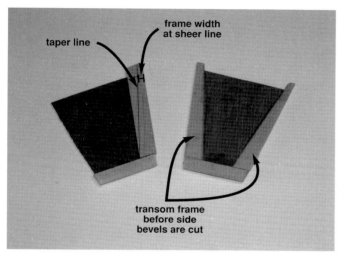

Side frames require taper cuts before you glue them in place. Determine the width of frame at the top, or sheer, line; establish the taper line; and then sand, saw, or whittle the frame to the line. Glue as shown, with enough overlap to accept the bevel once the bond is secure.

Attach Panels to Stem Post

Locate the side panels and stem post. To avoid making an error, mark the sides of the stem post that are to receive the side panels. Align the first panel to the stem so the inside leading edge of the panel is matched to the leading edge of the stem post. There should be excess stem above the sheer and below the chine. Use a clothespin or two to hold the stem in place. Run a bead of thin CA along the inside joint.

Attach the first panel to the stem post with the frame lines to the inside of the boat. Align the leading edge of the panel to the leading edge of the stem blank. Use clothespins to clamp the pieces in place. Run a bead of thin cyanoacrylate (CA) glue down the seam.

Align the Second Panel to the Stem

Both hands are needed for this one. Align the second panel so it is juxtaposed to match the position of the first panel. Are the station lines to the inside? The critical alignments are the bottoms of the panels and the leading edge of the panel to the leading edge of the stem. Do not overlap the leading edges of the panels. If the tops of the panels don't line up exactly, don't worry—you can sand

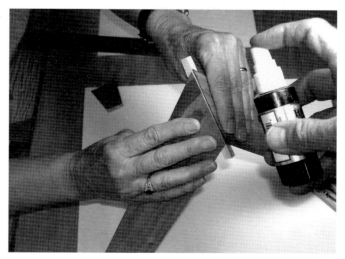

For the second panel, use thicker CA. Spread it on the stem blank with a flat toothpick or scrap piece of fiber. Adjust the second panel to the stem post's leading edge so the second panel is juxtaposed to the first. The most important alignment is at the bottom. Hold the panel in place for a couple minutes, or have a second set of hands give the joint a shot of accelerator.

them to match later. Use gap-filling CA for the second panel. Apply it to the stem post. This will provide more time to adjust the panel to the stem without lousing up your fingers with the adhesive. When the panel is in place, hold it for a couple of minutes, until the bond is secure, or have a second set of hands give it a shot of accelerator so it will bond more quickly. The panels are now attached to the stem post, and the station lines are to the inside of the boat. Set the partially formed hull aside.

Frames

The frames give the boat its distinctive shape. Your frame material is the $^1/_{16}$-by-$^5/_{16}$-inch basswood strips. To complete the frames, you will need white paper, an architect's rule, a sharp number 2 pencil, half a dozen craft pins, a corkboard or foam board surface on which to lay out the frames, clear waxed paper to lay over your lofted frames lines, a razor saw, a sanding board (80- or 100-grit paper will work nicely), and thick CA glue. The frames require several steps.

Lofting the Frames

To model this boat, each set of frame lines must be laid out to scale on paper. Study the frames' lines in the plans. Note that the half-breadth measurements are provided for each frame from the centerline of the boat along the base line to the chine and again at the sheer, or top line, of the boat at that point. The lines are to the inside of the panel. Also provided is the elevation at each frame, the vertical distance from the baseline of the frame to the sheer line. These three measurements, drawn to scale, create the template for each frame. For the model, disregard for the time being the standing bevels and underbevels needed to receive the panels. Unlike when building the full-size boat, the bevels will be added immediately before they are installed.

Forming the Frames

You may craft all the frames before they are installed to the hull. I prefer to craft each one prior to each installation. This allows me to catch a mistake sooner. Use a sharp pencil, and keep it sharp. Begin with the centermost frame. It is the first to be installed.

Use the $^1/_{16}$-by-$^5/_{16}$-inch material. Place the lofted lines on your corkboard or foam board, and cover with waxed paper. The waxed paper will prevent the frame from bonding to the board's surface if there is any glue spillage. Cut a length of material, and align it with the bottom frame line. Place a piece of frame material so that the bottom of the material is aligned with the horizontal line of frame #5 on the template. Mark the corners with about $^1/_{16}$-inch excess beyond the line of the side frame, and cut with a razor saw. Carefully realign the bottom of this piece of the frame to the template. Use six craft pins to bracket and hold the piece in place.

Form each side frame next. Cut two lengths that extend above and below the sheer line and baseline. Mark the sheer line and baseline per the template. Use a spacer to keep the frame on the same plane. Measure and mark the taper of the frame. Once the taper cut is complete, use gap-filling CA to bond the pieces. Note that the side frames should extend beyond the sheer line a scaled inch or two and lie true to the template lines. Give the CA a couple of minutes to set up.

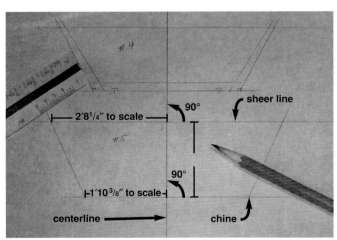

Frame #5 is the centermost frame on the McKenzie double-ender with a transom. The frame's centerline is perpendicular to its baseline. Mark the elevation of the frame—the boat's profile at that point—and establish a line parallel to the baseline. Use the half-breadth measurements to mark points on the baseline and sheer line, and connect these points. Extend the lines of the side frames a couple scaled inches beyond the sheer line.

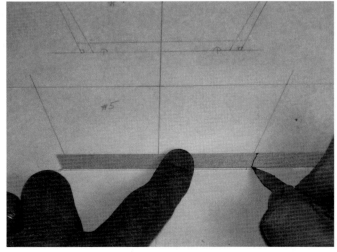

Lay the bottom frame material to the frame's bottom line. Mark the ends at the angles of the side frames about $^1/_{16}$ inch beyond the chine line. Cut with a razor saw or other tool.

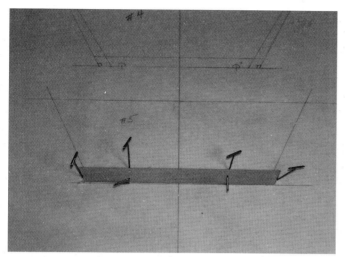

Pin the bottom frame to the foam or corkboard. Alternatively, you can tape the piece in place, but I find the pins to be more convenient. Double-check the alignment. Cover the lines with wax paper to protect them from glue spills.

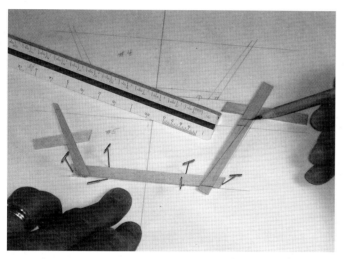

Lay the side frame material over the bottom frame and a spacer, and align the material with the side frame line. Mark the inside taper line, and then cut or sand it. Realign and glue the side frame in place. The thick CA works best here. Simply daub the glue on the joint and hold in place until bond is secure.

Beveling the Frames

Frame bevels are usually cut before assembly on the full-size boat, or they may be crafted after assembly with a hand plane. For the model, the bevels will be made after assembly using the sanding board. Align the upright frame to the station on the half-breadth line drawing at the chine. This will allow you to approximate the bevel needed to fit comfortably against the side panels when it is installed. The centermost frame requires very little or no bevel. An underbevel on the bottom frame is unnecessary now. It will be done after all frames are installed.

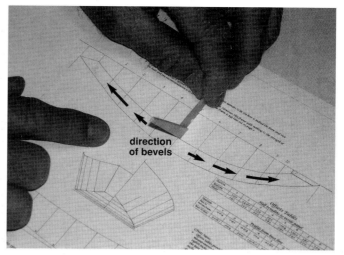

Estimate the bevels. Place the frame upright on the half breadth to estimate the bevel. This is a boat, not an airplane, and your best estimate will work fine.

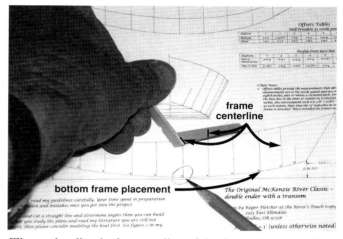

The station line is the centerline of the frame. You therefore need to know on which side of the station lines the bottom frame sits when sanding the bevel. In this drawing, the placement of the bottom frame is designated by an X.

When sanding bevels, support the side frame and bottom frame in your off hand, and use the sanding board to create the bevel.

Marking and Cutting Limber Holes

Mark and create the limber holes, openings that allow water to pass back and forth through the bottom frames should some river find its way onto the boat.

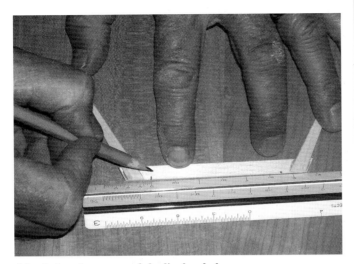

Mark the placement of the limber holes.

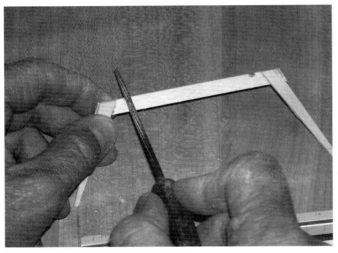

Use a $^1/_8$-inch-diameter round file to craft the notches or cut square notches.

Marking and Cutting Chine Notches

Finally, mark and cut the chine notches. The illustration shows a notch that will accept a beveled chine. The chine is usually beveled so the top of the chine sits roughly parallel to the floor. Water will not collect atop the notch and be trapped next to the panel. If you choose not to bevel the chine, then mark and cut the chine notch so the top line is perpendicular to the outside line of the side frame.

Use these same procedures for each frame.

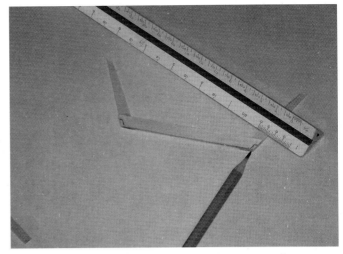

Mark the chine notch, using the dimensions to scale as shown on the plans.

Take into account the bevel, and trust your eye when making the cuts. Make the vertical cut first and then the horizontal. Remove the notch waste. The completed frame is ready to be installed.

Installing the Transom

Dry-install the boat's centermost frame to the side panels. In doing the full-size boat, you are advised to use several frames. Clamp the frame to the appropriate station line on the first panel. Alignment to the station line doesn't need to be precise yet. Pull in the second panel, and clamp the frame in place. With the frame reasonably secure, adjust it so the centerline of the frame is aligned to the station line. Leave it clamped; do not glue.

Locate the transom and study the placement of the transom to the first side panel. Once you have it clear in your mind, apply the thicker CA to the transom side and affix it to the panel. Hold the transom in place until the bond is secure, or give it a shot of accelerator. A clamping system will work when you build the full-size boat. Here, use your hands.

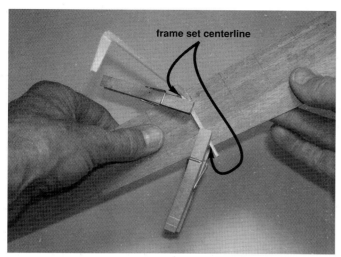

To complete the formation of the hull, dry-fit the centermost frame to the appropriate station line on one of the side panels. Mind the direction of the standing bevel and the position of the bottom frame. See the plans. Clamp in place with two clothespins.

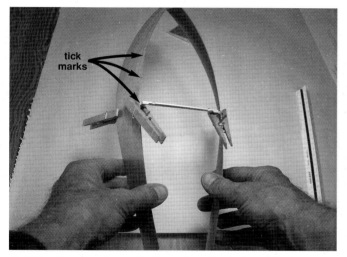

Pull in the second panel, align the other half of the frame to the appropriate station line, and clamp in place. Adjust the frame so that the side frame lines run along the side frame and through the joint of the bottom frame. Use the tick marks you placed at the top of each station line as guides for adjusting the bottom frame. Clamp in place.

I use my lap to apply just enough pressure to bring the panels together for the final attachment of the transom. Daub some thicker CA onto the transom side, align the pieces, and hold them in place until they are secure, or have a second pair of hands give the joint a shot of accelerator. The basic shape of the hull is achieved.

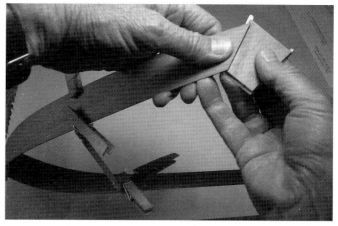

Locate the transom—or stern post—and orient it to the first side. Apply thicker CA to the transom side to be installed. Align the transom to the corner of the side panel. The standing edge of the panel is flush with the aft side of the transom piece. The top of the transom extends beyond the sheer of the side panel. This excess will be removed after the hull is complete. Note the alignment of the underbevel to the panel's chine.

Attach the second side of the transom to the remaining side panel. Apply the thicker CA to the transom edge. Place the boat stem on a surface, and gently align the transom and hold it in place. Take care with the alignment. (Accelerator may be applied to speed the cure time).

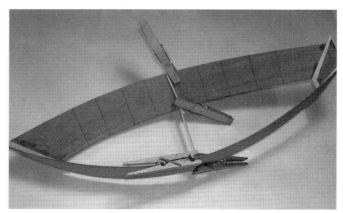

The basic hull is ready for installation of the frames.

Installing the Frames

The frames give the hull its shape. It is now time to complete the frame installation. Use the thin CA after alignments have been confirmed and you are ready to lock everything in place.

The model doesn't provide enough dimensions to apply fasteners. You are dependent on the CA. Application of the thin CA may take a little practice. Not much, but a little. The key is to let a small amount of glue run the length of the seam between the side frame and the panel. It is easy to overapply the material. If you find that the frame was a misfit after applying the glue, carefully separate the frame from the panel with the X-acto blade, sand, and reinstall the frame correctly.

Install the remaining frames, alternating each frame fore and aft of the center frame. This protocol will allow you to spot any mistakes sooner rather than later. You want to be sure the chine and sheer lines are running fair. If you run into an anomaly, adjust the frame, check it against your template, or double-check your template against the plans.

At some point after the frames are in and before the chine logs are fitted, cut the base of the stem flush with the boat's bottom line. The razor saw will work. This step is unnecessary in the full-size boat, but the absence of the excess stem will make the placement of the chine against the stem a bit easier.

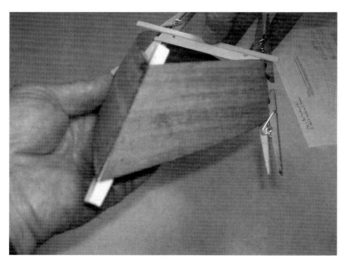

Prepare to install the centermost frame. Use a straight batten to assist with the bottom alignment. Reestablish proper alignment of the frame and then clamp. Now fine-tune the alignment. Since the bottom frame was not beveled, expose enough underside meat so that the frame may be beveled once all the frames are in. Double-check to see that the frame's centerline is aligned to the station line on the panel. Tweak as necessary.

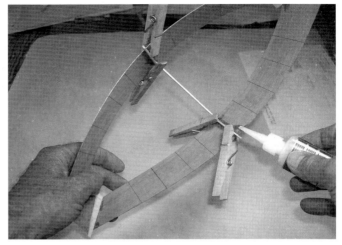

When the frame's alignment is set, apply a bead of thin CA along the seam of each side frame. Don't overdo on the glue, which will run.

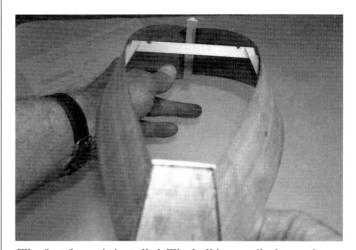

The first frame is installed. The hull is very limber and may appear to be out of square. I have straightened this one for the photo by slightly twisting the transom end while holding the stem end steady.

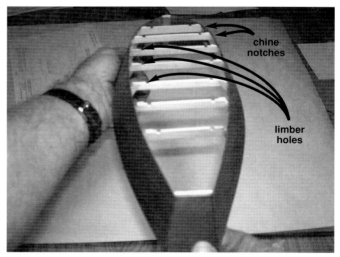

Install the remaining frames fore and aft of the center frame until all are in. The chine notches show a bevel that parallels the panel, and the limber holes show symmetry along the bottom.

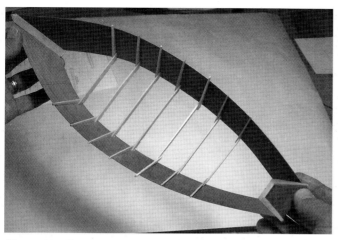

Two more frames to go.

After the frames are in, and before work begins on the chine logs, remove the excess stem on the underside of the boat. Cut the stem flush with the razor saw while holding the bow flush to the cutting surface. It's not necessary to do this now on the full-size boat, but its removal from the model will make siting the chine at the stem a little easier.

Chine Logs

The two chines are the boat's keystones. The chines receive the fasteners for the bottom panel. The side panel is similarly secured at the chine. The chine log fits into the frames' chine notches and snugly against the stem and stern pieces. Study the Sam Manning drawings in chapter 11 that relate to fitting and installing the chine logs. We describe the use of a limber measuring stick to transfer measurements to the chine log. For the model, these "limber sticks" are the chine pieces.

The two chine logs should be 16 to 18 inches long. If they are not beveled per the plans, then their orientation to the boat doesn't matter. Beveled chines, however, are oriented so that topside of the bevels are parallel to the floor of the boat.

I have beveled $^{1}/_{16}$-by-$^{5}/_{16}$-by-18-inch basswood strips (right) to serve as this model's chine log. This is a more difficult piece to bevel, so if you are limited on skill and tools, use $^{3}/_{64}$-by-$^{3}/_{16}$-by-18-inch basswood strips without the bevel (left). The purpose here is to learn how to fit and install the chines.

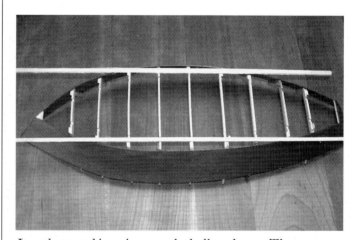

Lay the two chine pieces on the hull as shown. These are 18-inch lengths. If you have beveled them, you want to make sure they are oriented correctly. I beveled the top and bottom of the chine so that they are parallel.

Align the chine with the outside panel to verify its orientation. If the chine is not beveled, then it doesn't matter which side chine is installed on which side.

Fit the chine to the stem end of the boat. Leave some of the chine exposed beyond the bottom line of the boat. You will sand this excess off later to ensure a flat surface for the bottom panel. Mark the angles for the stem fit. This can be done freehand. Once the angles are marked, remove the chine and cut it to the angles. My preferred tool here is the X-acto knife with a sharp blade. It makes a nice clean cut, and the cut can be easily modified when necessary. The chine end at the stem should fit snugly.

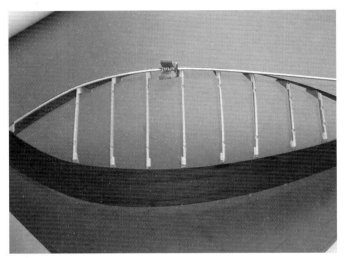

Heel the chine into the chine notches, and abut the piece against the stem post. Align it so that some surplus is exposed above the side panel. Clamp the chine in place, and then turn the hull right side up in order to mark and cut the piece.

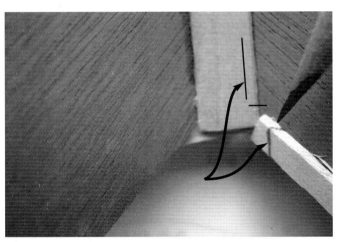

Mark the compound bevel lines as indicated. The top line parallels the face of the stem, and the second line mimics the stem's upward angle. The space is too tight to spile these angles with a compass, as demonstrated in chapter 11, but you can do it with your eye and hand. It may take a couple of tries, but you'll get it.

Remove the chine, and cut the piece as you have marked the angles. The razor saw would work, but I prefer my sharp X-acto knife, which makes a clean cut. Refit the chine to the stem, and modify the cut if necessary.

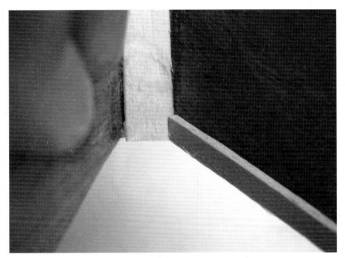

The chine should fit snugly to the panel and base of the stem post. If the bottom of the chine is beveled, it must be flush to the panel or some surplus chine must be exposed.

Use the following for the model only. Refit the chine to the stem end, and insert it into the chine notches. The rocker of the boat will allow this without conflict at the transom end. Double-check the fit. Mark the chine at the midsection of frame #4 or #5. Remove and cut the chine log at the mark. Install the first half of the chine, and then repeat the procedure for the second half of the chine log. The two chine log pieces will join at the midsection of frame #4 or #5, thus hiding the cut joint. Do not do this for the full-size boat. The technique I describe here is for the models only.[2]

Don't overdo the glue. You'll notice that I was a little sloppy on the chine application. This is no problem if you wipe off the excess before it cures. It is best to apply the glue as shown, though you may prefer to flip the model over and apply the CA to the inside. Modeler's choice.

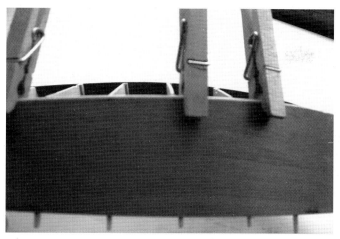

With the 16- to 18-inch chine in place at the stem, fit it to the chine notches through the boat's midsection. Leave a bit of chine exposed above the bottom line.

At frame #4 or #5, mark the chine at the midsection of the frame. Now cut the chine at the mark, and refit it against the stem and into the notches.

Use the thin CA to glue the stem end of the chine in place. If you get a little sloppy with the CA, wipe the excess off quickly with a paper towel. Let the chine set for a couple of minutes.

Take the other half of the chine and fit it to the transom, using the same technique as for the stem fit.

Once you are satisfied with the fit, carefully measure and cut the remainder of the chine on the other end so that it abuts the first piece. The chine is cut and fit so that the frame will hide this joint after the bottom is installed.

Repeat the procedure for the second chine. The installed chines are balanced and juxtaposed to each other. When setting the second chine, use your eye to estimate this balance before gluing. Note the left chine is a tad bit lower than the right. I had to do this to ensure there is some excess chine on the underside.

Note the equal juxtaposition of chines on the stem. That's it for the chines.

Prepare Hull for Bottom Panel

The next step is to prepare the hull for the bottom panel. The side panel, chine log, stem post, transom, and frames should all provide a uniform surface to receive the bottom panel. A hand plane, a straightedge that will span the boat amidships, and a sanding board are recommended for the full-size boat. For the model, simply use a flat sanding board with 80- or 100-grit paper. The board is simple to make, and the paper can be secured to the board with the CA.

This sanding procedure will create some dust, so take care to protect yourself with a dust mask. Regularly check your progress, and adjust sanding pressure where needed. The bottom panel will lie flush to the chine, transom, stem, and frame surfaces.

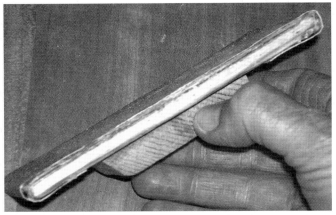

Now you will use the sanding board to prepare the under-hull for the bottom panel. The sanding board is a 3-by-6-inch piece of ¼-inch plywood. I have fashioned and glued on a small grasp piece for the topside. Use thicker CA to glue 80- or 100-grit sandpaper to the board.

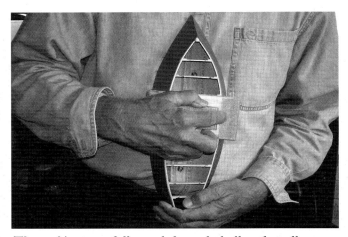

The goal is to carefully sand the underhull so that all surfaces are flat in relation to each other. The sanding board spans the boat bottom while you use up-and-down strokes to remove the surplus chine, stem, and bottom frames.

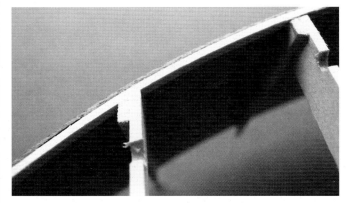

Note that sanding has beveled the frames' undersides. If any of the frame is loosened by the sanding procedure, simply reglue it in place. Your job is done when all surfaces are uniform and the bottom panel lies flat to the underhull. The bottom frames of the full-size boat, though, are beveled when built.

Rub Rails

In chapter 11, I offer the builder a choice of installing rub rails before or after the bottom goes on. The McKenzie double-ender with a transom calls for rub rails, so we'll take care of them now. The plans call for 9-foot rub rails, so the scaled model rails will be 9 inches long. Use the 1/32-by-5/16-inch basswood strips. The eye of the builder shapes the pieces, and each rub rail is positioned similarly on each side panel.

Apply thin CA to the underside of the rub rail. Because of the bend of the panel, the ends may take a little extra glue. If you have trouble, daub some thicker CA on the underside of the rail's ends, and hold in place with the end of the knife or some object with a small surface.

The next step is to make rub rails from two 9-inch pieces of 1/32-by-5/16-inch basswood strips. With an artistic eye or precise measurements, mark and fashion the ends of each rub rail as shown. Use a sanding board or an X-acto knife to trim ends. Quarter-inch plywood is a good choice for the full-size boat.

The finished rails will be evenly balanced in appearance as you rotate the boat and examine it from different angles.

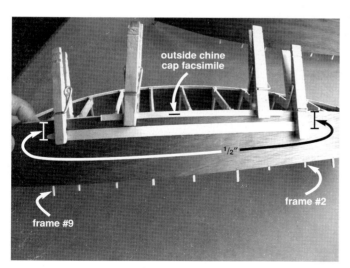

outside chine cap facsimile

1/2"

frame #2

frame #9

The rail is placed at the leading edge of frame #9 in this boat, and the aft edge trails off past frame #2 toward #1. Position the rails so that the centerline of each sits 1/2 inch above the chine line. Use clamps to hold the piece in place, and adjust as necessary. The temporary piece clamped along the bottom is the material to use for the outside chine cap and allows you to evaluate the spacing between the chine cap and the rub rail.

Prepare and Install Bottom Panel

Before the bottom panel is installed, check the limber hull for squareness. Some people can do this by eye. I prefer to check the hull against a taut string that spans the centerline of the boat. It is rare that a limber hull doesn't require some attention. When you are satisfied with the alignment, a rubber band can hold the boat square, or as with the full-size boat, a batten may be set.

The hull is very limber, which will be the case with the large boat too. The next step is to square the hull and secure it. Make a pencil mark at the dead center of each frame, transom, and stem. Run a taut string down the center, and lightly twist the hull until all center marks are aligned with the string. You can also mark a straight line on paper and visually align the boat, upside down, with your marks. Once you have achieved the proper alignment, the trick is to hold the hull in place.

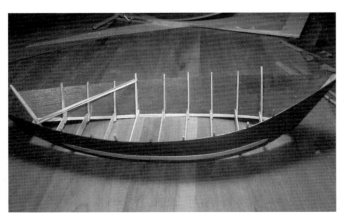

I use a rubber band to hold the hull in position. It may take two or three different-size bands to do the job. Alternatively, you can run a small batten cut and fit diagonally to the frames. As you go through the next steps to prepare and attach the bottom panel, double-check that the hull remains in the proper position.

Use $1/16$-inch mahogany for the bottom panel. Outline the panel as shown, then cut it using an X-acto knife, scroll, saw, or band saw. Place the panel so it is flush to the underside of the hull and there is "excess material" around the perimeter. Use masking or painter's tape to secure the panel in place. When you are satisfied with the alignment, apply the CA glue.

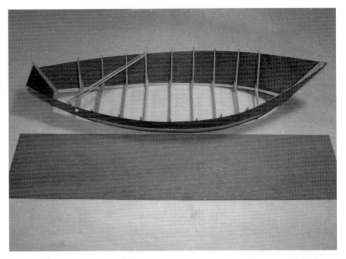

The bottom panel is $1/16$-inch mahogany, 4 inches wide by 16 inches long.

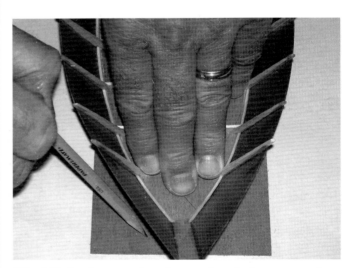

The full-size boat requires that you lay the bottom panel over the underhull. Here you'll turn the boat over with one hand and carefully mark the perimeter, allowing about $1/8$ to $1/4$ inch surplus around the chine. Make sure the boat alignment amidships falls within the width of the blank. Rock the boat fore to aft as you scribe the line.

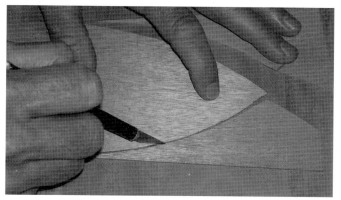

Remove the roughly scribed bottom panel from the 4-by-16-inch piece. Draw and redraw the X-acto knife over the lines several times to cut the piece, or use a scroll saw.

Use masking or painter's tape to temporarily secure the bottom panel to the hull. Double-check the bottom alignment to ensure that there is surplus panel around the entire perimeter.

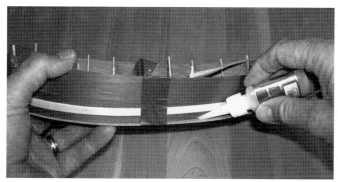

Run a bead of thin CA along the seam as shown, moving successively from the boat's midsection to the stern and then the stem. Apply pressure with the off hand as needed to close any open seams when applying the CA. It helps to use some accelerator here.

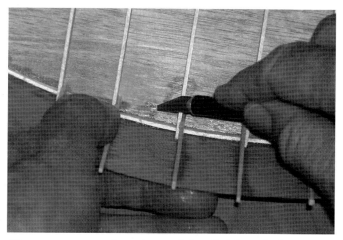

If you want to apply a nice semigloss finish to the boat when it is complete, you must remove any excess glue lest it shine through the finish. To do this, snap the end off an old X-acto blade and use it as a scraper.

Trim the excess bottom panel flush with the side panel. Use the sanding board for the final stages. The side panel is your guide, but take care not to gouge the panel with the knife or oversand.

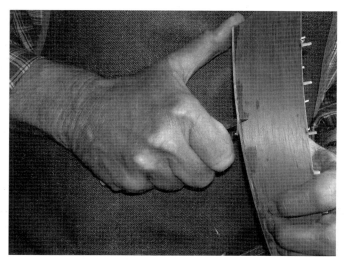

Once the bottom is secure, remove the excess panel. I like to use a small modeler's plane, but the careful application of the X-acto knife works very well too. Angle the blade so that it parallels the flare of the boat, and carefully whittle away at the excess. Observe the direction of the grain.

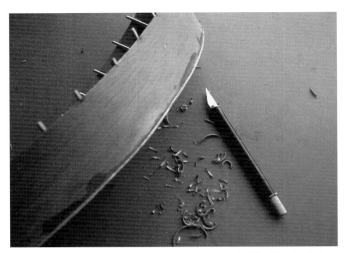

Don't whittle all the way to the side panel. Finish the job with your sanding board.

Use 80- or 100-grit sandpaper on the sanding board to make the remaining edge of the panel flush with the side panel. Use the flare of the side panel as a guide, but take care not to sand through the thin side panel.

The chine line should be sharp and clean.

Stem Cap and Transom Trim

With the sanding board, square the outward face of the stem post about $1/8$ inch. Fit and then glue the stem cap, which provides added protection to the stem and covers the end grain of the plywood panels.

Now cut and fit the transom trim. Fit and install the bottom piece first, followed by the side pieces. Fit them so the inside edge of the trim matches the transom and side panels. This leaves some "meat" that you will sand off flush with the side and bottom panels. The chine cap and outside sheer rails will then lie flush over the transom trim.

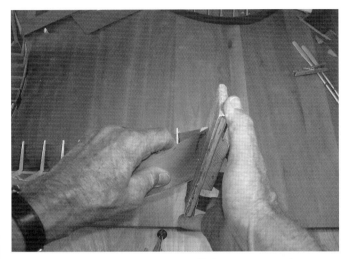

Use the sanding board to square off the stem to receive a $1/16$-by-$1/8$-by-4-inch piece of strip wood.

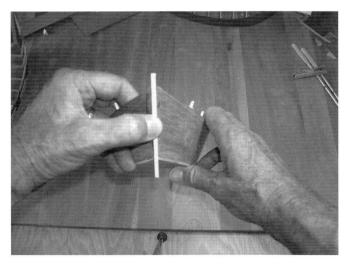

Apply thicker CA to the backside of the stem cap, center, and let the glue cure.

Remove the surplus stem cap so that it is flush with the bottom panel, leaving a little excess at the top. The stem cap may be left square or sanded flush with the side panels. For the model, I recommend the latter, since it eases the job of fitting the chine cap and outside sheer rail to the stem cap.

Cut and fit the transom trim if called for. Use the ³/₆₄-by-³/₁₆-inch strip wood. Install the bottom piece first and then the two side pieces. Fit the trim to the edges of the panels. As soon as the glue is set, sand the surplus trim so that it lies flush with the panels.

Chine Caps and Outside Sheer Rails

Use six ³/₆₄-by-³/₁₆-by-18-inch basswood strips for the chine caps and outside and inside sheer rails (gunwale and inwale). Notice how the chine cap and rail lie flush to the stem cap and transom trim. The excess can be trimmed and shaped once the installation is complete.

Install the chine caps, using the thicker CA. Place and glue an inch or two at a time after the cap is started. The application of an accelerator will provide an instant cure of the glue.

Carefully place the inside edge of the chine cap along the chine edge of the boat. You will sand the surplus flush with the bottom following installation.

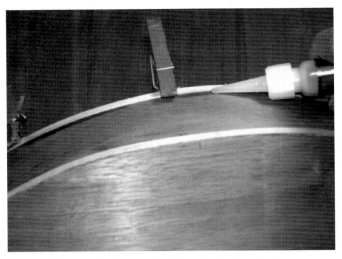

Install the outside sheer rails. Use the clothespin clamps to adjust and hold the rail in place. Check the alignment of the two side panels at the stem. If one is slightly lower, install the first rail so that the alignment begins there. You can then match the second outside rail to the first, and sand the surplus side panel of the second flush with the first after the hull is completed. Apply a bead of thin CA to the underside of the rail. Trim the ends so that they will not impede the installation of the second rail, and repeat the procedure.

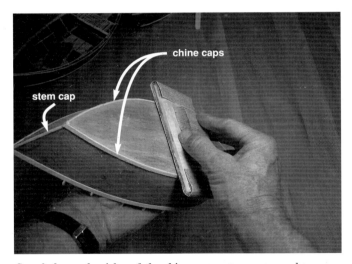

Sand the undersides of the chine caps, stem cap, and transom trim to ensure that they are flush with the bottom panel. It's important that the bottom, from port to starboard, remain flat.

The chine cap and sheer rails may be shaped as shown or beveled to a squared stem cap.

Inside Sheer Rail

The inside sheer rail may be tight-fitted in a manner as described for tight-fitting the chines in chapter 11. First, however, it is necessary to bevel the inward face of each frame so it parallels the side panel at each point. This will allow the rail to lie flush with the frame and run in fair line along the sheer of the boat.[3]

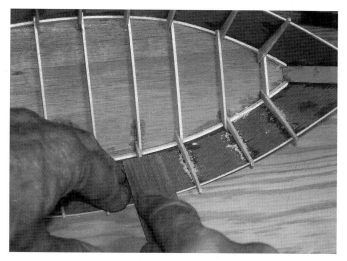

Sand the inward face of the frames so that they parallel the side panel at that point. It helps to lay the boat on its side against a flat surface and sand the frame square to the surface. The bevel will be more accurate.

Then cut and fit the inside rail. The ends should be beveled to join the stem post and transom frame in an appealing manner. Clamp the rail in place, and use thin CA at each frame and the unions with the stem and transom frames. As with the chine logs, the inside rails should appear on the same plane at the stem and transom when completed.

Fit the inner rail, clamp, and glue. Be certain the rail sits square to the outward side panel. A small square will help. Apply just a drop of thin CA where the rail joins the stem post and then at each frame, including the transom frame. Take care that the second sheer rail is juxtaposed to the first at the stem and the stern when it is installed.

Symmetrically installed inside sheer rails are nicely juxtaposed on the transom frames.

Your eye is the best test for judging placement.

Remove the surplus frames, after the sheer rails are installed. The razor saw will work nicely. Cut the frames flush with the rails. This is also a good time to shape the top of the transom. Some people like a rounded transom, but others like to square them off to the sheer line. My preference is to shape them as shown.

The completed hull. Pretty, isn't it?

The Completed Hull

There you have the completed hull. I apply a flat finish and sometimes complete the boat's interior appointments. When I do, I measure and loft the lines for each part per the plans, pin them to my drawn template on the foam board, glue, and install.

It takes some time, but the completed model is a thing of beauty in itself. Most important, however, is having completed the hull. I dare say your confidence in tackling the full-size boat will be greatly increased.

Endnotes

1. Harold "Dynamite" Payson, *Boat Modeling with Dynamite Payson,* (Camden, ME: International Marine, McGraw-Hill Companies, 1989), and Harold "Dynamite" Payson, *The Dory Model Book,* (Brookline, ME: WoodenBoat Books, 1997).

2. Remember that in the full-size boat, measurements taken with the limber sticks are applied to the chine log, and the whole piece is installed.

3. The frames on the full-size boat are notched to receive the rail, or the inside bevels are formed when the frames are built.

A school of completed McKenzie River drift boats.

PART 4

The Boats' Lines

"Like steelhead, a drift boat is the perfect union of form and function, all beauty and business and one of the most honest things on the planet. Few other craft will perform the same function, and none with such elegance. A white water raft will transport you down river, but it is sluggish and clumsy, handling like precisely what it is—an ungainly bag of gas. But the hull of a drift boat is geometric grace, a curvature in space defined by smooth, arced planes that intersect like the vault of a cathedral. It holds no hint of ugliness. A drift boat has a simplicity, a clearness of vision, and sense of purpose so absolute that it might have sprung from the uncluttered heart of a Shaker."

—*Ted Leeson*, The Habit of Rivers: Reflections on Trout Streams and Fly Fishing

CHAPTER 14

The Light McKenzie River Boat

*It would pivot on a dime, seemed to be tough as nails,
had a shallow draft, and was a charm to row.
This was a huge contrast to the
more heavily timbered boats of the day.*

I removed my sketches from the folder and presented them to the Man in front of me. I had sought him out for advice regarding a modeling project I thought might have some merit. He was shorter than I had expected, and his cautious welcome suggested curiosity more than suspicion, although Down East men of the sea were known to cast a wary eye at strangers with paper in their hands. Visitors frequented his place, however, always to meet the man and to talk about boats. A couple from Australia had recently been there. They had come to the States to visit friends in Detroit. The Aussie had built one of the Down Easter's boats and was anxious to meet this Maine legend, and since they were "in the neighborhood," they thought they would drop by. It was like that around this place: people simply dropping in, usually unannounced, from all over the country and world, to meet and visit with this man. He's always home. Why go anywhere when you believe you reside in a heavenly place? Besides, the man saw enough of the world during a stint in the navy, and nothing he saw compared to his little corner of the Maine coast.

Four things caught my eye that day. The first was his hat, a white touring cap that sat squarely over the bridge of his nose. Somehow the cap didn't fit my preconceived notion of a Maine lobsterman and boatbuilder nestled in his shop, but the 1930 Chevrolet Roadster parked outside may have been the answer. The second was his hands, seasoned by the toil of lobster fishing, boatbuilding, and now, for the past twenty-five years or so, boat modeling. As we shook hands, I marveled at how such stubby fingers could do such delicate work. The third was his shop, a pole structure about 15 by 25 feet with

8-foot walls. The rustic red exterior gave way to an interior cluttered with boat models atop a table that ran the length of the shop. A pair of center poles formed an aisle between the table and a band saw, table saw, and well-used woodstove. The seasoned 2-by-8 tongue-and-groove floor was a kaleidoscope of paint blotches and varnish from building myriad boats and models. His dad had helped him build the shop when the man was a young adult and recently wed. While that building experience was still fresh, the Down Easter turned around and built a small shed across the yard from the shop. He's an experiential learner. Here he has remained lobstering, building boats, modeling, and writing.

Yes, writing. The man has written ten books about small-boat building, their ease of construction, boat modeling, and tool care. His innate ability to speak simply and directly, without the limitations of formal education, led some good friends to encourage him to write about what he does. He never graduated from high school, although in 1990 the local school awarded the man a high school diploma in recognition of the impact his writing has had on boatbuilding aficionados, young and old. Hesitantly at first, and then more boldly, he committed pen to paper. Over the years, his how-to books have offered the timid, wannabe boatbuilder encouragement and confidence.

The fourth item that caught my eye that day was Amy, the man's effervescent and loquacious wife of fifty years. They appeared as point and counterpoint, yin and yang, salt and pepper, milk and cream, a nice match. It was clear that with Amy, this man of few words didn't have to hold up his end of the conversation. She was delightful.

Harold "Dynamite" Payson stood among a soft pile of shavings, and the ambient air hinted of pine, cedar, and the faint odor of lacquer. A stool at the workbench supported him. I felt as if I were standing on hallowed ground. It was September 1997.

Dynamite reviewed my sketch. "What the hell is that?" he asked. I explained that it was a drift boat. "I've never seen one before," he said. "What are they used for?" I told him it was a dory-type boat specifically built for running and fishing rivers of the Northwest, and that their use and popularity have spread to other parts of the country. "See here," he said, as he rummaged through papers on the corner of his workbench. "I got a letter from a fella in Salem, Oregon, a while back asking me to model a boat for him. I wrote back and told him I didn't know the boat, but I could do it from a set of plans." The request was for a McKenzie River drift-boat model. I was in that moment reminded just how small this world is. The query was from Dr. William Girsch, a Salem-area endodontist and neighbor to me! I didn't know Bill at the time, but since then we have become very good friends. Bill and his wife, Kathy, had recently traveled through Camden, Maine, and had spotted a Bank dory in a local gallery. Dynamite had modeled the dory. The boat's lines favored that of the contemporary drift boat, and Bill wondered whether the artist could replicate a drift boat. One reason Bill had moved to Oregon was to be in close proximity to steelhead and trout fishing, and the drift boat had become his favorite fishing platform. I

explained to Dynamite the boat's characteristics. The boat intrigued him. Could he model the boat if I found a set of lines for him? He replied, "E-yeah." Returning to Oregon, I found a way for Dynamite to model a drift boat. I shipped some patterns to him. Dynamite modeled the boat, Bill Girsch received his wish, and I found two new friends.

The problem with Bill Girsch's request of Dynamite was the absence of lines drawings of the McKenzie River drift boat. There are very few. Worse still, there are no recorded lines of any McKenzie or Rogue River boat as they evolved over time. It was then that I decided to try my hand at recovering the lines and construction details of an early McKenzie River drift boat. Little did I know then where that decision would lead.

Leroy Pruitt believes his dad, Veltie, built the first light McKenzie River boat in the mid to late 1920s. I decided to start with this boat. It would be a good test for me. Veltie's light board-and-batten boat no longer exists. Leroy Pruitt, however, had an abundance of photographs of the boat in use, and he had clear recollections of the boat's details. As a little tyke, he had assisted Veltie when one of the light board-and-batten boats was built. The little boat, the friendship it helped forge between Veltie and Prince Helfrich, and the rivers the boat made accessible to these men drew me to the boat like a bear to a honey tree. Between Leroy Pruitt's recollections of the boat, an abundance of pictures he had of the boat in use, and some counsel from Dyna-

Harold "Dynamite" Payson frames a Friendship sloop he is modeling for a midwestern transplant from the boat's place of origin in the Musongus Bay area of Maine, circa 2000. All of Dynamite's work is done from scratch, from milling his own material to lofting the boat parts to scale. A trip to his shop is a step back in time to when the quality of work was completely dependent on the eye and hand. COURTESY OF HAROLD "DYNAMITE" PAYSON

mite Payson, I thought I may be able to replicate the boat. I had also located an excellent reference, *Boats: A Manual for Their Documentation*.[1] I decided to give the boat a try.

I visited Leroy at his home on the McKenzie River several times during the winter of 1997–98. He said the boat was 13 feet long stem to stern, with a bottom length of about 11 feet and a bottom width amidships of about 3 feet. He remembered the width because when Tom Kaarhus milled the wood for Veltie, each plank was about 1 foot wide, and the bottom required three planks that ran the length of the boat. The beam at the sheer amidships was about 5 feet. The bottom planks were milled to about $^{1}/_{2}$-inch thickness, and the two strakes for the sides, or side planks, were milled down to $^{3}/_{8}$ or $^{1}/_{4}$ inch. The bottom strake required a width of at least 14 inches in order to conform to the boat. Old-growth spruce was still plentiful in those days, and planking of this dimension was easy to acquire. The planking was spruce and the frames were Port Orford cedar, the makings for a light boat. The boat had eleven frames, a goodly number for a craft that size. Because the boat was planked with thinner material than was customary, it seems likely that Veltie added frames for security and strength to the lighter planking. The little boat's siblings on the McKenzie were more heavily timbered.

I studied Leroy Pruitt's photographs of Veltie and the boat for several days, and then I put pencil to paper on my drafting table. With the basic data Leroy provided me about the boat's overall dimensions and the photographs, I laid down a scaled lines drawing of the boat's breadth, or plan view. I fussed with the drawing for a couple of days to make sure the lines ran fair. And then I was stumped. Photographs are one-dimensional, and I had difficulty establishing a reasonable profile, or elevation, view of the boat. I knew that whatever I came up with, it wouldn't be perfect, but I wanted it to be close.

Along came my kid brother, Jim. In the late spring of 1998, Jim and his wife, Dee, visited us. They were still thawing out from a typical Minnesota winter in Pelican Rapids, where Jim taught art, video production, and leadership to junior and senior high students. His family, students, and the community in great part adore him, because his vivid imagination brings to life a world of possibilities for his students. He has the ability to unlock one's creative genius, something he believes lies within every person. Jim spent fourteen difficult, and sometimes traumatic, months in Vietnam in 1965 and 1966 as a forward observer with the 101st Airborne. His readjustment to civilian life was troublesome. Jim has always had a creative side, but his recovery from his experiences in Vietnam were greatly aided by three things: a great woman, Dee, who rekindled Jim's trust in people; two adopted children, whose initial presence in his life triggered a renewed sense of responsibility and commitment; and expressive paintings that allowed him to treat the horrors of his more immediate past as incentives to make a difference in the lives of others. He's a little brother I look up to.

During Jim's visit, I presented the boat's photos to him and explained my problem in establishing the craft's profile. His response was, "Piece of cake." There was one photograph in particular that Jim found most helpful— a photo of Veltie standing in his newly built boat flyfishing. We spent an afternoon examining the photos as Jim pieced together a three-dimensional view of the boat. I was impressed. He's either very good, or he found it very easy to con his one-dimensional brother.

I think he is very good. From the photographs and Veltie's body size, he helped me deduce the overall view of the boat. We established a profile that looked and felt right. I completed the drawings: a half-breadth, profile, and body, or cross-sectional, view of the boat to scale. The next step was to model the thing. When I met and visited Dynamite Payson the previous fall, I had purchased several of his books. Two of them, *The Dory Model Book* and *Boat Modeling with Dynamite Payson*, I found particularly helpful.[2]

About the time I was ready to start whittling on the boat, my wife and I returned to Maine. Sue's grandfather had purchased property on Johns Bay, McFarland's Cove, in 1927. The property has remained in the family through four generations and today serves as a gathering point for kin who now reside in several corners of the country. I placed my line drawings of Veltie Pruitt's boat in a tube and took them along in hopes that I could go over them with Dynamite, whose home is 35 miles from the Cove, half that distance as the crow flies.

At the first opportunity, once I had touched base with Sue's siblings and cousins, I called Dynamite. He remembered me. I was pleased. He said, "E-yeah, bring the lines up and let's take a look at them." I was in his shop the next day. I told Dynamite the story of the boat as he fondled the lines. "Hmmm. Everything's runnin' fair," he commented to himself as he held the 18-by-24-inch sheets of vellum up as if he were sighting a rifle. He flipped through the two remaining sheets, which contained the frames layout, stem cross section, transom, and interior appointments. The drawings were 1 inch to the foot in scale. Dynamite thought for a moment and said, "The best way to test these plans is to model the boat." I explained that I planned to do that when I returned to Oregon. "How long are you in Maine?" he asked. "Two weeks." "What kind of free time do you have?" he continued. "I'm free as the breeze," I said, hiding my uncertainty about family plans. "Look, if you have the time and the interest, let's build the damn thing. It'll take a week, but you have all the stuff laid out on these sheets. I'll work with you. We'll first craft the plug, lift the side panels, and then model the boat." I was incredulous. "I'll show you how to do it, but you'll learn best if you model the boat yourself." I stood speechless long enough for Dynamite to break the silence. "Well?" he asked again. In my head, my response rang out: "Are you kidding me? Work side by side with the famous Dynamite Payson? In his shop? Rubbing shoulders with the man? Crafting my first model? Here on hallowed ground? Are you kidding me?" All I could say was "E-yeah."

On my way back to the Cove, I began to process all that had happened. Normally I visit with Sue before making a major time commitment, but true to her nature, she was delighted by this opportunity for me. For the next six days, I left the McFarland's Cove at about 7 A.M. and arrived at Dynamite's shop an hour later. For eight hours each day, I learned from the man. Dynamite showed me how to use first the profile lines and then the half-breadth lines to handcraft a three-dimensional plug.[3] At each step, the station lines for the frames were marked and re-marked. As the plug took shape, the futtocks, those lines created by the unveiling of each laminated board, served as a guide to crafting a fair and square plug. Dynamite's hands were sure, his tools were sharp, and Shirley Temple's tightly curled locks fell around his feet. We lifted the side panel and station lines from the plug, and then milled the material for the boat. Dynamite mills the material for every model from scratch and to scale. He's an artist with wood.

We each crafted a model of the Veltie Pruitt boat that week. The boat came together nicely. Dynamite led the way, and I followed suit. Bells and lights continually went off in my head with exclamations: "Oh, that's how it's done! Wonderful!" Each day my confidence grew a little, and each day I arrived at the shop a bit earlier, until one morning Dynamite hollered from his bedroom window at the twilight of dawn, "You're early!" The additional hour or so provided me the opportunity to catch up with Dynamite, listen to the calls of distant loons on the pond, and savor the shop environment. Except for the inner sheer rail and finish, my model was complete by Saturday. Dynamite had finished his boat. I left Dynamite and Amy that week secure in my new knowledge and with the treasure of two new, genuine, and inviting friends.

I returned to Oregon, completed Veltie's boat, and at the first opportunity I arranged to meet Leroy Pruitt in Springfield, Oregon, downriver from his home in Vida. I

Dynamite eyes the lines of a plug he is crafting. This hull is carved to the lines of a boat he is planning to model and is an essential first step in employing a modeling technique he calls the lift method. It is this technique he taught me with the Veltie Pruitt boat. COURTESY OF HAROLD "DYNAMITE" PAYSON

simply explained to Leroy that I had something I wanted him to examine. Over coffee at a local restaurant, I pulled the model from a box and handed it to him. His eyes widened as he examined the craft, they welled up a bit, and then he said, "This is my Daddy's boat! How did you do that?" I have had many gratifying moments over the course of my research, but this moment was one of the tops. As important, in that moment I realized that I can do this work, and I committed myself to the recovery and re-creation of the McKenzie River boats.

Dynamite and I continue our collaboration. Bill Girsch expanded his interest in drift boats to include the originals. In fact, his office is adorned with four different McKenzie River boats crafted from my lines, along with several Maine originals, all by Dynamite Payson. It was serendipity. Bill Girsch and I, unknown neighbors, find Payson on the other side of the continent at about the same time, with parallel interests, and new relationships are formed. Go figure.

Veltie Pruitt's light riverboat has not been built full-size, although it is on my list. You may beat me to it. I dream of building the boat and running some of the same water Veltie and Prince ran seventy-five years ago. Impediments to building a replica of the boat include the difficulty in locating Sitka spruce board widths suitable for the strakes and bottom planks. Instead, I will build the boat with a single sheet of 4-by-14-foot 1/4-inch marine-grade

Here I am placing a model of the light board-and-batten boat on its stand. I handcrafted this model at Dynamite's side in Maine, and it is my sentimental favorite. COURTESY OF ANDY WHIPPLE

plywood for the side panels and a 12-foot sheet of $^1/_2$-inch plywood for the bottom. Built with this material, the boat will conform to the lines of the original light McKenzie River boat, and it will be easier to construct. The downside to this boat is the same as was experienced by Veltie and Prince—more limited carrying capacity and a lower profile that allowed the boat to ship water from time to time. The downside is also its upside: a lighter, more versatile and maneuverable craft. I would not use the vessel for fishing, given my other fishing-boat options, but I would use it for simple pleasures such as sneaking off with my wife, Sue, to reap the benefits of more remote stretches of streams in the area. My fly rod would be with me, however, in the event we encountered rising fish. To use the boat on more populated streams would draw considerable attention and inquiries, and conversation would interrupt the peace and solitude Sue and I seek.

Endnotes

1. Museum Small Craft Association, Paul Lipke, Peter Spectre, Benjamin A.G. Fuller, editors, *Boats: A Manual for Their Documentation* (Nashville, TN: American Association for State and Local History, 1993).

2. Harold "Dynamite" Payson, *The Dory Model Book*, (Brookline, ME: WoodenBoat Books, 1997), and Harold "Dynamite" Payson, *Boat Modeling with Dynamite Payson*, (Camden, ME: International Marine, McGraw-Hill Companies, 1989).

3. "Plug" is the term Dynamite uses to describe a model that is carved from a perfectly squared block of wood that is comprised of laminated pieces of $^3/_4$-inch clear vertical grain boards, in this case eastern white pine. The profile of the boat is first carved precisely to the lines of the plans, and then the half-breadth (chine and sheer) lines are marked and carved precisely to the lines. The result is a three dimensional "plug" of the boat, a lovely art form in itself.

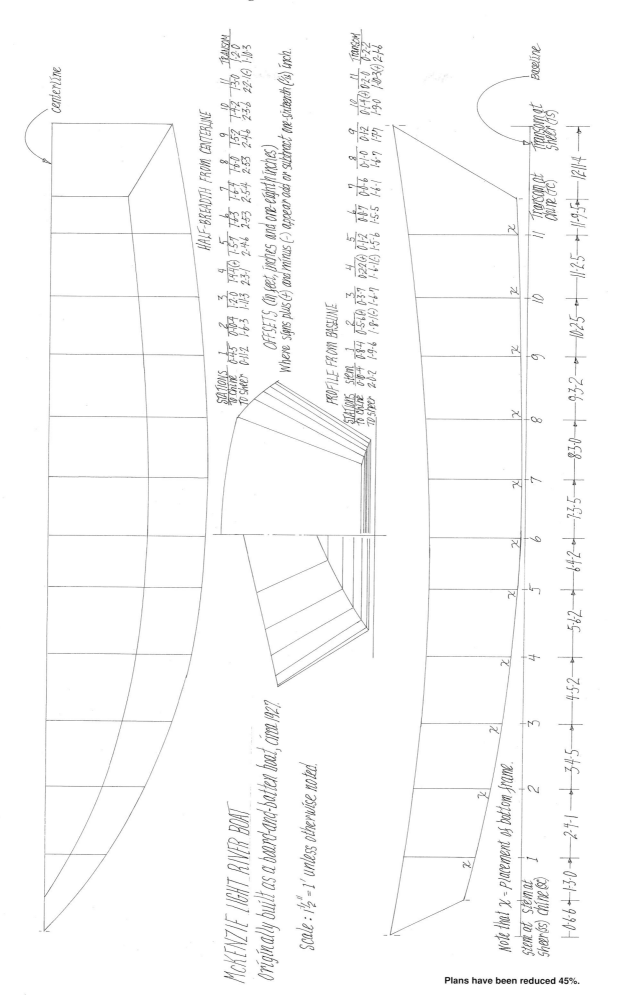

centerline

HALF-BREADTH FROM CENTERLINE

STATIONS	1	2	3	4	5	6	7	8	9	10	11	TRANSOM
To Chine	0-4.5	0-0.4	1-2.0	1-4.4(+)	1-5.7	1-6.3	1-6.7	1-6.0	1-5.2	1-4.2	1-3.0	1-2.0
To Sheer	0-11.2	1-6.3	1-11.3	2-3.7	2-4.6	2-5.3	2-5.4	2-5.3	2-4.6	2-3.6	2-2.1(-)	1-11.3

OFFSETS (in feet, inches, and one-eighth inches)
Where signs plus (+) and minus (-) appear add or subtract one-sixteenth (1/16) inch.

PROFILE FROM BASELINE

STATIONS	STEM	1	2	3	4	5	6	7	8	9	10	11	TRANSOM
To Chine	0-1.4	0-8.4	0-5.6(+)	0-3.7	0-2.2(+)	0-1.2	0-0.7	0-1.6	0-1.0	0-1.2	0-1.4(+)	0-2.0	0-2.2
To Sheer	2-0.2	1-9.6	1-8.1(-)	1-6.7	1-6.1(-)	1-5.6	1-5.5	1-6.1	1-6.7	1-7.7	1-9.0	1-10.3(+)	2-1.6

MCKENZIE LIGHT RIVER BOAT
Originally built as a board-and-batten boat, circa 1927.

Scale: 1½" = 1' unless otherwise noted.

Note that x = placement of bottom frame.

	stem at	1	2	3	4	5	6	7	8	9	10	11	Transom at	Transom at
Stem at													Chine (TC)	Sheer (TS)
Sheer (S) Chine (SC)														

| 1-0-6.6 | 1-3.0 | 2-4.1 | 3-4.5 | 4-5.2 | 5-6.2 | 6-4.2 | 7-3.5 | 8-3.0 | 9-3.2 | 10-2.5 | 11-2.5 | 11-9.5 | 12-1.4 |

baseline

Plans have been reduced 45%.

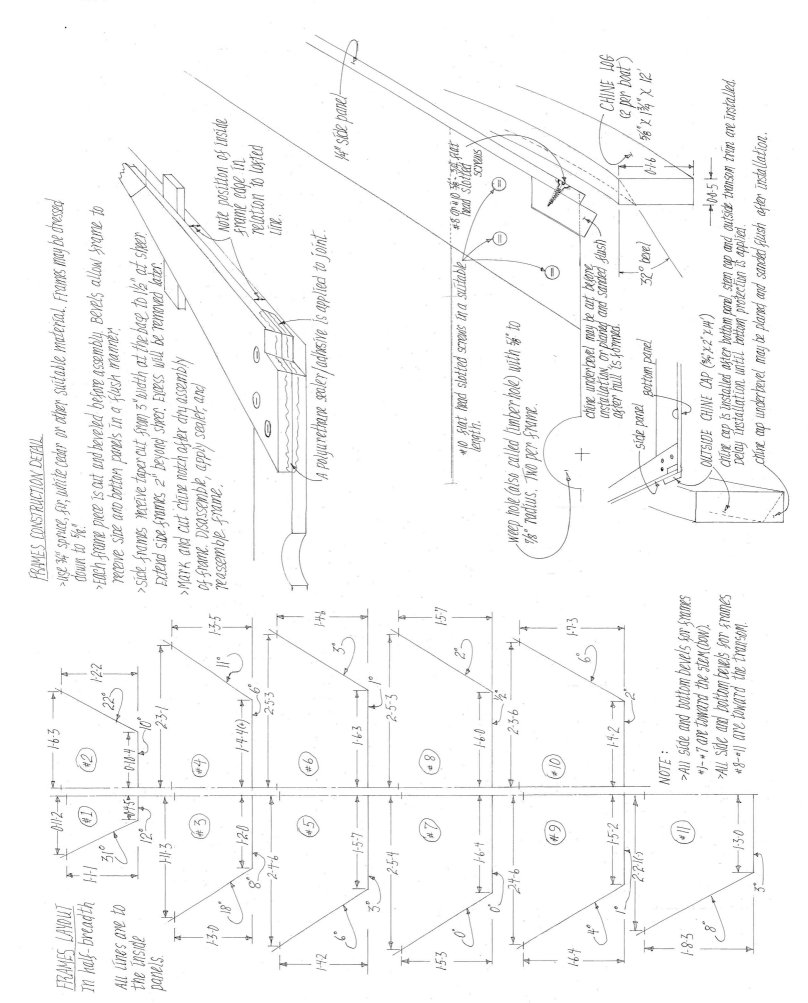

FRAMES CONSTRUCTION DETAIL

> Use 3/4" spruce, fir, white cedar or other suitable material. Frames may be dressed down to 5/8".

> Each frame piece is cut unbeveled before assembly. Bevels allow frame to receive side and bottom panels in a flush manner.

> Side frames receive taper cut from 3" width at the base to 1 1/2" at sheer. Extend side frames 2" beyond sheer. Excess will be removed later.

> Mark and cut chine notch after dry assembly of frame. Disassemble, apply sealer, and reassemble frame.

Note position of inside frame edge in relation to lofted line.

A polyurethane sealer/adhesive is applied to joint.

44" side panel

CHINE LOG (2 per boat)
5/8" X 3/4" X 12'

#8 or #10 5/8"-3/4" flat head slotted screws

52° bevel

OUTSIDE CHINE CAP (3/4" x 2" x 14')
Chine cap is installed after bottom panel, stem cap and outside transom trim are installed. Delay installation until bottom protection is applied. Chine cap underbevel may be planed and sanded flush after installation.

side panel
bottom panel

chine underbevel may be cut before installation or planed and sanded flush after hull is formed.

#10 flat head slotted screws in a suitable length.

weep hole (also called limber hole) with 5/8" to 7/8" radius. Two per frame.

FRAMES LAYOUT
In half-breadth

All lines are to the inside panels.

#1   #2
#3   #4
#5   #6
#7   #8
#9   #10
#11

NOTE:
> All side and bottom bevels for frames #1-#7 are toward the stem (bow).
> All side and bottom bevels for frames #8-#11 are toward the transom.

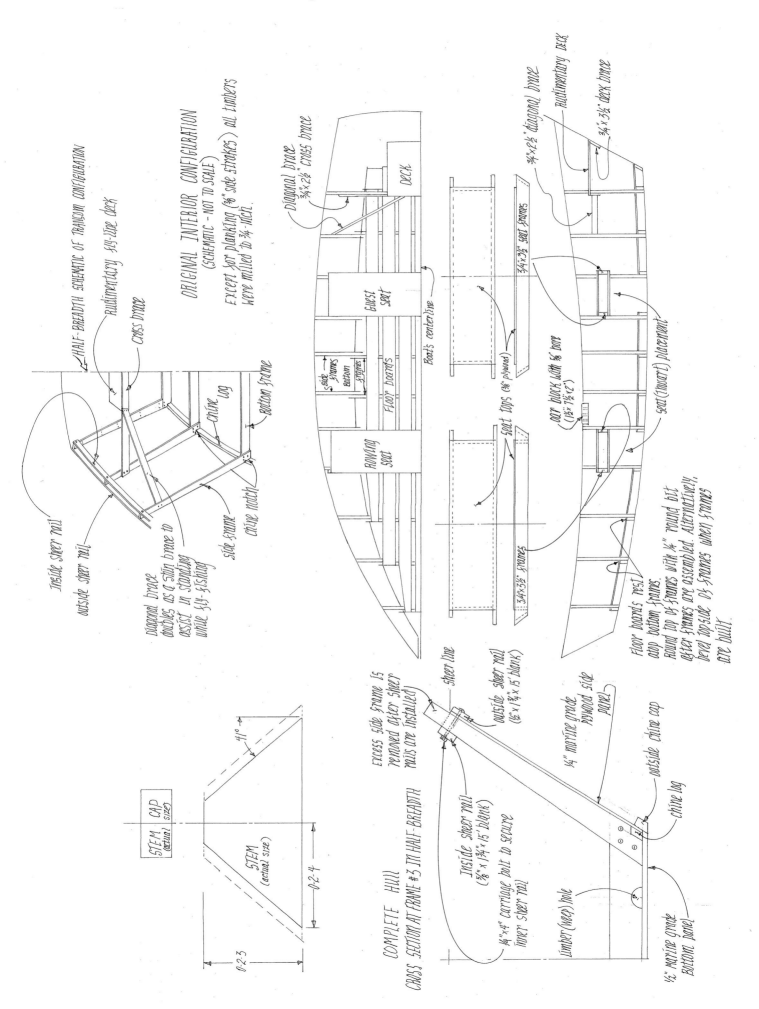

HALF-BREADTH SCHEMATIC OF TRANSOM CONFIGURATION

Inside sheer rail

outside sheer rail

Diagonal brace doubles as a stiff brace to assist in standing while fly-fishing

Rudimentary seat-size deck

cross brace

chine log

chine notch

side frame

bottom frame

ORIGINAL INTERIOR CONFIGURATION
(SCHEMATIC - NOT TO SCALE)

Except for planking (⅜" side strakes) all timbers were milled to ¾-inch.

Diagonal brace

¾"x2½" cross brace

DECK

Guest seat

side frames

bottom frames

Rowing seat

Floor boards

Boat's centerline

¾"x3½" frames

seat tops (⅜" plywood)

¾"x3½" seat frames

oar block with ⅝" bore
(1½"x 7½"x2")

seat (insert) placement

Rudimentary deck

¾"x3½" deck brace

¾"x2½" diagonal brace

Floor boards rest atop bottom frames.
Round top of frames with ¼" round bit after frames are assembled. Alternatively, bevel topside of frames when frames are built.

STEM CAP (actual size)

41°

STEM (actual size)

0-2-4

0-2-3

COMPLETE HULL
CROSS SECTION AT FRAME #3 IN HALF-BREADTH

sheer line

Excess side frame is removed after sheer rails are installed

outside sheer rail
(½" x ¾" x 15' blank)

Inside sheer rail
(⅝" x ¾" x 15' blank)

¼"x4" carriage bolt to secure inner sheer rail

¼" marine grade plywood side panel

limber (weep) hole

outside chine cap

chine log

½" marine grade bottom panel

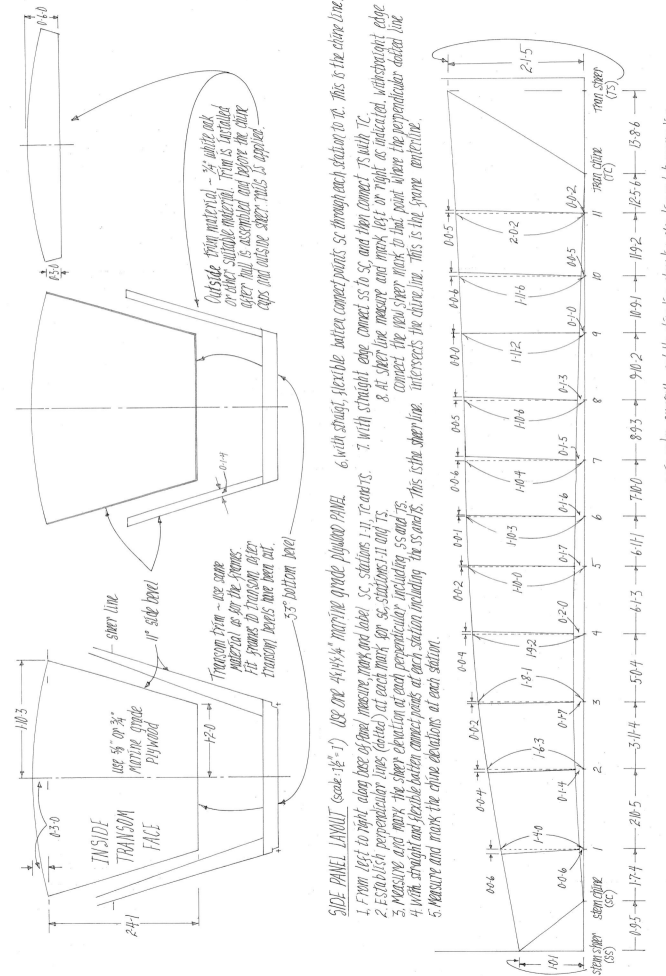

SIDE PANEL LAYOUT (scale: 1½" = 1') USE ONE 4×14×¼" marine grade plywood PANEL

1. From left to right along base of panel measure, mark and label SC, stations 1–11, TC and TS.
2. Establish perpendicular lines (dotted) at each mark for SC, stations 1–11 and TS.
3. Measure and mark the sheer elevation at each perpendicular including SS and TS.
4. With straight and flexible batten connect points at each station including the SS and TS. This is the sheer line.
5. Measure and mark the chine elevations at each station.
6. With straight, flexible batten connect points SC through each station to TC. This is the chine line.
7. With straight edge connect SS to SC, and then connect TS with TC.
8. At sheer line measure and mark left or right as indicated, with straight edge connect the new sheer mark to that point where the perpendicular dotted line intersects the chine line. This is the frame centerline.

9. In order, carefully cut the chine line, sheer line, stem line and transom line.
10. Use this panel as a template to mark and cut second panel.

INSIDE TRANSOM FACE

use ⅝" or ¾" marine grade plywood

sheer line
11° side bevel
53° bottom bevel

Transom trim ~ use same material as for the frames. Fit frames to transom after transom bevels have been cut.

Outside trim material ~ ¾" white oak or other suitable material. Trim is installed after hull is assembled and before the chine caps and outside sheer rails is applied.

CHAPTER 15

The Trapper
McKenzie 12-Foot Square-Ender

"The functionality, the lighter-weight design, no need for a trailer—I love it.
We have a lot of rivers here in Pennsylvania without proper boat launch access.
We can carry this guy if we have to."

—DAVID ZIELINSKI

This boat is ideally suited for the person who wants to slip away from the crowd alone or with a friend and enjoy the privacy of a pristine stream other boats won't navigate. The 12-foot-long side panels give it a stem-to-stern length of just over 11 feet, and it is light enough to hand-load onto a pickup with an 8-foot bed, offload, and hand-carry to the stream. The traditional McKenzie rocker gives the boat maneuverability in tight places, and in the hands of a deft oarsman, it will handle any big water assumed by the boat's larger cousins. Suitable for the solitudinarian or the adventurous duo that seeks out-of-the-way water, this boat will put the fisher in places larger boats cannot reach. It has considerable carrying capacity and will accommodate light gear for day trips, an overnight drift, or other equipment.

I recovered its lines from a boat Woodie Hindman built for Prince Helfrich in 1939. The boat type is typical of the Kaarhus design. Prince had the boat built to run his traplines in the off-season. He desired a boat that was easy to handle alone, could be dropped into or retrieved from a river where access was limited yet convenient for him, and had capacity enough to carry all his traps and critters. Trapping seasons ran from November through March, and they provided another source of income to the guide and his family. Prince's oldest son, Dave, recalls one trip with his dad. Prince had roughly 100 miles of traplines, and he invited Dave to join him on a few runs closer to home. One run was from Vida, Oregon, on the McKenzie to Peoria on the Willamette River and required an overnight stop along the stream. Mink were particularly profitable at the time, and Dave

recalls laying out twenty-eight mink in the boat to show his mother, Marjorie, when she picked them up in Peoria. Dave remembers Prince's pride with his catch that day. The furs were worth $100 each. In 1940, $2,800 for two days' work was extraordinary.

Prince continued to use the boat, which I've named the *Trapper*, for his traplines through the 1940s. The little craft saw other uses too. Prince's kids found it a comfortable boat to handle on the McKenzie, and their experiences helped sharpen their river rowing skills. In 1952, however, Prince sold the *Trapper* to another Vida resident, Frank Wheeler, a family friend. Since that time, the boat has remained in the Wheeler family, and it saw considerable use over the years for family outings and fishing trips, and as a training tool for Frank's children, who also delight in the river.

One river guide was impressed enough with the boat that he built a copy from patterns he lifted off the *Trapper*. The guide took the boat to Montana for use on a ranch he managed. For the past twenty years, however, the wooden boat has seen little use and instead sits in Frank's barn loft, dry, secure, and resting on its laurels. I learned about the boat and its history from Dave Helfrich. Coincidentally, I was at that time reviewing Woodie and Ruthie Hindman's diaries. Ruthie's journal notes that Woodie completed a boat for Prince on May 5, 1939, and that Prince picked it up the next day.[1] I have deduced that the boat was the *Trapper*. Excitement about the find overtook me, and I asked Frank if he would let me take the necessary measurements so I could record the boat's lines and ultimately make them available to anyone interested.

In January 2000, my good friend Dr. Bill Girsch and I traveled to Vida to meet up with Frank, Dave Helfrich, and Leroy Pruitt. We lifted the boat from its loft and set it on the floor of Frank's shop. Once the boat was leveled, we made the appropriate measurements: its breadth and profile, or elevations, at each frame, stem, and transom. As we worked, conversations gravitated toward Woodie Hindman, Prince Helfrich, and Veltie Pruitt, and we pondered the marvels of these men. At noon, the group retreated to Frank's home, where LuElla, Frank's wife, treated us to a lavish lunch. As we sat in the dining room, my eyes were continually drawn to the McKenzie flowing past the Wheelers' tightly manicured backyard, and I couldn't help but marvel at Frank's foresight in hanging on to the little *Trapper*, a treasure now made available to sentimental folks like me and you.

Frank died in 2003. His love for rivers and this boat, however, did not die with him. A re-creation of the *Trapper* today quietly glides the small streams of western Pennsylvania at the hands of David Zielinski and Robert Bell, two fly fishers who love to leave the beaten path and explore inaccessible waters. An electrical engineer who lives in Irwin, Pennsylvania, Dave is a home boat builder who is attracted to the history of these special craft and the eastern streams they might bring to the reach of his flies. Dave learned about the work I was doing to record the lines and stories of these boats in January the year Frank died. We corresponded infrequently for a time, and on March 11, 2004, I sent Dave a set of McKenzie double-ender plans. I was impressed with his ability to build a fine drift boat from my plans. It was this experience with his first drift boat and our continuing correspondence that led us to discuss the *Trapper*. I finally laid down the lines and modeled the boat in the fall of 2004. I lamented that I wasn't going to have time to build the first-off from the plans in time for this book and explained that I thought it was important to build the boat full-size to verify the efficacy of the plans. His interest was immediately piqued, and within a few short e-mails, we were talking about his building the boat.

He liked the idea of a smaller, portable boat that could handle both big water and smaller streams. I sent the model, a set of plans, and guidelines for building the boat to him. Within a short period of time, he was into the project, and his goal was to complete it in time for the boat to accompany him and a couple friends on the upper Delaware River for their annual spring fishing trip. He did, and they did.

When Dave evaluated the *Trapper* on the water, he wrote:

Leroy Pruitt and Bill Girsch examining the Trapper *after we lifted it from Frank Wheeler's loft.*

Frank Wheeler's daughter, Mary Ellen, looks at the Trapper *in the light of day. She plans to restore it to its original condition, not for use but for show. The years have finally caught up with the little boat.*

I like its size and the way it sits in the water. It feels light, easy to work, and it makes a killer one-man boat. Unfortunately, I made it too heavy, especially the floorboards. The boat is fine on bigger water, but I would like it lighter for smaller streams. I will solve that little problem by removing the floorboards for my solo trips. I like its size, but one frame longer would make it a sweet two-man boat. But then we would essentially have a Rapid Robert. Built with standard marine-grade materials, this small boat can be constructed for less of an investment than standard 16-foot drift boats. It is the go-to boat for quick trips to the river.[2]

The Trapper under construction in Dave Zielinski's garage.
COURTESY OF DAVID ZIELINSKI

Two of Dave Zielinski's friends, Mark Stanley (left) and Joe Osborne, relax in the finished boat during a fishing trip on the upper Delaware River in May 2005. The Trapper *has considerable carrying capacity for its size. It is a charm to row and easy to load and offload. It's pretty, too.*
COURTESY OF DAVID ZIELINSKI

Dave has found that the boat handles best with 8$^{1}/_{2}$-foot oars, and the shorter fore-to-aft length makes distribution of weight a factor in handling. Both he and Bob are surprised that the boat will comfortably tolerate their combined weight and gear, and it fishes the two of them nicely. There is limited storage room in the boat, but Dave says he will remedy that with a boat box under

each seat. The high transom and sides can also create a challenge in a stiff breeze. The high, broad transom can act like a sail that makes control difficult on the broader, flat water of the upper Delaware. The other disadvantage is that other fishermen want to stop and inquire about the boat. This gets in the way of fishing. That is the price one pays for introducing a unique riverboat onto an eastern river.[3]

Dave and Bob have given the boat several names, depending on their circumstance and mood. It's been called the "tub," the "little green tub," and the "heavy little bastard." This last name was assigned to the boat as the pair hoisted it into the pickup with all the gear, anchors, and 3 inches of water under the floorboards. Dave tells me they still hold on to the *Trapper* name in deference to Prince Helfrich's use of the boat. But what's in a name? The real questions are these: Does the boat put you in places where the fish reside and where few others can go? Is it easily portable? Is it safe? Is it fun? The answer to all is yes!

Endnotes

1. Ruthie Hindman's daily diary entries cover the period 1937 through 1943, and then periodically from that time until Woodie's death in 1967. Woodie also kept a diary, but his notes were very cryptic. Credit for permitting me to examine and use the diaries goes to their owner, Ruth Burleigh, Ruthie Hindman's niece and the recipient of Woodie and Ruthie's memorabilia.

2. Dave Zielinski, e-mail correspondence, October 31, 2005.

3. Ibid., May 9, 2006.

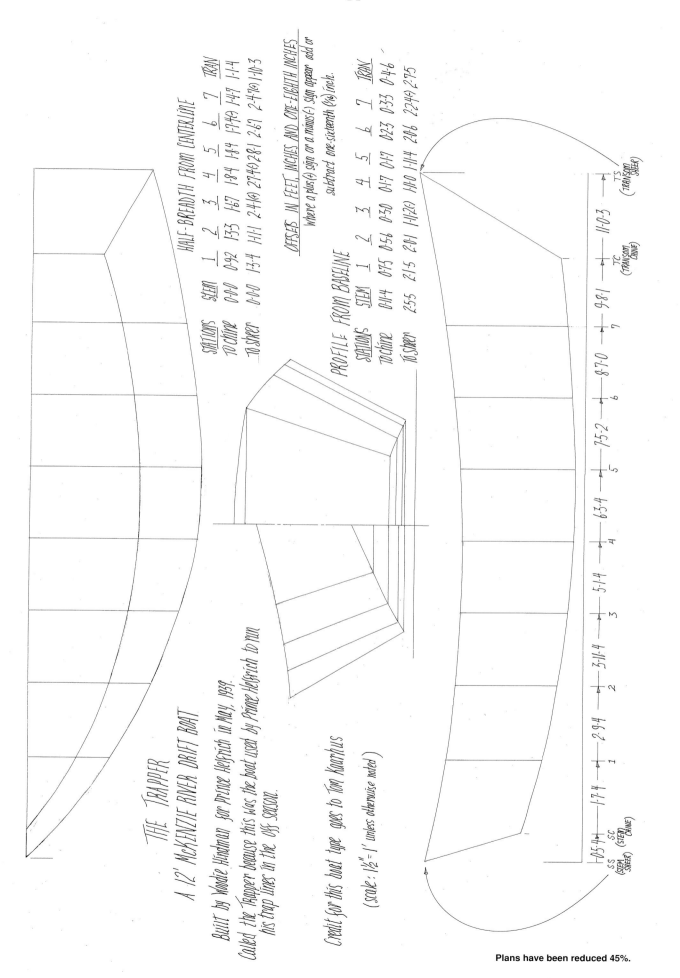

THE TRAPPER

A 12' McKENZIE RIVER DRIFT BOAT

Built by Woodie Hindman for Prince Helfrich in May, 1959.

Called the Trapper because this was the boat used by Prince Helfrich to run his trap lines in the off season.

Credit for this boat type goes to Tom Kaarhus

(scale: ½" = 1' unless otherwise noted)

HALF-BREADTH FROM CENTERLINE

STATIONS	STEM	1	2	3	4	5	6	7	TRAN
To chine	0-0-0	0-9-2	1-3-3	1-5-7	1-8-4	1-8-4	1-7-4(-)	1-4-7	1-1-4
To sheer	0-0-0	1-3-4	1-1-1	2-4(+)	2-7-4(-)	2-8-1	2-6-7	2-4-7(0)	1-10-3

OFFSETS IN FEET, INCHES AND ONE-EIGHTH INCHES
where a plus(+) sign or a minus(-) sign appear add or subtract one-sixteenth (1/16) inch.

PROFILE FROM BASELINE

STATIONS	STEM	1	2	3	4	5	6	7	TRAN
To chine	0-11-4	0-7-5	0-5-6	0-5-0	0-1-7	0-1-7	0-2-3	0-3-3	0-4-6
To sheer	2-5-5	2-1-5	2-0-1	1-11-2(0)	1-11-0	1-11-4	2-0-6	2-2-4(+)	2-7-5

Plans have been reduced 45%.

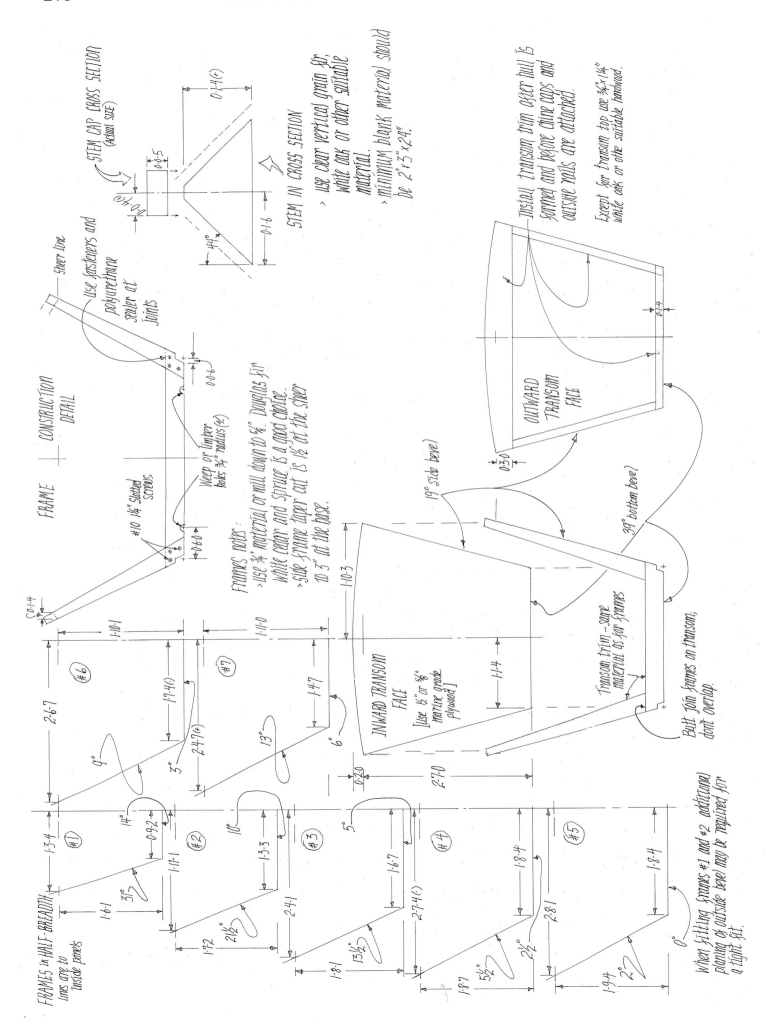

STEM CAP CROSS SECTION
(actual size)

STEM IN CROSS SECTION

> use clear vertical grain fir,
  white oak or other suitable
  material.
> minimum blank material should
  be 2"×5"×24".

Install transom trim after hull is
sanded and before chine caps and
outside rails are attached.

Except for transom top use 3/4"×1¼"
white oak or othe suitable hardwood.

FRAME CONSTRUCTION DETAIL

Sheer line

Use fasteners and
polyurethane
sealer at
joints

#10 1¼" Slotted
Screws

Weep or limber
holes 3/4" radius (±)

FRAMES notes:
> use 3/4" material or mill down to 5/8". Douglas fir,
  white cedar and spruce is a good choice.
> side frame taper cut is 1/2" at the sheer
  to 3" at the base.

OUTWARD
TRANSOM
FACE

19° side bevel

39° bottom bevel

INWARD TRANSOM
FACE
[use 1/2" or 5/8"
marine grade
plywood]

Transom trim—same
material as for frames

Butt join frames on transom;
don't overlap.

FRAMES in HALF-BREADTH
Lines are to
inside panels

#6   #7

#1   #2   #3   #4   #5

When fitting frames #1 and #2 additional
planing of outside bevel may be required for
a tight fit.

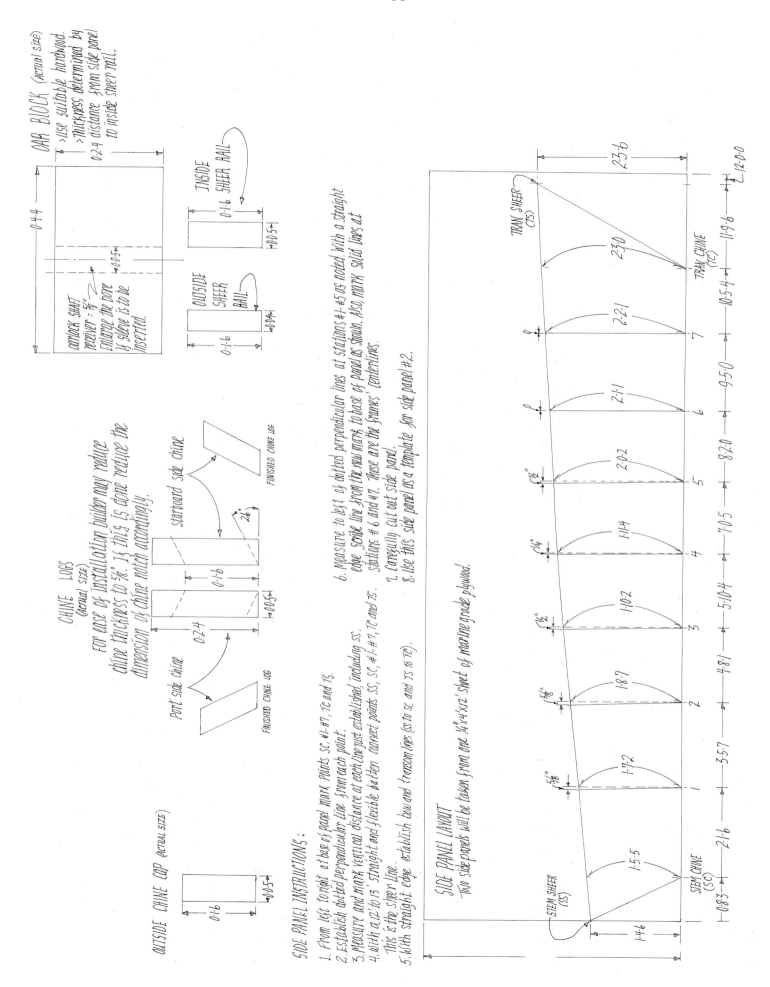

OAR BLOCK (actual size)
- use suitable hardwood
- thickness determined by 0-2-4 distance from side panel to inside sheer rail.

camlock shaft recover = ⅝"
Enlarge the bore if sleeve is to be inserted.

INSIDE SHEER RAIL
0-1-6

OUTSIDE SHEER RAIL
0-1-6

CHINE LOGS (actual size)
For ease of installation builder may reduce chine thickness to ⅝". If this is done reduce the dimension of chine notch accordingly.

Port side chine
Starboard side chine

FINISHED CHINE LOG
FINISHED CHINE LOG

0-2-4
0-1-6

OUTSIDE CHINE CAP (actual size)
0-1-6

SIDE PANEL INSTRUCTIONS:

1. From left to right at base of panel mark points SC, #1-#7, TC and TS.
2. Establish dotted perpendicular line from each point.
3. Measure and mark vertical distance at each line just established.
4. With a 12' to 13' straight and flexible batten connect points SS, SC, #1-#7, TC and TS.
5. With straight edge establish bow and transom lines (SS to SC and TS to TC). This is the sheer line.
6. Measure to left of dotted perpendicular lines at stations #1-#5 as noted with a straight edge scribe line from the new mark to base of panel as shown. Also mark solid lines at stations #6 and #7. These are the frames' centerlines.
7. Carefully cut out side panel.
8. Use this side panel as a template for side panel #2.

SIDE PANEL LAYOUT
Two side panels will be taken from one ¼" x 4' x 12' sheet of marine grade plywood.

STEM SHEER (SS)
STEM CHINE (SC)

TRAM SHEER (TS)
TRAM CHINE (TC)

1-5-5
1-7-2
1-8-7
1-10-2
1-11-4
2-0-2
2-1-1
2-2-1
2-3-0

⅝" ⅝" ½" ¾" ¾" 1½" 0 0

0-8-3 2-1-6 3-5-7 4-8-1 5-10-4 7-0-5 8-2-0 9-5-0 10-5-4 11-9-6 12-0-0

1-4-6
2-3-6

SS 1 2 3 4 5 6 7

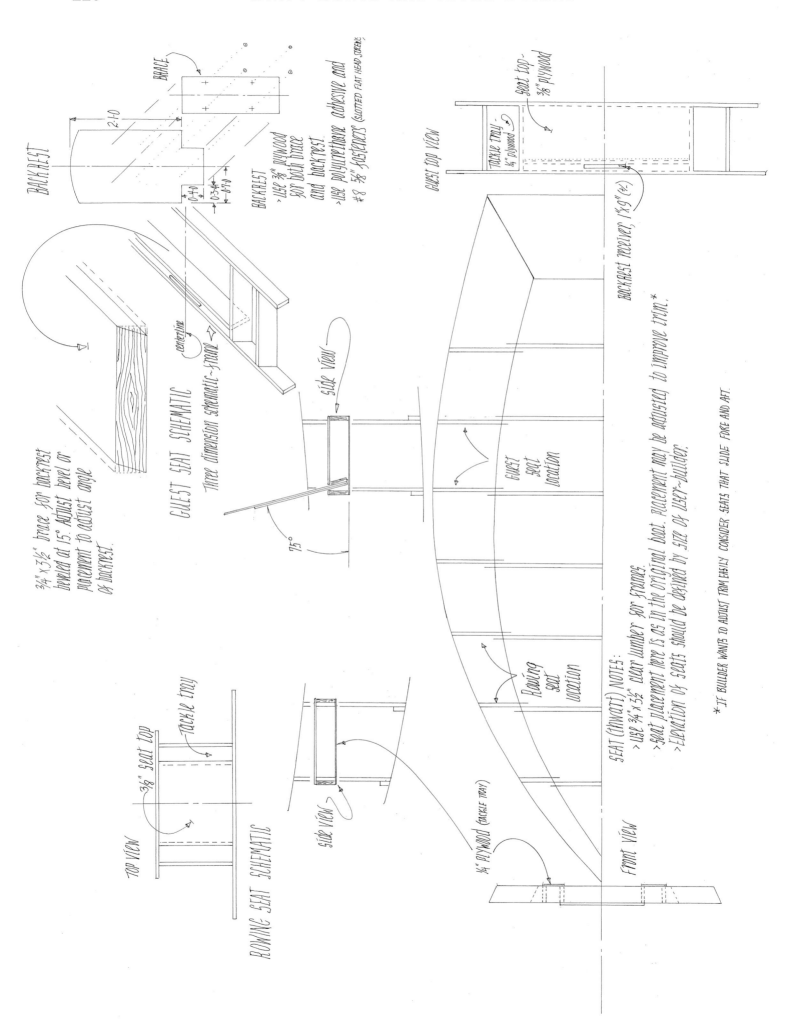

BACKREST

BRACE

2-0

BACKREST
> use ⅜" plywood
for both brace
and backrest.
> use polyurethane adhesive and
#8 ⅝" fasteners (slotted flat head screws)

¾" x 3½" brace for backrest
beveled at 15°. Adjust bevel or
placement to adjust angle
of backrest.

GUEST SEAT SCHEMATIC
Three dimension schematic~stone

centerline

side view

75°

GUEST TOP VIEW

Tackle Tray ~
¼" plywood

Seat top~
⅜" plywood

Backrest receiver, 1"x9" (4)

Guest
seat
location

Rowing
seat
location

SEAT (THWART) NOTES:
> use ¾" x 3½" clear lumber for seats.
> seat placement here is as in the original boat. placement may be adjusted to improve trim.*
> Elevation of seats should be designed by size of user~builder.

¼" plywood (tackle tray)

Front View

* If builder wants to adjust trim easily consider seats that slide fore and aft.

TOP VIEW

Tackle Tray

⅜" Seat Top

side view

ROWING SEAT SCHEMATIC

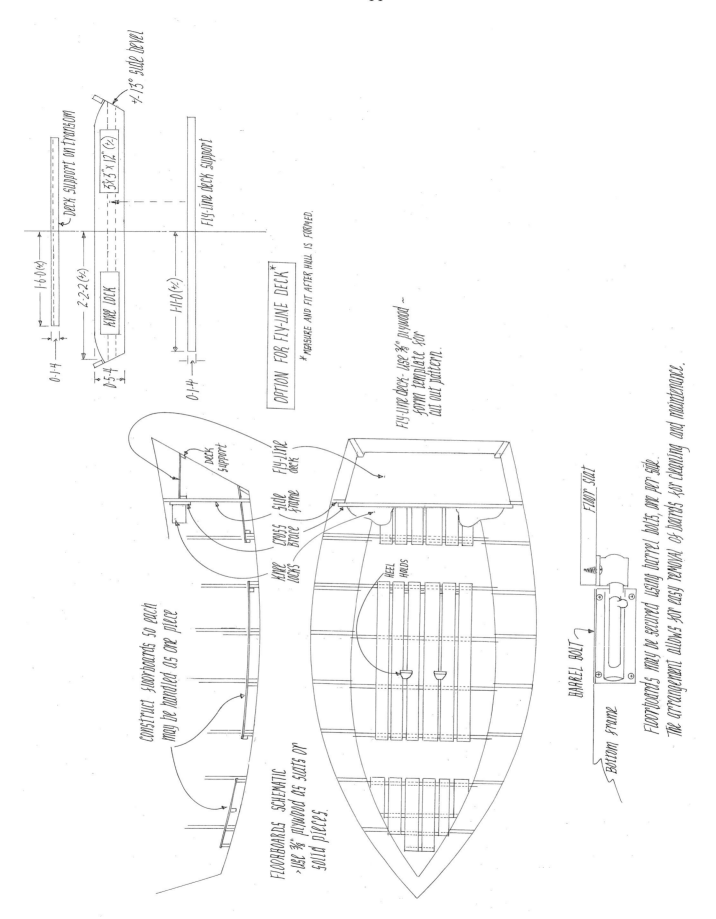

Deck support on transom

+/-15° side bevel

3"x5"x12" (½)

KNEE LOCK

Fly-line deck support

1-6-0 (½)

2-2-2 (½)

1-11-0 (½)

0-1-4

0-5-4

0-1-4

OPTION FOR FLY-LINE DECK*

*MEASURE AND FIT AFTER HULL IS FORMED.

Fly-line deck - use ⅜" plywood ~ form template for cut out pattern.

deck support

Fly-line deck

CROSS BRACE

SIDE FRAME

KNEE LOCKS

HEEL HOLDS

construct floorboards so each may be handled as one piece

FLOORBOARDS SCHEMATIC
> use ⅜" plywood as slats or solid pieces.

FLOOR SLAT

BARREL BOLT

Bottom frame

Floorboards may be secured using barrel bolts, one per side.
The arrangement allows for easy removal of barrels for cleaning and maintenance.

CHAPTER 16

The Rapid Robert
The Kaarhus McKenzie Square-Ender

*This is the unsung hero of the McKenzie.
It doesn't have the sexy lines of the double-enders,
but it's the best dual-purpose riverboat one will find.*

Tom Kaarhus's 14-foot plywood McKenzie square-ender is in my view an unsung hero of the McKenzie River. Its tradition dates back to John West's "bathtub with oarlocks," but it wasn't until Kaarhus applied the new plywood material to riverboat construction that the popularity of this boat grew beyond McKenzie River country. This boat provided the McKenzie guides with maneuverability and carrying capacity, two features that allowed them to comfortably venture afield for several days with their clients. It was this boat type that Woodie and Ruthie Hindman used to make their first solo run down the Middle Fork of the Salmon River in August 1939. Prince Helfrich and Veltie Pruitt both speculated, the first time they saw this boat during the filming of *Abe Lincoln in Illinois*, that it would make a fine whitewater boat. It did, and it still does.

Kaarhus built his first 14-foot plywood square-ender in 1938 after he successfully tested the integrity of the newer waterproof material. The boat became the standard for riverboat construction. Several guides continued to build board-and-batten boats for a time. Once the lighter and more versatile plywood boat was tried, however, conversion to plywood construction was a no-brainer. The material was easier to work, and Kaarhus discovered that the boat could be built without a bracing, jig, or strongback. This simplified the boatbuilding process. In response to the vessel's growing popularity, Kaarhus offered the boat as a kit, something he later may have regretted because of the time-consuming questions he received from novice builders.

How and when it happened, I don't know, but sometime in the mid to late 1940s, Kaarhus discovered that the square-ender performed well with a small motor. His test may have occurred about the time that Everett Spaulding asked Woodie Hindman to remove the bow of his dou-

ble-ender and install a small transom. Tiring of the long pulls through flat water, Spaulding wanted to save time on the river with the application of a motor. Perhaps Tom Kaarhus realized that the broader transom of the square-ender would perform better under power than the double-ender and its narrow transom. The double-ender with a transom under power often invited impolite comments. It still does. The narrow transom burdened with a motor and its accentuated rocker drives the transom down and the prow up, making it ungainly, tentative, slow-moving, and susceptible to the wind.

Whatever his rationale or timing, when Kaarhus modified the boat's transom to accept a motor, he created a wonderful dual-purpose boat. On the one hand, the boat handled whitewater comfortably. The modest rocker gave the boat great maneuverability, and the broad transom provided greater width amidships to the downriver end of the boat and therefore more displacement and greater carrying capacity. He learned that with proper weight distribution, the boat would trim easily under power and move with a grace unavailable to its McKenzie and Rogue River cousins. The boat was ideally suited for river trips and lake, bay, and estuary fishing.

The boat seems to have lost it appeal, however, over time. Its lines are not as poetic and graceful as those of the double-enders. In whitewater, the broad transom creates enough resistance in downriver movement to risk a stall on the crests of large standing waves, and the boat can be slapped around a bit if the transom isn't angled properly into a wave. Notwithstanding these minor annoyances, an oarsman can learn to manage the boat in various classes of rivers. John West, Prince Helfrich, Veltie Pruitt, and others of their ilk used this boat type safely and successfully for years. You can learn to do it too.

It is the boat's dual-purpose nature that I predict will cause this vessel to reemerge as a popular drift boat. One of the Northwest's premier drift-boat builders, Ray Heater, admired this craft when he first saw it on an Oregon coastal stream in the mid-1950s. Ray writes about the boat: "I found the Rapid Robert attractive because it could be used as more than a drift boat. A person with limited means could use this boat with a small outboard motor and troll and fish lakes and bays very well. The boat offers a variety of uses in one craft. I have even sailed this boat! The boat represents simplicity in this complicated world."[1]

The double-enders and Rogue dories are also used on lakes and bays. Their high prows and small transoms make them slow and awkward. The higher prows act as sails in the slightest breezes, so that on the oars or with a motor, the helmsman has to constantly correct the boat's direction. The square-ender, however, is more like a water bug, able to skitter hither and thither without the annoyances its sexier cousins experience. The lower profile in the bow, the broad base of the transom, and the less-pronounced rocker make for a suitable drift boat under power. For the person who seeks the better of two worlds, rivers and lakes, this boat won't be beat.

The lines and construction details of this boat were recovered over a four-year period, beginning in the mid-1990s. Fishing an Oregon coastal stream one day for steelhead, I spotted the outline of an abandoned boat in a brier patch of Himalayan blackberries along the bank. With my patient wife's permission, I beached my dory, struggled up the bank, pulled away the blackberry canes,

and examined the boat. The decay-resistant frames, probably white cedar, held the rotting side and bottom panels in place, barely. It had to be an old Rapid Robert! I made a mental note of its location, and then unsuccessfully tried to locate the boat's owner.

Within a couple weeks, I soloed that same stream with measuring tapes, loppers, notebook, and pencil on board. When I located the boat, I was able to capture measurements that provided basic information. These included frame placements along the side and bottom panels, the lengths of the side panels at the gunwale and chine, dimensions of the stem, transom and transom cutout for the motor, and reasonable estimates of the stem and transom bevels to receive the panels. The measurements reinforced my suspicions that this was a Rapid Robert. To accurately capture the lines of a boat, it's important to square it up and put it in that imaginary box. I was afraid to touch this boat for fear it would crumble, so I did the best I could with what I had. Later that week, with the numbers and recollections of the boat's construction still fresh in my mind, I laid the boat's lines down on paper. The breadth measurements of the boat faired out well, but the profile was a wild guess. I was not unsatisfied. A subsequent trip down the river the following spring showed no signs of the old boat. Unusually high waters that winter may have taken it, and now it may reside in a tidal mudflat somewhere. I don't know.

My attempt to re-create the lines of this relic remained dormant for a year. One day in 1998, Ray Heater's partner, Cyrus Happy, told me that he knew a man who had

Ray Heater and a customer test a Rapid Robert under power. The boat moves efficiently under power, and in the hands of a skilled oarsman, it handles class III water nicely. COURTESY OF RAY HEATER

One builder was anxious to get his Rapid Robert on the river and launched it before the stem post, frames, or top of the transom were trimmed. That's the way it is with many home boat builders—they just can't wait to put their craft on the river.
COURTESY OF JEFF BUHL

recently restored a Rapid Robert. Bob Mahoney owned the boat, which was not far from Cyrus and Ray's shop. At my first opportunity, I contacted and then visited Bob. Bob let me take profile measurements at the stem, transom and amidships. I then made another stab at the boat's profile matched to the boat's half-breadth measurements and came up with a reasonable set of lines.

I was certain that the old coastal boat was a Rapid Robert, but not sure enough that I wanted to invest time and energy into modeling the boat. In the meantime, Sam Johnson, one of Oregon's well-known small-boat aficionados, had recently completed a compilation of northwestern small boats for the Oregon Historical Society. I discussed with him my interest in recovering and recording the lines of the early drift boats and river dories. Sam graciously volunteered to share some of his notes and articles with me. It was a treasure trove of information, leads, and insights.

In that pile of material was a copy of an article by Thomas E. Riley about the Rapid Robert. The same article was apparently published twice, once in 1950 and again in 1955 by *Science and Mechanics*. In the articles, the author presented information to build the boat. The articles are the first reference I've seen to the boat as the Rapid Robert, a name that remains a conundrum to me.[2]

I immediately pulled out my line drawings of the old boat and compared them with the dimensions provided in Riley's article. The match was uncanny. Except for

frame #4, the elevations and half-breadth measurements were within 1/8 inch of the Riley data. I attributed the variation at frame #4 to my awkward eye (I was on my back for most of the measurements) or a frame warped by the boat's position and deteriorated condition. Nonetheless, I was thrilled by the comparison, and I wondered if I were really that good or simply lucky. I concluded that I do have the skills for this work, but I am also fortunate to have discovered people who share my interest in these boats and who have been unselfish in their support of this work. Indeed, one of the blessings I have received is the wealth of new friends.

Endnotes

1. Ray Heater, e-mail correspondence, November 11, 2005. Ray Heater owns and operates Ray's River Dories with his business partner Cyrus Happy. Ray considers this craft the traditional McKenzie River drift boat. Ray's boats may be viewed online at www.raysriverdories.com.

2. To date I have not located the original article, only copies. John Gardner in his July 1980 article about the McKenzie River drift boats *(National Fisherman)* cites a secondhand reference to the piece: Thomas E. Riley, "Rapid Robert, Craft Project No. 33," *Boat Builders' Handbook,* (Science and Mechanics, 1955), 162–165. Gardner then cites another copy of the article he found in his own files, vol. 3, (1956), 62–65. My search for the original article(s) continue.

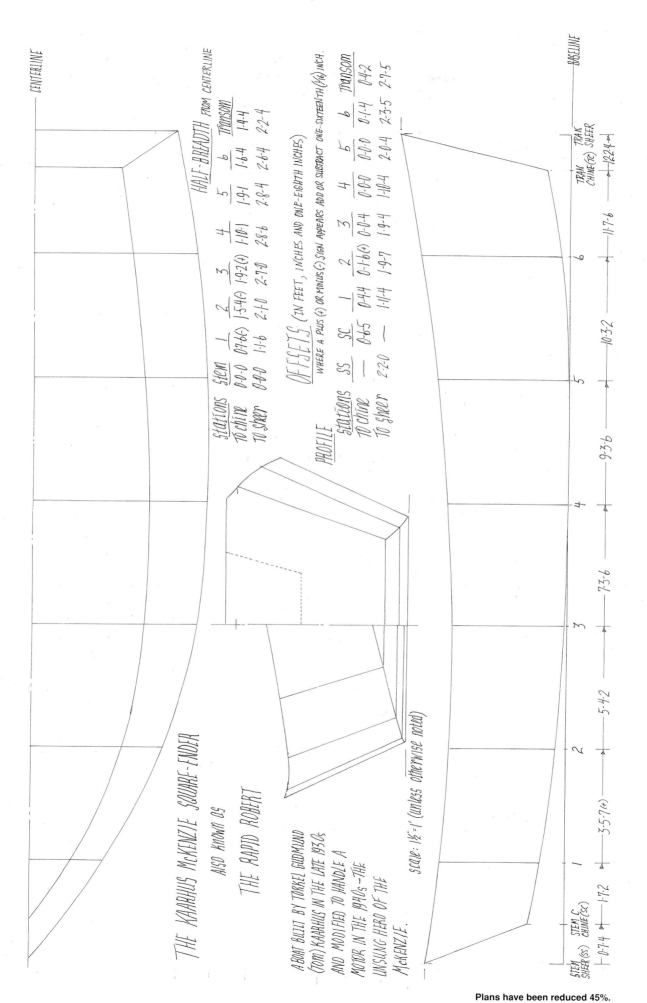

THE KAARHUS McKENZIE SQUARE-ENDER

ALSO KNOWN AS

THE RAPID ROBERT

A BOAT BUILT BY TORKEL GUDMUND (TOM) KAARHUS IN THE LATE 1970s AND MODIFIED TO HANDLE A MOTOR IN THE 1940s — THE UNSUNG HERO OF THE McKENZIE.

SCALE: 1½" = 1' (UNLESS OTHERWISE NOTED)

OFFSETS (IN FEET, INCHES AND ONE-EIGHTH INCHES) WHERE A PLUS (+) OR MINUS (-) SIGN APPEARS ADD OR SUBTRACT ONE-SIXTEENTH (¹⁄₁₆) INCH.

HALF-BREADTH FROM CENTERLINE

STATIONS	STEM	1	2	3	4	5	6	TRANSOM
TO CHINE	0-0-0	0-7-6(-)	1-5-4(-)	1-9-2(+)	1-10-1	1-9-1	1-6-4	1-4-4
TO SHEER	0-4-0	1-1-6	2-1-0	2-7-0	2-8-6	2-8-4	2-6-4	2-2-4

PROFILE

STATIONS	SS	SC	1	2	3	4	5	6	TRANSOM
TO CHINE	—	0-6-5	0-4-4	0-1-6(+)	0-0-4	0-0-0	0-0-0	0-1-4	0-4-2
TO SHEER	2-2-0	—	1-1-4	1-9-7	1-9-4	1-10-4	2-0-4	2-3-5	2-9-5

CENTERLINE

BASELINE

STEM SHEER (SS) 0-7-4 STEM C CHINE (SC) 1-7-2 1-7-2 3-5-7(+) 5-4-2 7-3-6 9-3-6 10-3-2 11-7-6 TRAN CHINE (TC) 12-2-4 TRAN SHEER

Plans have been reduced 45%.

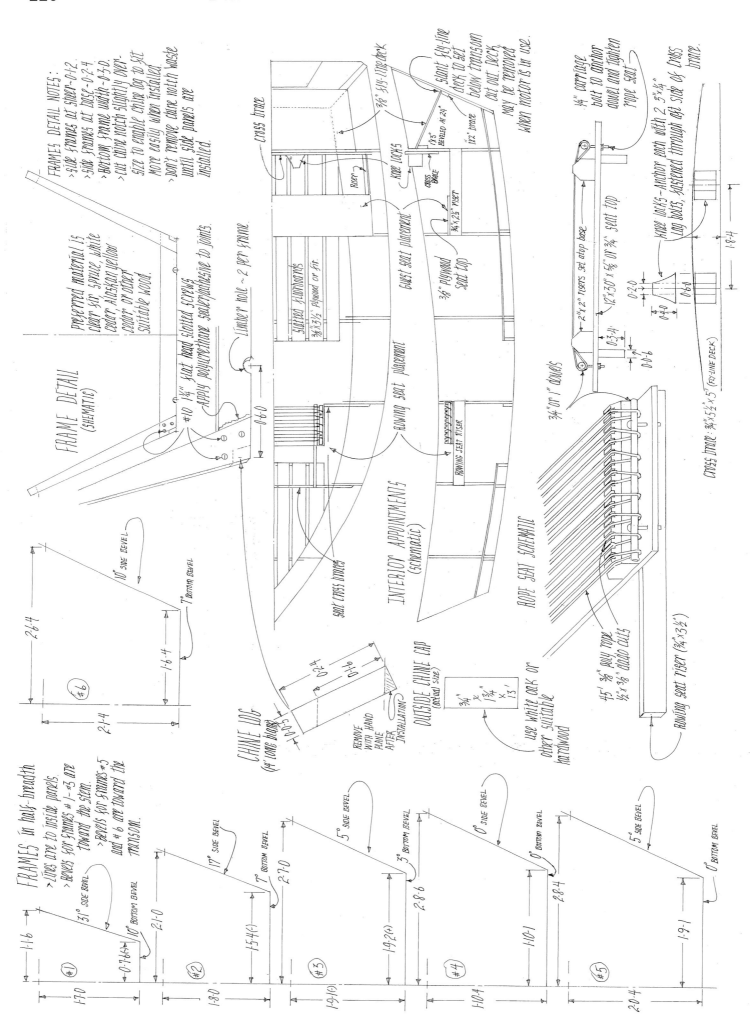

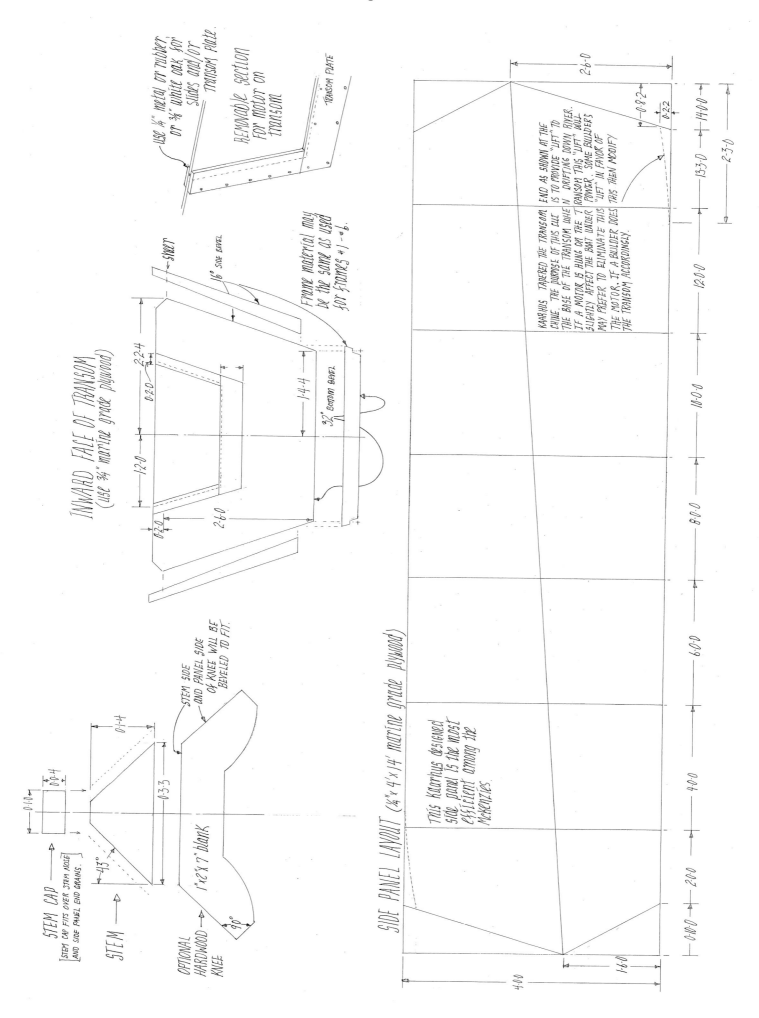

CHAPTER 17

The Bridges
A Kaarhus-like 16-Foot
Rapid Robert

"I like the versatility of this boat. It's roomy, handles my little 5 horsepower motor nicely on flat water, and has exceeded my expectations for handling on the river. I even use it salmon fishing and crabbing on salt water. The boat receives lots of compliments."

—DOUG BRIDGES

Tom Kaarhus built a few 16-foot square-enders, but the popularity of these boats waned when the double-enders came into their own in the 1940s. Kaarhus built several double-enders for his clients, but demand for the square-enders quietly faded. Over the years, I have kept my eyes open for an original Kaarhus 16-foot square-ender. The only boat that might be a Kaarhus original serves as a flowerbed in the hills west of Dallas, Oregon.

A few years ago, I found a 16-foot side panel on a burn pile near the McKenzie River. The landowner said it was part of an old Kaarhus boat, the remnants of which had long been scattered. He allowed me to pull the side panel off the burn pile. It was sorely rotted along its edges, but the locations of the boat's frames were clearly marked by the color contrasts created between wood protected from the sun and the exposed panel. Finding a flat spot adjacent to the burn pile, I laid the panel out and used some lath I had in my truck to sharpen the perimeter of the panel. The lath outlined an approximation of the original section's appearance. If this was indeed a 16-foot panel from a Kaarhus square-ender, the frames would have been installed perpendicular to the imaginary baseline of the boat. I therefore needed one set of measurements along the chine.

Each frame has a centerline. It is that line represented by the union of the bottom and side frame. The few Kaarhus boats I have examined show that Tom consistently installed his frames perpendicular to the imaginary baseline of the boat. If I captured the distances of each frame from the stem along the chine, I could loft the lines square to the bottom panel. I also puzzled over which side of the bleached frame marks was the center-line, that side of the rib that was matched to the bottom frame. The deterioration on the edges of the chine stole evidence that once existed about the bottom frames' locations. I guessed that Tom faced the bottom frames on the stem side of the ribs, a practice I have noted in his 14-foot boats. My regret that afternoon was that I didn't have my camera. A return to the area a few months later showed only the ash heap of the burn pile.

I decided that to re-create Tom's version of a 16-foot Rapid Robert would require more time than I was able to give the project. I vacillated between its inclusion and exclusion in this book.

And then Doug Bridges called me. It was February 2004.

Doug is a drift-boat aficionado from Sequim, Washington. He fishes rivers such as the Bogacheil in northwest Washington, and he enjoys the protected areas of the Strait of Juan de Fuca, Puget Sound, and the Hood Canal. Doug's first drift boat was built from a Don Hill set of plans, the double-ender with a transom.[1] Doug loves his Don Hill boat, but he was interested in creating something more versatile.

During Doug's telephone call, we discussed the 16-foot Rapid Robert. He told me that he had considered modifying the lines of the Don Hill boat to look more like an Oregon "mini dory" but had learned about the Rapid Robert from Ray Heater, Jackson Hole guide A. J. DeRosa, and my website. The more he learned about the boat, the more he liked the idea of a vessel that performs well both as a drift boat on the river and under power on open water. He told me that he didn't want to build a kit boat; his next boat had to be from scratch. He desired a boat with ample interior room, stability, and good performance. I was impressed with his knowledge, interest, and seeming woodworking abilities. During this visit, I told him that I had intentions of developing plans for a 16-foot Rapid Robert, but it would be a year or two before they would be ready.

Subsequent conversations were by e-mail. He asked if the 14-foot version of the boat could be modified to 16 feet. We talked about the challenges associated with such a modification. I don't know if it was his enthusiasm and knowledge or my presumptuousness, but I recall asking him if he would like to partner with me in designing the boat. Clearly he didn't want to wait a couple years for my plans. With a partner, I might be able to complete the boat's plans in time for this book. The risks were that we had not met personally, that he would build the first-off from plans with potential errors that could be costly to him, and that I would place considerable trust in a person who talked the talk but might not be able to walk it.

Doug notified me that he was interested in the project. I remember thinking, "This guy has a creative side screaming to get out." He saw the project as an opportunity to re-create something of historical value to the fishing and boating community and practical value to him. I have since learned that Doug's wife, Susan, also favored the idea of the project and encouraged him to use the best materials, employ a bright finish on the boat, and acquire a new trailer. Wow! Atta girl, Susan. It was heartwarming to learn that Doug has a partner as supportive of his work as my spouse is of mine.

Ed Reschke worked for Tom in the 1940s. He had sent me a sketch of his recollections about how the boat was built.[2] To reduce the rocker, Ed says that Tom removed up to 1½ inches of chine from the side panel in a fair and gradual arc from just aft of the stem to a point about two-thirds the distance to the transom. I drafted a couple sets of lines accordingly and attempted several models of the hull. I sent my lines drawings and a troubled model of the hull to Doug for his review. He checked my work and then crafted his own model, which he sent me with two recommendations: first, that we keep the chine lines of the side panels straight, reasoning

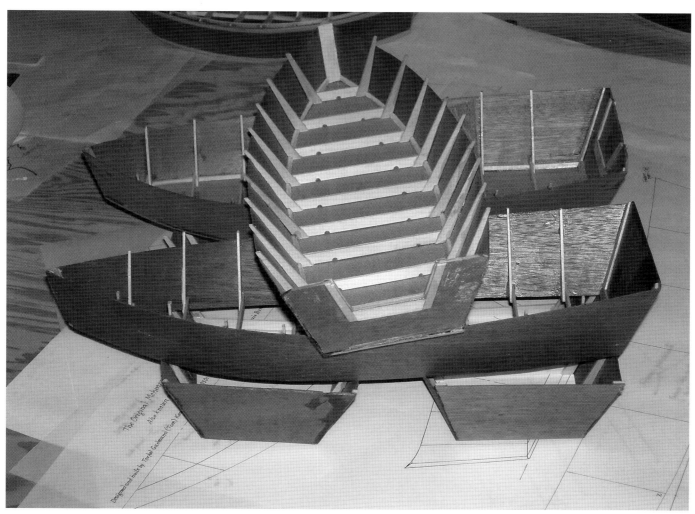

I didn't hand-carve a half-model plug for this boat. Doing so would have saved Doug and me the effort of working through five troubled hull models before getting it right. I can hear Dynamite Payson: "Serves you right, Roger."

The hull was framed free-form and is now ready to receive the bottom panel. COURTESY OF DOUG BRIDGES
Inset: *Doug encountered one anomaly at the base of the stem: The 1/4-inch side panel conformed nicely to the stem post, but the outside chine cap had difficulty making the bend. A couple small kerf cuts solved the problem. Alternatively, Doug could have faired the stem slightly with a hand plane.* COURTESY OF DOUG BRIDGES

that a novice builder would have less trouble marking and cutting panels without the curvature of the side panel's chine, and second, that we reduce the length of the required 16-foot 1/4-inch sheet to 15 feet, 9 inches. This adjustment would require the joining of two 4-by-8-foot panels rather than three. Properly married panels require a scarf joint beveled at a twelve-to-one ratio, or a 3-inch feather bevel on a 1/4-inch panel. Three inches of panel length is lost with the bevel.

I carefully examined Doug's hull model. It ran fair along the chine and sheer and sat square to my bench. Like me, he had difficulty fairing the chine, but the model looked good. Since I didn't have access to one of Tom's few 16-foot square-enders from which I could lift the lines, I thought, "What the heck." The goal was to design and build a Kaarhus-like 16-footer that would offer similar performance. We would design and offer a "bridge" from the early Kaarhus boat to a more contemporary, easier-to-build model of the original. With that decision, I modified the lines a bit, especially the side-panel layout. The change allowed for a little more elevation at the transom, from 29 to 29³/4 inches, with a

corresponding reduction at the bow, from 19 to just over 18 inches. I shortened the 4-by-16 panel to 15 feet, 9 inches and moved the base of the stem forward slightly, which faired the chine. I kept the same frame placements as appeared on the deteriorated panel I had found on the burn pile.

I shipped the revised lines to Doug, and he began work on his project. Doug was confident that any glitch he encountered with the lines could easily be corrected on the full-size boat. Indeed, Doug says that one of his most memorable moments was fitting the frames to the hull using the free-form construction technique. With minor modifications, he was able to fair the hull. Once the hull was complete, Doug was confident that everything else was okay. But there was one remaining challenge: fitting the outside chine cap to the stem. The bend into the stem was a little more than the white oak chine cap could handle. We had anticipated that this might be a problem. It could have been minimized by crafting a floating stem bevel to receive the side panels. The degree of bevel at the base of the stem is greater than the degree of bevel at the top of the stem. Instead, I calculated the difference between the two angles and gave Doug the average bevel for the stem. This allowed him to cut the stem on his table saw. To solve the problem with the chine cap, Doug cut a couple shallow kerfs on the underside of the chine at the offending point of contact into the stem. It worked nicely and is not noticeable to the casual observer.

Doug then completed the hull. The rest of the project took the greatest amount of time, but it was merely carpentry work. The hull hung together nicely, and now it was a matter of designing his interior space so that it met his fishing and family needs. He decided to install sliding seats for the helmsman, oarsman, and guests in order to keep the boat trim under different weight distributions. The boat has considerably more interior space and carrying capacity than his 16-foot Don Hill drift boat. Doug was now confident that his goal of building a great dual-purpose drift boat and flat-water boat had been achieved. He had only to test it.

Doug completed the boat in the late spring of 2005. Rivers were too low to run, but Sequim Bay on the Strait of Juan de Fuca offered the opportunity to test the boat under power on open water. Doug's little 5-horsepower long-shaft motor pushed the boat nicely, but he quickly learned to keep the boat in the sheltered areas of bays and estuaries. He fashioned a removable davit to increase the ease of pulling crab pots. It's common for multi-tasked salmon fishermen in the Northwest to drop crab pots while fishing, checking them periodically throughout the day. Doug's satisfaction with the boat and motor was obvious in his comments to me.

That fall, Doug was finally able to drop his new boat into the Bogachiel River to test its handling. River conditions were still low and provided a good test of the boat. "I am happy to say the 16-foot Rapid Robert exceeded my expectations for handling on the river," he says. "It has the feel of a bigger boat but doesn't handle much differently than my 16-foot Don Hill boat. It holds the current as well as or better than my Don Hill boat and turns more quickly than I thought it would. My sixteen-year-old son, Jared, took the boat through a very shallow but fast run. It is common to bang rocks here when the river is so low. We went right through without ever touching bottom. While we were fishing the hole below, two aluminum drift boats came through, and you could hear them banging on the rocks all the way down the river. I've got a keeper."[3] The broader bottom fore to aft and the reduced rocker provide more displacement and therefore a shallower draft.

It wasn't until April 2006 that I was able to meet Doug for the first time and test the boat. Doug and Susan accepted our invitation to attend the Depoe Bay

The first time Doug Bridges and I met face-to-face was at the April 2006 Depoe Bay (Oregon) Wooden Boat Festival, more than a year after Doug's completion of the boat. Doug and Susan brought the boat down for the show. COURTESY OF DOUG BRIDGES

Doug tests the boat's trim, with our spouses seated fore and aft, on the North Santiam River south of Salem. It seemed that regardless of weight placement, a safe trim was maintained. COURTESY OF DOUG BRIDGES

Wooden Boat Festival and to spend a day on the river. Our work together had been done entirely by phone, e-mail, and snail mail.

Four things impressed me about the boat. First was its roominess and carrying capacity. I don't think the draft was more than 4 inches, and regardless of the location of weight the boat remained trim in the water. Second, it is light on the oars. In other words, the boat moves with minimal effort and pivots as easily as my more fully rockered 16-foot McKenzie. It seems to glide across the surface. Third, I didn't notice any chine dip when I purposely moved the boat into a strong eddy 90 degrees to the current. Finally, I am very impressed with Doug's workmanship. He did a superb job of crafting the boat. It stands out.

With encouragement from Susan, Doug applied a bright finish to the exterior of the boat. "It is like a magnet for compliments everywhere we go. I have yet to see a Rapid Robert in this neck of the woods, so I imagine most people on the river will think that we are pretty bizarre."[4] "Envy" may be a more appropriate descriptor of coming reactions. The boat's carrying capacity and dual-purpose nature make it a great fishing and family riverboat.

It should be no mystery why I have chosen to call this boat the *Bridges.* Doug Bridges was instrumental in creating a bridge from the original Rapid Robert to a contemporary and highly functional craft that honors the originator, Tom Kaarhus. I think Tom would be pleased.

Endnotes

1. Don Hill built his first drift boat in 1961 at the age of fifteen. Hill has been a lifelong boatbuilder and McKenzie River fishing guide. His website is www.dhdriftboats.com/.

2. Ed Reschke correspondence, April 15, 2002.

3. Doug Bridges e-mail, November 20, 2005.

4. Ibid., July 31, 2005.

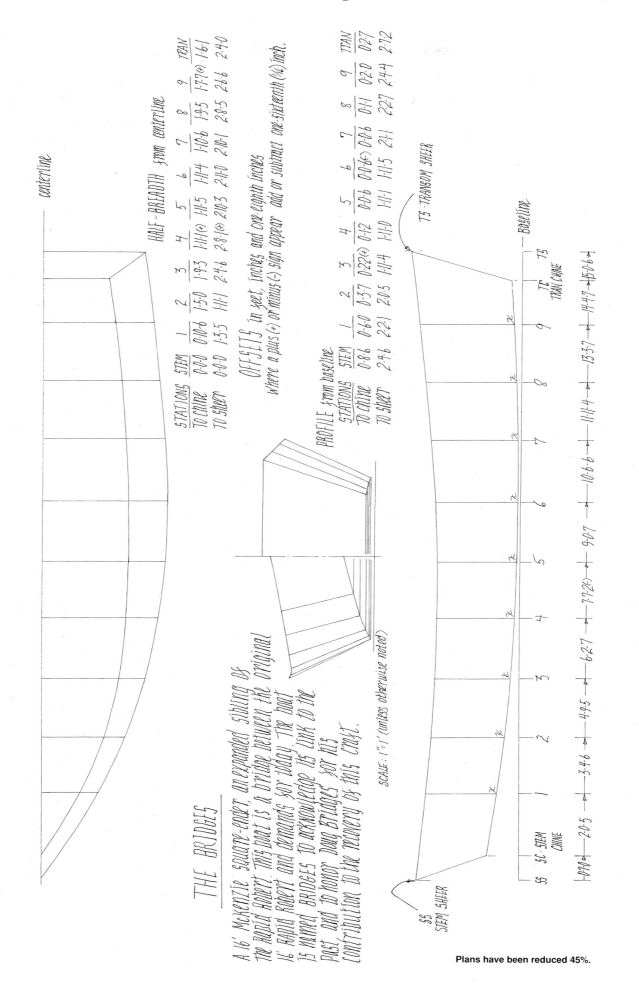

THE BRIDGES

A 16' McKenzie square-ender, an expanded sibling of
the Rapid Robert. This boat is a bridge between the original
16' Rapid Robert and demands for today. The boat
is named BRIDGES to acknowledge its link to the
past, and to honor Doug Bridges for his
contribution to the recovery of this craft.

HALF-BREADTH from centerline

OFFSETS in feet, inches and one-eighth inches
where a plus (+) or minus (-) sign appear add or subtract one-sixteenth (1/16) inch.

STATIONS	STEM	1	2	3	4	5	6	7	8	9	TRAN
TO CHINE	0-0-0	0-10-6	1-5-0	1-9-3	1-11-(+)	1-11-5	1-11-4	1-10-6	1-9-5	1-7-7(+)	1-6-1
TO SHEER	0-0-0	1-3-5	1-11-1	2-4-6	2-8-1(+)	2-10-3	2-11-0	2-10-1	2-8-5	2-6-6	2-4-0

PROFILE from baseline

STATIONS	STEM	1	2	3	4	5	6	7	8	9	TRAN
TO CHINE	0-8-6	0-6-0	0-3-7	0-2-2(+)	0-1-2	0-0-6	0-0-6(+)	0-0-6	0-1-1	0-2-0	0-2-7
TO SHEER	2-4-6	2-2-1	2-0-5	1-11-4	1-11-0	1-11-1	1-11-5	2-1-1	2-2-7	2-4-4	2-7-2

SCALE: 1"=1' (unless otherwise noted)

Plans have been reduced 45%.

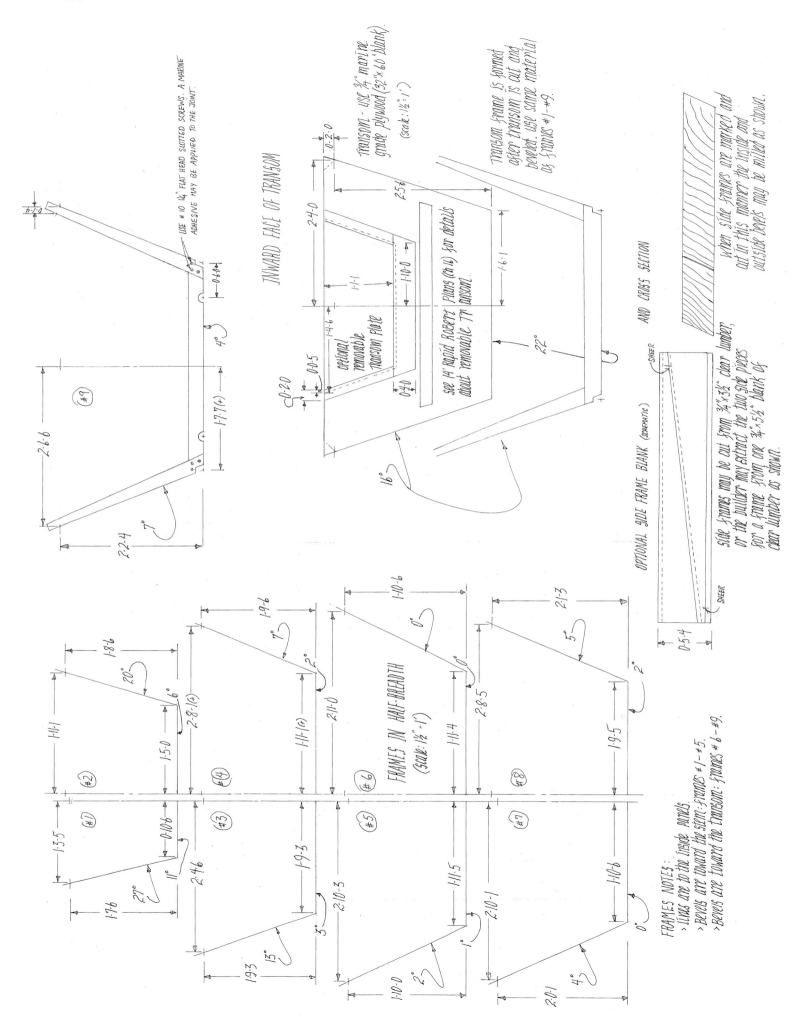

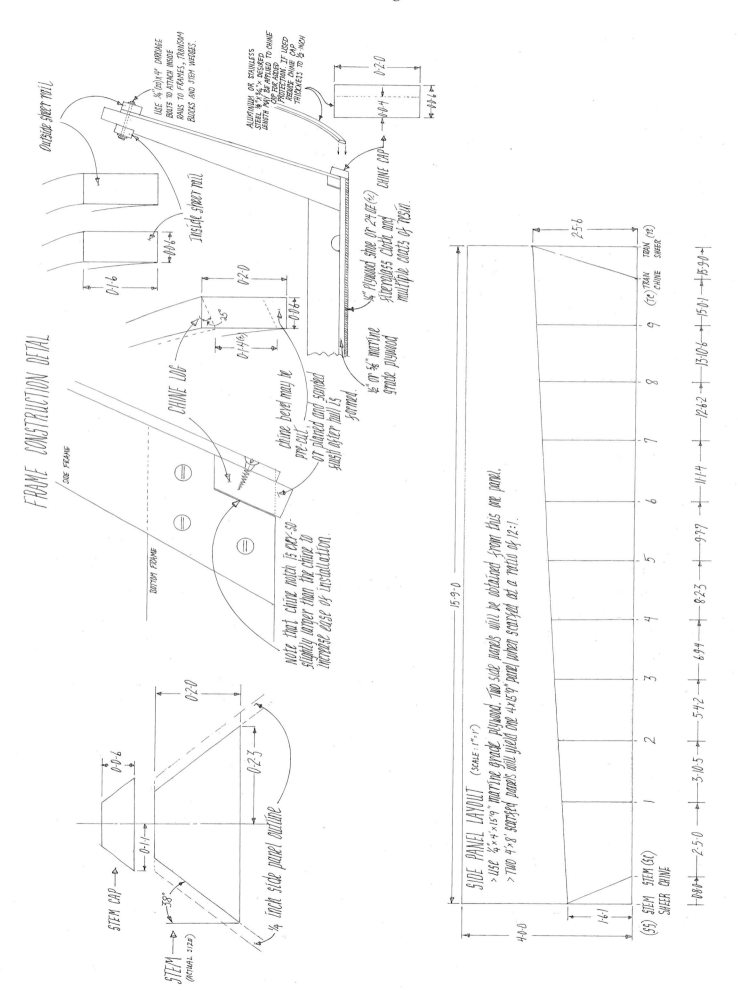

FRAME CONSTRUCTION DETAIL

Outside sheer rail

Inside sheer rail

USE ¼" (20)x4" CARRIAGE BOLTS TO ATTACH INSIDE RAILS TO FRAMES, TRANSOM BLOCKS AND STEM WEDGES.

ALUMINUM OR STAINLESS STEEL ⅛"x¾"x DESIRED LENGTH MAY BE APPLIED TO CHINE CAP FOR ADDED PROTECTION. IF USED, REDUCE CHINE CAP THICKNESS TO ½-INCH.

CHINE CAP

¼" PLYWOOD SIDE OR 24 OZ (½) FIBERGLASS CLOTH AND MULTIPLE COATS OF RESIN.

½" or ⅝" MARINE GRADE PLYWOOD

CHINE LOG

Chine bevel may be pre-cut, or planed and sanded flush after hull is formed.

SIDE FRAME

BOTTOM FRAME

Note that chine notch is over-so-slightly larger than the chine to increase ease of installation.

STEM CAP

STEM (ACTUAL SIZE)

¼ inch side panel outline

38°

SIDE PANEL LAYOUT (SCALE: 1"=1')
> USE ¼"x4'x15'9" MARINE GRADE PLYWOOD. TWO SIDE PANELS WILL BE OBTAINED FROM THIS ONE PANEL.
> TWO 4'x8' SCARFED PANELS WILL YIELD ONE 4'x15'9" PANEL WHEN SCARFED AT A RATIO OF 12:1.

15-9-0

2-5-6

4-0-0

1-6-1

(SS) STEM STEM (SC)
SHEER CHINE

(TC) TRAN
CHINE

TRAN (TS)
SHEER

1   2   3   4   5   6   7   8   9

0-8-0 2-5-0 3-10-5 5-4-2 6-9-4 8-2-3 9-7-7 11-1-4 12-6-2 13-10-6 15-0-1 15-9-0

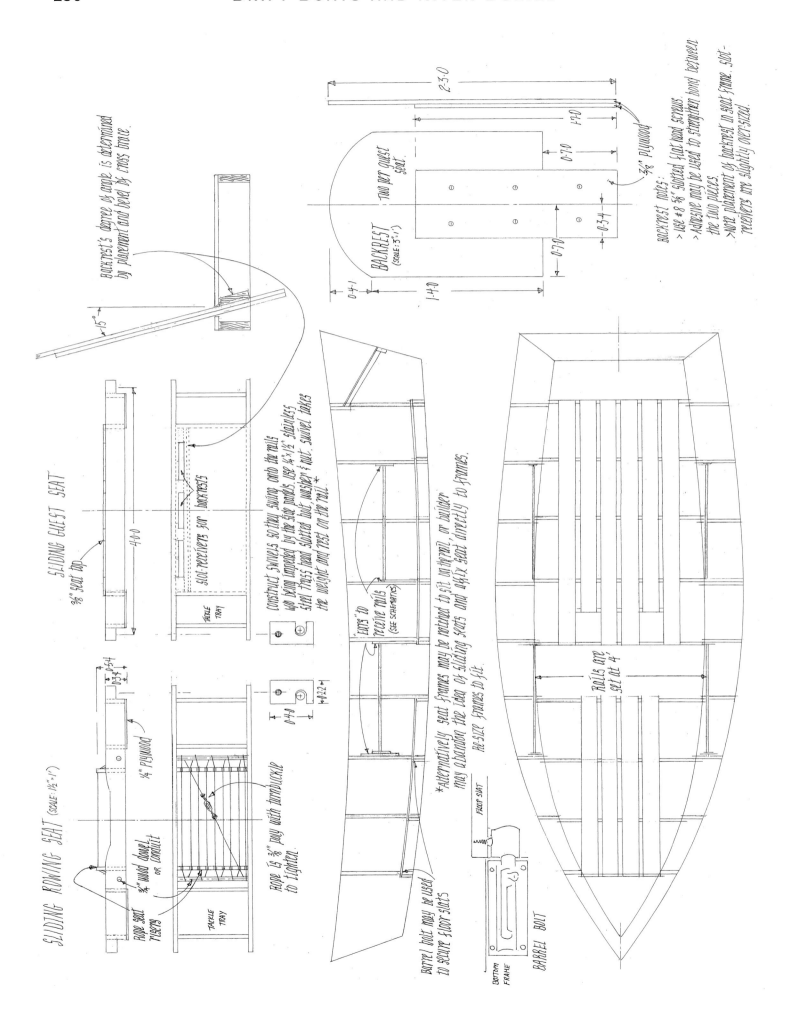

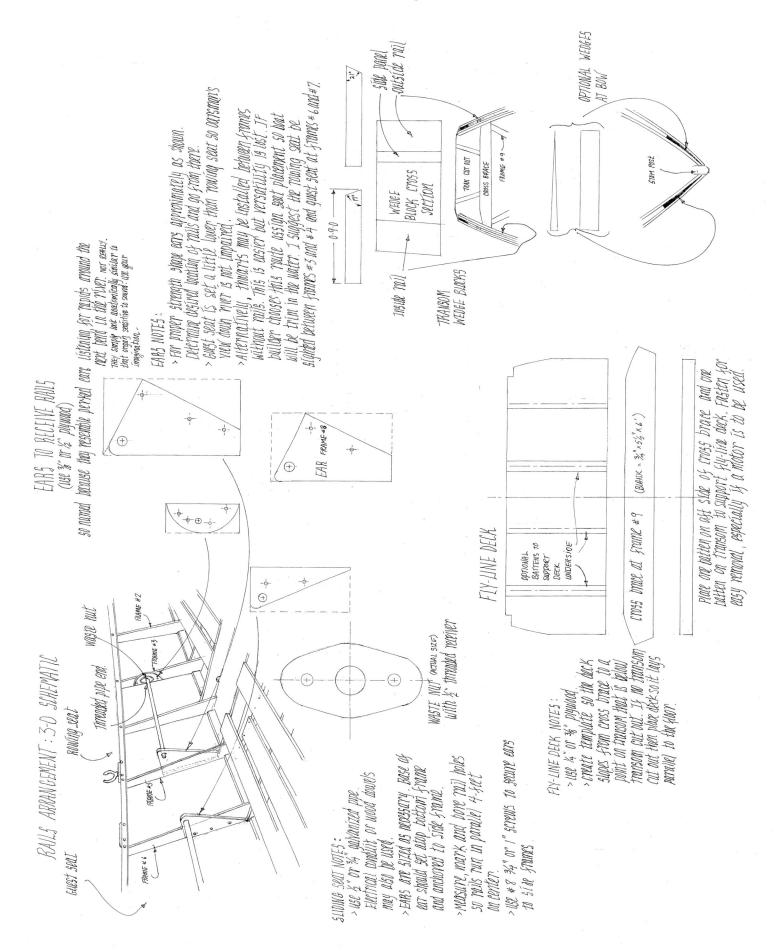

CHAPTER 18

The Double-Enders
Three Boats by Woodie Hindman

In the eyes of many, the double-ender is the apotheosis of McKenzie River drift boats.
In pure numbers, the double-ender with a transom is the most popular type,
with a hull design recognized and used across the North American
continent and in many parts of South America and New Zealand.

Finding Woodie's First Double-Ender

I studied the Glen Wooldridge sled in the grove for a few minutes, trying to decide if I wanted to capture her lines. The boat was one of Glen Wooldridge's early sleds he used to run up the Rogue River. Shortly after his 1915 run from Grants Pass to Gold Beach, Wooldridge said that someday he would design a boat that he could run up the whitewater of the Rogue under power, a vision most people of the area would have thought pure fancy. Wooldridge, however, had a knack for translating ideas into concrete reality, and in 1947, he made his first successful run from Gold Beach to Grants Pass in a powered river sled. He went on to run a variety of northwestern rivers, and today he is considered the father of whitewater jet boating. Commercial jet-boat operators on the Rogue talk fondly about the "old man of the river" and his influence on their livelihood today. I am singularly interested in drift boats and river dories, but it seemed fortuitous that this boat and I were at this place. I decided to take her measurements.

The trip to and from this place was an event in itself. It was February 1998. Bob Schroeder, son of a former colleague of mine at Oregon State University, Walt Schroeder, invited my wife and me to Paradise Lodge on the Rogue River for a winter weekend. It was to be a working weekend. Walt Schroeder had begun a tradition of sorts several years earlier to help the Paradise Lodge owners prune the fruit trees on the property. In typical learn-by-doing fashion, Walt used the event as an educational workshop for Paradise Lodge staff and others. The capstone of Walt's OSU Extension career was in Curry County. His office was in Gold Beach. The annual pruning event began with Allen Boice and then continued with Court Boice, Allen's son and new lodge proprietor. It seems that the sons continued a tradition of their fathers, though the focus became getting the job done, not using it as a teaching experience. Paradise Lodge has since been sold.

The draw for me, of course, was not the work. It was the place. The location is a wilderness lodge accessible only by boat. For the bold pilot with keen reflexes and intimate knowledge of the area, the lodge is also reachable by small plane. My motives for accepting Bob Schroeder's invitation were three. First, it was a nice midwinter trek to an area we frequent on our Rogue River trips. Second, I could exercise my limited horticultural skills on some fruit trees in a remote enough area that others wouldn't scrutinize the quality of my work. Most important, however, it was an opportunity to examine and capture the lines of the Wooldridge boat.

Court Boice met our small group of fruit tree experts at Foster Bar (see map on page 46). Our party included Bob Rackham, an extension horticulturist from Corvallis; Bob Schroeder, the son of a horticulturist; our wives; and me. Our 15-mile upriver trip was by jet boat, a twin-engine, twin-impeller silver thing with *Paradise* emblazened on its hull. The low, guttural throb of the engines as they patiently idled while we boarded showed more life as Court backed off the shore, and then surged with a steady hum as we powered upriver. We scaled rapids like Tacoma and Clay Hill and skimmed over shallow riffles that appeared no more than a few inches deep. The river didn't exhibit the spring or summertime color I was accustomed to. Leafless oaks, evergreen madrone trees, grassy slopes, and the ribbon of aqua blue river against a graying sky were beautiful nonetheless. Our trip to Paradise Lodge was uneventful, and we made a long trek up the steps to the lodge to be greeted by the warm smiles of the staff. It was Friday. Our return trip to Foster Bar two days later was a little more trying.

Earlier phone conversations with Court Boice drew me to the dory. I was disappointed to discover on arrival at Paradise, however, that the boat was a Wooldridge wooden sled and not one of the early dories he had built to navigate the Rogue on his many downriver trips. Perhaps it's a gender thing, that two men can talk about the same boat within the context of their experiences—Court a jet-boat aficionado and me a drift-boat man—and in fact talk about two different boat types unbeknownst to the other. Clearly the sled boat was historically significant, although it didn't address my immediate research needs. Nonetheless, as I examined the sled, I decided that it would be prudent to take its measurements.

As I turned to walk back to the cabin and retrieve my equipment, something in the pole structure at the center of the grove caught my eye. In the early-morning twilight, I could make out the sharp crescent lines of a small boat. As I walked toward the boat, each step created the illusion of movement in the boat's profile. It was strange.

The boat was a small double-ended drift boat. I guessed its stem-to-stern centerline length at about 13 feet, with a bottom width at the chine of about 3 feet, perhaps a little more. The boat had the greatest rocker fore to aft of any drift boat I have yet seen. It very much had the tight, crescent shape of standing waves in a rapid, and I recalled Woodie Hindman's comment that he liked to build his boats so they conformed to the shape of the river's waves.

Court Boice was stirring in the lodge, and I asked him about the little double-ender. He said that one of the Helfrich brothers had brought it downriver and loaned it to him for his little museum. Court knew that it was a McKenzie double-ender and that Prince Helfrich had built it. Prince had made several boats of this type for his Skyline Boys Camp on the McKenzie. I decided then and there to take her lines and then visit

the Helfrich family on my return home. The Wooldridge boat would have to wait.

I squared the boat on its stand as best I could, and with Sue's help, I took its measurements. The boat measured 14 feet, 6 inches around the sheer, and its lines were about as poetic a set of lines as I had yet seen in a drift boat. I imagined the vessel as the Porsche of the McKenzie: smart looking and agile, with an ability to pirouette on a dime. My visions of the boat proved real when I first put its re-creation on the water.

When we returned home, I immediately went to work on the boat's lines drawings. I plotted my measurements to scale, and slowly the profile, breadth, and body views of the boat emerged on paper. I was still insecure enough in my ability to lay down a credible set of lines that I shipped the lines to Dynamite for his review. One of several things I have learned about Dynamite is that when his interest is piqued, he'll jump into a project without a life preserver. I asked him for his analysis of the lines, and in return I received a hand-carved plug and a scaled model of the boat. I was stunned. When I called to thank him, he said, "Well, you wanted my evaluation. This is the best way I know to test a set a set of lines. This boat can be built. Ya done good." I was pleased.

The boat was not built, however, until I confirmed its niche in the scheme of things. Woodie Hindman and Prince Helfrich were very good friends, and there was

Home boatbuilder Kevin Kean of Woodinville, Washington, installs thwarts on his newly constructed double-ender. He worked on the boat on and off over a two-year period.
COURTESY OF KEVIN KEAN

Kean's finished boat, a project he says was worth the time and effort. COURTESY KEVIN KEAN

much give and take in boats and knowledge about their performance between the two. An innocuous reference in Woodie's diaries about a set of boat patterns and Prince Helfrich, coupled with their friendship, led me to conclude that Woodie loaned his 14-foot double-ender patterns to Prince for his boys camp. I had been unable to locate a boat that approximates Woodie's first small double-ender—until now. It seemed to me that the boat at Paradise Lodge was as close as I would come to the original double-ender that Woodie built during the winter of 1939–40. I decided to add the boat to my collection of drift-boat types on the McKenzie.

Ray Heater built the first of these plans in 2000.[1] His shared interest in the origins of the McKenzie River drift boats led him to offer to build the boat for me. I was elated at the offer, and the drift boat is a beautiful piece of work, reflective of a skilled craftsman. The result is a boat that is light to handle, has extraordinary maneuverability, and thus far has comfortably handled the biggest water an Oregon river can throw at it. The boat is a great one-

person boat. I understand Prince Helfrich's interest in the boat as a learning tool for his campers. It has the capacity for two people, but that's it. The accentuated rocker causes the boat to draft more than the other McKenzies. Moreover, the narrower bottom width amidships makes her more tender, tipsy. My boating partner Ken Brown discovered that when I shifted my weight while he was standing behind the rowing thwart. My movement threw him off-balance, accentuated by a reaction of the boat, and over he went. Fortunately, Ken has the reflexes of a cat, and his derriere was the only piece of his anatomy that got wet when he caught the gunwales, legs draped in the boat. I rediscovered two things that trip: first, that safety must remain a priority, and second, that it is very difficult to pull someone back into a boat while laughing uncontrollably.

The little double-ender whetted my appetite to find and re-create Woodie's two other double-enders: his 16-foot true double-ender and his 16-foot double-ender with a transom.

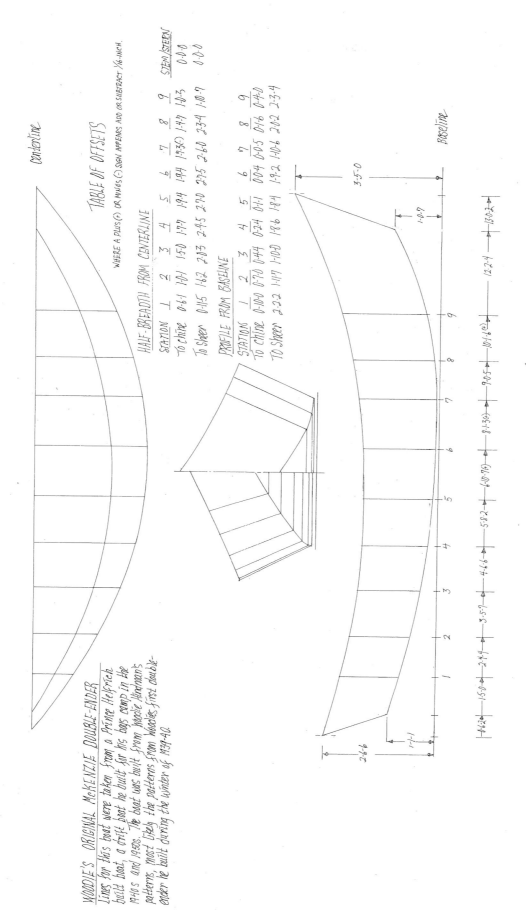

WOODIE'S ORIGINAL McKENZIE DOUBLE-ENDER

Lines for this boat were taken from a Prime Helfrich built boat, a drift boat he built for his boys camp in the 1940s and 1950s. The boat was built from Woodie Hindman's patterns, most likely the patterns from Woodie's first double-ender he built during the winter of 1939-40.

TABLE OF OFFSETS

WHERE A PLUS (+) OR MINUS (-) SIGN APPEARS ADD OR SUBTRACT 1/16-INCH.

HALF-BREADTH FROM CENTERLINE

STATION	1	2	3	4	5	6	7	8	9	STEM/STERN
To Chine	0-6-1	1-0-1	1-5-0	1-7-7	1-9-4	1-9-4	1-9-3(-)	1-4-7	1-10-3	0-0-0
To Sheer	0-11-5	1-6-2	2-0-3	2-4-5	2-7-0	2-7-5	2-6-0	2-3-4	1-10-7	0-0-0

PROFILE FROM BASELINE

STATION	1	2	3	4	5	6	7	8	9
To Chine	0-10-0	0-7-0	0-4-4	0-2-4	0-1-1	0-0-4	0-0-5	0-1-6	0-4-0
To Sheer	2-2-2	1-4-7	1-0-0	1-0-0	1-8-4	1-9-2	1-10-6	2-0-2	2-3-4

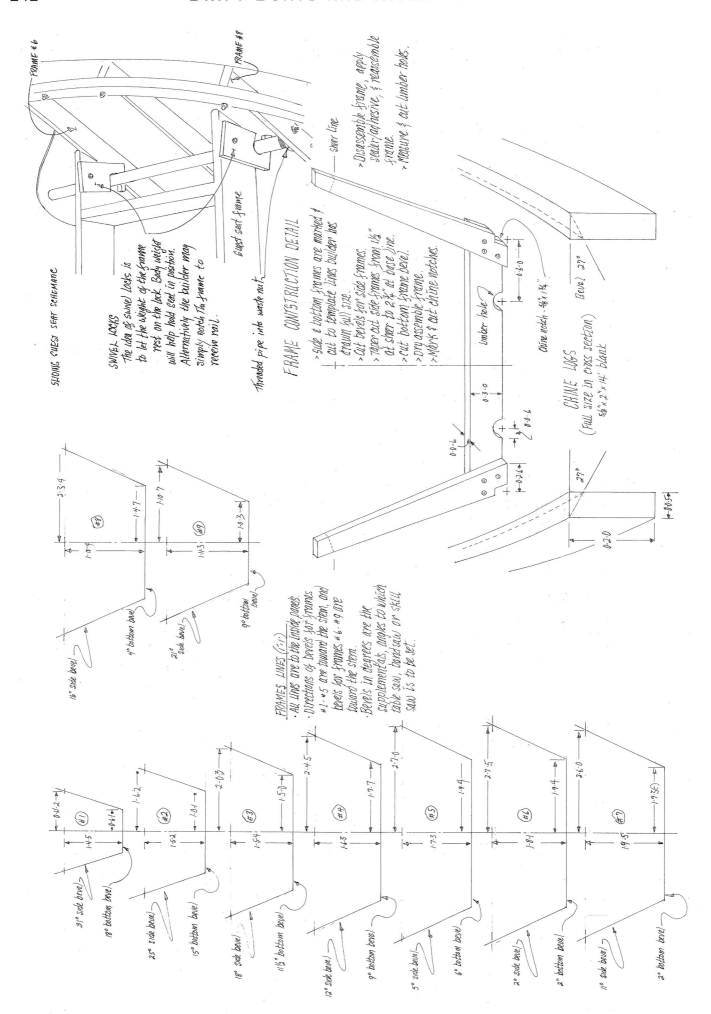

SLIDING GUEST SEAT SCHEMATIC

FRAME #6

FRAME #8

Guest seat frame

Threaded pipe into waste nut

SWIVEL LOCKS

The idea of swivel locks is to let the weight of the frame rest on the lock. Body weight will help hold seat in position. Alternatively the builder may simply notch the frame to receive rail.

FRAME CONSTRUCTION DETAIL

- Side & bottom frames are marked & cut to template lines builder has drawn full size.
- Cut bevels for side frames.
- Taper cut side frames from 1½" at sheer to 2¾" at base line.
- cut bottom frame bevel.
- Dry assemble frame.
- Mark & cut chine notches.
- Disassemble frame, apply sealer/adhesive, & reassemble frame.
- Measure & cut limber holes.

Sheer line

Limber hole

Chine notch - ⅝ x ¾

0-6-0
0-3-0
0-2-0
0-0-7
0-0-0
0-0-6

CHINE LOGS
(full size in cross section)
⅝" x 2" x 14' blank

Bevel 27°

27°

0-2-0
0-0-5

FRAMES LINES (1½":1')
- All lines are to the inside panels.
- Directions of bevels for frames #1 - #5 are toward the stem, and bevels for frames #6 - #9 are toward the stem.
- Bevels in degrees are the supplements, angles to which table saw, bandsaw or skill saw is to be set.

#8
0-2-3-4
1-4-7
1-10-9

16° side bevel
4° bottom bevel

#9
1-10-7
1-0-3
1-11-3

21° side bevel
9° bottom bevel

#1
0-11-2
0-11-1
1-6-2
1-4-5

31° side bevel
18° bottom bevel

#2
1-0-1
2-0-3
1-5-2

25° side bevel
15° bottom bevel

#3
1-5-0
2-4-5
1-5-4

18° side bevel
11½° bottom bevel

#4
1-7-7
2-7-0
1-4-3

12° side bevel
9° bottom bevel

#5
1-9-4
2-7-5
1-7-3

5° side bevel
6° bottom bevel

#6
1-9-4
2-6-0
1-8-1

2° side bevel
2° bottom bevel

#7
1-7-3½
1-9-5

11° side bevel
2° bottom bevel

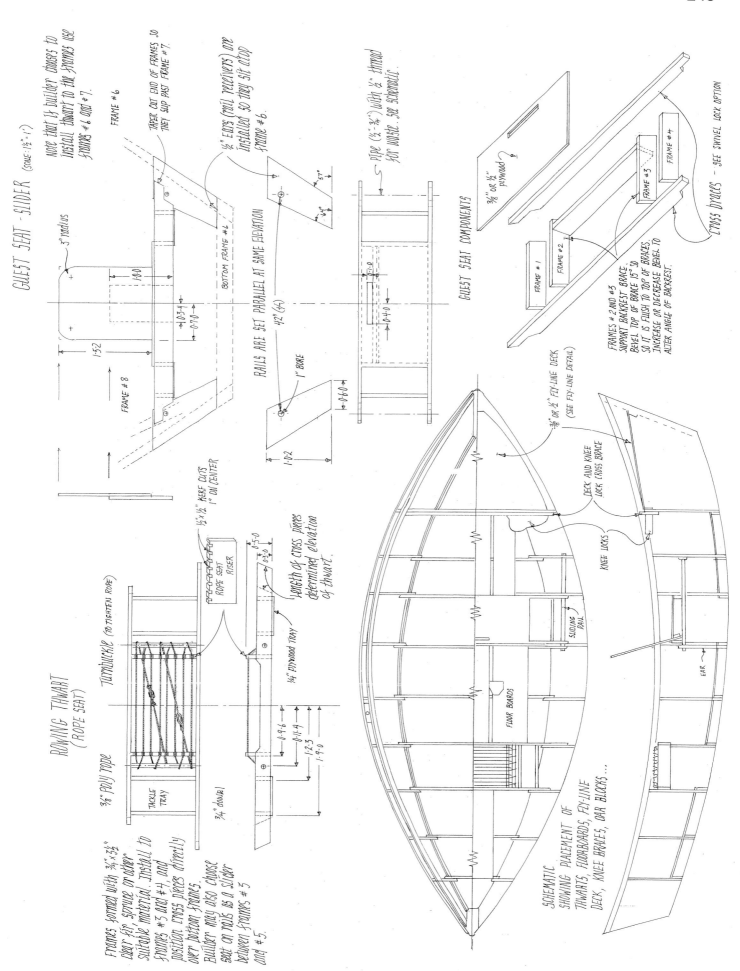

GUEST SEAT - SLIDER (SCALE 1½"=1')

Note that if builder chooses to install thwart to the frames use frames #6 and #7.

FRAME #6

TAPER CUT END OF FRAMES SO THEY SLIP PAST FRAME #7.

½" EARS (RAIL RECEIVERS) ARE INSTALLED SO THEY SIT ATOP FRAME #6.

3" radius

FRAME #8

BOTTOM FRAME #2

RAILS ARE SET PARALLEL AT SAME ELEVATION

PIPE (½"-¾") WITH ½" THREAD FOR NOOSE. SEE SCHEMATIC.

42" (A)

1" BORE

GUEST SEAT COMPONENTS

⅜" OR ½" PLYWOOD

FRAME #3

FRAME #4

FRAME #1

FRAME #2

CROSS BRACES - SEE SWIVEL LOCK OPTION

FRAMES #2 AND #3 SUPPORT BACKREST BRACE. BEVEL TOP OF BRACE 15° SO IT IS FLUSH TO TOP OF BRACES. INCREASE OR DECREASE BEVEL TO ALTER ANGLE OF BACKREST.

ROWING THWART (ROPE SEAT)

TURNBUCKLE (TO TIGHTEN ROPE)

½"×½" KERF CUTS 1" ON CENTER

ROPE SEAT RISER

length of cross pieces determined elevation of thwart

¼" PLYWOOD TRAY

⅜" POLY ROPE

TACKLE TRAY

¾" dowel

Frames formed with ¾"×3½" clear fir, spruce or other suitable material. Install to frames #3 and #4, and position cross pieces directly over bottom frames. Builder may also choose boat on rails as a slider between frames #5 and #5.

⅜" OR ½" FLY-LINE DECK (SEE FLY-LINE DETAIL)

DECK AND KNEE LOCK CROSS BRACE

KNEE LOCKS

SLIDING RAIL

FLOOR BOARDS

EAR

SCHEMATIC SHOWING PLACEMENT OF THWARTS, FLOORBOARDS, FLY-LINE DECK, KNEE BRACES, OAR BLOCKS...

SIDE PANEL INSTRUCTIONS - This double-ender has the greatest rocker fore to aft of all the McKenzies.

1. From left to right along base of panel measure and mark points S.C. stations #1-#9, S.C. and S.F.S.
2. Establish perpendicular lines (dotted) at each mark just established.
3. Measure and mark chine at each perpendicular line.
4. With a straight, flexible batten connect chine points S.C. stations #1-#9, and S.C. This is the chine line.
5. Measure and mark sheer at each perpendicular (S.S. stations #1-#9 and S.F.S).
6. With a straight, flexible batten connect sheer points. This is the sheer line.
7. Connect points S.S. to S.C. with a straight edge, and connect points S.F.S. to S.F.C. these are the bow and stern lines. The panel's lines are thus established.
8. At sheer measure to left of dotted perpendicular as noted and mark (stations #1-#9).
9. With straight edge scribe a line from the new sheer mark to intersection of dotted line and the chine line. This is the centerline for each frame.
10. Cut out the side panel. Use the panel as a template for the second panel. Done correctly the second panel will be taken from the remnant 4'x5' sheet.

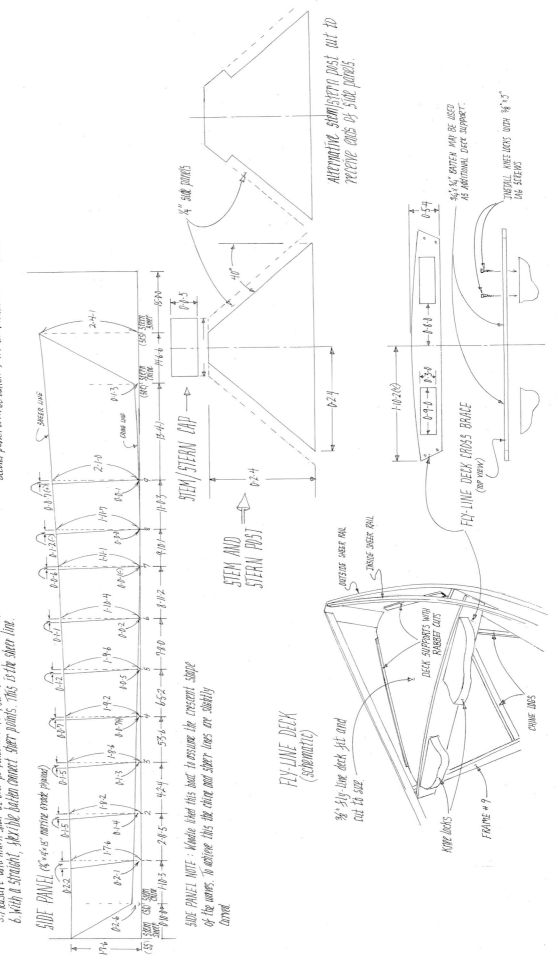

SIDE PANEL ("4"x4'x15' marine grade plywood)

SIDE PANEL NOTE: Woodie likes this boat to assume the crescent shape of the waves. To achieve this the chine and sheer lines are slightly curved.

STEM/STERN CAP

STEM AND STERN POST

FLY-LINE DECK (schematic)

⅜" fly-line deck jig and cut to size

knee locks

FRAME #9

Alternative stem/stern post cut to receive ends of side panels.

¼" side panels

FLY-LINE DECK CROSS BRACE (top view)

¾"x¾" batten may be used as additional deck support.

Install knee locks with ⅜"x3" lag screws

OUTSIDE SHEER RAIL

INSIDE SHEER RAIL

DECK SUPPORTS WITH RABBET CUTS

CHINE LOGS

The 16-Foot Double-Ender

When reliable 16-foot plywood panels became available toward the end of World War II, Woodie built his first 16-foot double-ender. It was roomier and had more carrying capacity than the 14-foot boat, and the boat quickly became popular among the guides. It also became Woodie's boat of choice for guiding and pleasure.

I don't know if his attachment to the double-ender was a result of his attraction to the lines or was because this was truly his boat. He had been building the Kaarhus square-ender, a boat he couldn't claim as his own, for several years. The double-ender, however, was his adaptation. He created it. Woodie could call it his own. Like Tom Kaarhus, Woodie wasn't proprietary about his boats, but like most men, he was probably a bit territorial. He wanted to leave his mark somewhere, and that mark was the double-ender.

Remnants of Woodie's 16-foot double-enders are rare. Leroy Pruitt has one, though Marty Rathje built it. Marty built Woodie Hindman's double-enders after he purchased Woodie's boatbuilding business in 1954. I have taken a few measurements off the boat. There is an anomaly in the boat: It measures just over 15 feet around the sheer. That may have been a function of the plywood lengths Rathje had to work with for this boat, or the original buyer may have specified the length. I am confident that when Woodie built his boats, he chose to get as much out of his material as possible. Boatbuilder Ray Heater, who built a 15-foot double-ended Hindman replica a few years ago, has that same tendency today.

My confidence in trying to re-create the lines of the Hindman 16-foot double-ender didn't surface until I uncovered a set of patterns that had been drawn up in 1968. President Herbert Hoover was born in Iowa but raised in Oregon. Over the years, he developed a fondness for fishing the McKenzie River and was a frequent visitor there before, during, and after his presidency. Several guides claimed to have squired Hoover, a number that has probably grown a bit over the years. The novelty of the patterns is the name given the boat type, the Herbert Hoover McKenzie River Boat Plan, although it is curious that the patterns carry a date four years subsequent to Hoover's death. Someone developed the plans at Weyerhaeuser in Cottage Grove, Oregon, and the copyright belongs to the company. An off-and-on two-year search for the person responsible for the plans was fruitless. No one in Cottage Grove was familiar with the plans. I then turned to research archivist Megan Moholt at the Weyerhaeuser headquarters in Federal Way, Washington. She was unable to locate either a copy or the person responsible for the patterns.

In 2005, I decided that I had enough information to lay down the lines of the 16-foot double-ender with confidence. The Herbert Hoover plans were a great help, because the frames, stem, and stern post bevels closely matched my own calculations. After all, there aren't many variables when building a 16-foot double-ender. Woodie always extracted two side panels from one 4-foot-wide ¼-inch sheet of plywood, and he took full advantage of the 4-foot plywood width on the bottom panel. I also concluded, perhaps erroneously, that the person who developed the Herbert Hoover McKenzie River Boat Plan did so either from a set of patterns or from boat measurements, quite possibly Woodie Hindman's. The Weyerhaeuser plans appeared a year after Woodie's death. Other boat builders were on the scene at that time and it is possible they were the source for the Weyerhaeuser plans. Regardless of the source, the plans represent Woodie Hindman's 16-foot double-ender. Though my plans for this double-ender are an amalgam of information—measurements, my calculations, and the Weyerhaeuser plans—much of the credit for my line drawings goes to Weyerhaeuser. The Herbert Hoover pattern offered me the confidence to proceed.[2]

Leroy Pruitt and his oiled 15-foot double-ender, at Vida, Oregon.

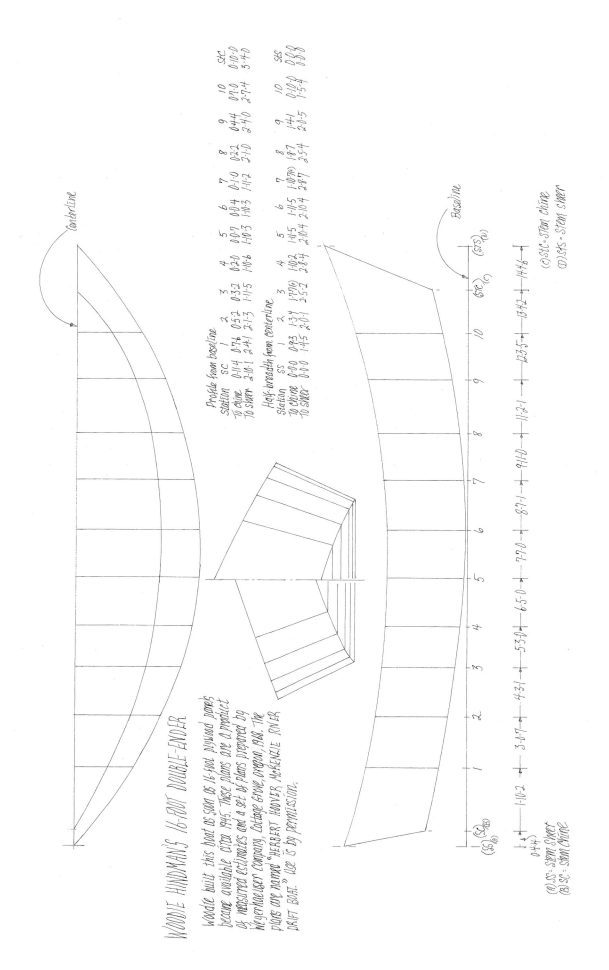

WOODIE HINDMAN'S 16-FOOT DOUBLE-ENDER

Woodie built this boat as soon as 16-foot plywood panels became available circa 1945. These plans are a product of measured estimates and a set of plans prepared by Weyerhaeuser Company, Cottage Grove, Oregon, 1961. The plans are named "HERBERT HOOVER McKENZIE RIVER DRIFT BOAT." Use is by permission.

Profile from baseline

Station	SC	1	2	3	4	5	6	7	8	9	10	StC
To chine	0-11-4	0-7-6	0-5-2	0-3-2	0-2-0	0-0-7	0-0-4	0-1-0	0-2-2	0-4-4	0-7-0	0-10-0
To sheer	2-10-1	2-4-1	2-1-3	1-11-5	1-10-6	1-10-3	1-10-3	1-11-2	2-1-0	2-4-0	2-7-4	3-1-0

Half-breadth from centerline

Station	SS	1	2	3	4	5	6	7	8	9	10	StS
To chine	0-0-0	0-9-3	1-3-7	1-7-7(+)	1-10-2	1-11-5	1-11-5	1-10-7(+)	1-8-7	1-4-1	0-10-2	0-3-3
To sheer	0-0-0	1-4-5	2-0-1	2-5-2	2-8-4	2-10-4	2-10-4	2-8-7	2-5-4	2-0-5	1-5-4	0-3-3

(A) SS = stern sheer
(B) SC = stern chine
(C) StC = stem chine
(D) StS = stem sheer

Plans have been reduced 45%.

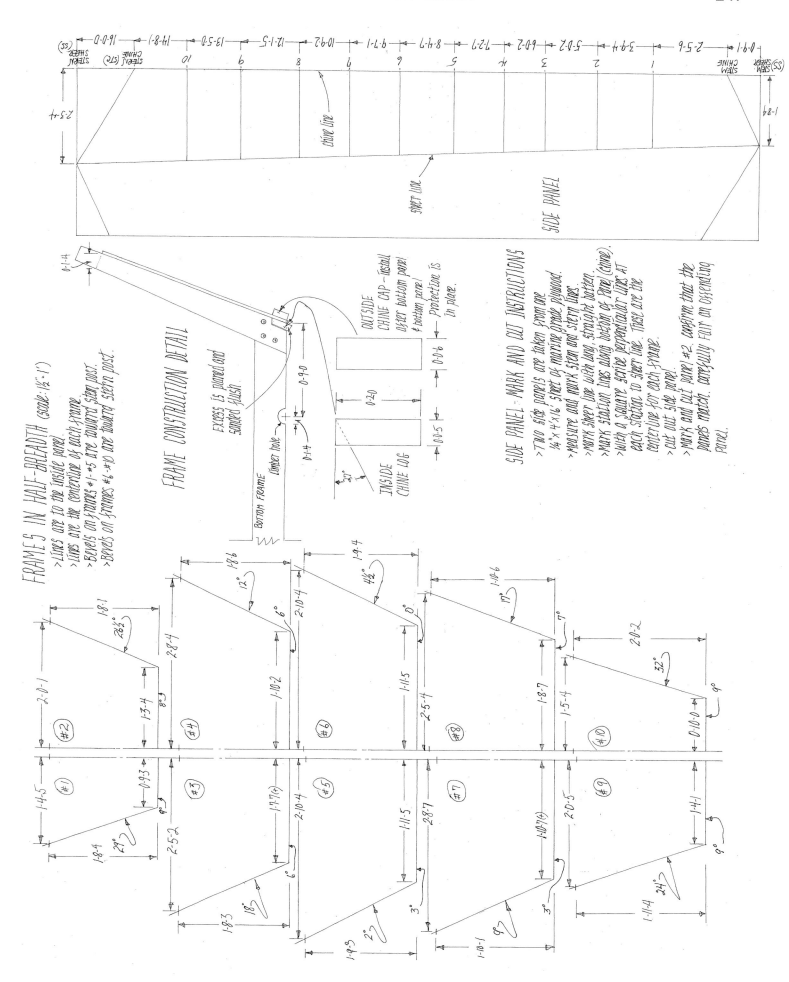

SIDE PANEL - MARK AND CUT INSTRUCTIONS

>Two side panels are taken from one
¼"×4'×16' sheet of marine grade plywood.
>measure and mark stem and stern lines.
>mark sheer line with long, straight batten.
>mark station lines along bottom of panel (chine).
>with a square, scribe perpendicular lines at
each station to sheer line. These are the
centerline for each frame.
>cut out side panel.
>mark and cut panel #2. confirm that the
panels match. carefully fair on ascending
panel.

FRAME CONSTRUCTION DETAIL

OUTSIDE
CHINE CAP - install
over bottom panel
& bottom panel
Protection is
in place.

INSIDE
CHINE LOG

Excess is planed and
sanded flush.

Limber hole

BOTTOM FRAME

FRAMES IN HALF-BREADTH (scale: 1½"=1')

>Lines are to the inside panel.
>Lines are the centerline of each frame.
>Bevels on frames #1-#5 are toward stem post.
>Bevels on frames #6-#10 are toward stern post.

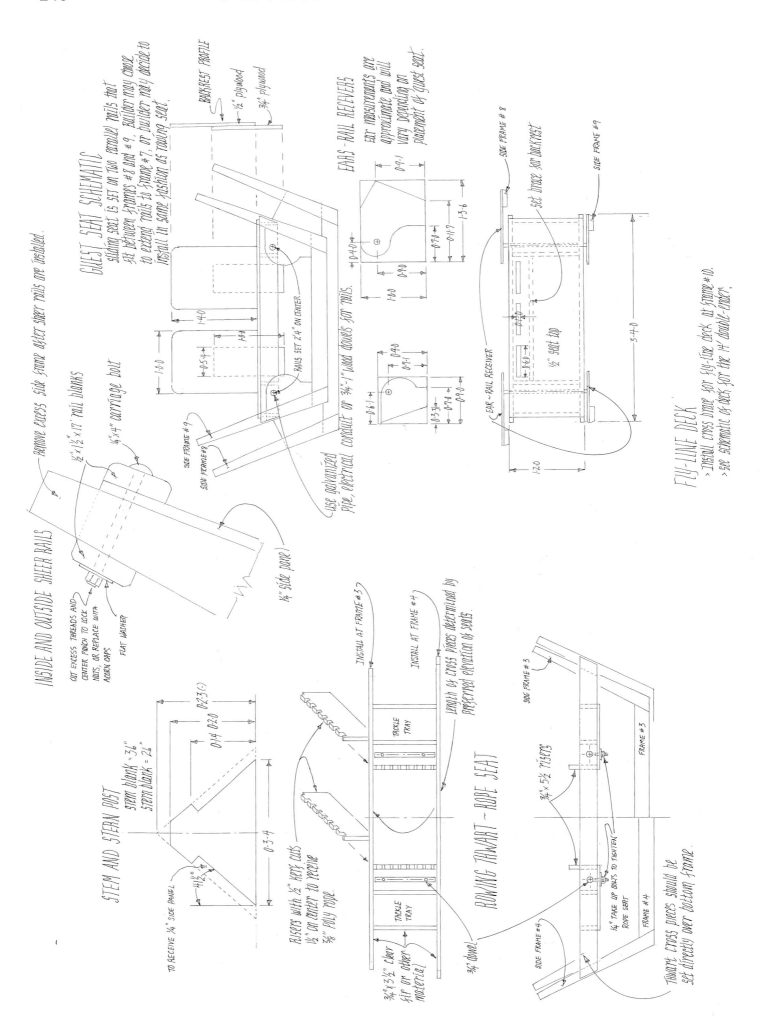

INSIDE AND OUTSIDE SHEER RAILS

Remove excess side frame after sheer rails are installed.

½" × 1½" × 17' rail blanks

¼" × 4" carriage bolt

Cut excess threads and center punch to lock nuts, or replace with ACORN CAPS

FLAT WASHER

¼" side panel

SIDE FRAME #9

SIDE FRAME #8

GUEST SEAT SCHEMATIC

Sliding seat is set on two parallel rails that fit between frames #8 and #9. Builder may choose to extend rails to frame #7, or builder may decide to install in same fashion as rowing seat.

BACKREST PROFILE

½" plywood

¾" plywood

RAILS SET 2¼" ON CENTER

Use galvanized pipe, electrical conduit, or ¾"-1" wood dowels for rails.

EAR - RAIL RECEIVERS

Ear measurements are approximate and will vary depending on placement of guest seat.

EAR ~ RAIL RECEIVER

½" seat top

SIDE FRAME # 8

SIDE FRAME #9

Set brace for backrest

FLY-LINE DECK

> Install cross brace for fly-line deck at frame #10.
> See schematic of deck for the 14' double-ender.

STEM AND STERN POST

TO RECEIVE ¼" SIDE PANEL

Stem blank = 34"
Stern blank = 26"

ROWING THWART ~ ROPE SEAT

INSTALL AT FRAME #3

INSTALL AT FRAME #4

TACKLE TRAY

Length of cross pieces determined by preferred elevation of seats.

Risers with ½" kerf cuts 2" on center to receive ⅜" poly rope.

¾" × 5½" Clear fir or other material

TACKLE TRAY

¾" dowel

Thwart cross pieces should be set directly over bottom frame.

SIDE FRAME # 3

¾" × 5½" risers

FRAME #3

4" TAKE UP BOATS TO TIGHTEN

ROPE SEAT

FRAME #4

SIDE FRAME #4

The 16-Foot Double-Ender with a Transom

The third double-ender designed and built by Woodie was the double-ender with a transom. Woodie at first resisted constructing this boat, but his good friend and guiding companion Everett Spaulding insisted that he build it. Thus it's ironic that this boat became the pre-eminent McKenzie River drift boat, a boat recognized today across this continent and on at least two others as the McKenzie River drift boat. The boat type has become a favored fishing platform. The transom provides the boat with more interior space, and the craft's sleek lines and characteristic ease of maneuvering are maintained.

In the spring of 1999, Ray Heater and I traveled to Eugene to examine and take the measurements off a Woodie Hindman boat. Neil Prien owned the craft. The boat carried some Hindman trademarks: less flare to the side panels than found in contemporary drift boats, beveled chine logs, an unnecessary tenth frame under the fly-line deck, and a metal identifying plate with Woodie's name. I couldn't tell, however, if the boat had been built before or after Marty Rathje bought Woodie's boat shop and business in 1954. Marty continued to build Woodie's boats and tagged each boat built with Woodie's nameplate. I have since learned that Rathje used a plate that read,

When Marty Rathje purchased Woodie's boat shop in 1954, he modified the brass plate to read, "Built by Woodie Hindman Boats, Springfield, Oregon." Boats built by Woodie Hindman carried nameplates that read, "Built by Woodie Hindman, Springfield, Oregon."

Trevor Kilpela built this McKenzie River double-ender with a transom from the plans presented here. He launched the boat in 2006 on Michigan's Au Sable River at McMasters Bridge. COURTESY OF TREVOR KILPELA

Gracie Zielinski loves her dad's boat, the McKenzie double-ender with a transom. COURTESY DAVID ZIELINSKI

"Built by Woodie Hindman Boats, Springfield, Oregon," whereas boats built by Woodie carried a nameplate that read, "Built by Woodie Hindman, Springfield, Oregon." Neither Ray nor I can recall specifically how the plate in this boat was worded. My field notes recall the words "built by Woodie," but I can't tell whether that was a conclusion I noted or was my reference to the nameplate. Regardless, it was a Hindman boat. Ray, Neil, and I spent a good part of the afternoon taking its measurements.

When I laid the boat's lines down on paper, I was struck by the narrower symmetry of the boat. Scarfing technology was such that Woodie confined his boat to the width of the panels, 4 feet or slightly less. His boats were relatively light, and the continuous rocker fore to aft made the craft highly maneuverable. Colorado River guide and author Brad Dimock rowed my McKenzie for a time on our Rogue River commemorative run in 2002. I watched him explore parts of the river other boatmen in our party refused to go. Of the boat, he said, "This is the sweetest row I can remember. I actually find it easier to handle than your little double-ender, Roger." That's the way it is with this boat: very good carrying capacity and highly maneuverable. It has the added attraction of beautiful lines that make her an eye-catcher.

My search for the Hindman double-enders began fortuitously at Paradise Lodge. It could have ended there also, so my wife thought, save for the jet-boat skills of Court's son, Justin. The rain started Friday evening, gently at first, but steadily. By midmorning Saturday, the rainstorm was getting worse, not unusual for this time of year. These rains will last a few hours and then let up, allowing the earth to recover a bit and then perhaps hitting again. By late Saturday afternoon, we were in a deluge that persisted through the night and well into Sunday morning. By that time, the Rogue had risen a dozen feet or so and looked more like a mudflow. As we observed the river from the safety of the lodge 40 feet above, our conversation recalled the 1964 flood. A heavy snowpack melted by a rain such as this had brought the river to and into the lodge that year. Though the snowpack this year was comparatively light, we were worried that river conditions might preclude our departure and we might be stranded at Paradise for a time. It's a great place to be stranded, but there were also schedules to keep.

About 10:00 or 11:00 Sunday morning, I heard the low, throaty rumble of boat engines as the jet boat backed into the torrent. The engines came to life, and the jet boat sped downstream. It was Justin testing to see whether travel back to Foster Bar would be safe. Justin returned within half an hour and reported that he could take us out. We loaded our gear, and with the usual farewell comments, we left. Other than river debris plugging an impeller a few times, the trip to Foster Bar was uneventful. The river, however, was spectacular. Huggins Canyon, for example, is a placid stretch of river that this morning sported huge standing waves that towered over the boat. Justin deftly skirted them on the north side. Tacoma and Clay Hill Rapids, class III water under normal conditions, were flat, but Clay Hill Stillwater was a cascade of fast-moving water. A jet boat's speed must exceed that of the river's current for control. I think our trip out to Foster Bar must have been in record time.

Endnotes

1. Ray Heater's website is www.raysriverdories.com.
2. Weyerhaeuser gave me permission to incorporate into my line drawings much of the information from the Herbert Hoover McKenzie River Boat Plan.

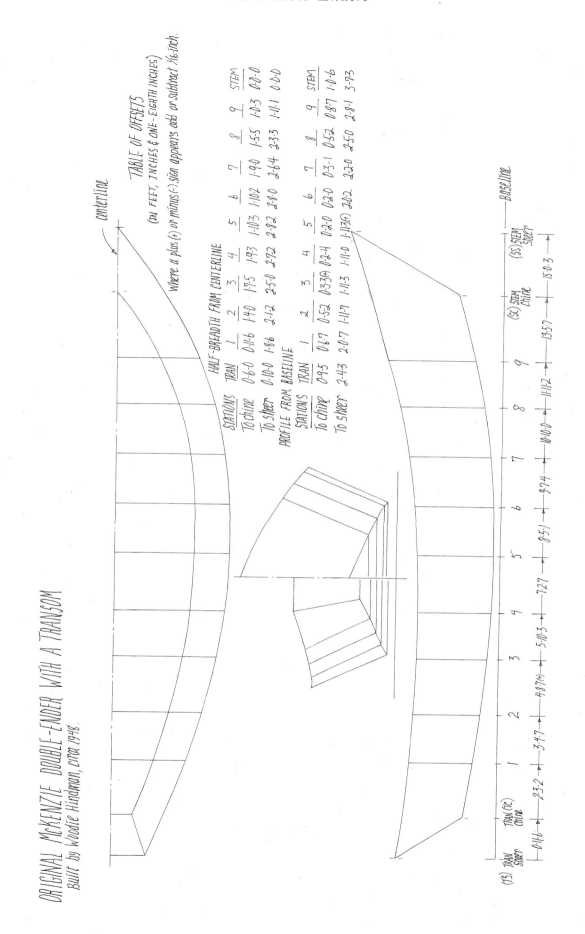

ORIGINAL McKENZIE DOUBLE-ENDER WITH A TRANSOM
Built by Woodie Hindman, circa 1948.

TABLE OF OFFSETS
(IN FEET, INCHES & ONE-EIGHTH INCHES)

Where a plus (+) or minus (–) sign appears add or subtract ⅛-inch.

HALF-BREADTH FROM CENTERLINE

STATIONS	TRAN	1	2	3	4	5	6	7	8	9	STEM
To chine	0-6-0	0-11-6	1-4-0	1-7-5	1-9-3	1-10-3	1-10-2	1-9-0	1-5-5	1-0-3	0-2-0
To sheer	0-10-0	1-8-6	2-1-2	2-5-0	2-7-2	2-8-2	2-8-0	2-6-4	2-3-3	1-1-1	0-0-0

PROFILE FROM BASELINE

STATIONS	TRAN	1	2	3	4	5	6	7	8	9	STEM
To chine	0-9-5	0-6-7	0-5-2	0-3-3(+)	0-2-4	0-2-0	0-2-0	0-3-1	0-5-2	0-8-7	1-0-6
To sheer	2-4-3	2-0-7	1-11-7	1-11-3	1-11-0	1-11-3(+)	2-0-2	2-2-0	2-5-0	2-8-1	3-9-3

(TS) TRAN SHEER — 0-11-6 — TRAN (TC) CHINE — 2-3-2 — 3-4-7 — 4-8-7(+) — 5-10-3 — 7-2-7 — 8-5-1 — 9-2-4 — 10-10-0 — 11-11-2 — (SC) STEM CHINE 13-5-7 — (SS) STEM SHEER 15-0-3

Baseline

Plans have been reduced 45%.

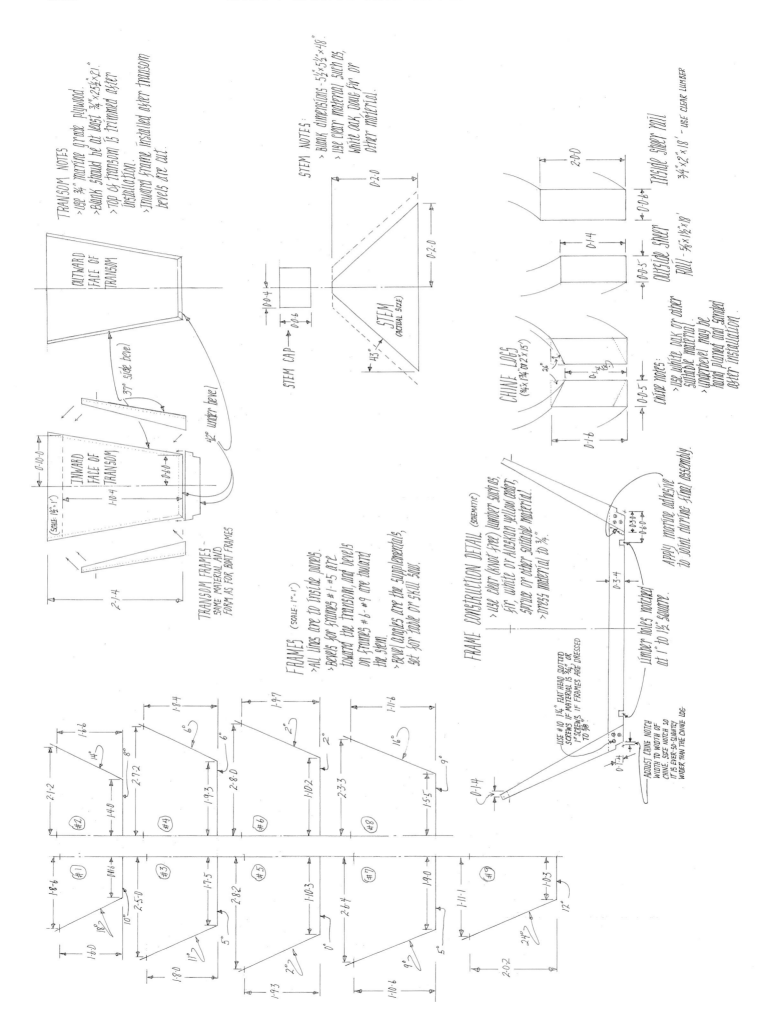

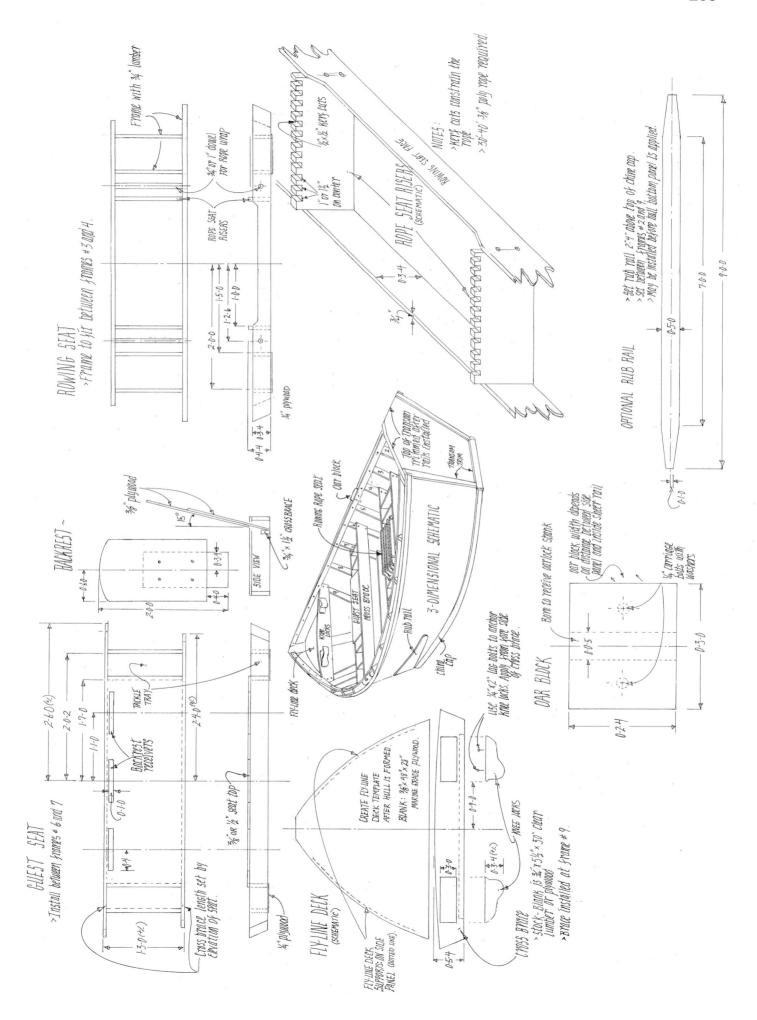

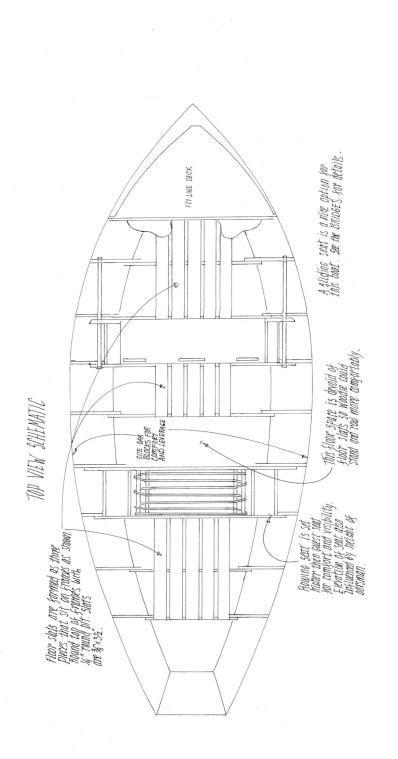

TOP VIEW SCHEMATIC

FN LINE DECK

SITE OAR BLOCKS FOR COMFORT AND LEVERAGE

Floor slabs are formed as three pieces that sit on frames as shown. Round top of frames with ¼" round bit. Slats are ⅜" x 3½".

Rowing seat is set higher than chair seat for comfort and visibility. Elevation of seat also influenced by height of oarsman.

This floor space is devoid of floor slats so novice could stand and row more comfortably.

A gliding seat is a nice option for this boat. See the BRIDGES for details.

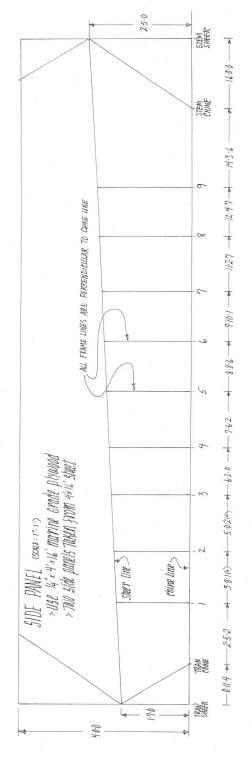

SIDE PANEL (SCALE: ¾"=1')

> Use ¼" x 4' x 16' marine grade plywood
> Two side panels taken from ½16' sheet

ALL FRAME LINES ARE PERPENDICULAR TO CHINE LINE

sheer line
chine line

STEM SHEER
STEM CHINE
2-5-0

9   16-0-0
    14-3-4
8   12-4-7
7   11-2-7
6   9-10-1
5   8-8-6
    7-6-2
4   6-2-0
3   5-0-2(+)
2   3-8-1(+)
1   2-5-2
    0-11-4

TRAN CHINE
1-7-0
TRAN SHEER
4-0-0

CHAPTER 19

The Rogue River Driver
The Boat at Winkle Bar

"They looked heavy and clumsy to me, but upon trying one I found to my amaze, that, empty, it rowed remarkably easily . . . and altogether delighted me. . . . We drifted into a hollow, reverberating canyon, where the river boiled and eddied in an endless solitude. No one except myself had any trouble. My boat now seemed large and heavily laden, and in swift currents or slapping waves I could only with extreme difficulty handle her."

—ZANE GREY, *TALES OF FRESHWATER FISHING*

I had never run the fish ladder at Rainie Falls. The thin strip of water cascaded over and around boulders of various sizes, all of which were slick as hell along its bank, and it offered a chute through which drift boats and other assorted craft could be safely lowered. Lining a boat through this channel is slow, tough work that requires 100 feet of rope and a couple of agile people who step and jump from slick rock to slick rock as the boat is lowered through the ladder. From top to bottom, the distance is about 100 yards, but when you're working a boat down the chute, it can seem like a mile. One misstep, which happens frequently, and a person can land in the life-threatening drink, with the boat, if not securely anchored to a second or third person, slipping noisily away to any one of several boat graves downriver.

I had not floated in a raft on the Rogue River before, either. The normal rhythmic pitch and roll of my drift boat was replaced by the gentle yawning of a 16-foot sac of gas as its bottom side rarely lost contact with the river, even in heavy water. The resulting ride was akin to the kindly roll of obesity down an undulating hill, feeling the ground beneath but never losing contact with it. I was also wet. I don't know what I was thinking. My carefully handled drift boat, with its sharp prow and nicely flared sides, cut through the chop and crested each wave. The boat kept me dry even in the most turbulent water. The raft, however, with its tubular frame, plowed through the

waves, leaving its occupants soaked, which explains why my two experienced rafters were adorned in raingear, something I'd thought was a bit odd on this warm, sunny April day. I discovered the reason immediately downriver from our put-in at Grave Creek landing. We lumbered through Grave Creek Falls and I was left drenched and cold, a chill that persisted until we stopped and I was able to put on my own raingear.

As we approached Rainie Falls, the oarsperson made no attempt to pull in along the north bank above the fish ladder. This is standard operating procedure in a drift boat. Instead, she slowed the raft and angles it into the headwaters of the chute. I nervously asked, "Uh, what are we doing?" She said, "We'll just run this," whereupon she reangled the raft, shipped the oars, and proceeded down the chute, the raft bouncing left and right as we careened from one boulder to another and then shot out into the mainstream just below the falls. The raft did a casual 360, and then we proceeded normally downriver. I threw a furtive glance at the oarsperson, who was in the midst of an indifferent yawn. I wasn't sure whether the yawn was for effect or because we had gotten a pretty early start. Nonetheless, I was impressed with her.

This trip had begun several months earlier. In my search for a replica of the Rogue River driver, I decided that the historic boat on display at Zane Grey's old cabin at Winkle Bar was my best choice. The Bureau of Land

Management (BLM) oversees the Wild and Scenic section of the river. Winkle Bar is located in the heart of this stretch (see map on page 46). The BLM Rogue River program manager at the time was Jim Leffmann, whose office was in Medford. I had met Jim when I was searching for historic photos of the Rogue. During that visit, I explained the nature of my research and took the liberty of showing him several models of the boats I had already recovered. On a subsequent visit, I told Leffmann of my desire to retrieve the lines of the Zane Grey boat at Winkle Bar, and why. I also mentioned that I wanted to do this before the start of the Rogue River permit system on May 15. After that date, travel by river on the Wild and Scenic section was by lottery permit only. He suggested that I visit with the person in charge of the Rand Visitor Center, now expanded and remodeled. Today it is called the Smullin Visitor Center. The facility is located a couple of miles downstream from Galice and is the place where boaters check in and pick up their permits for the Rogue River trips.[1] Robyn Wicks managed the private-party permit system.

Robyn Wicks is a Grants Pass native who has a deep appreciation for the Rogue and its history. She is a tall,

Robyn Wicks (left) and Louise Richards at the Smullin Visitor Center at Rand, Oregon, in May 2006. They had not seen each other for an extended period. Robyn now writes environmental impact statements in another part of the BLM world at Medford. Louise is the commercial permit administrator for the National Wild and Scenic Rogue River and the Grants Pass and Glendale Resource Areas. Her office is in Grants Pass.

effervescent lady with a spontaneous smile that quickly puts people at ease. She listened attentively as I explained the nature of my work and my interest in capturing the lines of the Rogue River driver at the Zane Grey cabin. The only logical way in there with the equipment I needed was by boat. I had two constraints: time and logistics. The pass over the Siskiyou Mountains to the coast, the most direct route to the public takeout point at Foster Bar, was made impassable by remnant winter snow. I asked Robyn about the possibility of hitchhiking with one of her crew as they readied for the upcoming spring and summer river traffic. The crews use rafts to run the river to Marial, just above Mule Creek Canyon and below Winkle Bar. They check out camp sites, collect debris and flotsam, and attend to the few pit toilets above the high-water line. The toilets no longer exist. Today river travelers pack everything out. Everything.

Robyn pondered my inquiry and thought that might be a possibility. I don't know what conversations she had up the chain of command, but I suspect that with Robyn's endorsement and Jim Leffmann's approval, the trip was a go. April 18, 1998, became the target date for the trip. I assumed that I would indeed hitchhike with one of the crew, but instead Robyn and a colleague decided to make the trip. The plan was to leave Rand in early morning, travel to Winkle Bar, take the boat's measurements, float on down to Marial, load the raft at the BLM takeout, and drive back to Rand—all within the day. Whew!

Louise Richards was the second person. Louise is the BLM's commercial permit administrator. She's not native but acts every bit the part. She, too, sports a quick smile but is the more reserved of the two. I saw in Robyn and Louise the long and the short of it; two women who each knew their business, loved the river, and seemed a nice complement to the other. It was my lucky lot to have this pair squire me that day, although I admit to mild apprehension. There's just something about oars and me. I feel much more comfortable if they are in my hands. Before we shoved off, there was polite conversation between Robyn and Louise about who would take the oars, and as with my daughters, who would squabble over the opportunity, I wanted to jump in and say, "I'll take 'em." Instead, Louise offered to take the oars, Robyn said okay, and off we went. I think the decision may have been made ahead of time. Louise is the more diminutive of the two. I suspect one of their goals was to remind this river nimrod that rowing expertise is not confined to men. Rowing expertise also resides in finesse and grace and, when needed, the strength to pull a raft away from a river hazard. Louise's yawn at the bottom of the fish ladder at Rainie Falls was for effect.

each measurement, especially for the profile. The technique worked because there is nominal rocker to the boat. This is where I got even with Robyn and Louise: I put them to work. Both were willing helpers. Louise held the standard for the transit, I called out the measurements, and Robyn recorded. Occasionally we switched roles, as each built confidence in the task at hand. The project took several hours.

We were back at Rand by 6:00 that evening. I didn't think the one-day trip was possible with all that had to be done, but Thelma and Louise were more than up to the task. Did I say Thelma? I meant Robyn.

On my return home, I busied myself in the shop. I transferred the measurements to my drafting table and established the boat's lines. I completed the lines and hand-carved a half model to the lines over the next three weeks, and then spent night and day crafting the first-off model. On June 12, 1998, I presented the model to Robyn and her staff at a little ceremony in Galice. As far as I know, the model remains on display at the Smullin Visitor Center. If you ever see the boat, you'll know the story.

Zane Grey's river driver is a double-ended boat just over 22 feet long stem to stern. The rocker is modest and gives the boat considerable carrying capacity. In beam, it is 2 feet, 11 1/2 inches at the chine and 5 feet, 6 inches at the sheer. Floor timbers and side frames are the only internal structure, and the boat has no evidence of longitudinal support, such as a keel, chine log, or battens. Two rowing stations provide ample room fore and aft for equipment. If a trip required the use of poles, there was also room at the stem and stern for a person to assist in pushing the boat upriver. The boat was obviously built for a one-way trip into the canyon, to be dismantled for its lumber or used along this section of river for local transport. The frames and planking are substantial, all four-quarter lumber. Fastenings are nails. The frames appear to be Douglas fir, and the long bottom planks and side strakes are redwood. The garboard is anchored directly into the bottom plank. This suggests that the boat may have been built right side up in traditional dory fashion: lay and secure the bottom planks, define the bottom planks' camber, build the frames, and install the strakes. On the other hand, as I suggest in the plans, it's more likely that the boat was built upside down. It was a very heavy and cumbersome boat compared with today's river dories. The boat performed well in its day and has secured its place in riverboat history.

I'm not sure who will want to build this boat. Perhaps someone who is looking for a sense of place, a boat with great carrying capacity, and a unique conversation piece. Unless the builder is an expert whitewater person, I wouldn't advise this boat for anything above a class II river. Estuaries, bays, frog water, and lakes would be ideal

A severely deteriorating boat at Winkle Bar.

My equipment for the boat at Winkle Bar included battens, levels, a plumb bob, two level lines, a measuring stick and measuring tape, pencils, and a field notebook. Also included was a transit. When the family that owned the property gave their permission to measure the boat, their one request was that the craft not be disturbed. The boat is in a sorry state, and any movement could cause further collapse of the structure. Of course, I agreed, but I needed to determine how to obtain reasonably accurate measurements. It is essential that the baseline of the boat be true in order to put the boat in a measurable box that serves as anchor points for each measurement. The boat is typically leveled. That was not possible in this case. The transit allowed me to calculate the chine's variance fore to aft from the baseline, and then factor that variance into

Glen Wooldridge and Cal Allen's first boat and the Winkle Bar boat are very much like this river driver used for commercial salmon fishing from Grants Pass to Gold Beach. COURTESY OF THE BLM, ROGUE NATIONAL WILD AND SCENIC RIVER

locations for its use. Even though Zane Grey described the boat as easy to row and very maneuverable, the extended chine line makes it unsuitable on technically difficult rivers. Grey and his party lined many more rapids than they were able to run.

I have modified the plans for the boat so that it can be built using the free-form construction technique. The boat's lines remain true to the original. Should anyone be interested in building the boat true to the original, I will be pleased to provide the layouts for the bottom planks and side strakes.

As Louise, Robyn, and I took the boat's measurements that day at Winkle Bar, I kept thinking about Glen Wooldridge and his comment about the boat he and Cal Allen built for their first trip down the Rogue in 1915. That boat was very much like this one. "It was a hell of a looking thing. Heavy! It was made of cedar planks and 2 x 4s, and was about 20-feet long. We caulked up the cracks and dragged it down and heaved it over the bank just below the old dam. We rustled up some oars from someplace and got ready to start."[2]

Nonetheless, this boat type built today with a plywood skin would be lighter, more maneuverable and functional. Who knows? Perhaps someday soon we'll see this boat somewhere on the water again, bringing pleasure to its builder and conversation to his friends.

Endnotes

1. Bureau of Land Management, Smullin Visitor Center at Rand, 14335 Galice Road, Merlin, OR 97532.

2. Florence Arman, *The Rogue: A River to Run* (Grants Pass, OR: Wildwood Press), 51.

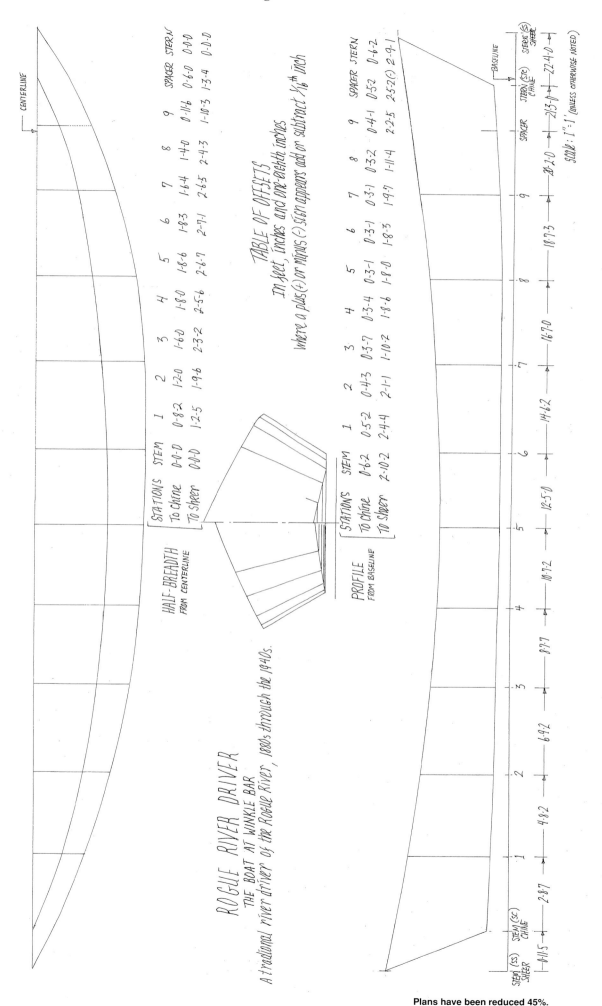

ROGUE RIVER DRIVER
THE BOAT AT WINKLE BAR
A traditional river driver of the Rogue River, 1880s through the 1940s.

TABLE OF OFFSETS
In feet, inches and one-eighth inches
where a plus (+) or minus (-) sign appears add or subtract $\frac{1}{16}$th inch

HALF-BREADTH FROM CENTERLINE

STATIONS	STEM	1	2	3	4	5	6	7	8	9	SPACER	STERN
To Chine	0-0-0	0-8-2	1-2-0	1-6-0	1-8-0	1-8-6	1-8-3	1-6-4	1-4-0	0-11-6	0-6-0	0-0-0
To Sheer	0-0-0	1-2-5	1-9-6	2-3-2	2-5-6	2-6-7	2-7-1	2-6-5	2-4-3	1-10-3	1-3-4	0-0-0

PROFILE FROM BASELINE

STATIONS	STEM	1	2	3	4	5	6	7	8	9	SPACER	STERN
To Chine	0-6-2	0-5-2	0-4-3	0-3-7	0-3-4	0-3-1	0-3-1	0-3-1	0-3-2	0-4-1	0-5-2	0-4-2
To Sheer	2-10-2	2-4-4	2-1-1	1-10-2	1-8-6	1-8-0	1-8-3	1-9-7	1-11-4	2-2-5	2-5-2(-)	2-9-1

SCALE: 1"=1' (UNLESS OTHERWISE NOTED)

Plans have been reduced 45%.

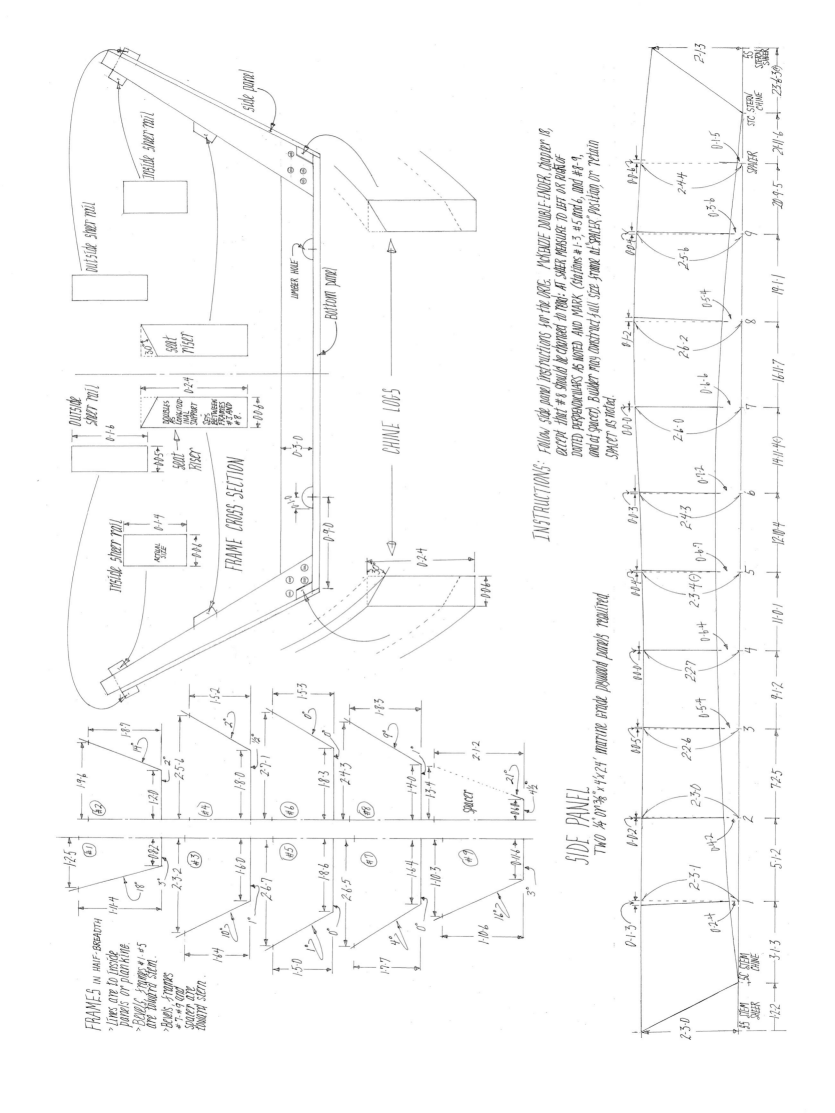

FRAMES IN HALF-BREADTH
> Lines are to inside panels or plankine.
> Bevels, frames #1-#5 are toward stem.
> Bevels, frames #7-#9 and spacer are toward stern.

FRAME CROSS·SECTION

side panel

inside sheer rail

outside sheer rail

inside sheer rail

ACTUAL SIZE

outside sheer rail

seat riser

seat riser

DOUBLES AS LONGITUD-INAL SUPPORT. SETS BETWEEN FRAMES #3 AND #8.

LIMBER HOLE

bottom panel

— CHINE LOGS —

INSTRUCTIONS: Follow side panel instructions for the ORIG. McKENZIE DOUBLE-ENDER, Chapter 18, except that #8 should be changed to read: AT SHEER MEASURE TO LEFT OR RIGHT OF DOTTED PERPENDICULARS AS NOTED AND MARK (Stations #1-3, #5 and 6, and #8-9, and at Spacer). Builder may construct full size frame at Spacer "position or retain Spacer as noted.

SIDE PANEL
Two 1/4" or 3/8" x 4'x 24' marine grade plywood panels required.

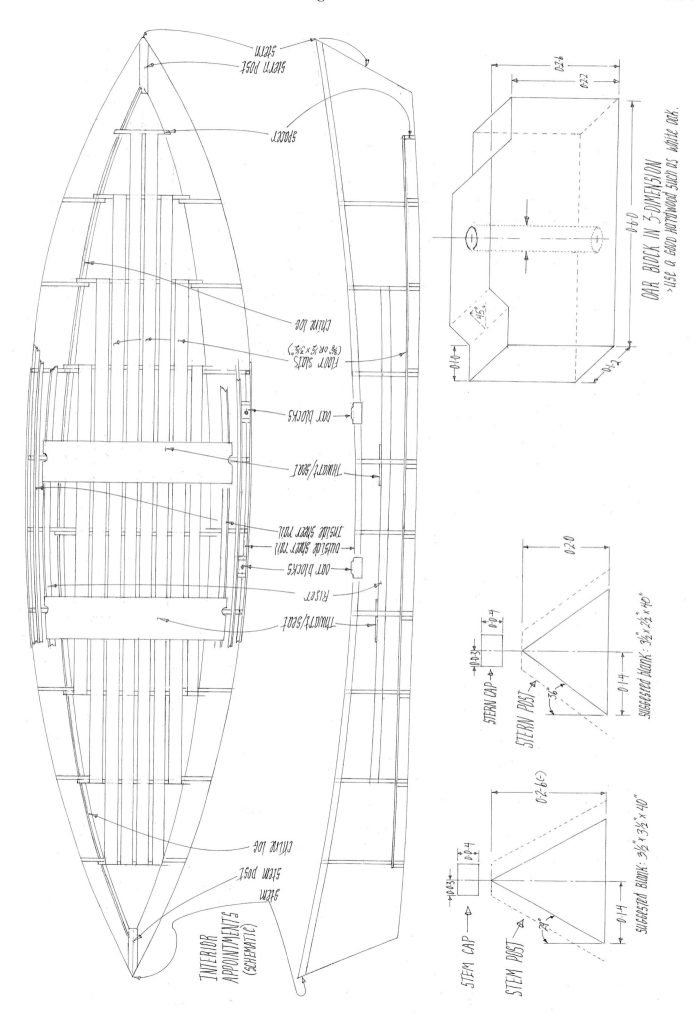

INTERIOR
APPOINTMENTS
(SCHEMATIC)

stem
stem post
chine log

chine log

Thwart/seat

RISER

oar blocks
outside sheer rail
inside sheer rail

Thwart/seat

oar blocks

FLOOR SLATS
(⅜" x ¾" OR ⅜" x 3½")

chine log

spacer

stern post
stern

stern post
stern

STEM CAP

STEM POST

0-2-6(-)

0-0-4
0-0-3

0-1-4

29°

SUGGESTED BLANK: 3½" x 3½" x 40"

STERN CAP

STERN POST

0-2-0

0-0-4
0-0-3

0-1-4

36°

SUGGESTED BLANK: 3½" x 2½" x 40"

OAR BLOCK IN 3-DIMENSION
>use a good hardwood such as white oak.

0-2-6

0-2-2

0-9-0

0-1-0

0-1-2

45°

stem post

stern post

stern post support

strongback

Bottom planks

ceiling braces force the longitudinal bottom planks to conform to sawn camber of the strongback.

strongback supports elevate hull and frames off the floor.

Frames

- sheer strake -
- strake #3 -
- strake #2 -
- strake #1 -
- garboard -

The ROGUE RIVER DRIVER, at Winkle Bar, was constructed of 4-quarter material throughout: 4-quarter frames and planking. Frames were Port Oxford cedar with reduced planking.

It is likely that the boat was built upside down on a longitudinal strongback made from a heavy plank sawn to the desired bottom rocker. The strongback was notched to receive the 4-quarter floor timber stumps which were squared and secured to accept the five to six 4-quarter longitudinal bottom planks. The stem and stern posts were also secured to the strongback. The planks were fastened to the floor timbers and a combination of oakum, pitch, tar and cotton sealed the joints and seams. The footprint of the boat was cut to an angle acceptable to the garboard, bottom strake.

Four-quarter reduced strakes were cut and laid into the frames, garboard first. The strakes were carvel planked. This sheet shows the strakes' layout and size of lumber needed to mark and cut each strake to dimension. The garboard was nailed to each frame about 3 inches on center and directly into the beveled edge of the bottom plank. The boat didn't have an inside chine log.

Built with this material, the boat was very heavy and awkward to handle on the river. Most rapids were lined or portaged. The boat's advantages included stability and carrying capacity.

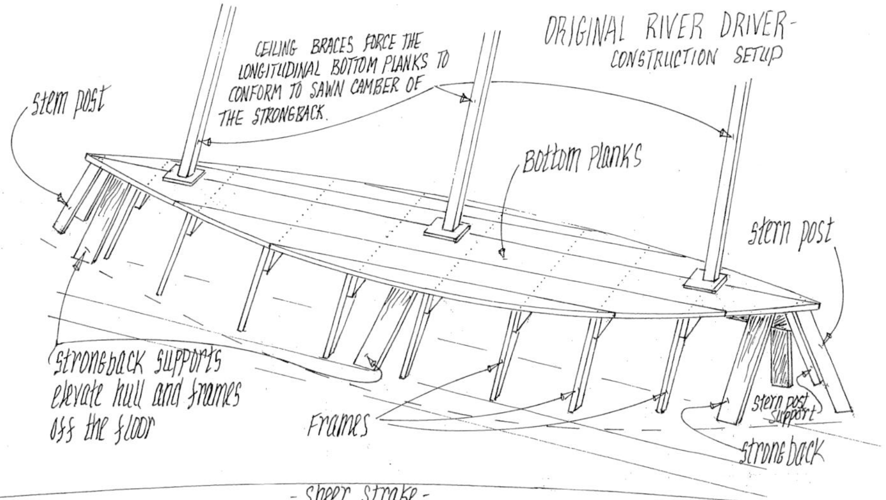

MINIMUM STRAKE BLANKS REQUIRED FOR PLANKING

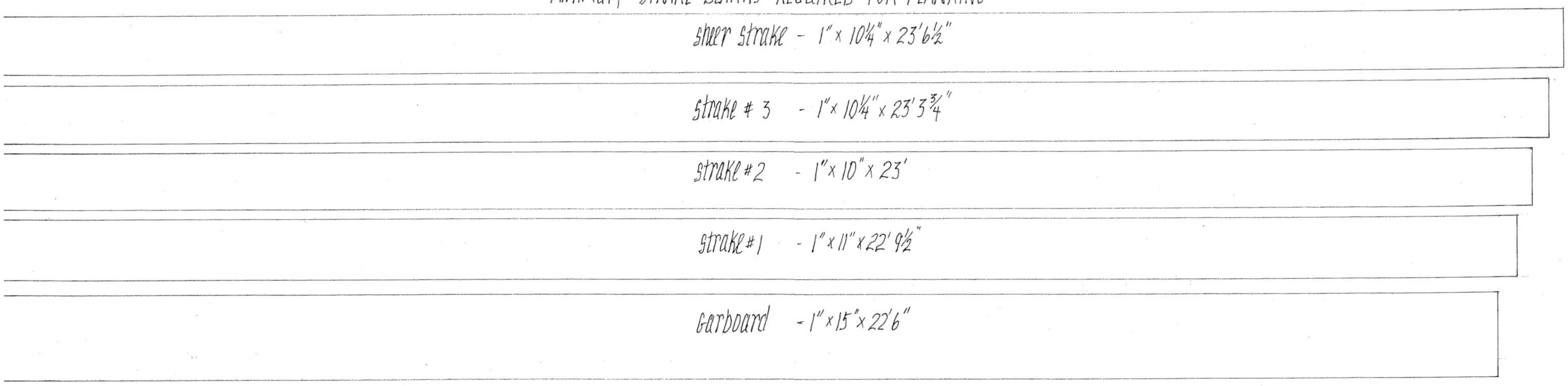

sheer strake - 1" x 10¼" x 23'6½"

strake #3 - 1" x 10¼" x 23'5¾"

strake #2 - 1" x 10" x 23'

strake #1 - 1" x 11" x 22'9½"

garboard - 1" x 15" x 22'6"

CHAPTER 20

The Classic Rogue River Dory

Bob Pritchett's Last Boat

It sits there as the culmination of more than forty years of experience on the Rogue, the epitome of perfection . . .

There was reverence in Steve Pritchett's voice as he talked about his dad and his dad's boats. We stood in Steve's small shrine, a tribute to Bob Pritchett, Press Pyle, Glen Wooldridge, and other boating pioneers of the Rogue River. I was impressed with his collection and the care he exercised in preserving photographs, correspondence, posters, oars, Wooldridge-like jackass lift, and a motor, the type used by Glen on his 1947 run up the Rogue from Gold Beach to Grants Pass. I'd walked into a treasure trove. Two items that immediately caught my eye were the Rogue River dories parked in separate bays. One was a dory built and used by Press Pyle. The other was more prominently displayed. It was the first thing I saw as I entered the building. The dory was the last boat Bob Pritchett built before his death in 1989. Steve completed the unfinished project and has kept the boat in his museum since. The boat has never been launched and sits there as the culmination of more than forty years of experience on the Rogue, the epitome of perfection, and the classic Rogue River dory.

Steve eyed me carefully, and I sensed caution in his demeanor. I had called him unannounced, introduced myself, and explained my interest in learning about the evolution of the Rogue River dories. Robyn Wicks of the Rand Visitor Center near Galice on the Rogue River had suggested that Steve might be a good source. He invited me to his Grants Pass home.

The third of Bob and Virginia Pritchett's four children, Steve is much like his dad: quiet, introverted, confident, private, and physically impressive. I remember thinking that if I were in a dark alley, fearful of what's around the corner, this is a guy I'd want at my side. He is stocky with a very firm handshake that lets you feel his athleticism. I think that Steve, like his dad, could break an oar with his bare hands. He doesn't smile, and I look for small signs that he resonates with my research. People of the Rogue River view strangers with suspicion until a level of trust is developed that causes them to drop their guard a bit, but never completely. I liked Steve. He's genuine, honest, and straightforward, but I couldn't tell how I was being received. The fact that I was there suggests he was surreptitiously curious about my work.

Following our initial visit, I concluded that Bob Pritchett's final boat is the capstone to a tradition of Rogue River dories that merits preservation. I wanted to record this boat. Rogue River boatbuilders typically kept records of their patterns on a shingle that hung in their shop or were retained in their heads, but there were no recorded lines or construction details as records of their existence. I drew up the courage to call and ask Steve if he would allow me to record the lines of his dad's boat. He agreed. I was pleased.

In June 1998, I visited Steve, and together we took measurements of the dory. Because of the various circumstances and conditions, each boat I have recorded has required slightly different strategies. The keys to a good record are two: The boat should sit parallel to its imaginary baseline, and consistent reference points should be established for taking the measurements. In every case, the boat is square to an imaginary box I create for the boat. But Steve didn't want to remove the boat from its trailer. This made measurements from the boat's baseline problematic. Alternatively, I established an elevated level line that ran the length of the boat's centerline. With two sets of hands and eyes, a pair of battens—one calibrated—and a flexible tape, we recorded the boat's profile at each sta-

Steve (left) and his dad, Bob Pritchett, before Bob's death in 1989. COURTESY OF VIRGINIA PRITCHETT

tion. Half-breadth measurements were from the centerline to the inside panel at the sheer and the chine. Adjustments to these measurements were made to accommodate the inside sheer rail and chine log. To complete the boat's profile, we used a level and batten to measure the angles and lengths of the transom and stem post. The next steps were to record the boat's construction details: frames, transom, stem post, sheer rails, chine logs, thwarts, oar blocks, floor boards, and so on.

As Steve and I worked, I learned that there had been one or two previous attempts to replicate this boat. I was not the first. Steve said they were well-intentioned locals who wanted to build a boat like his dad's. "They just couldn't get it right." I accepted that revelation as a challenge and quietly decided there and then to present Steve with a model of Bob Pritchett's boat, the first-off from these lines.

As soon as I returned to my studio, with the measurements and sketches still fresh, I laid the lines down to scale. Most drift boats today are built free-form, without a jig. I decided that Pritchett's boat could be replicated using this technique. The challenge, however, would be to calculate all the bevels, angles, and bilge and side panel dimensions. Using the scaled lines, I handcrafted a half model, or plug: first the profile, and then the half breadth to the lines. Carefully done, making handcrafted plugs is a failsafe method for capturing the side panel dimensions and station lines and evaluating the fairness of the boat's lines.

Confident that I had the lines, side panel, and station lines, I completed the plans for the boat. To test their efficacy, I modeled the boat using the free-form con-

struction technique. I milled wood customary for these boats to scale, and then, following the plans, I handcrafted the model. The scaled plans are key to modeling this boat. The frame lines and side panel layout served as templates for both. Since Steve was to receive this boat, I took care to replicate Bob Pritchett's boat in both detail and color. Several weeks later, I presented the boat to Steve. My satisfaction with the boat was confirmed when Steve told me, "You've got it." Since then, several people have built Bob's boat in other parts of the continent: Alaska, Idaho, Michigan, British Columbia, and the Yukon Territory. I am gratified that the legacy of this boat and the man behind it lives on.

Several features of this dory make it distinctive. Form follows function. Pritchett and his colleagues built boats to achieve certain tasks, and although the boat appears similar to the McKenzie River double-enders, it is quite different. First, the flare of this boat approximates 40 degrees off vertical. This accentuated flare does two things: It minimizes splash into the boat by throwing water outward when encountering whitewater, and it adds more stability. It's almost impossible to flip the boat by standing on the sheer rails. The flared side panels become an extension of the bottom.

Pritchett's dory has a 60-inch flat spot on the bottom fore to aft amidships, from frame #3 to frame #8, coupled with some rake under the prow and transom. This flat spot gives the boat great carrying capacity because of the increased displacement. Fully loaded with two guests, the oarsman, and gear, with a 15-horse motor hanging on the transom, the dory maintains a shallow draft. Neither the base of the transom nor the base of the stem sits below the waterline. The extended flat spot also allows more chine to be in contact with the river, which means that the boat will tend to hold its line in a rapid. In some situations, this characteristic is very useful. I have footage of Bob Pritchett, courtesy of Steve, running Grave Creek Falls on the Rogue. These rapids aren't particularly treacherous so long as the correct line is held and the boat remains parallel to the current. The initial drop and subsequent standing waves, however, are impressive. In the footage, Pritchett inadvertently broke one of his oars on the port side of the boat at the top of the falls. A risk in such a situation is that the force of the current may push the dory broadside into the rollers and swamp or, worse, flip the boat. Then you've got real problems! In the film, as soon as the oar breaks, Pritchett scrambles to replace the lost oar with his spare. It takes a few seconds, enough time that he's in serious trouble if the boat turns 45 or more degrees to the direction of the current. That didn't happen. Instead, the boat held its line perfectly, and Pritchett replaced the lost oar without mishap. The extended chine line served as something of a rudder and helped keep the boat straight in the current.

As a fishing platform, the boat was most often used to trail flies or hardware while the oarsman slowed the boat relative to the current. Other times he would slow the boat enough that pockets, slicks, and attractive water could be fished without having to set an anchor. The oarsman was continually working. The extended chine line, however, allowed the current to slip around the boat, making it far less work to hold the dory in the current. At the end of the day, an oarsman on a Pritchett dory was less tired than if he had been rowing a McKenzie River drift boat. With the McKenzies, their bottom rocker fore to aft causes the river to pillow up under the transom as the oarsman rows against the current to slow the boat's descent. This "pillow" of water continually pushes the drift boat so that the oarsman is working against it in addition to the current and the weight of the boat.

Another feature of the extended chine contact with the river relates to a motor. Bob Pritchett liked to use a motor to move through slow water more quickly and complete the last 30 miles of the trip on the lower

Rogue. The plans show a hip near the transom, a sharp downward slope. This is a feature of most traditional Rogue dories. This profile accommodates a long-handled tiller for the outboard motor. Bob Pritchett liked to operate the motor while standing just aft of the rowing thwart. With his weight slightly forward and the longer chine line, the dory remained more trim under power. Drift boats and river dories generally are not well suited for a motor, but among the dories, this boat is a good bet.

The boat's assets can also be a liability, especially in technical water that demands maneuverability. The boat's longer chine line makes it slower to pivot and requires that the oarsman calculate the route farther ahead. But for ease of rowing, carrying capacity, holding a line in the current, and holding the boat in a current, this dory is excellent.

The plans for this dory remain true to the Pritchett boat except for two minor modifications. Bob placed two $1/2$-inch chine logs per side panel to achieve a full inch of chine. The chine logs were not beveled. They sat flush against the side panel at 90 degrees. He crafted the side frames in two pieces. One extended down the side panel flush with the top of the chine and its inside edge, and the

Bob Pritchett with his dory being built right side up in a jig. This same boat may be built free-form as described. PHOTO COURTESY OF STEVE PRITCHETT

I gave Steve Pritchett this model of his dad's dory as a gift. COURTESY OF PATRICK FARRELL

other ran straight down the first shim to the bottom frame. The first piece was in effect a shim for the second, and the technique eliminated the need to cut a chine notch into a completed frame. These plans instead require the builder to preform the frames and cut a chine notch before assembly. Moreover, the chine logs are 3/4 inch and beveled so that the topside sits roughly parallel to the bottom of the boat.

The classic Rogue River dory is an excellent fishing platform and whitewater boat. As Steve nods his head in approval over this dory, I like to think that if Bob Pritchett were still alive, he would agree with his son.

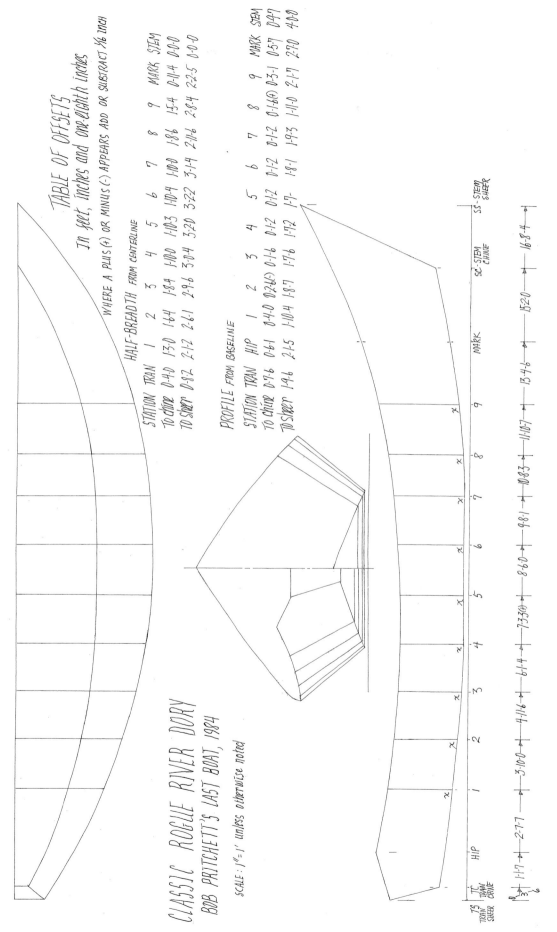

TABLE OF OFFSETS
In feet, inches and one-eighth inches

WHERE A PLUS (+) OR MINUS (-) APPEARS ADD OR SUBTRACT ⅛ INCH

HALF-BREADTH FROM CENTERLINE

STATION	TRAN	1	2	3	4	5	6	7	8	9	MARK	STEM
To Chine	0-4-0	13-0	16-4	1-8-4	1-0-0	1-0-3	1-10-4	1-0-0	1-8-6	1-5-4	0-11-4	0-0-0
To Sheer	0-8-2	2-1-2	2-6-1	2-9-6	3-0-4	3-2-0	3-2-2	3-1-4	2-11-6	2-8-4	2-2-5	0-0-0

PROFILE FROM BASELINE

STATION	TRAN	HIP	1	2	3	4	5	6	7	8	9	MARK	STEM
To Chine	0-7-6	0-6-1	0-4-0	0-2-6(-)	0-1-6	0-1-2	0-1-2	0-1-2	0-1-2	0-16(-)	0-3-1	0-5-7	0-4-7
To Sheer	1-9-6	2-1-5	1-10-4	1-8-7	1-7-6	1-7-2	1-7-	1-8-1	1-9-3	1-11-0	2-1-7	2-7-0	4-0-0

CLASSIC ROGUE RIVER DORY
BOB PRITCHETT'S LAST BOAT, 1984

SCALE: 1" = 1' unless otherwise noted

Plans have been reduced 45%.

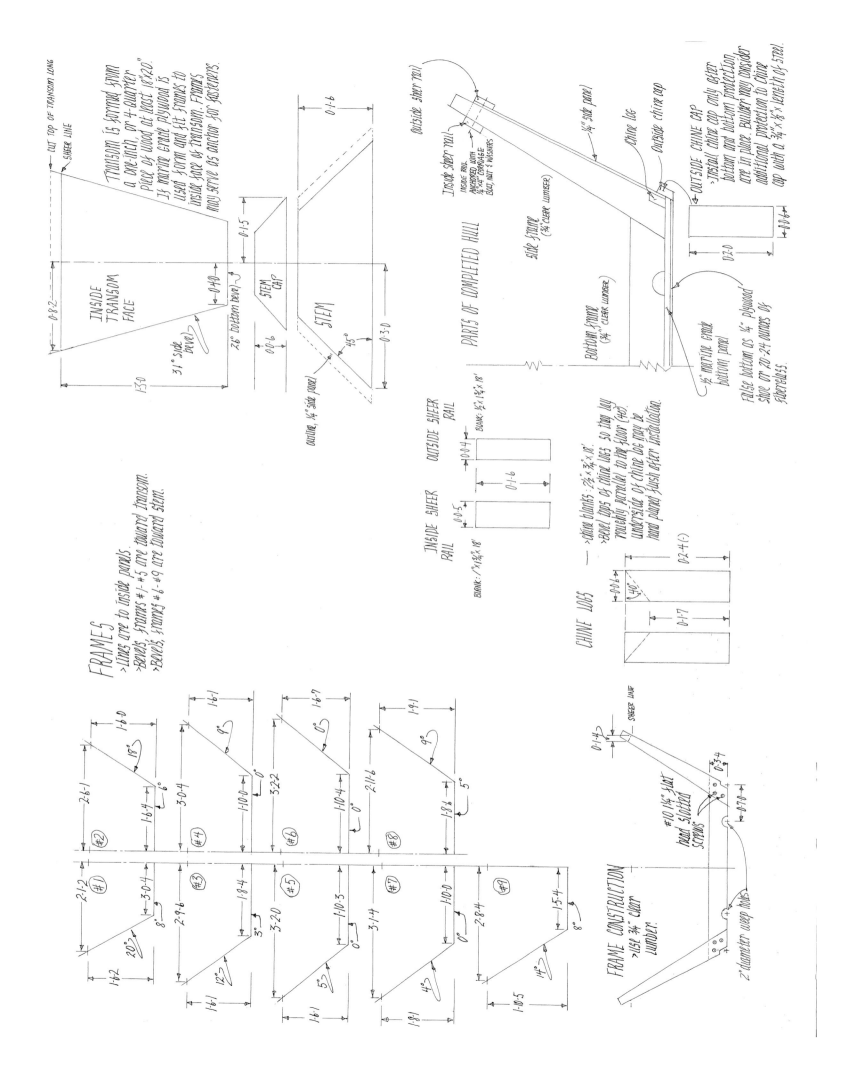

CUT TOP OF TRANSOM LONG
SHEER LINE

Transom is formed from a one-inch, or 4-quarter, piece of wood at least 18"×20". If marine grade plywood is used form and fit frames to inside face of transom. Frames may serve as anchor for fasteners.

INSIDE TRANSOM FACE

31° side bevel

26° bottom bevel

outline, ¼" side panel

0-2-8
13-0
0-4-0
0-1-5

STEM CAP

STEM

45°

0-1-6
0-0-6
0-3-0

FRAMES
> Lines are to inside panels.
> Bevels, frames 1- #5 are toward transom.
> Bevels, frames #6-#9 are toward stem.

#2   18°   1-4-0
2-6-1   1-4-1
1-6-4   6°
#1   3-0-4
2-1-2   0°
8°   8°
2-9-6
1-6-1   12°

#4   9°   1-6-1
3-0-4   1-10-0   0°
#3   5-2-2
1-8-4   3-2-0
1-6-1   5°   3°

#6   0°   1-6-7
5-2-2   1-10-4   0°
#5   3-2-0
1-10-3   3-1-4
1-3-1   5°   4°

#8   9°   1-9-1
2-11-6   9-8°   5°
#7   1-10-0
1-10-5   2-8-4
1-10-5   4°   0°

#9
1-5-4
8°

INSIDE SHEER RAIL
BLANK: 1"×3¾"×18'

OUTSIDE SHEER RAIL
BLANK: ½"×1¾"×18'

0-0-4
0-1-6
0-0-5
0-1-6

CHINE LOGS
> chine blanks: 2½"×¾"×18'
> Bevel tops of chine logs so they lay roughly parallel to the floor (40°). underside of chine log may be hand plained flush after installation.

40°
0-0-9(+)
0-2-4(-)
0-1-7

PARTS OF COMPLETED HULL

Outside sheer rail
Inside sheer rail
INSIDE RAIL
ANCHORED WITH
¼"×4" CARRIAGE
BOLT, NUT & WASHERS

¼" side panel

side frame (¾" CLEAR LUMBER)

Chine log
Outside chine cap

OUTSIDE CHINE CAP
> Install chine cap only after bottom and bottom protection are in place. Builder may consider additional protection to chine cap with a ¾"×8" length of steel.

0-0-4(-)
0-2-0

bottom frame (¾" CLEAR LUMBER)

½ marine grade bottom panel

False bottom as ¼" plywood shoe or 20 or 24 ounces of fiberglass.

FRAME CONSTRUCTION
> Use ¾" clear lumber.

SHEER LINE
0-1-4
0-3-4
0-7-0

#10 1¼" slot head slotted screws

2" diameter weep hole

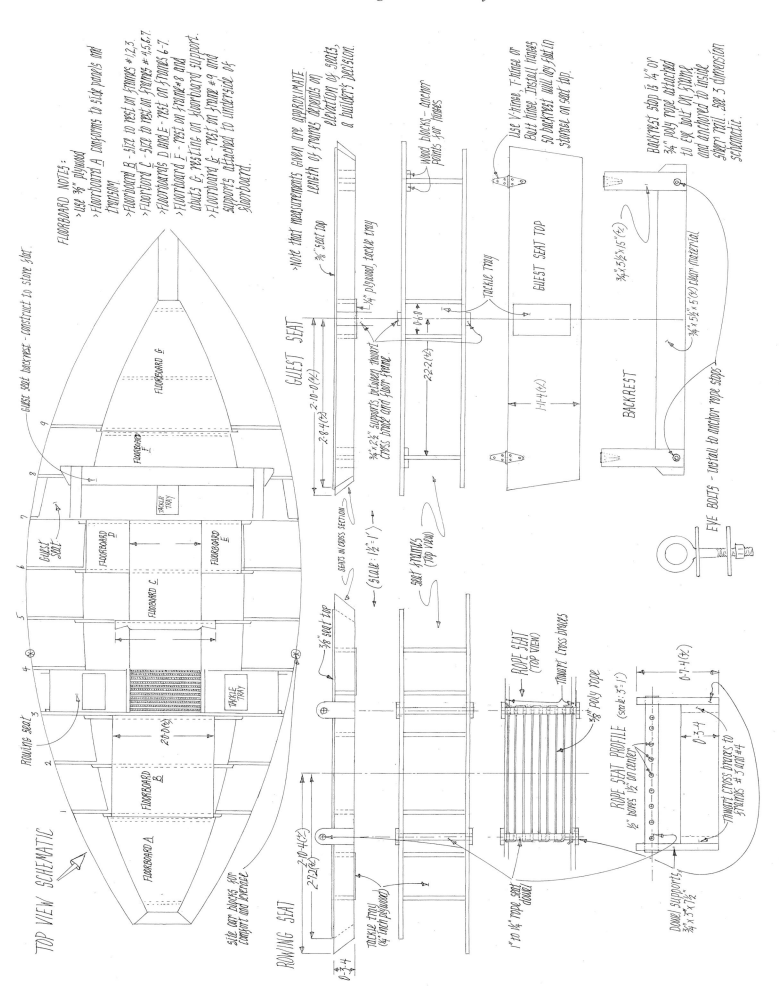

FLOORBOARD NOTES:
> use ⅜" plywood
> Floorboard A conforms to side panels and transom.
> Floorboard B - size to rest on frames #1,2,3.
> Floorboard C - size to rest on frames #4,5,6,7.
> Floorboards D and E - rest on frames 6-7.
> Floorboard F - rest on frame #8 and adds & resting on floorboard support.
> Floorboard G - rest on frame #9 and supports attached to underside of floorboard.

GUEST SEAT BACKREST - construct to store flat.

TOP VIEW SCHEMATIC

Rowing Seat

site oar blocks for comfort and leverage

Floorboard A
Floorboard B
Floorboard C
Floorboard D
Floorboard E
Floorboard F
Floorboard G
Guest Seat
Tackle Tray
2-0-0 (±)

> Note that measurements given are APPROXIMATE. Length of frames depends on elevation of seats, a builder's decision.

GUEST SEAT

⅜" seat top
¼" plywood, tackle tray
0-6-0
2-8-4 (±) 2-10-0 (±)
2-2-2 (±)
1-1-4 (±)
¾" x 2" supports between thwart cross brace and floor frame

seats in cross section
(SCALE: 1½"=1')

seat frames (Top View)

ROWING SEAT

tackle tray (¼" inch plywood)
2-10-4 (±)
2-2-2 (±)
0-3-4
⅜ seat top
1" to ¼" rope seat dowel

ROPE SEAT (TOP VIEW)
thwart cross braces
⅜" poly rope

ROPE SEAT PROFILE (scale: 3"=1')
½" bores ½" on center
Dowel supports, ¾" x 3" x 7½"
0-7-4 (±)
0-3-4
thwart cross braces to frames #3 and #4

use V-hinge, T-hinge or Butt hinge. Install hinges so backrest will lay flat in storage on seat top.

wood blocks—anchor points for hinges

GUEST SEAT TOP
tackle tray

BACKREST
¾" x 5½" x 5 (±) clear material
¾" x 5½" x 15" (±)

Backrest slats 15 ¼" or ¾" poly rope attached to eye bolt on frame and anchored to inside stern rail, see 3 dimension schematic.

EYE BOLTS - Install to anchor rope steps

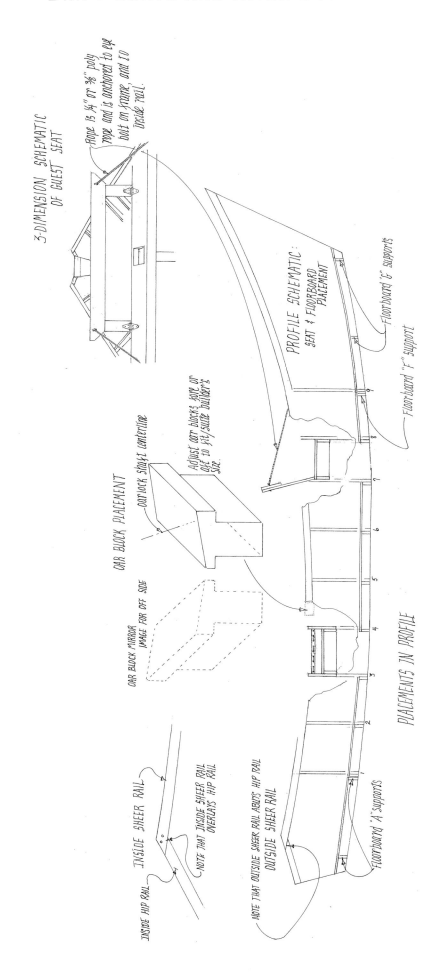

3-DIMENSION SCHEMATIC OF GUEST SEAT

Rope is ¼" or ⅜" poly rope and is anchored to eye bolt on frame, and to inside rail.

PROFILE SCHEMATIC: SEAT & FLOORBOARD PLACEMENT

Floorboard "G" supports

Floorboard "F" support

OAR BLOCK PLACEMENT

Oarlock straps centerline

Adjust oar blocks fore or aft to fit/suite builder's size.

OAR BLOCK MIRROR IMAGE FOR OFF SIDE

INSIDE SHEER RAIL

INSIDE HIP RAIL

NOTE THAT INSIDE SHEER RAIL OVERLAYS HIP RAIL

NOTE THAT OUTSIDE SHEER RAIL ABUTS HIP RAIL

OUTSIDE SHEER RAIL

Floorboard "A" supports

PLACEMENTS IN PROFILE

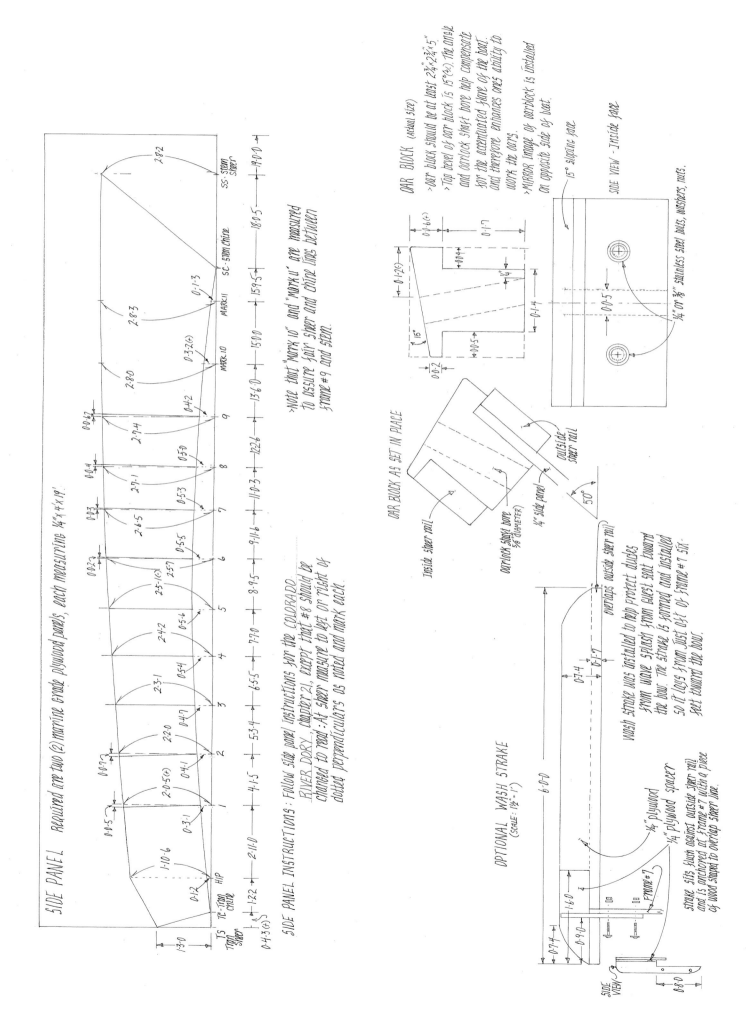

SIDE PANEL Required are two (2) marine grade plywood panels, each measuring ¼" x 4' x 19'.

SIDE PANEL INSTRUCTIONS: Follow side panel instructions for the COLORADO RIVER DORY, chapter 21, except that #8 should be changed to read: At sheer measure to left or right of dotted perpendiculars as noted and mark each.

>Note that "mark 10" and "mark 11" are measured to assure fair sheer and chine lines between frame #9 and stem.

OAR BLOCK (actual size)

>Oar block should be at least 2¾"x2¾"x5".
>Top bevel of oar block is 15° (±). The angle and oarlock shaft bore help compensate for the accentuated flare of the boat and therefore enhances one's ability to work the oars.
>Mirror image of oarblock is installed on opposite side of boat.

SIDE VIEW - inside face

15° sloping face

¼" or ⅜" stainless steel bolts, washers, nuts.

OAR BLOCK AS SET IN PLACE

Inside sheer rail

oarlock shaft bore ⅝ (diameter)

¼" side panel

outside sheer rail

50°

OPTIONAL WASH STRAKE
(SCALE: ½" = 1")

overlaps outside sheer rail

Wash strake was installed to help protect ducks from wave splash from guest seat toward the bow. The strake is formed and installed so it tops from just aft of frame #7 six.. bent toward the bow.

¼" plywood

¼" plywood spacer

Frame #7

Strake sits flush against outside sheer rail and is anchored at frame #7 with a piece of wood shaped to overlap sheer line.

SIDE VIEW

CHAPTER 21

The Colorado River Dory

"Briggs and others [eventually went] to aluminum, which although initially tougher, lacks the capacity for clean repairs, dooming them to the eventual appearance of a much worried beer can. On the other hand, there's nothing prettier to look at or sweeter to handle than a Briggs dory. She is 'naked elegance' in the pristine environment of the Grand Canyon."

—BRAD DIMOCK, HIBERNACLE NEWS, 1994

I looked across the valley from a vantage above Grants Pass and marveled at the beauty of the place. The valley's surrounding mountains and hills impede air movement through the basin, and it's an increasingly rare day that the ambient air is so clear and striking. But it was April, and the place was fresh from spring showers that moved through the night before. The day's activity in the valley below hadn't yet fouled the air with its emissions. It soon would, though, but that moment was captured in my mind's eye, and I paused to relish the clarity of view. I noticed that Jerry Briggs was caught by the scene too, and as if to pinch himself, he muttered, "Beautiful, isn't it?" We turned and walked into the garage to examine the frame.

Jerry spent the two previous days locating his construction frame for the Colorado River dory. His generosity was working against him. He had loaned the apparatus to a friend, who in turn had loaned it to another. Over time, Jerry had lost track of the piece. It took some doing, but Jerry found it at the hilltop home owned by an acquaintance who someday plans to build the boat. I was there to examine the frame and determine whether it would provide the information necessary to record the boat's measurements. Jerry seemed unconcerned by its absence, but I was relieved that he found it. It saved me considerable time, and I recognized the frame as a piece of riverboat history that should be safeguarded somewhere, somehow.

Formed from 2-by-6s, 2-by-4s, 2-by-3s, and 2-by-2s, the construction frame is the skeletal structure that gives the dory its shape and provides for precise placement of the stem, transom, frames, and plywood skin. The thing was surprisingly heavy. One man could not move it. For two of us, it was a struggle, so we decided to examine it in place. It was immediately clear to me that measurements from the centerline of the frame at each key point would provide the distances to the inside panel, and measurements from the top of the frame would give me the boat's profile. Perfect. Jerry and I spent the next couple of hours recording measurements at each station, including the bow and stern.

As we worked, Jerry told me the story of the frame's creation. When Martin Litton approached him about building a dory for the Colorado River, Jerry was struck by similarities between Litton's requested design and his own Rogue River Special. "I had a friend who wanted to build his own boat off my design, so I gave him the patterns for this frame. He built the frame and then he built the boat, so I asked him if I could have his frame." Jerry's friend agreed. Briggs modified the frame to reduce the flare of the sides a bit. He extended a flat spot on the bottom fore and aft amidships to increase chine contact with the river, and he straightened the chine lines between frames #4 and #7 so they ran parallel to each other. Jerry retained an upward rake under the bow and stern. The profile of the Rogue River Special shows a hip at the transom end. The hip allows the use of a long-handled tiller for a motor. The operator is able to stand behind the rowing thwart and comfortably operate the boat when it's under power. Jerry removed the hip from Litton's boat, but he kept the tombstone-shaped transom, which provided a little more floor space than a true double-ender and could handle a motor should Litton choose not to row out the tail end of his trips on Lake Mead. These slight modifications of the Rogue River Special were a good match for Martin Litton's needs.

When Jerry and I finished with our measurements, I double-checked to make certain I had everything I needed to lay down the boat's lines on paper. I did, except for the angles. Rather than calculate angles and bevels from the lines, I decided to take them directly off the frame. Jerry asked me, "Why are you doing that?" I explained my need for the information, and he said, "I understand the need, but why are you bothering to do that? I've got all that information." I slapped my forehead—a part of my anatomy that has been flattened over time from similar Ahas!—and said, "Of course you do!" Jerry had a record of all bevels, angles, frame lengths, and other information. Like most other Oregon boatbuilders, Jerry recorded the information on a board hanging in his shop. He loaned the board to me.

After I lay the lines down to scale, I typically hand-carve a scaled half model to the lines of the boat. I use the profile and then the half-breadth lines as a guide. This work accomplishes several things, but foremost, the completed project provides the bilge dimensions and lets me lift an accurate side panel off the modeled hull. An accurately marked side panel that includes the station lines is necessary for free-form construction. I explained this next step to Jerry, and he said, "You know, I think I can find the side panel template I used for the full-size boat in my shop."

The next morning, Jerry and I rummaged through an area where he recalled seeing the panel. One corner of my shop harbors things that haven't seen the light of day for years, and I know of no other place more difficult to get to—until I joined Jerry on this treasure hunt for the side panel. We searched for half an hour or so, with Jerry making comments like "No wonder I never found that anvil" and "Oh, that's where that went; little wonder I couldn't find it," until we located a 20-foot-long ¼-inch plywood panel leaning against the shop wall. This was it! The dory's side panel had been carefully extracted, and the hole that remained provided the necessary template.

We spent another half hour clearing an area on the floor in order to secure a flat space large enough to handle the plywood template. We laid down a clean sheet of white Tyvek, placed the panel on it, and scribed the side panel outline with an indelible marker. We were both satisfied with the outcome. As it later turned out, however, I was forced to carve the half model in order to verify the placement of the station lines on the panel. Once the hull is pulled together, the frames are perpendicular to the baseline of the boat. To achieve that, several of the station lines on the side panel are off vertical a bit because of the curvature of the panel. The only way for me to mark those lines accurately was with the half model.

I was ready to develop the boat plans.

Several telephone conversations and a few weeks later, I sent the first set of line drawings to Jerry Briggs. The hull was right on. My interpretation and representation of the boat's watertight compartments, however, were slightly off amidships. The other minor complication was the need for a self-bailer. Jerry marked up my drawings, we talked by phone, and I finally nailed down the boat. During our conversations, Jerry told me, "Building the hull is the easy part; it's all the carpentry work that takes the time." He painstakingly constructed the frames for the bulkheads, decks, and hatch lids, and sealed all seams with tape and resin. "The trickiest part of the carpentry project," he said, "was fitting the decks around the frames."

What makes this boat so special for the river of the Grand Canyon? It's how it interacts with the river. The boat's response to any set of river conditions is immediate. It doesn't absorb energy like a raft, as it slogs and burps it way through hellish water; the dory *is* energy. The boat meets the river head-on as it gathers momentum to catapult through and over big water. It catches every nuance of the river. If there's any pause, it's from the oarsman who hesitates, misreads, or blunders into rapids unprepared. There, too, the boat may be forgiving. Its extended chine line acts like a keel to help keep the dory parallel to the current should the oars lose contact with the river. The high prow splits most normal waves, and the boat's interior remains dry, though the huge waves of the Colorado come right over the top. Hundreds of gallons swash the decks. The sloping decks amidships direct the water to the oarsman's foot well, where a simple self-bailer handles the excess. The oarsman is free to remain on the oars without interruption, so long as he keeps his seat. The pitches and rolls of some rapids have dumped the best, despite the installation of some ingenious foot and leg braces to help the oarsman sit tight. Water over the top also fills the passenger foot wells. While the added weight may add some stability, the sloshing side to side can be unnerving to the oarsman. Self-bailing designs for the passengers' foot wells require elevated passenger seats. This raises the center of gravity and makes the boat less stable, so it remains to the passengers to keep the foot wells empty. Boatmen consider it a golden run when the foot wells remain dry through huge water. In the end, however, it's only the way the boat is handled that will keep the big water from dumping you, no matter what. The slightest miscalculation or inept maneuver means you'll swim.

All food, clothing, camp gear, equipment, and libations for seventeen to twenty-one days are stored in the dory's holds. This weight, tightly packed, maintains a low center of gravity and helps keep the craft stable. If

Vince Welch squires his Briggs dory through Lava Falls on the Colorado. Skilled hands on the oars coupled with watertight compartments and a self-bailing rowing cockpit keeps the boat afloat and upright. COURTESY OF RUDI PETSCHEK

rapids succeed in upsetting a Briggs dory, the watertight compartments buoy the craft, and the lifeline that circumvents the hull is a security blanket for its passengers. Rarely, but occasionally, an uncontrolled dory will mistake rocks for the river and incur some damage. In the boat's hold are enough supplies and equipment to do the necessary repair. A Briggs dory is never left behind, even if it means airlifting one out by helicopter.[1]

Martin Litton was delighted with his new boat, and through the 1970s, Jerry built thirty-two more wooden Colorado River dories. Briggs then went to the shallow end of the pool and built nine aluminum dories, beginning in 1979. Quality marine-grade wood material was getting harder to find, and labor costs for a wooden boat were high. It was simply more profitable to have someone else manufacture aluminum dories to Jerry's specifications than to continue with wood.

A run through any rapids in a Briggs boat leaves its occupants exhilarated and inspired. The Briggs dory does what Martin Litton hoped: provides hundreds of guests each year a river experience like no other. They leave the Colorado River and the Grand Canyon with a new sense of place and an appreciation for a craft that puts one in touch with this river environment like no other.

Professional builders and do-it-yourselfers have copied the Briggs boat. I see this as a tribute to Jerry Briggs's boat design and building abilities and to Martin Litton's insight into a meaningful Colorado River experience. Plastic, fiberglass, and aluminum have replaced traditional frame construction of this dory, for all practical purposes, along with wood and foam core encapsulated in resin. Despite these advanced technologies, there is something about the quiet wakes of wood on water and the history of this boat that leads to me believe we'll see a few more frame-constructed Briggs dories on the river. It's been almost forty years since Jerry built his first boat for Litton. Most of Jerry's boats are still in use today, and only one has gone to its grave. Framed boats last.

Endnote

1. In an April 28, 2006, interview, Martin Litton recalled that one of his boats, probably the Emerald Mile, became firmly wedged between the Big Black Rock and the shore. He had no choice but to leave it. However, he returned later to airlift the boat out of the canyon by helicopter. "On another occasion, in a trip-ending stunt by Mike Taggett, the entire expedition—people, boats, and all—was airlifted out of the canyon from the beach at the foot of Lava Falls by chopper. It was pretty wild."

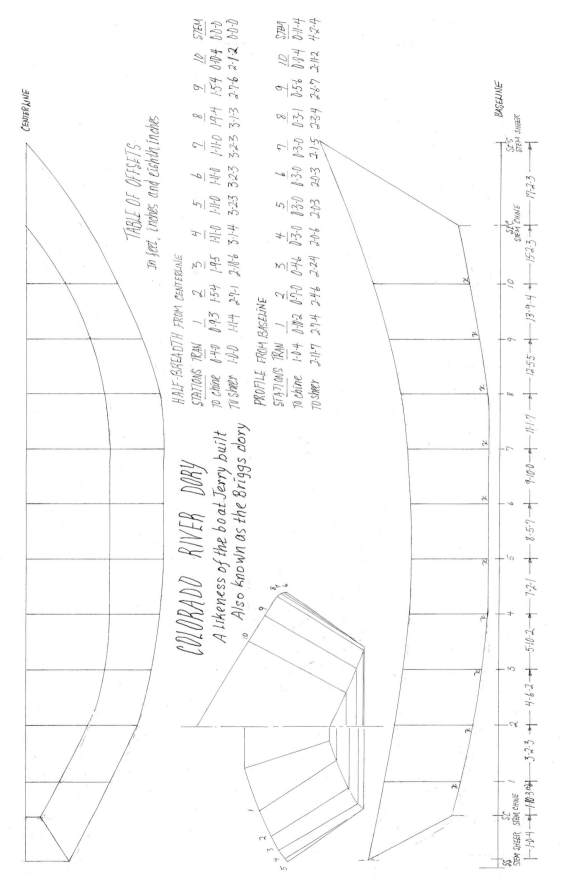

COLORADO RIVER DORY

A likeness of the boat Jerry built
Also known as the Briggs dory

TABLE OF OFFSETS
In feet, inches and eighth inches

HALF-BREADTH FROM CENTERLINE

STATIONS	TRAN	1	2	3	4	5	6	7	8	9	12	STEM
To Chine	1-4-0	0-9-3	1-5-4	1-9-5	1-11-0	1-11-0	1-11-0	1-11-0	1-9-4	1-5-4	0-10-4	0-0-0
To Sheer	1-0-0	1-11-4	2-9-1	2-10-6	3-1-4	3-2-3	3-2-3	3-1-3	2-7-6	2-1-2	0-0-0	

PROFILE FROM BASELINE

STATIONS	TRAN	1	2	3	4	5	6	7	8	9	12	STEM
To Chine	1-0-4	0-10-2	0-7-0	0-4-6	0-3-0	0-3-0	0-3-0	0-3-0	0-3-1	0-5-6	0-8-4	0-11-4
To Sheer	2-11-7	2-9-4	2-4-6	2-2-4	2-0-6	2-0-3	2-0-3	2-1-5	2-3-4	2-6-7	2-11-2	4-2-4

CENTERLINE

BASELINE

SS STEM SHEER · STEM SHEER
SC STEM CHINE
—1-10-4— —3-2-3— —4-6-2— —5-10-2— —7-2-1— —8-5-7— —9-10-0— —11-1-7— —12-5-5— —13-9-4— —15-2-3— —17-2-3—

SFS STEM SHEER
SFC STEM CHINE

Plans have been reduced 45%.

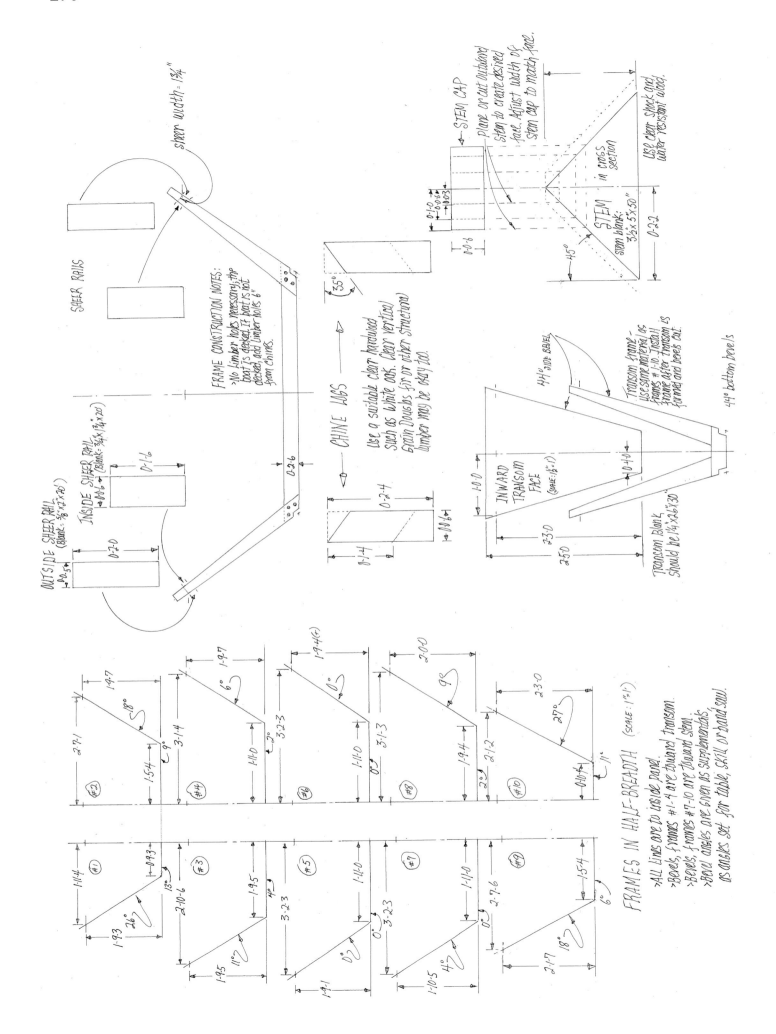

SIDE PANEL

Requires two ¼" x 4' x 19' marine grade plywood panels

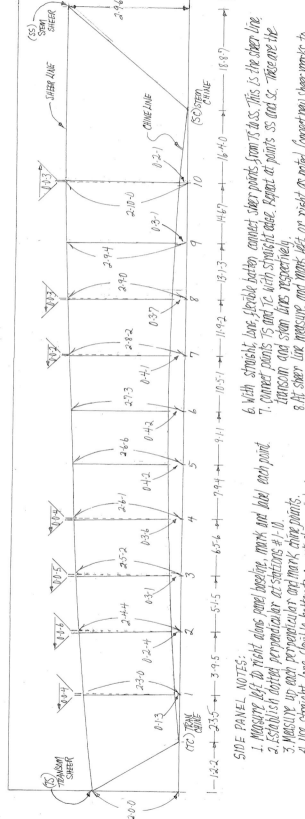

SIDE PANEL NOTES:
1. Measure left to right along panel baseline, mark and label each point.
2. Establish dotted perpendicular at stations #1-10.
3. Measure up each perpendicular and mark chine points.
4. Use straight, long, flexible batten to connect chine points from TC to SC. This is the chine line.
5. Measure and mark points of the sheer at TS, stations #1-10 (dotted perpendicular lays) and SS.
6. With straight, long, flexible batten connect sheer points from TS to SS. This is the sheer line.
7. Connect points TS and TC with straight edge. Repeat at points SS and SC. These are the transom and stem lines respectively.
8. At sheer line measure and mark left or right as noted. Connect new sheer marks to the chine, these points where dotted perpendiculars intersect the chine line. These are the side frame centerlines.
9. Cut out side panel and use as a template for second side panel.

OPTIONAL RUB RAIL
> Use ¼" or ⅜" plywood.
> Install so base is 2"-to-3" above top of chine cap.

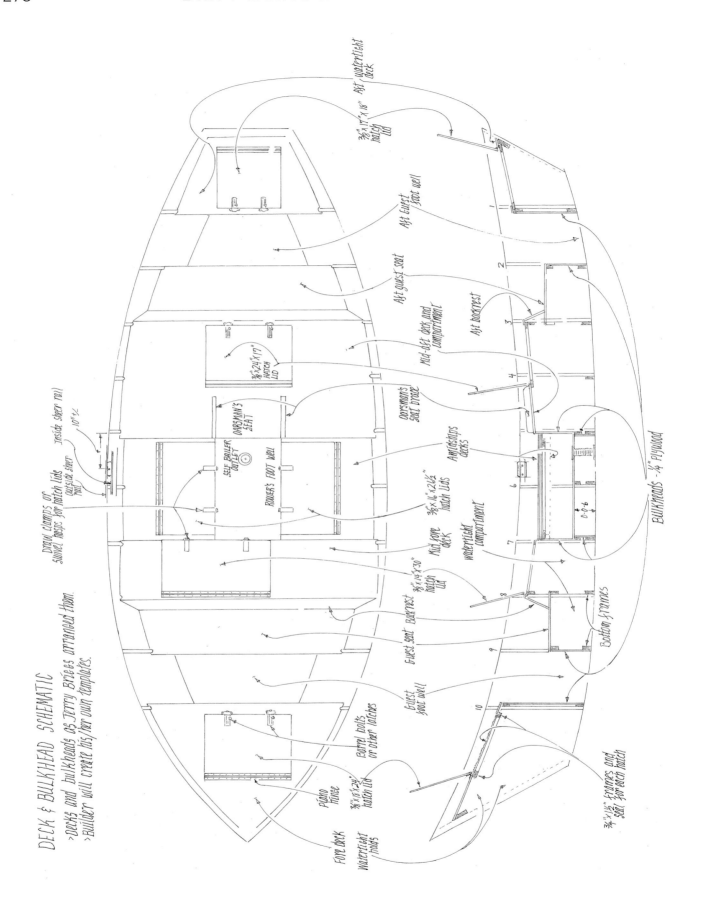

DECK & BULKHEAD SCHEMATIC
> Decks and bulkheads as Jerry Briggs arranged them.
> Builder will create his/her own templates.

Fore deck

Watertight holds

Piano hinge

⅜"x18"x24" hatch lid

Barrel bolts or other latches

Guest foot well

Guest seat

Backrest

⅜"x14"x30" hatch lid

Mid core deck

⅜"x16"x24½" hatch lids

Watertight compartment

Bottom frames

¾"x1½" frames and seal for each hatch

Draw clamps or swivel hasps for hatch lids

Inside sheer run

Outside sheer rail

10½"

SELF-BAILER OUTLET

OARSMAN'S SEAT

ROWER'S FOOT WELL

⅜"x24"x17" HATCH LID

Oarsman's seat brace

Amidships decks

Mid-aft deck and compartment

Aft guest seat

Aft backrest

Aft guest foot well

⅜"x17"x18" hatch lid

Aft watertight deck

BULKHEADS - ¼" plywood

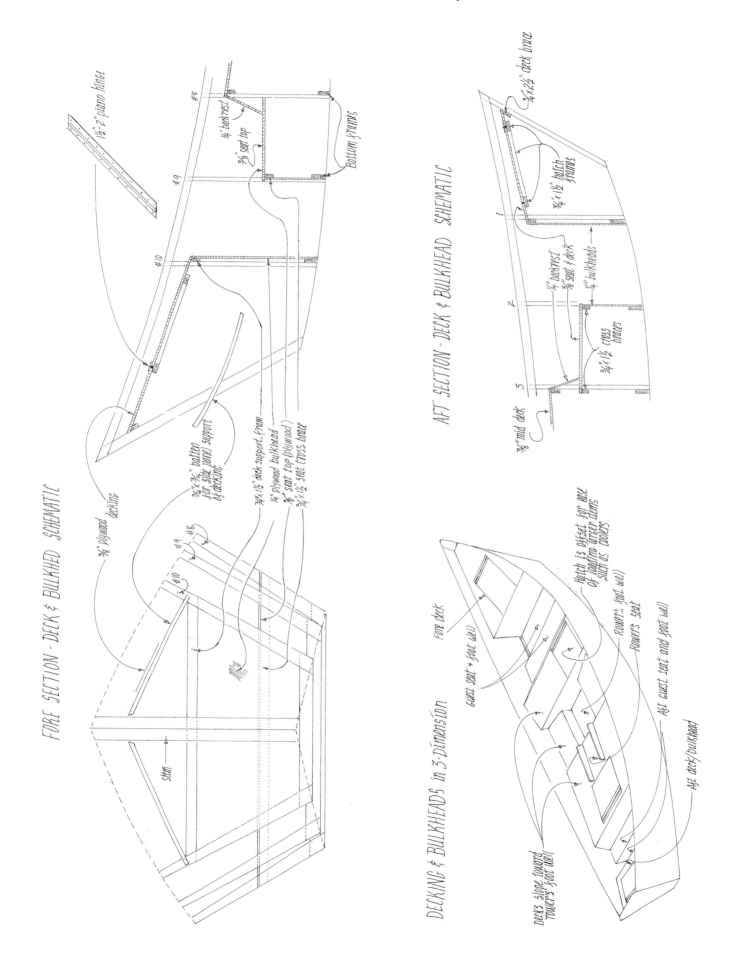

FORE SECTION - DECK & BULKHEAD SCHEMATIC

½"-2" piano hinge

#9

#8

#10

3/8" plywood decking

3/4" x 3" batten for side panel support of decking

3/4" x 1½" deck support frame

¼" plywood bulkhead

3/8" seat top (plywood)

3/4" x 1½" seat cross brace

#10

#9

#8

stem

#8

#9

#10

¼" backrest

3/8" seat top

Bottom frames

AFT SECTION - DECK & BULKHEAD SCHEMATIC

3/4" x 2½" deck brace

3/4" x 1½" hatch frames

¼" backrest
3/8" seat & deck
¼" bulkheads

3/4" x 1½" cross braces

3/8" mid deck

3   2   1

DECKING & BULKHEADS in 3-Dimension

Fore deck

Hatch is offset for ease of loading larger items such as coolers

Guest seat & foot well

Rower's foot well

Rower's seat

Aft guest seat and foot well

Deck's slope toward rower's foot well

Aft deck/bulkhead

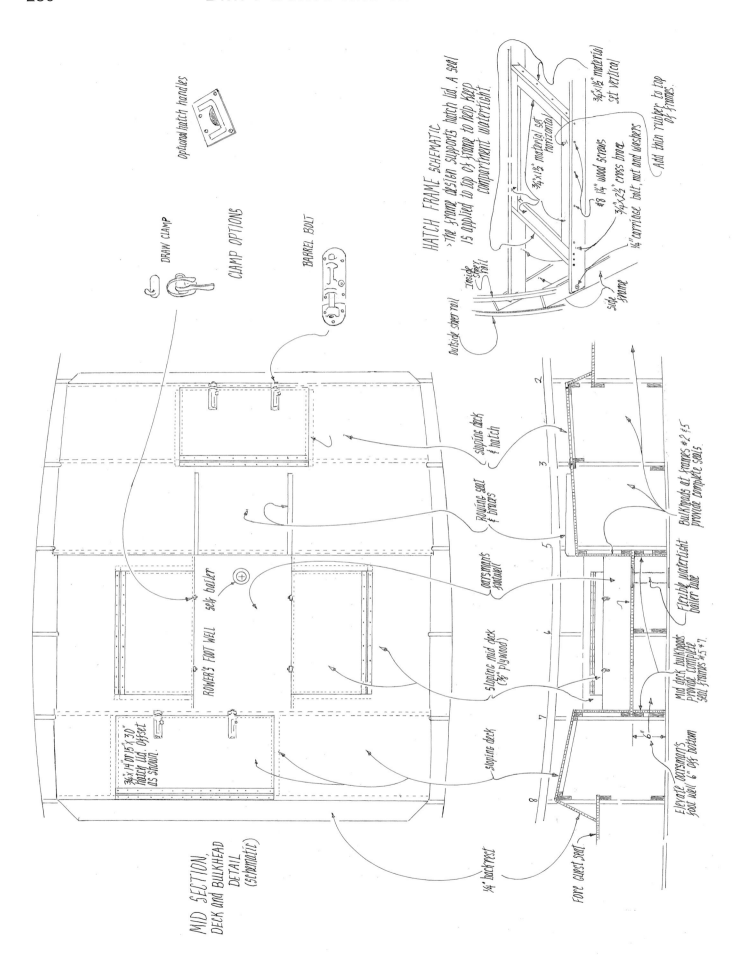

optional hatch handles

DRAW CLAMP

CLAMP OPTIONS

BARREL BOLT

HATCH FRAME SCHEMATIC
> The frame design supports hatch lid. A seal
is applied to top of frame to help keep
compartment watertight.

3/4"x1/2" material set horizontal

3/4"x1/2" material set vertical

#8 1/4" wood screws

3/4"x2 1/2" cross brace

1/4" carriage bolt, nut and washers

Add thin rubber to top of frames.

inside sheer rail

outside sheer rail

side frame

MID SECTION,
DECK and BULKHEAD
DETAIL. (schematic)

3/4"x 14"OT 15 x 30'
hatch lid. Offset
as shown.

ROWER'S FOOT WELL

self bailer

sloping deck

sloping mid deck
(3/8" plywood)

4" backrest

Fore guest seat

Elevate oarsman's
foot well, 6" oak bottom

Mid deck bulkheads
provide complete
seal. Frames #5 + 7.

Flexible watertight
bailer tube

Bulkheads at frames #2 +5
provide complete seals.

oarsman's
footwell

Rowing seat
& braces

sloping deck
& hatch

1 2 3 4 5 6 7 8

EPILOGUE

Lessons on Handling a Drift Boat

The common denominator to all great river boatmen is the ability to read the water. All were students of the river's flow . . .

I wish I had another lifetime to develop my river skills." These are words from river guide Willard Lucas. Willard was born and raised on the Rogue River near Agness, about 30 miles upriver from its mouth at Gold Beach. During a visit with him, I commented on others' impressions of him as an oarsman. Many of the older river guides I've talked to consider Lucas to have been one of the best. "Oh, I suppose I was pretty good," he says, "but there is so much more I could learn." To prove his point, he showed me a contraption in the backyard. It was an old washing machine that had been rebuilt so water could be pumped into a long, sloping trough. In the trough were rocks, sticks, and other obstacles. When the machine was turned on, it pumped water to the head of the trough. The water ran through the trough, and Lucas rearranged the obstacles to study the different hydraulics he created. Willard Lucas is a student of the river. "Running a drift boat is a really an art form," he says. "If I can catch the flow and use it to my advantage, then I reduce the amount of work required of me on the oars."[1]

Bobby Pruitt, another guide from Rogue River country and Veltie Pruitt's nephew, enjoys telling a story about Willard Lucas. Willard was rowing for Bobby on the Owyhee River, a southwestern Oregon river that can be run only in the spring when there is enough winter snowpack in the Owyhee Mountains. Bobby and his guides had pulled over to scout a particularly troublesome set of rapids. Bobby decided to line the rapids. Willard was upriver when the party pulled over, and Bobby tried to wave him down. "Willard stood in the boat, looked the rapids over, sat down, and zip, zip—ran the thing without

a hitch. It was amazing," says Bobby. "You never really saw him work hard on the oars. He made it look simple."[2]

As we visited, Lucas became less modest about his oarsmanship on the river. "I suppose I was pretty fair, but the thing I enjoyed most about the drift boat was trying to be in harmony with the river. If I can go with the flow, then I capture the river's energy and I'm at one with it. Sure, there are times when I had to work real hard. Some rapids require heavy use of the oars. But on the right kind of water, I could stay pretty relaxed."[3]

Prince Helfrich's sons, Dave, Dick, and Dean, are excellent boatmen in their own right. When I asked Dave whether he could recall how he developed his river skills, he replied: "Ya know, I feel like I've always had a set of oars in my hands. At my seventieth birthday party, with my mother present, I commented on my delivery at birth. I was a small baby, but she had a difficult delivery. I think it was because I was born with a set of oars in my hands. Boating is just a part of my life."[4]

Dave's youngest brother, Dean, believes that one of the better boatmen he observed in his early years was Everett Spaulding, who persuaded Woodie Hindman to add the transom to the double-ender. What does Dean think made Everett so special? "He could read the water. Spaulding could look at a stretch, pinpoint the hidden obstacles, site a course, and execute it beautifully." Dean admits that he and his brothers are all very good, "but we had a great teacher in my dad and excellent mentors like Veltie and Everett." Dean says he was probably in his prime as a boatman when he was forty-five years old, when he had the knowledge, dexterity, and strength to exude confidence. "I don't have the strength I once had, or

A younger Willard Lucas rests on the gunwale of his dory. Though he is big and strong, he chooses instead to master the river with finesse and intelligence. "Learn how to read the water," he says. "That is the trick." COURTESY OF WILLARD LUCAS

the reflexes. I like to think, though, that I have gained a lot of wisdom about the river, and it's that wisdom that keeps me safely in touch with the river and out of trouble."[5]

In *A River to Run,* the Rogue River's Glen Wooldridge recounts his days as a youth when he went to the river, lay out on a flat rock above the stream, and watched the currents swirl and eddy and ripple over rocks. At first he dropped pieces of wood in the current to see how they reacted to the currents, and then he crafted little boats to do the same. I suspect that in his mind's eye, he calculated how these pieces of bark and little "boats" might be influenced to take a little different track.[6]

As a little boy, Leroy Pruitt developed a hands-on technique for understanding how stream currents affect a boat. Too young to row but not too young to fantasize, Leroy crafted Douglas fir bark into rough boat shapes. The pieces were longer than they were wide. In the concave topside of the bark, he posted a couple wooden pegs on each side to replicate the placement of oarlocks. With upward of 20 feet of light string coming off each peg, he released the bark boat into a little stream that ran through their property. Standing upstream, often in the middle, he let the bark boat tug against the strings, one in each

hand. If he tugged on the left string, he could envision himself in the boat pulling on the right oar. The tug caused the bark boat to swing 45 degrees to the current, and immediately the current pushed the boat to his right. A tug on the right string had the reverse effect. The bark boat now moved to his left. Leroy also maneuvered the boat around obstacles he encountered in the creek. By holding tightly to both strings, he could lower the boat down the creek at a speed slower than the current. Then, by tugging on one string or the other, he moved the boat to one side of the creek and then the other, around obstacles and obstructions. He would do this for hours and take himself to other places where rivers ran wild and awaited him, just like his dad, the Preacher, and Prince Helfrich were doing in real time. Leroy Pruitt's experiences as a child in the creek with his bark boats was an excellent training ground for his career as a river guide.[7]

The common denominator to all the good river boatmen is the ability to read the water. All were students of the rivers' flows, whether they realized it or not. My early attempts at running a river were under the tutelage of my good friend and boating partner Ken Brown. My first encounter with whitewater was on the lower Deschutes

River just below Shearer's Falls at a place called Wreck Rapids, a tricky little rascal. After studying the rapids for a few minutes, Ken suggested that I do as he did and follow him through. Our wives were on the access road above the river watching the scene. With sweaty palms, a rapid heartbeat, and a body full of adrenaline, I shoved off at Ken's heels. He was about 20 yards below me. My eldest daughter, Wendy, accompanied him. I focused on Ken and his boat, insecure in the maelstrom, but I did as he did.

Suddenly there was a loud report of wood on rock, and I marveled as Ken's boat did a complete 360 in the rapids' tailout. I thought to myself, "So that's the way it's done," and followed suit. My McKenzie's prow rose over the crest and slammed down on a rock hidden below the riley water. It sounded like a muffled rifle shot. The impact pitched the boat to port, and I did exactly as my friend and executed a perfect pirouette as the boat rode through the rapid's trailing standing waves. We pulled into an eddy downriver, and like many boatmen before us, we were giddy with the thrill of survival. I learned two important lessons that day. First, I am ultimately responsible for my occupants, my boat, and myself. Second, I must learn to read the water with confidence and know what must be done to navigate a stretch safely.

If you are unfamiliar with drift boats and river dories, you may realize by now that rowing a drift boat is unlike handling a rowboat on a lake. The oarsman usually faces downriver, the direction of travel, and rows against the current to slow the boat's descent. A stronger pull on one oar pivots the boat slightly and allows the current to catch the upside chine, and the oarsman can move the boat laterally across the current with an even application of the oars. The reverse happens when the opposite oar is used to pivot the boat in the other direction. Generally, the boat is held parallel to the direction of the current. When pivoting the boat to move across current, a rule of thumb is not to swivel the craft more than 45 degrees to the flow. If the boat were to hit an unseen obstruction below the surface, the blow would be glancing, and it's unlikely to upset the boat. On the other hand, if the boat is 90 degrees to the flow of the current and an obstruction is encountered, the boat may swamp, be damaged, or flip. Drift boats and river dories are very stable craft, but as with any tool, if they are used inappropriately, the consequences could be dire.

It is not my intention here to provide you with lessons on reading the water, river navigation, or oarsmanship. I simply encourage a new drift boat user to learn river safety, river etiquette, and navigation skills. It is incumbent on you to be a prudent and thoughtful student.

There are a couple of ways you can learn about rivers and drift boats. One is to capitalize on the good graces of an experienced boatman or go to the expense of hiring

Young Dave and Dick Helfrich in a small boat Woodie Hindman gave them circa 1940. The Helfrich children grew up with oars and fly rods in their hands. COURTESY OF DAVE HELFRICH

As a boy, Leroy Pruitt always dreamed of becoming a guide.
COURTESY OF LEROY PRUITT

a river guide to teach you. Another option is to capitalize on the resources available through electronic and print media. Frank Amato Publications sells a book titled *Drift Boats: A Complete Guide,* which features the basics of rowing and reading the water, as well as drift trip and safety checklists. It's a pretty decent drift-boat primer.[8]

Drift boats and river dories are wonderful watercraft. Originally designed and built as fishing platforms, these boats have increasingly become pleasure and adventure craft that provide escape from the busy world in which we live. As my boating partner and I launch our boats for a three- or four-day fishing trip down the Deschutes River, we simultaneously cut loose with a "Yahoo!"—our announcement that we have returned and expect to have a superb trip.

Two final observations about drift boats, river dories, and rivers: Pack out what you pack in. Everything. Over the years, we humans have done much to foul our free-flowing streams, sometimes by unwitting deeds and other times by thoughtless acts perhaps influenced by the seeming remoteness of a river. I encourage every drift boater and doryman to observe the concept of no-trace river running. In other words, leave no evidence, seen or unseen, of having been there. If it's possible to leave the river a better place for having been there, do that too.

Second, and most important, insist that all your boat occupants wear life jackets, including yourself. Mishaps can occur in an instant. Hundreds of lives are lost each year in water for want of a personal flotation device (PFD). The U.S. Coast Guard requires their use and many states now impose a hefty fine if PFDs are not present or in use. PFDs are essential for all drift boats and river dories. Use them.

My drift boat is my therapy. Whether I'm doing some maintenance work on the boat or I'm on the river, the experiences put me in another place. One of my favorite drifts is a short, six-mile run on the Willamette Valley's Santiam River. It's just minutes away from my home. The launch site is immediately adjacent to Interstate 5, the main Washington-Oregon-California artery that links the three states. It's busy and noisy, not the most pleasant place to put on the river. Oftentimes that's the way I am when I launch: busy, noisy, and with a cluttered mind.

As the drift boat leaves shore, the sound of traffic crossing the freeway bridge becomes muted by my anticipation of the solitude ahead. As I round the first bend, the clutter and noise that filled me begin to drain away, just as the river itself drains the Cascade Mountains of its winter snowpack. The screech of an osprey is the first sign to alert me to this other world. The freshly leafed cottonwoods glide by, a doe browses on fresh growth, a clutch of goslings skitter across an eddy, a salmon breaks water, and I become relaxed, at peace and seemingly at one with this world. Three hours later, as I load the boat to head home, I am refreshed and look forward to my next trip.

Endnotes

1. Willard Lucas interview, June 15, 2006.
2. Bobby Pruitt interview, April 26, 2005.
3. Lucas interview.
4. Dave Helfrich interview, May 24, 2006.
5. Dean Helfrich interview, June 1, 2006.
6. Florence Arman, *The Rogue: A River to Run,* (Grants Pass, OR: Wildwood Press), 11.
7. As told by Leroy Pruitt, boat handling workshop, Vida, OR, April 19, 2005.
8. Dan Alsup, *Drift Boats: A Complete Guide,* Portland, OR: Frank Amato Publications, 2000.

Glossary

Aft. In direction, toward the stern.

Amidships. The midsection of the boat from fore to aft.

Baseline. A line parallel to the waterline from which measurements are taken to define a boat in profile. Often drawn along the centerline of the hull.

Batten. A relatively thin length of wood that can be laid through a series of reference points to determine or mark a fair line. Also refers to a length of wood laid along the outward hull to assist in sealing a carvel-planked riverboat.

Bevel. The angles put on edges or butts of boat frames, planking, and other parts to ensure tight fits.

Body plan. The end-on views of the boat as measured using the same points as in the other two views, profile and half breadth. The lines are to the inside planking.

Bottom frame. The bottom timber of a boat frame to which bottom planking is attached. Defines the boat's width between the chines.

Cant. An angle off perpendicular. Also, an oblique line or surface that cuts off the corner of a square or other geometric appearance that may be more functional or aesthetically pleasing.

Carvel-planked. Describes a planked boat in which the strakes or planks are fastened to the frame edge to edge.

Centerline. The line that divides a boat into two equal halves fore to aft. It is the basis for all half-breadth measurements for lofting and frame assembly in river dories.

Chine. The lowest joint fore to aft where the side planking meets the bottom planking; the bottom fore-to-aft edge of the boat.

Chine cap. A board that extends longitudinally along the outward chine from stem to stern. The cap is added after the bottom plank and is intended to protect the chine from river rocks and other abrasions and protect the end grain of the bottom plank.

Chine dip. An event that occurs when the river current catches the chine of the boat and causes the boat to heel over noticeably. This occurs when the boat enters a competing strong current such as an eddy or when moving the boat from slack water into the current. The dip can be alarming to a beginning drift boater. It is also easily avoided.

Chine log. A length of suitable wood that extends from stem to stern along the chine, where fastenings are applied to anchor the bottom planking and side planking. This piece is a keystone in a river dory. Also called the *inside chine.*

Cross spall. A temporary wooden brace that extends across a frame for added strength when forming the hull of a drift boat.

Dory. A flat-bottom boat with flared sides and narrow stern that is more stable when weighted with gear. Drift boats meet the definition of dory except when defined by method of construction. A traditional dory is built right side up, and the floor timbers are first to be laid. A drift boat is built upside down, and the bottom panel is the last to be laid.

Double-ender. A drift boat with a pointed end at both stem and stern.

Double-ender with a transom. A drift boat with a small transom to replace the upriver end of the boat, the bow. McKenzie guides continue to call this boat a double-ender in spite of the transom.

Drift boat. A wide, flat-bottom boat with flared sides and a continuous rocker fore to aft that is specifically designed for river running and as sportfishing platforms. The term *drift* indicates that the boat moves downstream from a put-in to a takeout point.

Fair. Describes a line that is smooth and graceful in its arc, without any aberrations; pleasing to the eye.

False bottom. An additional layer of planking on the outward bottom, providing river rock protection. In river dories, these can be strips of oak lath that run longitudinally on the underside, a plywood shoe, or more popular today, fiberglass and epoxy resin.

Fastenings. Ring nails, screws, nuts, bolts, washers, sealers, and adhesives that are used to anchor pieces of the boat to others. In this book, *fastenings* is used interchangeably with *fasteners.*

Flare. The outward angle of a boat's sides between the chine and the sheer when viewed in cross section.

Fore. Any forward point on a boat when used in connection with *aft.*

Frame centerline. A perpendicular line beginning at the union of a bottom frame and side frame and extending upward along the inside edge of the side frame.

Freeboard. The elevation at the sheer above the waterline at any given point along the hull.

Garboard. The side plank, or strake, that joins with the bottom on a hull. Usually the lowest plank on the hull.

Gunwale. A strengthening board that runs along the sheer of a hull, usually anchored to the outside face of the planking. Also called the *outside sheer rail.*

Half-breadth plan. Presents the lines as half width of the boat's stem and stern at the chine and sheer, and at all stations between. The lines are to the inside planking.

Inboard. Within the limits of the hull area.

Inside sheer rail. A strengthening board that complements the gunwale and runs along the inboard edge of the sheer. Also called the *inwale.*

Keel. The lengthwise backbone of a hull, usually extending below the hull to keep the boat on track. In drift boats the chine serves as a keel.

Knee locks. Shaped support blocks of wood affixed to a permanent cross spall to support a standing fisher as the boat migrates downstream.

Lapstrake. Planking that overlaps the garboard and each additional strake, giving the appearance of clapboards.

Limber holes. Openings in the bottom frames or bulkheads that allow water to move from one section of the hull to another. Also called *weep holes.*

Loft. To draw and lay out parts of the hull full-size.

Meat. Additional width of stock required to cut a standing bevel, and the added dimension of stock needed to ensure a surface will receive another piece, such as the bottom panel to the frames, chine log, stem, and transom.

Outside sheer rail. The gunwale.

Outward. The outside limits of the hull.

Perpendicular. Describes lines that are set 90 degrees to the baseline.

Planking. Boards applied to frames and forms in building the hull. Most of the boats in this book require plywood panels for the planking.

Plans view. The lines of a boat in half breadth, in profile, and ends-on (body plan), allowing the builder to visualize the boat in three dimensions.

Profile. The side view of the boat's lines as measured from the baseline to the chine and the baseline to the sheer at each station, stem and stern. The end stations are the perpendiculars established at the sheer points of the stem and stern.

Rake. A departure from a horizontal chine line that parallels the waterline and moves up toward the stem or stern. Also means a departure from perpendicular of any boat member such as stem and transom.

Rapid Robert. A name attributed to the McKenzie square-ender by the builder, Tom Kaarhus.

River dory. The same as a drift boat except that there is not a continuous rocker fore to aft. Instead, a flat spot at the chine may extend up to 30 inches fore and aft of amidships. This flat spot is typical of the Rogue and Colorado River dories.

Rocker. The crescent arc of the chine line fore to aft in a drift boat.

Rub rail. A $^1/_4$- to $^3/_8$-inch-thick protective strake added to the side planking 2 to 4 inches above the chine that extends from frame #2 to frame #9.

Scarf joint. Two beveled pieces of wood joined end to end or edge to edge and glued so the joint's thickness remains true to the thickness of the boards joined.

Scrive board. A portable piece on which parts of a boat may be lofted full-size, such as a piece of plywood to loft frames.

Sheer. The uppermost line of a boat as viewed in profile, stem to stern. Also called the *sheer line.*

Spanish windlass. A length of rope placed around a portion of the boat's hull used to pull the planking into position by means of a lever that twists and constricts the rope.

Spile. To scribe a line that defines the shape of a piece to be joined to a part of the boat, usually by means of a compass. The technique helps ensure a tight fit and is especially useful in marking compound angles, such as in fitting the chine log to the stem and stern.

Square-ender. A drift boat with a broad, squared transom that serves as a wash strake in whitewater and a motor mount on quiet water.

Standing bevel. Angle upward from the front surface of a board that requires wider stock [meat] to achieve the finished width.

Station line. A perpendicular line that marks the centerline of each frame. These lines are numbered or lettered sequentially from left to right on the lines plan.

Stem post. The foremost structural member of a boat's hull, to which the converging planks are fastened.

Stem and stern post caps. An outward piece that lies over the planking joint at the stem or stern. Sometimes called a *false stem.*

Stern post. The aft structural member of a boat's hull, to which the converging planks are fastened.

Strake. One of two or more units of planking that closes in a boat's hull. Also called *side strakes.* The uppermost plank that forms the sheer line is often called the *sheer strake.* The bottommost strake is the *garboard.*

Strongback. A timber that is marked and cut to the profile of the chine with sufficient meat to mark, set, and square the frames, stem and transom, or stern post in the inverted position. The strongback is usually set on an elevated platform.

Thwart. A member that spans the interior of the hull, usually as a seat for guests or the oarsman.

Transom. The after face of the boat's stern, usually the entire stern.

Transom trim. External wooden trim that caps, or overlays, the planking joints of the transom.

Under bevel. Angle downward from the front surface of a board, which may be cut into the finished width.

Yahoo! A sound usually heard when a river dory or drift boat is launched into a river for the first time, and every time thereafter.

Index